SOVIET ARCHITECTURAL AVANT-GARDES

SOVIET ARCHITECTURAL AVANT-GARDES

ARCHITECTURE AND STALIN'S REVOLUTION FROM ABOVE, 1928–1938

Danilo Udovički-Selb

BLOOMSBURY VISUAL ARTS
LONDON • NEW YORK • OXFORD • NEW DELHI • SYDNEY

BLOOMSBURY VISUAL ARTS
Bloomsbury Publishing Plc
50 Bedford Square, London, WC1B 3DP, UK
1385 Broadway, New York, NY 10018, USA
29 Earlsfort Terrace, Dublin 2, Ireland

BLOOMSBURY, BLOOMSBURY VISUAL ARTS and the Diana logo are trademarks
of Bloomsbury Publishing Plc

First published in Great Britain 2020
Paperback edition first published in Great Britain, 2022

Copyright © Danilo Udovički-Selb, 2022

Danilo Udovički-Selb has asserted his right under the Copyright, Designs and Patents Act, 1988, to
be identified as Author of this work.

For legal purposes the Acknowledgments on pp. xxiii–xxvi constitute
an extension of this copyright page.

Cover design by Eleanor Rose
Cover image: Vesnin brothers, Palace of Culture, 1937, Photograph © Danilo Udovički-Selb

All rights reserved. No part of this publication may be reproduced or transmitted in any form or by
any means, electronic or mechanical, including photocopying, recording, or any information
storage or retrieval system, without prior permission in writing from the publishers.

Bloomsbury Publishing Plc does not have any control over, or responsibility for, any third-party
websites referred to or in this book. All internet addresses given in this book were correct at the
time of going to press. The author and publisher regret any inconvenience caused if addresses
have changed or sites have ceased to exist, but can accept no responsibility for any such changes.

Every effort has been made to trace copyright holders and to obtain their permission for the use
of copyright material. The publisher apologizes for any errors or omissions.

A catalogue record for this book is available from the British Library.

A catalog record for this book is available from the Library of Congress.

ISBN: HB: 978-1-4742-9986-2
PB: 978-1-3502-8842-3
ePDF: 978-1-4742-9984-8
eBook: 978-1-4742-9985-5

Typeset by RefineCatch Limited, Bungay, Suffolk

To find out more about our authors and books visit www.bloomsbury.com
and sign up for our newsletters.

To my two Mimis

CONTENTS

Comparative Chronology	viii
List of Illustrations	xviii
Acknowledgments	xxiii
Introduction	1
1 A Call for the Party to Defend Modern Architecture: Stalin's "Cultural Revolution" and the Aporia of "Proletarian Architecture"	7
2 Continuity and Resistance: Designed Before 1932, Completed Down the Decade	43
3 Building Modern Architecture: "In an Atmosphere of Genuine Creativity," 1933–1939	83
4 The Shaping of Architecture Ideology within the Stalinist Project: Unreachable "Proletarian" Architecture Yields to Unattainable "Socialist"	123
5 The Improbable March to the Congress: "Soviet Architecture Eaten by a Gangrene"	157
Conclusion	201
Bibliography and Sources	209
Index	223

COMPARATIVE CHRONOLOGY

	SELECTED ARCHITECTURAL & CULTURAL EVENTS	PARTY & POLITICAL EVENTS
1919	Founding of the VHUTEMAS	
	Tatlin's Tower to the III International	
	V. Kandinsky: Named Head of Russian Museums	
1921		End of Civil War
		Lenin introduces the New Economic Policies (NEP)
20 December	El Lissitzky's First PROUNs. Founds journal *Veshch* in Berlin	Founding of Union of Soviet Socialist Republics (USSR)
1922	Kandinsky leaves Russia	
	Palace of Labor competition (Brothers Vesnins 3d Prize)	
1923		12th Party Congress [All-Union Communist Party (Bolsheviks)]
	Ladovskij founds ASNOVA	Stalin appointed General Secretary
	MAO, Pre-revolutionary Moscow Association of Architects reestablished	
	Ljubov Popova: Street installations & theatrical collaboration with Aleksandr Vesnin and Vsevolod Meyerhold	
1924		
21 January		Lenin dies
	Popova dies of scarlet fever at 35	
	J. Protozanov: film Aelita *Queen of Mars*	
1925	Vesnin Bros: "Leningrad Pravda" competition	14th Party Congress [All-Union Communist Party (Bolsheviks)]
18–31 December		
		L. Kamenev expelled from the Politburo
	Founding of RAPP [Proletarian Writers]	End of Zinovev-Kamenev-Stalin Triumvirate
	S. Eisenstein: Film: *Battleship Potemkin*	Kamenev calls for removal of Stalin as Secretary
	M. Ginzburg *Style and Epoch*	L. Trotsky removed from the Politburo
1926		New Alliance: Zinovev-Kamenev-Trotsky
	VHUTEMAS renamed VHUTEIN	
	V. Pudovkin, Film: *Mother*	
	M. Ginzburg: Gosstrah apartments (Malaja Bronnaja Street, Moscow). Founds OSA	

Comparative Chronology

	SELECTED ARCHITECTURAL & CULTURAL EVENTS	PARTY & POLITICAL EVENTS
1927	(Society of Contemporary Architects), and the journal *Sovremenaja Arhitektura (SA)* designed by Alexej Gan [dies in the "Gulag" around 1942] House Communes: Ginzburg calls for a "Comradely competition" on new Housing Typologies	
October		L. Kamenev expelled from the Central Committee (Further: C.C.)
	Vesnin Brothers: Moscow Department Store	
12–19 December		15th Party Congress: Trotsky and G. Zinovev expelled from the Party
		Kaganovich replaces Zinovev in the Politburo
		N. Buharin (editor of *Pravda*) named head of the Komintern, replacing Zinovev
		Collectivization of farmlands (not yet forced) N. Krupskaja adamantly against it, calling on Lenin's refusal of any collectivization before the country would have at least 200,000 tractors
		Kaganovich tours Moscow Party cells for damage control
		Calls voiced in C.C. for the elaboration of a Five-Year-Plan
		Zinovev and Trotsky organize a failed rally
1928	First Congress of the RAPP	Trotsky exiled to Alma-Ata (Central Asia)
		NEP abolished
May		The "Shahtij" show trial" against "bourgeois" engineers
	A. Dovzhenko, Film: *Arsenal*	
	Results of first competition entries for the Lenin Library	Kamenev expelled from the party
16 December		Buharin meets secretly with Kamenev. In disagreement with Stalin, warns of creation of a "police state" if attitude towards peasants persists. Opposes Stalin's theory
	Ginzburg completes Government Building in Alma-Ata	that the advance towards socialism will meet ever greater resistance of the "class enemy"
	Ladovskij leaves ASNOVA to form ARU (Association of Russian Urbanists). First "ARU Declaration"	M. Tomsky removed as Trade Union leader
		End of year Buharin, A. Rykov & Tomsky offer resignation. Stalin refuses: offers verbal concessions

Comparative Chronology

	SELECTED ARCHITECTURAL & CULTURAL EVENTS	PARTY & POLITICAL EVENTS
1929		
February		Trotsky arrested and expelled from the USSR Buharin, Tomsky and Rykov try to prevent it
	Boris Iofan's Sanatorium in Barviha in vicinity of Moscow, 1929–1936	
		Maximalist variant of the Five-Year-Plan adopted
	Ginzburg completes (partially) his experimental Narkomfin Communal housing project	
		C. C. Plenum: Buharin confronts Stalin openly for first time. Declaration to Stalin: "Collective decisions have been replaced by one man's will"
	Protests against the imposition of Shchuko's Lenin Library project	
26 June– 13 July		16th Party Conference: *First Five-Year-Plan adopted.* Crash accelerated industrialization and forced collectivization of land
August		Kaganovich secretly sponsors creation of VOPRA
	Dziga Vertov, Film: *Man with a Movie-Camera*	
	Competition for the Commissariat of Light Industry	Buharin removed from his post as editor of *Pravda* and Chairman of the Komintern
1930 5 January	E. May, H. Schmidt and Mart Stam invited to plan new towns	Decree on the stages of the collectivization of agrarian land
	Third (stone) Mausoleum of Lenin, attributed to Architect Shchusev	Half of peasantry collectivized from January to May [from 4 million to 14 million]
	Competition for the ZIL Palace of Culture	
		Ill prepared collectivization prompts peasants to start leaving the kolkhozes
14 March		*Pravda:* "The struggle against the distortions of the party line in connection with the Kolhoz affairs"
7 April	Founding of VANO (independent groups united)	Stalin's article "Dizziness from Success" blames collectivization disaster on local party members' excesses
12 April		Buharin, Tomsky and Rykov fail to take advantage of Stalin's defeat
14 April	Majakovskij commits suicide	
		Resolution on expansion of labor camps
4 April	Leningrad exhibition: "Soviet Artists in Recent Years," with one of Malevich's "Arhitektons" topped with a statue of Lenin	
26 June– 13 July		16th Party Congress Stalin's consolidation of power not yet complete: Stalin: "The USSR has entered the Socialist phase"

Comparative Chronology

	SELECTED ARCHITECTURAL & CULTURAL EVENTS	PARTY & POLITICAL EVENTS
	VHUTEIN closes for good at the end of the Spring semester	"Cleansing of enemy and kulak elements in Kolkhozes" Kaganovich *Announces massive Party Purges* Bukharin attacks forced collectivization: Accuses Stalin of reducing peasantry to feudal exploitation
	N. Miljutin, *Sotsgorod: Problems of building Socialist Cities*	Recreating the order of State functionaries
28 July		New IZO Head, arch. A. Mordvinov, Condemns I. Leonidov's architecture as epitome of "petit bourgeois trends" in architecture Calls it "Leonidovshchina" in moral lynching of the talented young constructivist. Consequently his teaching position revoked
	Last issue of Ginzburg's *SA*	
20 August		12th Party Conference on City vs. Country Rykov expelled from Politburo
	Hannes Meyer arrives in Moscow with his students	
25 November to 7 December		Second Show Trial: "Industrial Party" against notable economists and engineers (25 Nov–7 Dec)
1931		
27 February		CC Resolution on workers-peasant police force
25 May	First issue of *Sovetskaja Arhitektura* Nikolaj Miljutin editor	
15 Jun	*Izvestija:* announces competition for the Palace of the Soviets	C.C. June decree on housing and urbanism. Resolution drawn from Kaganovich's speech on the Moscow city economy
18 June		Stalin orders to start building the Moskova-Volga-Baltic sea canal
	Stalin speech at meeting of planners: seven paragraphs	Using Gulag inmates, ending with massive deaths as consequence of work conditions (Building begins in 1932)
23 June		Demotion of Nikolaj Miljutin from the position of People's Commissar of Finance
	First Meeting Moscow architects:	
27 June	Resolution on sponsorship of design and construction of Palace Soviets under City Council (Mossovet)	

xi

Comparative Chronology

	SELECTED ARCHITECTURAL & CULTURAL EVENTS	PARTY & POLITICAL EVENTS
7 September		Stalin First Conference of Workers in Socialist Industry "Involvement of Bol."
2 October	BAUHAUS exhibition opens in Moscow Hannes Meyer curator	"Technology determines everything"
23 October		Stalin's protest letter to the editorial board
	La Construction Moderne Special issue on Soviet architecture	of *Proletarskaja Revolucija* regarding issue 6, 1930, an "anti-party and semi Trotskyist article"
1931–1933	First, Second and Third competition for the Palace of Soviets	
1932		L. Kamenev and Zinoviev readmitted into party after a second expulsion
23 April	C.C. decree on the dissolution of all independent Art Associations	Beginning of Famine
	["*O Perestrojke LITHUDORG*"]	Lasts through 1934
		Year of completion of ruthless forced collectivization
20 July	Consultative meeting under Viktor Vesnin's Presidency. Present: VANO, VOPRA, ASNOVA, ARU, SASS, OSA. Topic: Create an All-Union of Soviet Architects [SSA]	Medvedev: in *1932 381,000 peasant families deported, 1933–34*: "at least three million children died"
		Kamenev and Zinoviev sent into exile
	New SSA Board discusses the possibility of forming "creative units"	Politburo: divided between *moderates* and *extremists*:
8 August	within the SSA. They are de facto recreated	Moderates: Kirov, Ordzhonikidze, Kuibyshev, Kalinin. The left opposition revived without organized opposition.
2 September	First general meeting of SSA	Stalin takes care of it with occasional deportations
3 September	A Draft of SSA Statutes presented for Government approval	
9 November	VOKS debates "anti-Soviet comments" in *La Construction Moderne*	
23 December	Alfred Agache: Speaks in Moscow: "Not to forget that a city has an anthropo-geographic past that cannot be ignored"	
	Agache criticizes Le Corbusier's *tabula rasa* for Moscow	
27 December	Le Corbusier accepts to give a paper on Urbanism in Moscow. Did not occur.	
		Kamenev's and Zinoviev's second expulsion from the Party
	Mihail Ohitovich, a sociologist, admitted into the SSA	
		Reintroduction of internal passports Lenin had denounced as the worst form of Tsarist despotism
	SSA directorate to discuss Ohitovich's "Theory of inhabitation" ["*Teorija zhilishcha*"]	

Comparative Chronology

	SELECTED ARCHITECTURAL & CULTURAL EVENTS	PARTY & POLITICAL EVENTS
1933		
12 January	Bruno Taut's lecture in Moscow	C.C. Plenary session on purges: "PARTY PURGES COMPLETED"
9 February	Hannes Meyer's lecture in Moscow	Kamenev and Zinoviev readmitted to the party on recantation
10 May	Stalin at meeting of the Council for the construction of the Palace of the Soviets asks that the entire building be a base for Lenin's statue	
	Perret's 1937 Museum published in *Arhitekturnaja Gazeta*	
	B. Iofan named Project Director of PS in collaboration with V. Gel'freih & V. Shchuko	
15 May	First Metro line started	
22 June	First issue of *Arhitektura SSSR*	
	E. Maj : *"Two Years Experience Working in the USSR"*	
2 July	*L'Architecture d'Aujourd'hui* asks VOKS on June to contribute to a questionnaire on Modern Arch., which was sent to French architects. and the "Critiques les plus connus"	
	Letter sent through Lurçat	
2 August	Krejcar gives a lecture at VOKS on contemporary Czechoslovakian architecture	The GPU awarded medal for completion of Volga Baltic Canal. Hundreds of inmates dead
	The constructivist Oblispolkom, (Novosibirsk Government Building) by Boris A. Gordeev and Sergej Turgenev (Vhutemas alumni), completed	
	Letter from Vesnins, Ginzburg Ladovskij and Leonidov to *L'Architecture d'Aujourd'hui* refuting claims in its article "Artistic Reaction in the USSR"	
14 October		Kaganovich at plenary session of the C.C., To the Komsomols: "Excuse me, but the proletariat wants to have pretty buildings"
	A. Shchusev appointed Head of "Hotel Moscow" Project. Actual authors (L. Savel'ev & Stapran)	
22 October	Decree to raise several buildings for specialists in Moscow. Confided to Iofan	
	Academy of Architecture inaugurated (Graduate Studies)	
25 November	Stalin speaks w/authors of Palace of the Soviets	
	Lurçat in Moscow	

Comparative Chronology

	SELECTED ARCHITECTURAL & CULTURAL EVENTS	PARTY & POLITICAL EVENTS
29 November	Charlotte Perriand arrives in Moscow with the intention to stay and work in the USSR	
	Stalin speaks with the authors of the Palace of Soviets	
1934	NARKOMTJAZHPROM competition	
26 January–10 February		17th Party Congress
		Stalin: "Congress of the victors"
	Sovetskaja Arhitektura folds	Asserts full, unquestioned power
	Perriand leaves Moscow disappointed. Official reason: dramatic events in Paris (Aborted fascist coup)	Stalin: "Of course we are far from enthusiastic about Fascist regime in Germany. But Fascism is besides the point, if only because Fascism in Italy, for example, has not kept the USSR from establishing the best relations w/ that country"
19 February	Final project for Palace of Soviets approved	
	Article by Lurçat in *Art Vivant*: sympathetic remarks about new trends in Soviet Architecture	
10 June		Kamenev and Zinoviev expelled from party for the third time
14 July		
	Directorate of House of Architects named: Kolli, Zaslavskij, Bumazhnij, Kozhin, Hannes Meyer, S. Lisagor	
	Planners Meet w/ Stalin: Reconstruction of Moscow. Stalin: "Anyone who tries to impede the plan has to be called to order"	
	"Voroshilov" Army rest-home by Merzhanov opens in Sochi 1931–1934	
17 August	First Congress of Writers opens	
	Rostov-Na-Donu: Hotel "Rostov" inaugurated	
1 December	ZIL Palace of Culture's small theater completed	Murder of Sergej Kirov
	"Organization Committee" for the Arch. Congress created by government decree	Kamenev and Zinoviev arrested as "objectively" responsible for murder
7 December		Leonid Nikolaev [Kirov's assassin] executed
	Baku, Arch. S. Pen News Agency Building completed (1931–1934)	
	P. Golosov's *Pravda* Headquarters Moscow 1931–1934	
	First issue of *Arhitektura za Rubezhom*	
30 December	First issue of *Arhitekturnaja Gazeta*	

Comparative Chronology

	SELECTED ARCHITECTURAL & CULTURAL EVENTS	PARTY & POLITICAL EVENTS
	Frank Lloyd Wright sends congratulations to first issue of *Arhitekturnaja Gazeta*	
	Letter from J. J. Oud to editors of *Arhitekturnaja Gazeta*: Assails architectural conditions in USSR	
1935		
15–16 January		First Zinoviev-Kamenev trial
	M. Ohitovich presents "National Form and Socialist Architecture" at the House of Architects, in discrepancy with Stalin's position	
8 January	Ohitovich expelled from SSA and party. Arrested soon after. [Executed in 1937]	
15 January	Architects send letter to Stalin in connection with his "brilliant speech about cadres," addressing him as "the great architect of socialist society" Signed; Shchusev, Burov, Kolli, I. Golosov, V. Vesnin, Ginzburg, H. Meyer et al.	Civil War hero, Vladimir Nevskij, Director of Lenin Library, arrested. Executed May 1937 SSA Party cell begins investigating Ohitovich
14 May	First Metro Line completed A. Shchusev's Hotel "Moskva" inaugurated	SNK (government) and C.C. decree on General Plan of Moscow Stalin's first radio broadcast at the inauguration of the Metro
15 May	MALEVICH dies	
		Society of old Bolsheviks abolished
22–28 September	International Congress of Architects in Rome. Soviet delegation lead by M. Ginzburg	
1936		
27 January		C.C. & Government Decree: About "Improvement of Architectural Production"
12 February	I. Golosov's modern housing lock in Moscow Iofan's Barviha Sanatorium near Moscow completed	Party hierarchy intervenes directly for the first time in matters of architectural style
20 February	*L'Architecture*, publishes Soviet projects *Pravda* article ritually read at Party meetings	*Pravda* articles: against "Dom Korobki" (Boxy houses) and "formalism" *Pravda*: "Cacophony in Architecture" ("Kakofonija v Arhitekture") signed ambiguously as "ARHITEKTOR"
27 February	Moscow-wide meetings of architects debating new official guidelines	

xv

Comparative Chronology

	SELECTED ARCHITECTURAL & CULTURAL EVENTS	PARTY & POLITICAL EVENTS
	Arch. Solomon Lisagor, Ginzburg's collaborator, arrested and executed	Trial of former Mensheviks
20 April		Virulent attack on the Architecture Academy. Arrests and executions follow to the end of the year
	Trip of Moscow architects to NKVD labor camp at Bol'shevo (Gulag)	"Trotsky-Zinovietvite terrorist center" (includes Kamenev) goes on trial [Second Zinoviev trial]
18 June	Maxim Gorky dies	Academy Vice-rector Ja. Aleksandrov expelled from the SSA as "Trotskyist enemy and double dealer:" arrested and executed
19 August	Mel'nikov's "Gosplan" garage completed—his last project	
5 December		New Constitution adopted beaming with civic, political, religious and human rights. Buharin sees it as a great chance for the "humanizing of Bolshevism ..."
1937		
	M. Ohitovich executed in the Gulag	
18 February		Ordzhonikidze Politburo member dies, probably by suicide, after a violent altercation with Stalin
25 February		Stalin calls for Plenary meeting: for the expulsion from party and arrest of Buharin and former Prime Commissar Alexej Rykov
27 February		Buharin and Rykov expelled from Party
28 February		Rykov and Buharin arrested
March	Second Metro line completed	
3 April		NKVD chief G. Jagoda arrested. Shot a year later. Replaced by Jezhov
	Last Issue of *Za Rubezhom* D. Fridman, Modern Standard High School, Moscow Soviet Pavilion in Paris International Exhibition, by Iofan and V. Muhina	Stalin speech: about the presence of "thousands and thousands of wreckers, spies, terrorists throughout the country." Including spies in army. C.C. calls for increased repression
20 May	M. Ginzburg's "Ordzhonikidze" Sanatorium in Kislovodsk completed	Zinoviev's new trial (this time under Yezhov): known as "Trotskyist–Zinovietvite Terrorist Center"

Comparative Chronology

	SELECTED ARCHITECTURAL & CULTURAL EVENTS	PARTY & POLITICAL EVENTS
5 December	Second stage of the Vesnin ZIL Palace of Culture's main body inaugurated with fanfare	
1938		
16 January	Third Metro line started	
26 February	Gustav Klucis arrested and shot reportedly with 100 other Latvian communists	
2–13 March		"Trial of "The Twenty-One," most former members of Lenin's Politburo with Bukharin and Rykov as main defendants. Bukharin executed (two days after the completion of trial)
15 March	Arrest of poet Osip Mandelstam for second time. Dies in the Gulag of cold and hunger	
5 May		Beria named Yezhov's deputy
22 August		Yezhov arrested. Replaced by Beria
1939		
10 April	Meyerhold arrested. Executed the following year Soviet Pavilion in New York Sverdlovsk, completion of the Constructivist "Gorodok Chekistov" Architects I. Antonov and V. Sokolov 1931–1939	
1940		
4 February	Novosibirsk: Constructivist University Chemical Institute inaugurated Ginzburg publishes his Kislovodsk "Ordzhonikidze" sanatorium	Yezhov executed
1941		
21 June		Hitler invades the USSR
October	A. Gan arrested (executed September 1942)	
10 December	El Lissitzky dies of tuberculosis	

ILLUSTRATIONS

1.1 LEFT: Baku, "Moresque" first electric train station, 1928 (Photographer unknown); RIGHT: Erevan, "Byzantine-like" administrative building, 1927. (National Museum of Architecture Erevan, Armenia) — 12

1.2 Lenin Library Competition: TOP: Fridman, Fidman, and Markov, First Prize. MIDDLE: V. Shchuko, Lenin Library, with Lenin's name on the "sarcophagus"-like pediment. BOTTOM: The Vesnin brothers' entry. (Courtesy Shchusev Museum of Architecture) — 13

1.3 M. Ginzburg, Narkomfin Housing Model, and View of Northern Entrance. (Courtesy Shchusev Museum of Architecture) — 27

1.4 Ivan Leonidov 1934 NKTP competition entry. (Courtesy Shchusev Museum of Architecture) — 40

2.1 Journal *Za Rubezhom* (*Architecture from Abroad*). (Photo by author) — 47

2.2 Boris Iofan, watercolor of the Rockefeller Center. (Private collection) — 49

2.3 A. Langman GOSPLAN building, Moscow 1935. (Photo by author). — 50

2.4 Site of the Simonov Monastery (Courtesy Shchusev Museum of Architecture); and extant towers (Photo by author) — 52

2.5 Small Theater completed in 1934 (remaining tower of Simonov Monastery in background); and plan of the entire Palace of Culture 1935–1937. (Courtesy Shchusev Museum of Architecture) — 53

2.6 a) Panteleimon Golosov, *Pravda* headquarters in Moscow, built from 1933–1935 (LEFT: Courtesy Shchusev Museum of Architecture; RIGHT: Canadian Center for Architecture—gift of Howard Schickler and David Lafaille); b) Front façade. Photo Hannes Meyer. (Canadian Center for Architecture—gift of Howard Schickler and David Lafaille); c) Front entrance, detail. (Canadian Center for Architecture—gift of Howard Schickler and David Lafaille) — 54

2.7 LEFT: Il'ja Golosov, D. D. Bulgakov multi-purpose housing block, Moscow, 1936. (Courtesy Shchusev Museum of Architecture); RIGHT: Adalberto Libera, fragment of the Palazzo Del Littorio, Italian Pavilion, Brussels, 1935, published in I.. I. Rempel's *Arhitektura Poslevoennoj Italii*, taken from 1934 German magazine. (Photographer unknown) — 55

2.8 LEFT: Hamilton's winning entry (Private collection). RIGHT: Iofan's 1933 version of the Palace of Soviets before Iofan's trip to New York. (Courtesy Shchusev Museum of Architecture [Canadian Center for Architecture—gift of Howard Schickler and David Lafaille]) — 57

2.9 B. Iofan winning entry in the first competition for the Palace of Soviets. (Courtesy Shchusev Museum of Architecture) — 58

Illustrations

2.10 Still echoing Hamilton's "Gothic" character, the Palace of Soviets starts growing heaven-bound, 1932. Fourth Round Competition. (Courtesy Shchusev Museum of Architecture [Canadian Center for Architecture, Gift of Howard Schickler and David Lafaille]) 60
2.11 LEFT: Malevich, 1922; *Arhitektony* RIGHT: Detail of the 1935 version of the Palace the Soviets. (Courtesy Shchusev Museum of Architecture) 62
2.12 LEFT: Raymond Hood's Rockefeller Center, 1933 (Courtesy Library of Congress); RIGHT: Close-up of the 1935 version of the Palace (Courtesy Shchusev Museum) 62
2.13 Elite Moscow housing (Photo by author) 62
2.14 LEFT: Langman, GOSPLAN Building, 1935 (Photo by author); RIGHT: Boris Iofan, Narkomtjazhprom (NKTP) competition entry, 1934. (Courtesy Shchusev Museum of Architecture) 63
2.15 Malevich's 1930 exhibition "Soviet Artists in the last 15 Years" at the Russian Museum in Leningrad, with Lenin's statue on top of some *Arhitektony*. (Photographer unknown, from Alberto Samonà, ed., *Il Palazzo dei Soviet 1931–1933* (Rome: Officina Edizioni), 1976) 64
2.16 RIGHT: Boris Iofan, Barviha exterior view of single rooms and apartments (Courtesy Shchusev Museum of Architecture); LEFT: Double-room apartments. (Courtesy Mariya Kostyuk) 65
2.17 Barviha's initial round rooms. (Courtesy Shchusev Museum of Architecture) 66
2.18 Tubular furniture in the Barviha Sanatorium, 1936 (Courtesy Shchusev Museum of Architecture) 67
2.19 The Voroshilov, 1934. Rest home in Sochi. (LEFT: Courtesy Shchusev Museum Of Architecture; RIGHT: Photos by author) 68
2.20 M. Ginzburg, Ordzhonikidze sanatorium, Kislovodsk. View of the eastern dormitory overlooking Leonidov's monumental stairs, and 1936 site model—comparable with 1933 Alvar Aalto Paimio Sanatorium. (Courtesy Shchusev Museum of Architecture) 69
2.21 LEFT: Leonidov, chairs for the House of Pioneers, Moscow, 1934. RIGHT: Leonidov lounge chair for the sanatorium, 1938. (Photographers unknown) 70
2.22 LEFT: Leonidov's 1938 landscaping with replica of the balconies of one of the three towers of his 1934 NKTP competition entry (Photo by author). RIGHT: Leonidov's park amphitheater. (Photographer unknown) 71
2.23 Eastern dormitory's roof mass "Dissolving into thin air" and trellised roof garden. (Photos by author) 74
2.24 General panoramic view of the sanatorium (from the south), with the central therapy building acting as a pivot between the west (architect Vantangov) and the east (Ginzburg) front dormitories. (Photographer unknown) 75
2.25 LEFT: Antonio Carminati, Camera del Lavoro, Milan, in "Novecento" Style (Rempel's *Arhitektura Poslevoennoj Italii*, taken from 1934 German magazine, photographer unknown); RIGHT: Kislovodsk Sanatorium Eastern Pavilion, using the same "carving" into the mass of the front façade

xix

Illustrations

	wall—a design feature Michelangelo was first to use in his Laurential Library and later the Capitoline palaces in Rome. (Photo by author)	76
2.26	Deeply "carved" corner of the eastern building and C. E. Vantangov's more sober 1938 western building. (Photos by author)	77
2.27	LEFT: Back of western building. (Photo by author); RIGHT: Gropius Bauhaus student dormitory. (Fragment, photo by author)	78
2.28	LEFT: Side of western building "levitating" balcony (Photo by author); RIGHT: Leningrad's ASNOVA (Ladovskij's rationalist school) Kitchen Factory (1930–1931), architects Barutchev, Gilter, Meerzon, and Rubanchik. (Photographer unknown)	79
2.29	LEFT: Secluded façade of western building (Photo by author); RIGHT: Villa La Roche interior. (Courtesy Artists Rights Society)	79
2.30	Brutalist stairs of the central medical facility. (Photos by author)	79
2.31	Double-glazed cylindrical inner garden in the core of the medical pavilion. (Photo by author)	80
2.32	Medical administrative buildings, administration and physicians' offices. (Photographer unknown)	81
3.1	The second part of the ZIL Palace of Culture on the front page of *Stroitel'stvo Moskvy*, published upon completion, 1937.	85
3.2	Palace of Culture: Coiled stairs leading to observatory. (Photos Vladislav Ogay, 2016)	86
3.3	Main entrance of the Palace of Culture with glass semi-cylinders above. (Photographer unknown, courtesy of Shchusev Museum of Architecture)	87
3.4	LEFT: Palace of Culture eastern round entrance on east-west long axis; RIGHT: Revealing of the structural system, forming inner terraces. (Photos Vladislav Ogay, 2016)	88
3.5	Palace of Culture interior: A flying symphony of undulating forms. (Photos by author)	88
3.6	Awkward marble veneering of curved surfaces. (Photos by author)	90
3.7	White abstractness: A. Dushkin underground station "Dvorec Sovetov," renamed today as Kropotnickaja. (Courtesy Shchusev Museum of Architecture)	93
3.8	LEFT: Kropotnickaja Station (Courtesy Shchusev Museum of Architecture); RIGHT: Malevich, Kazimir (1878–1935). Suprematist Composition: White on White. 1918. Oil on canvas, 31 1/4 x 31 1/4" (79.4 x 79.4 cm). 1935 Acquisition confirmed in 1999 by agreement with the Estate of Kazimir Malevich and made possible with funds from the Mrs. John Hay Whitney Bequest (by exchange). The Museum of Modern Art. (Digital Image ©The Museum of Modern Art/Licensed by SCALA/Art Resource, NY)	94
3.9	A. Dushkin, Majakovskaja, 1938. Lighting System And The Black Square. (Photos by author).	95
3.10	Section of Majakovskaja showing steel structural system, a technological feat "floating" within the tunnel, by R. A. Sheinfains and Je. M. Grinzaid. (Courtesy Shchusev Museum of Architecture)	96

Illustrations

3.11 Dushkin's competition entry for Majakovskaja. Note the importance given to murals on the ceiling and ornamented vaults, none of which survives in the built station. (Courtesy Shchusev Museum of Architecture)   97
3.12 Nikolaj Ladovskij, Krasnaja Vorota Metro entrance. (Courtesy Shchusev Museum of Architecture)   99
3.13 Ladovskij, Dzherzhinskaja station, 1935. (Courtesy Alessandro de Magistris)   100
3.14 Chistye Prudy, František Sammer (Nikolaj Kolli's Workshop), 1937. (Courtesy Shchusev Museum of Architecture)   100
3.15 View of night spectacles at the 1937 Paris world's fair. German (left,) and Soviet (right) pavilions framed by the Eiffel Tower in flames. (Personal collection. Photographer unknown)   102
3.16 LEFT: "The Comet" pointing to the transcendent path of humanity (Personal collection); RIGHT: El Lissitzky theater set for Malevich's "Victory over the Sun." (Photographer unknown)   103
3.17 LEFT: Malevich's Solo Arhitekton; MIDDLE: View of central stairs, framed by N. Suetin's Suprematist sculptures (Private collection); RIGHT: Iofan's early "Suprematist" sketches for the Soviet Pavilion in Paris. (Courtesy Shchusev Museum of Architecture)   104
3.18 LEFT: 1939 New York Pavilion (New York World's Fair 1939–1940 records, Manuscripts and Archives Division, The New York Public Library); RIGHT: 1937 Exposition Palais De Chaillot by Jacques Carlu with Laprade's "Pavillion De La Paix" and its obelisk. (Private collection)   107
3.19 Novosibirsk, Regional Government architect, Boris A. Gordeev completed in 1933. (Courtesy Balandin Museum of Siberian Architectural History of NSUADA. Architecture of Novosibirsk. Avant-Garde)   109
3.20 Architects Vengerov and A. Shiraev Administration of the West-Siberian Railroads –Tomsk Region. LEFT: Competition entry, 1933 (?). The actual Façade can be noticed behind the grid of the columns; RIGHT: Completed building 1935. (Courtesy Balandin Museum of Siberian Architectural History of NSUADA. Architecture of Novosibirsk. Avant-Garde)   110
3.21 Novosibirsk, 1933 Kuzbassugol Coal Mining Workers, by architects. B. Gordeev and Dmitrij Ageev. (Courtesy Balandin Museum of Siberian Architectural History of NSUADA. Architecture of Novosibirsk. Avant-Garde)   111
3.22 Gordeev and Turgenev Housing For Artists 1934–1939. Note the slanted composition of the photo, an echo of Rodchenko's style. (Courtesy Balandin Museum of Siberian Architectural History of NSUADA. Architecture of Novosibirsk. Avan-Garda).   112
3.23 Two views of B. Gordeev's Housing Project, "Dom-Kombinat"—polyvalent housing building with restaurant and community services for the OGPU members, 1936. LEFT: side façade; RIGHT: main entrance volumes and courts. (Courtesy Balandin Museum of Siberian Architectural History of NSUADA. Architecture of Novosibirsk. Avant-Garde)   113

xxi

Illustrations

3.24 a) Sverdlovsk (Ekaterinburg) "Gorodok Chekistov" housing for the NKVD (Secret Police), Administration Building 1931–1939 (Courtesy Vitaly Sumin, Deputy Director SOKM History Museum, Ekaterinburg/Sverdlovsk); b) Sverdlovsk (Ekaterinburg) "Gorodok Chekistov" model and view of single employees housing, 1931–1939 (Courtesy Shchusev Museum of Architecture); c) Sverdlovsk (Ekaterinburg) "Gorodok Chekistov" housing for NKVD families, 1931–1939 (Courtesy Vitaly Sumin, Deputy Director SOKM History Museum, Ekaterinburg/Sverdlovsk); d) Sverdlovsk (Ekaterinburg) "Gorodok Chekistov," general view and model, 1931–1939. (Courtesy Shchusev Museum of Architecture)   115
3.25 Hotel in Rostov-na-Donu by Armenian architects I. E. Cherkesjan and H. H. Chalkushjan, today "Marins Park Hotel," 1934. (Photographer unknown)   116
3.26 Apartment blocks on Budemovskij Prospekt, built between 1928 and 1936 with no alterations. (Photographer unknown)   117
3.27 "Utjuzhok" building, City Utilities Administration in Voronezh, 1934, by architects Popov and Shaman. (Photographer unknown)   117
3.28 Newspaper agency in Baku, Azerbaijan, architect S. Pen, 1929–1934. (Photographer unknown)   119
3.29 Standard High School Building in Moscow by architect D. Fridman. (Photographer unknown)   120
3.30 Konstantin Mel'nikov, GOSPLAN garage, Moscow, 1934–1936. (Courtesy Shchusev Museum of Architecture)   121
4.1 Konstantin Mel'nikov, Competition Entry for the Commissariat Of Heavy Industry (NKTP), 1934. (Courtesy Shchusev Museum of Architecture)   132
5.1 *Arhitekturnaja Gazeta* with Alabjan's Keynote Speech. Photo: Presidium Members (LEFT to RIGHT): N. Kolli, V. Vesnin, I. Golovko, N. Bulganin, President Of The Moscow Soviet, B. Iofan, V. Shchuko, A. Shchusev, I. Chernyshev. On the same page bottom right, the famous ¡NO PASARAN! with the salute by Manuel Arcas from The Architects Of The Republican Spain. (Author's scan)   182
5.2 *Pravda:* The tracing of the route the Soviet aviators flew from the USSR to Portland, United States, June 1937. (Author's scan)   183
5.3 Coffee recess. Attending, from LEFT, Kolli, Iofan, Wright, Ol'ga Sasso-Ruffo Ogareva, Iofan's wife. (Private collection, photographer unknown)   194
5.4 Soviet poster published towards the end of the civil war: Saint George as a red Bolshevik killing the dragon of capitalism. (Private collection)   196
5.5 Wright's "modified" speech in *Pravda*. (Author's scan)   197

ACKNOWLEDGMENTS

It is difficult, after two decades of research and publishing partial results of one's findings, not to risk forgetting some of the many people who played a role in the book's growth, and I apologize in advance to anyone whom I may have missed inadvertently.

My deep gratitude goes to the Shchusev Museum in Moscow, and its knowledgeable staff. I recognize with great appreciation the offer of the then Director of the Museum Irina Korobyna to give us the selected visual material without charge, in exchange for the editor's willingness to insert the museum's logo in the book. This offer was graciously upheld by the new Director E.S. Lihachëva whom I especially thank for it.

I am particularly grateful to Pavel Kuznetsov, Deputy Director of the Shchusev Museum without whose dedicated help the book would have been greatly impaired. The museum's photo archivist Lev Rasadnikov spent hours, days and weeks with me, steadily and patiently sifting through the museum's vast visual collection, with his peculiar way of grumbling along, but in a kind way, while searching for proofs for my thesis. Alissa Gorlova and Irina Finskaya opened with a keen and expert eye the Museum's "graphics" collections, allowing me to slowly scrutinize and select documents destined for scanning. Equally kind and helpful were the staff in the section of personal archival funds, allowing me to study and record the voluminous documentation of the brothers Vesnin. My warmest thanks go also to the young researcher of the Museum, Mark-Eduard Akopian, who spent time with me in long conversations, generously giving me three documents he had found in the course of his own research, and taking me around Moscow in search of lesser known constructivist work. My thanks go as well to the former photographer of the Shchusev Museum, Anatolij Popov who, in addition to making some of the best photographs for my work, also convinced me, despite my desperate reticence, that the best cure from poisoning with tampered vodka is to drink more vodka the next day. His and his family's hospitality warmed and comforted sometimes difficult moments in Moscow.

Jean-Louis Cohen, a fierce critique of my work over more than thirty years since we met at MIT, helped me generously at each stage of my career. His faith in my undertaking meant very much. I am also uniquely grateful to my colleague and dear friend Richard Cleary who read earlier versions of the manuscript with close attention to detail and rigorous scholarly advice; to Vladimir Paperny who read and critiqued some of my chapters from his unique point of view; to Alla Vronskaya for years of sustained scholarly exchanges, discussions and collaboration in more ways than can be expressed here; to Alexander Ortenberg, friend and collaborator, who read some early chapters, and pointed to significant works I would not have taken into consideration otherwise; to Vladislav Ogay, production and scenic designer in Moscow, for graciously donating a number of

Acknowledgments

his photographs of the current state of the brothers Vesnins' Palace of Culture; to Maria Kostyuk, chief curator of the Shchusev Museum collections and a Boris Iofan specialist, who shared her knowledge on Iofan—one of the central figures of the book—and gave me a photograph she took at the Barviha Sanatorium, access to which is strictly limited; to architectural historians Marina Khrustaleva and Natalia Melikova (a leader of the Novosibirsk "Konstruktivizm Proekt") for helping me hunt down elusive architecture works; to Olga Khajdurova who found time to take me to A.A. Velikanov, who, beyond significant information on Stalin's Soviet Union and its architecture, showed me how you can spend three hours discussing and sipping vodka without any apparent loss of lucidity.

The sojourn at the National Gallery of Art as a CASVA Senior Fellow was momentous, most of all for the interaction it facilitated with other distinguished scholars, including late Henry Millon whose observations about my talk were decisive, and Stephen Mansbach whose strong support and enthusiasm about my thesis were hugely uplifting. The long letter he wrote me after reading my December 2009 *JSAH* essay was sizable for my further work. Greg Castillo's challenge to prove my intuition about the role Kaganovich played in creating VOPRA pushed me deeper into the archives with successful results. In addition to the rich facilities CASVA offered, it opened wide the doors to the Library of Congress whose librarians confirmed my repeated experience that librarians are the kindest, most dedicated and patient people anywhere in the world. Beyond its incredible sources, the possibility to compare holdings from the Soviet Union (Stalin's Great Encyclopedia among others) to the same doctored in Moscow was revealing, while at the same time filling the gaps. I am also grateful to the University of Texas Alexander Library reference librarian Katie Pierce Meyer who helped me with bibliographic searches, and in particular to the School of Architecture's Director of the Visual Collection, Elizabeth Schaub for her relentless assistance in the production of the book's photographs. A generous grant from the Graham Foundation helped me with one of my research campaigns in Russia; while the University of Texas at Austin made possible, thanks to a significant Faculty Grant, a flight to Moscow, and, from there, a two days' journey by train to the mountain range of the Northern Caucasus, where I discovered Moisej Ginzburg's major 1938 work—the "Ordzhonikidze" Sanatorium in Kislovodsk—a work vaguely remembered only by name, and even misplaced on occasion, some one thousand kilometers west from its actual location—on the Crimean coastline. The excitement of this discovery was only matched by the incredible generosity and hospitality of the Kislovodsk people, including the taxi driver who, alerted by the train attendant claiming, in her own words, that she "had never seen a Professor before," entered the wagon and offered me a tour of the place—for free. The first stop was the dacha Alexander III built for his preferred Bolshoi ballerina. I owe to my special friend Sarah Williams Goldhagen the opportunity to present the first results of this discovery at an international conference of medicine in Groningen, Holland.

In Ekaterinburg (Sverdlovsk), frustrated that all the images I requested were in low resolution, Vice Director General of the History Museum, Vitaly Sumin, grabbed his

Acknowledgments

camera and, without telling me, went out to make his own photographs of the buildings I needed; and then sent them to me in Texas. Daria Garkusha, Head of the S. N. Baladina Novosibirsk Museum went out of her way to find what I was looking for, at times undertaking, as she put it, "real little detective searches." I thank her for what she managed to find. The reason for the difficulties with photographic material in both Ekaterinburg and Novosibirsk, as they explained it to me, is that those cities used to be part of closed regions even to Soviet citizens with strictly controlled photographic funds—let alone for images of the NKVD or GPU buildings I needed. Curiously, the latter were most often designed by constructivists even as late as 1939, like the important "Gorodok Chekistov" compound in Ekaterinburg. I thank former curator of the RGALI, Elena Tchougounova-Paulson for graciously printing from microfilms one thousand pages covering the First Congress of Soviet Architects. I also thank the two archivists of the Russian Academy of Sciences in Moscow—at its "Communist Academy" section—where I discovered that VOPRA was Lazar Kaganovich's brainchild. The location being almost impossible to find (and Moscow is full of Academies of all kinds), the chief archivist offered to meet me at the metro station on her way to work; from there we walked through long Dedalian parks and haphazardly dispersed buildings. The former Central Committee archives, now the RGASPI, was a model of professionalism while leaving the impression of being fully accessible. An altogether different story was the Moscow Party Committee archives, where the archivists, enjoying day after day the absence of any researcher, preferred to continue reading comfortably their daily papers, rather than paying attention to the nuisance of their accidental client. Selective censorship was also noticeable there, with the director withholding some important boxes with the claim that I did not need them, based on my research topic.

The two archivists of the Columbia University Avery Drawings were of greatest assistance and support helping me through Wright's archives to which I was guided by Anthony Alofsin who never missed an occasion to express his support for my work. My deep appreciation goes to my friends Miroslava Benes and Francesco Passanti, who read and commented with the most focused and dedicated attention the drafts of my 2009 essay for the *Journal of Architectural Historians* and other articles that served as a foundation to the present book; and most in particular to Christopher Long who read and commented almost everything I wrote, and supported me with his enthusiasm and remarks. Branka Bogdanov, curator of the Boston ICA, read my manuscript when it still consisted only of one chapter. Her response was solid fodder for the efforts to come. I also thank my colleague Igor Siddiqui for his steady support, and, on occasions in Paris, replacing me generously in outings with students to allow me uninterrupted time to write. I also gained from exchanges with Thomas Flierl who writes on related topics. Equally uplifting was the enthusiasm for my discoveries of Novosibirsk University Professor Konstantin Bugrov, editor of the distinguished culture and history journal *Questio Rossica*. The appreciation of my pursuits Alessandro de Magistris, Professor at the Politécnico di Milano, expressed through our discussions, and whose work is tangential to mine, was always of great significance.

Acknowledgments

The input of my graduate students in seminars and their research papers should not be underestimated, and among them in particular Elijah Montez and Jenna Ahonen. My former doctoral student, and today a distinguished scholar in Slavic Studies, Vladimir Kulić, played a significant role at every stage of our professional relationship.

Yet my greatest recognition of all goes to Jasminka Udovički for years of unwavering intellectual and moral support.

INTRODUCTION

Stalinism in architecture was abolished two and a half years after Stalin's death with the stroke of a pen—on November 4, 1955. What ended was known as "socialist" realism—onerous classicizing eclecticism—struck down in a joint statement of the Central Committee of the Soviet Communist Party and Government.[1] The injunction came in the wake of year-long consultations with the building elite Nikita Khrushchëv had initiated with a speech on December 7, 1954. He called for an end to wasteful "feudal" building ornaments, while people were housed worse than he was as a worker before the revolution.[2]

Using a language reminiscent of the modern movement's critique of historicism, the Soviet communiqué invited nothing less than the reintroduction of modern architecture in terms strikingly consonant with those the Congrès Internationaux d'Architecture Moderne (CIAM), formulated in the *Athens Charter*.[3]

In contrast to this swift official reinstatement of mainstream modern architecture—albeit applied miserably in the desert left behind by the uprooting of the avant-garde movement, two decades earlier—the Stalinization of Soviet architecture[4] had been a much longer and more complex undertaking, fully achieved only after the Second World War. Open support for progressive architecture was expressed publicly down the 1930s while producing masterpieces, such as the 1937 Soviet Pavilion in Paris—even Frank Lloyd Wright saluted this as "a master architect's conception that walks away with the Paris fair."

The present book's reevaluation of the architectural discourse of the 1930s addresses thus-far mostly unexplored fields, apt at reshaping heretofore received notions. Indeed, far from driven into extinction, soon after the April 23, 1932 Central Committee decree

---

[1] See Thomas P. Whitney *Khrushchev Speaks* (Michigan University Press), pp. 153–92, 1963.
[2] The name itself —"socialist" realism—continued, however, to be used for the new trend as well. See Reid, Susan E. "Toward a New (Socialist) Realism: The Re-engagement with Western Modernism in the Khrushchev Thaw." In *Russian Art and the West: A Century of Dialogue in Painting, Architecture, and the Decorative Arts*, edited by Rosalind P. Blakesley and Susan E. Reid, 217–39. (DeKalb: Northern Illinois University Press), 2007. See also Andrew Elam Day, "The Rise and Fall of Stalinist Architecture." In *Architectures of Russian Identity: 1500 to the Present*, edited by James Cracraft and Daniel Rowland, 172–90. (Ithaca, NY: Cornell University Press), 2003.
[3] The concept of Modernity continues to be debated, and interpreted in architecture and in other fields with respect to its relationship to history and historicism. For the purposes of this monograph, "modernity" is understood as the broad cultural term indicating a period or place having been marked by the results of "modernization," which in turn includes the dominance of post-Cartesian and especially post-Kantian rationalism, with pervasive assumptions of progress. "Modernity" is thus as much an ideological construct as it is a set of phenomena. "Modernism" tends to describe movements within modernity related here primarily to the avant-garde of the 1920s in Europe and the Soviet Union.
[4] What is meant by "Stalinization" is the gradual abandonment of avant-garde and progressive architecture in in favor of various forms of eclecticism and historicism, including American "corporate architecture" simile.

on the dissolution of independent artistic societies, Soviet modern architecture not only survived, but even branched into new vital modern forms. This argument was supported by no less than the leader of the Constructivist movement himself—Moisej Ginzburg—in an essay he titled "Liberated Creativity." The essay was published in *Arhitektura SSSR* in September 1934. The "liberation" in question referred to the ARHPLAN, a new organization of the architectural production Lazar Kaganovich, Stalin's right hand in the Politburo, helped create in 1933. The ARHPLAN was composed of twelve Moscow workshops, five of which were headed by the most prominent leaders of the avant-gardes, Konstantin Mel'nikov included.

The book questions the broadly held beliefs that the April 23, 1932 decree came with the imposition of a restrictive style. Quite to the contrary, as this study shows, in party meetings, Kaganovich actually expressed support for the constructivists he saw as a force that "housed millions of people," and would continue building in the future for "many millions more"—obviously implying that constructivism was there to stay.

The Communist Party leadership of the new All-Union of Soviet Architects (SSA), saw it otherwise. Their undeclared, if obvious goal, was to build a career by supplanting the leaders of the avant-garde movement, with monopolizing the architectural discourse. They promoted "socialist" realism, whose meaning they themselves were unable to elaborate. They just hoped, as a party member put it, that it would be "revealed" to them at some point.

The difficulty in agreeing what "socialist" realism ought to mean in architecture—a concept drawn uncritically from the 1934 First Congress of Soviet writers[5]—was compounded with the divergent stylistic preferences of the party's top leadership itself. In addition, the architectural apparatchiks were faced with the determined resistance of the avant-gardes, as well as of the younger generation of architects at large—the Communist youth (Komsomols) included. They were not ready to jettison modern architecture in the name of an obscure "socialist" realism that stubbornly refused to reveal itself. Given such uncertainties, the architecture communist leaders had no choice but to keep postponing their congress some five times, from 1933 to 1937.

Further proof of the avant-garde's vitality was that architecture party leaders, essentially Karo Alabjan, Arkadij Mordvinov, and Jakov Aleksandrov, harbored a genuine fear, uttered in secret party meetings, that the avant-gardes, presenting themselves as "an offended side" would "use the congress as a platform for propagating their own ideas." Ultimately, if still not fully in control, the SSA party cell had no choice but settle for 1937, the twentieth anniversary of the revolution they could not ignore.

Among the most notable examples of the architectural diversity throughout the 1930s were two singularly innovative Metro stations young Aleksej Dushkin inaugurated in 1935 and 1938 respectively with intriguing references to Malevich's "White on White" 1919 canvas for the first station; and to the latter's celebrated "Black Square" for the

---

[5] See *Problems of Soviet Literature: reports and Speeches at the First Soviet Writers' Congress* by A Zhdanov, Maxim Gorky, N. Bukharin, K. Radek, A. Stetsky (Moscow & Leningrad: Cooperative Publishing Society of Foreign Workers in the USSR), 1935.

second; the Vesnin brothers' main part of their Palace of Culture, built from 1935 to 1937, with its striking modernist interiors, still unexplored to this day; Mel'nikov's little-known 1936 GOSPLAN garage; Ginzburg's all-but-forgotten 1938 "Ordzhonikidze" sanatorium at Kislovodsk—published in a 1940 monograph—hidden in the forbidding mountain range of the Northern Caucasus.

A reassessment of the last, 1934 version of the Palace of the Soviets, a hyper-Stalinist project of oppressive monumentality offers, as the present book argues, another unexpected illustration of the surviving spirit of the avant-gardes in the USSR under Joseph Visarionovich Stalin's "Revolution from above." This spirit, in the work of Boris Iofan—virtually Stalin's personal architect—was echoed even more explicitly in the same architect's 1937 Paris Pavilion where Malevich's suprematism occupied a central place.

The present book explores the importance of these and other projects, offering a new interpretation of a historic turning point in Soviet architecture. This reconsideration includes both the architecture designed before the 1932 dissolution of independent avant-garde groups, but completed down the decade without alterations; and important modern work conceived and built entirely after 1932. The ambition of this study is not to present an exhaustive collection of the relevant work pertaining to its general argument, but rather to bring to light important examples that can support the claim of a strong presence of modern architecture under Stalin's "perestroika" (reconstruction) as he called it.

Beyond its architectural discoveries, the book shows that, unlike the Russian Association of Proletarian Writers (RAPP) and the Russian Association of Proletarian Musicians (RAPM), the All-Union Society of Proletarian Architects (VOPRA), far from being a spontaneous organization, was Kaganovich's 1929 brainchild, intended to accelerate the Cultural Revolution in the field of architecture. As such, after 1932, VOPRA was immediately morphed into a Communist Party cell that operated under the cover of secrecy into shaping the policies of the Union, with Kaganovich looming over it.

Not in the least irrelevant was Frank Lloyd Wright's correspondence with Soviet official architects throughout the 1930s. The mutual admiration was underscored by the triumphal reception Wright received at the congress, raising further questions about the nature and scope of the complex Soviet architectural discourse down the 1930s.

It is important to note, however, that, in the period under consideration what the Stalinist discourse collapsed into "constructivism," most often encompassed loosely the entire body of Soviet modern architecture, while arbitrarily blacklisting "formalism." Formalism included, by official fiat, even the eminently constructivist work of Ivan Leonidov, the pride of the second generation of constructivists, and the darling of his teacher—Aleksandr Vesnin. Therefore, Stalinist official critique operated with just two basic notions: "constructivism" and "formalism" in a politicized dichotomy where the latter was to be eliminated at all costs. Evidently, such approach to the avant-garde opened the door to perfunctory arbitrariness. While all three branches of the avant-gardes survived unambiguously to the end of the decade, that is, constructivism, rationalism, and suprematism—the politically ideologized distinction gradually reduced the critical architectural discourse to a meaningless construct.

By the late 1930s, the term "constructivism" described simply "modern architecture" in loosely CIAM terms having lost its specific distinction.

To further clarify the terminology, without falling into oversimplifications, one has to look at what constructivism meant originally, beyond Aleksej Gan's early Manifesto, *Konstruktivizm* (1922).

Born out of the "deconstruction" of traditional architecture (see the brother Vesnins' 1922 Palace of Labor competition entry), its "reconstruction," based on advanced technology and scientific knowledge, was theorized, as Manfredo Tafuri asserted, by two groups of linguists known today as "Russian Formalists." The most prominent group was the OPOJAZ—the "Society of Poetic Language." According to them, the true content of a work was its form. The new forms were the result of the montage of linguistic elements (materials, volumes, spaces), possibly even incongruous, into novel semantic series, acting on semantic displacements. In other words, their association would lead to the "estrangement" or "distanciation" (*ostranenie*) of its constitutive elements yielding an excess of meaning. Such constructive process or device (*priëm*) defining the work of art—"*Iskusstvo kak priëm*" (art as process) —was best illustrated in cinematic "editing" that the Formalist Viktor Shklovskij theorized in his writings; and filmmakers such as Sergei Eisenstein or Dziga Vertov used to synthesize into an innovative cinematic language. For Viktor Shklovskij, the work as such was "not an object, not a material, but a relationship of materials." Therefore, the accent was put on process (priëm), the "how" preceding the "what."

Such emphasis on the device in the work of art led the constructivists to reject the term "building" in favor of "editing" or "montage" of their architecture works. Ginzburg used explicitly the term on the occasion of his 1930 housing project, known as the "Narkomfin," because "We do not build anymore, we assemble: Architecture is montage." The Narkomfin, a constructivist work par excellence, thus had not been "built," but "edited." The result was the most accomplished example of constructivist architecture.

The negative connotation the Stalinists attributed to what they called "formalism" was likely derived from a convenient misuse, or abuse of the concept, based on the Formalists' principle that, as mentioned, the art-work's true content was its form.

***

The present book moves from the creation of VOPRA to the first repressive measures that curtailed the avant-gardes' institutions, replacing them with controlled and bureaucratized media. It shows how VOPRA, that Kaganovich created in response to the Lenin Library competition controversy, gradually eroded from within all the institutions of the architectural avant-gardes, like a virus implanted into a cell.

At the same time, the book argues that, despite such regressive realignment of the architectural condition, the leaders of the avant-gardes (with the tragic exception of the young Leonidov), maintained a leading position in most of the new architectural venues. The underlying argument of the second chapter is that the avant-gardes were able to continue implementing their progressive work either conceived before or after the disbanding of the autonomous groups. In this respect, the April 23, 1932 was not a "turning point" in terms of stylistic reversals. It only reframed the context within which architects were to operate. That hinge should rather be moved to 1936, when Ginzburg's call to generalize constructivism as the future of Soviet architecture caused a violent reaction of the most conservative factions in the central party institutions.

On the other hand, Stalin's infatuation with American corporate skyscrapers led to the cross fertilization, as the chapter's argument goes, not only between Boris Iofan's Palace of the Soviets and Raymond Hood's Rockefeller Center; it also points to Hood's apparent indebtedness to Malevich's own 1923 suprematist "skyscrapers" that Hood had the opportunity to see in a New York exhibition at the time he begins to design his Center. The latter might explain the abrupt and radical change in Hood's architectural expression.

Iofan's modernist Barviha sanatorium in the vicinity of Moscow, designed and redesigned from 1928 to 1936, demonstrates not only the significant versatility of the official architect—from the Palace of the Soviets to his 1940 Baumanskaja Metro station—all connected in one way or another to Malevich—but points generally to the diversity of the architectural expression found in the 1930s.

The third chapter addresses a wide range of modernist building types encompassing the realm of culture and education, underground transportation, administration, health and housing, and not in the least Soviet representation abroad—all designed after 1932, and built along the decade. A special consideration is given, in the third chapter, to Iofan's Soviet Pavilion in Paris. Some attention is also devoted to work in Novosibirsk, Ekaterinburg [Sverdlovsk], Rostov-na-Donu, Voronezh, and Baku, designed and built between 1931 and 1938. The chapter concludes with Mel'nikov's 1936 GOSPLAN garage, which was also to be his last.

The fourth chapter analyses the institutional environment within which the architectural avant-gardes were able to preserve the architecture discussed in the previous two chapters, while buttressing the first chapter with documentation and insights offered regarding the shaping of the architecture ideology within the Stalinist project.

The review of the professional press uncovers an *Arhitektura SSSR* trying to present itself as a neutral, detached medium, open to all that was called architecture on the professional scene of the country and abroad. Starting with 1936, however, it turns increasingly militant with intrinsic bias in the ideological and political sense, including regular reporting on the show trials and harangues against presumed "saboteurs" or "enemies of the people," while Stalin's name is always printed in red. Still, this did not prevent the journal from publishing in 1939 what was probably Moisej Ginzburg's last essay. Titled "The Organic in Architecture and in Nature,"[6] a topic integral to his concept of constructivism he developed in the mentioned 1940 book on his Kislovodsk sanatorium, while now aligning it with what he calls "socialist" realism.

As the decade progressed, the rubric on the so-called "architectural legacy" signaled "the critical assimilation of the architectural heritage" as an undeclared new direction. To this, Ginzburg and the Vesnins would respond sarcastically in a 1934 essay: "Which

---

[6] *Arhitektura SSSR*, 9, 1939, pp. 76–80.

legacy, Egyptian? Gothic? Greco-Roman?" —none of which, of course, was found in Russia. Finally, probably following Kaganovich's call (first formulated by Stalin) for an architecture that would be "national in form and socialist in content," ethnic architecture takes front stage as an "insatiable source of inspiration."

Still, *Arhitektura SSSR* continued to act, significantly, as an open forum for progressive architecture until the end of the decade. Despite an inevitable a priori political restrain, lingering self-censorship and ideological bias that mostly characterized the anonymous editorials, the journal maintained a serious intellectual discourse throughout the decade. Such were contributions by I. Vercman's discussion on "Hegel and Architecture"[7] (1936) or R. Higer's, D. Arkin's, N. Ladovskij's, N. Miljutin's, and M. Ginzburg's theoretical essays. In this respect, *Arhitektura SSSR* certainly appeared superior to mainstream, vocational architectural journals in Europe or in the United States. Wright himself noticed the fact, as he compared the vastly superior intellectual level of architects he met in Russia, to what he knew in the United States.

A close reading given to the party and SSA meetings in the fourth chapter is picked up in the fifth, which considers the entire decade. Unsuccessful efforts to figure out what "socialist" realism might mean in architecture were coupled with efforts to curb the recalcitrant leaders of the avant-gardes. These labors were referred to in the meetings as desperate "uphill battles" with the constructivists; along with often comic complaints such as the discovery that their own Komsomol members report to their constructivist workshop leaders all that was said about them in the secret party meetings; or that debates about Marxism in the workshops were not at all lead by the communists.

The fifth chapter concludes with a discussion of the Congress itself, which finally opens on June 17, 1937. It is there and then that Alabjan's worst fears about the congress unfolded into a nightmare, as Viktor Vesnin, deputy of the Supreme Soviet, and member of the Congress's presidium, unleashes a fiery defense of the historic significance of constructivism, naming, one by one, the attending upper crust architects who all built constructivist architecture for over ten years —including a livid Alabjan and the turncoat Kolli who had provoked Vesnin with his false claims that constructivism had been a fad limited to a misguided youth in the academia. Having been vividly interrupted throughout with enthusiastic applauses and laughter, Vesnin ended his speech, however, admitting tragically that constructivism had been defeated. The huge standing ovation of an elated audience clearly showed where the hearts of architects from all over the country still stood. The *Pravda* only published the part of Vesnin's speech where he declared the end of constructivism.

The other highlight of the week-long congress was Wright's speech with comic remarks pointing to his feeble understanding of the reality that surrounded him. The heavily censored report of his speech in the *Pravda* had him say the exact opposite of what he actually claimed. Francis Jourdain, a French Communist sympathizer, was the only foreign speaker who warned the Soviets about the dangerous direction they seemed to be taking. His speech was not published in the *Pravda*.

---

[7] *Arhitektura SSSR*, 6, 1936, pp. 65–71.

CHAPTER 1
A CALL FOR THE PARTY TO DEFEND MODERN ARCHITECTURE: STALIN'S "CULTURAL REVOLUTION" AND THE APORIA OF "PROLETARIAN ARCHITECTURE"

In 1928, when Stalin ended Lenin's New Economic Policy (NEP)—a mix of state capitalism and market economy[1]—he embarked in a system never tested before, a centrally planned economy. Lenin had introduced the NEP at the end of the Civil War in an effort to revive production and consumption. Antonio Gramsci, who addressed the Bolshevik Revolution in numerous writings, considered that this Revolution contradicted the logic of Marx's political economy. It is not to be excluded that such claim may have played a role in Lenin's decision to reintroduce some forms of capitalist economy after meeting Gramsci in Moscow in 1921. As founder of the Italian Communist Party, the latter saw the Bolshevik Revolution as premature, that is, "contradicting Marx's *Capital*," in a country with eighty percent of peasants, most of which were illiterate.

The reversal of the NEP meant no less than the overhaul of the entire economic and political system. Stalin referred to these transformations as *perestrojka* or "reconstruction," also popularly known, later on, as "revolution from above." To achieve such undertaking, he launched a vast social mobilization, including fabricated trials, to unsettle the economic and cultural protagonists of the NEP years.[2] As a justification for such systemic upheaval, indeed a "cultural revolution," Stalin declared that the successful building of socialism required an intensification of the "class struggle." This thesis did not go unchallenged of course. The resistance to curtailing the NEP, followed by accelerated industrialization and forced collectivization of farmland came from top members of the Central Committee, including such figures as Aleksej Rykov, head of the government (SNK) until 1930, Nikolaj Buharin (1888-1938) or Nadezhda Krupskaja (1869-1939)—Lenin's widow.[3]

As Sheila Fitzpatrick has claimed, "The party's leading organs encouraged groups of militant young communist 'proletarians' [...] to challenge, intimidate and humiliate their bourgeois elders and competitors in various spheres of cultural institutions."[4] This first

---

[1] See among others William G. Rosenberg, "NEP Russia as a 'Transitional' Society," in *Russia in the Era of NEP: Explorations in Soviet Society and Culture*, ed. Sheila Fitzpatrick, Alexander Rabinowitch, Richard Stites, (Bloomington: Indiana University Press, 1991).
[2] According to Roy Medvedev, the dissident Soviet historian, *Let History Judge: The Origins and Consequences of Stalinism* (New York: Alfred A. Knopf), 1972, p. 112. Based on an NKVD official's claim, the show trials for alleged "sabotage" against the technical *intelligencija* were aimed at "mobilizing the working masses," around the call for "intensified vigilance"—an opening for the brutal repression to come in the 1930s.
[3] See among others, Roy Medvedev "*Staline et le Stalinisme*" (Paris: Albin Michel), 1979, p. 97.
[4] Sheila Fitzpatrick, *The Cultural Front: Power and Culture in Revolutionary Russia* (Ithaca and London: Cornell University Press), 1992, p.192.

mobilization of the *perestrojka* involved preexisting groups of party members associated, among others, in proletarian organizations of arts and literature. Stirring up such associations from behind the scenes was a way of legitimizing the *perestrojka* as an alleged spontaneous grass-roots movement. The associations' simultaneous and "sudden rise to relevance and visibility between 1928–1929," can hardly be explained otherwise than by an orchestrated action from a single source. What clearly points into that direction is the Central Committee's swift creation of an additional "proletarian association"—the All-Union Society of Proletarian Architects (Vsesojuznoe Obshchestvo Proletarskyh Arhitektorov [VOPRA]) that Lazar Kaganovich, a top Politburo member, immediately put to task in the summer of 1929, in the wake of the Lenin Library controversy discussed later in this chapter.

Lazar Moisejevich Kaganovich (1893–1991),[5] of Jewish Ukrainian descent, had been a relatively minor figure in the Bolshevik Revolution. He held until 1928 the post of Secretary of the Ukrainian party. As part of his secret campaign to surround himself with unconditional supporters, as he gradually increased his power, Stalin brought Kaganovich to Moscow in 1928 where the latter rapidly rose to the top of Soviet leadership, second only to Stalin. In 1930 he joined the Politburo, while also taking the position of First Secretary of the Moscow Party, which was dominated by the Buharinist Right Opposition. Under Stalin's orders, he was to undertake an uncompromising purge of both Left and Right oppositions.

Adamantly devoted to his benefactor, he also played a sinister role in the forced collectivization that caused a devastating famine in 1932–1933, especially hitting southern Ukraine, the bread basket of the country. The confiscated wheat staple was used for the purchase of industrial machinery from the West. Stalin promoted Kaganovich to Secretary of the Central Committee in1928.[6] This gave him ample means to act as a top party organizer. As a pivotal figure of the "revolution from above," Kaganovich played a central role in the modernization of Moscow, notably the development of the subway, as discussed in the third chapter. While organizing the upcoming 16th Party Congress, he sought to obtain a rough estimate of how many party members were reliable, that is, how many were actually ready to fight for the new "party line." In the months that preceded the crucial Congress, Kaganovich thus noted casually on the corner of his copy of the congress program, with a red pencil: "Expel twenty-five percent of party members"[7]—a rogue estimate with well-known consequences down the upcoming decade of arbitrary "chistkas" (purges).

While Stalin's power was significantly increased at the end of the congress, his full, unchallenged control of the country occurred only at the next 17th Party Congress in 1934 soon christened, for good reason, "The Congress of the Victors." Once all cultural associations were dissolved in 1932, the "proletarians" were automatically turned into

---

[5] See among others, E. A. Rees, *Iron Lazar: A Political Biography of Lazar Kaganovich* (New York: Anthem Press), 2012.
[6] See among others Kathleen Benton *Moscow, an Architecture History* (London: I B Tauris) 1990, pp. 217–37.
[7] RGASPI Fond 81, op. 3, ed. hr. 4, p. 3

virtually secret party cells (*partgruppy*) incorporated into the new, centralized unions. This was, notably, the case of VOPRA, as discussed further. It mattered that the public did not associate the actions of the proletarians with the party's leading organs. Such "mobilization of the masses" and calls for an "increased vigilance against the counterrevolution" were essential aspects of what current historiography calls "cultural revolution"—albeit semantically very different from Lenin's acceptation of the term, as Fitzpatrick has pointed out.[8]

To situate the circumstances that ultimately allowed modern architecture to survive against all odds under Stalin's "revolution from above," we will turn to the dramatic effects the initial cultural revolution had on the realm of architecture between 1928 and 1930. The institutions of the existing spontaneous movements were to be gradually infiltrated and dissolved. Contrary to what has been argued thus far,[9] however, the actual circumstances need to be nuanced. Meaningful intellectual exchanges in architectural criticism and theory did survive almost to the end of the 1930s, prompting the visiting Frank Lloyd Wright to marvel about the Soviet architects' intellectual sophistication in comparison to those he knew in the US as argued in Chapter 4.

***

The pivotal event to be addressed here is the competition for the 1928 Lenin Library. The controversy about the contested results of the competition brought for the first time a highly public clash between the forces of the architectural avant-garde and the rising conservative movement. The assumption of the moderns was that the party, as had been the case at least implicitly, throughout the 1920s, accepted progressive, thus revolutionary architecture.

In the wake of the Lenin Library dispute, the second crucial moment to be considered is the party's creation behind the scenes of VOPRA—which aimed at monopolizing the public discourse on architecture. In what appeared as a paradox, VOPRA members adhered to a constructivist style all the way to and inclusive of the second competition for the iconic Palace of Soviets, while advocating the embrace of "proletarian architecture." Without ever being able to define what did they mean by "proletarian architecture"— later replaced by an equally obscure "socialist" realism—VOPRA used the term to disqualify a priori anything beyond its own work, that is, to primarily undermine the work of the living avant-gardes.

With this goal in mind, the first and major victim was to be, logically, the hotbed of Soviet modern architecture—the art and architecture school the avant-gardes created in

---

[8] The purpose of the famous "Shahtij" trial in the spring of 1928 against a group of "bourgeois" engineers, according to an NKVD official—as reported by Roy Medvedev and quoted by Sheila Fitzpatrick, was "to mobilize the masses," "to arouse their wrath against the imperialists," "to intensify the vigilance." Fitzpatrick, "Cultural Revolution as Class War" in Sheila Fitzpatrick, ed. *Cultural Revolution in Russia, 1928–1931* (Bloomington: Indiana University Press), 1984, p. 10. See other authors in Fitzpatrick's edited book for various aspects of that revolution. The trial can be taken as the beginning of the campaign.

[9] Hugh Hudson, *Blue Prints and Blood: The Stalinization of Soviet Architecture, 1917–1937* (Princeton University Press), 1994, pp. 136–47.

the wake of the revolution—the VHUTEMAS. Founded the same year as the Bauhaus (1919), the VHUTEMAS has often been compared to the former. VOPRA's next move were to be, as will be discussed, the cynical attempts at destroying morally and professionally the icon of the second generation of constructivists, Ivan Leonidov (1902–1959), set to lead the architectural revolution into the 1930s and beyond.

The next victim in line would be the innovative journal *Sovremenaja Arhitektura*, as the main vehicle for the dissemination of new architectural ideas—edited by two of the founders and leaders of constructivism—Aleksandr Vesnin (1883–1959) and Moisej Ginzburg (1892–1946). Parallel to these actions was the fateful Central Committee decision on April 16, 1930 to stop funding the workers' experimental house communes in which the avant-garde was invested in searching for alternative, "socialist housing" that would be mass produced without lowering their living and architectural quality.

Meanwhile, contradictions continued to abound as one of VOPRA's leaders, Arkadij Mordvinov (1896–1964)—responsible for Leonidov's violent character assassination and dismissal from his teaching position—organized in 1930 a major Moscow exhibition of no less than the Bauhaus itself. This can be explained to a large extent by the longstanding double standard that the Soviets cultivated, as they catered to the progressive *intelligencija* abroad—a vehicle of their international standing.

While this chapter registers the methodical demise of the avant-garde's institutions at home, it also shows that this did not preclude the state institutions from organizing, not only a major exhibition of the Bauhaus in 1930, but also making efforts to bring the Congrès internationaux d'architecture moderne (CIAM) to hold a congress in Moscow as late as 1935; or else invite Frank Lloyd Wright as a much worshiped guest to the founding Congress of Soviet Architects in the summer of 1937.

The Lenin Library Competition: The Avant-Gardes' First Loss

The effort to sustain the Russian modernist cause in the 1930s was launched through the complex events that surrounded the competition for the Lenin Library in Moscow, when the modernists appealed to the party to come to the rescue of progressive architecture.

The planning for a new central public library in the Soviet capital represented one of the most prestigious architectural undertakings since the 1917 October Revolution. It directly addressed a significant aspect of the regime's efforts, not only to raise the cultural level of the population in general, but to contribute as well to the young Soviet Republic's ambitions in the field of scientific research ingrained in the Revolution's ethos. The old Moscow main public library had no room left to accommodate rapidly growing collections. There was a sense of urgency as books piled up, inaccessible to the public.

Inevitably, the architectural concept to be adopted divided those who held that only a modern architecture could honor such enterprise and conservative circles who could not imagine a major library without its ponderous Roman orders. Not in the least was the issue compounded by the library's location facing the Kremlin's medieval walls.

The Moskovskoe Arhitekturnoe Obshchestvo (MAO), a prerevolutionary Moscow architectural society reinstated in 1923, juried the competition. Not unlike most competitions in the USSR, the latter was organized in two parts. One was open to the entire profession, the other only to invited architects. Because of its conservative jury, the open contest for the library attracted fewer than ten entries—almost certainly why young Leonidov, from the second generation of constructivists, did not take part in it. In addition to the four invited architectural teams, including the Vesnin brothers Aleksandr (1883–1959), Viktor (1882–1950), and Leonid (1880–1933), who heralded constructivism in architecture with their 1923 Palace of Labor, the entrants included several well-established academic figures from Tsarist times. Out of four invitees, only the Vesnin team had radically renounced their conservative pre-1917 architecture. The other invited participants included the engineer Ivan Rerberg (1869–1932, already active in the previous century); the Ukrainian classicist Vladimir Shchuko (1879–1939); and the presumed designer of Lenin's permanent mausoleum, Alexej Shchusev (1873–1949).

The new generation of architects that grew out of the 1917 upheavals was mostly trained at the Moscow VHUTEMAS (later VHUTEIN), one of the most innovative and largest schools of art and architecture in Europe that trained over one thousand students and more at any time. The school offered the students the possibility to choose between Masterskie (master workshops) directed by artists and architects adhering to different modernist orientations, but which also included a traditional academic curriculum run by established classicists.[10]

To resist countrywide reactionary trends of this sort, the VHUTEIN's Scientific and Technical Architectural Club called for a public debate at its premises on Miasnitckaja Street, in the vicinity of the designated building site for Le Corbusier's Centrosojuz.[11]

The public response to the call was overwhelming. Huge crowds of Moscow students, professors, and architects attended the meeting, turning it into a plebiscite against "architects who were active before the revolution and who belonged to aristocratic and bourgeois circles."[12] One speaker pointed out sardonically that Soviet architecture seemed to be undergoing its own "renaissance," with new projects and buildings boasting Palladian façades.

The debate ended with a unanimous resolution emphasizing the need for a "systematic and relentless struggle" against what the assembly regarded as "the indifference of the profession" to the country's actual conditions and against the rejection of contemporary materials and innovative structural systems.[13] The declaration stated emphatically:

---

[10] The VHUTEMAS (Vysshie Hudozhestveno-Tehnicheskie Masterskie, or Higher Artistic and Technical Workshops), was founded in 1919 by the People's Commissariat for the Enlightenment (NARKOMPROS) under the Commissar Anatolij Lunacharskij (1875–1933). The school was renamed VHUTEIN (Vysshie Hudozhestveno-Tehnicheskij Institut, or Higher Artistic and Technical Institute) in 1927.

[11] *SA* 2 (1928), p. 3. Ironically, this was also the street where in 1912 the Vesnin brothers contributed to the design of Moscow's Central Post Office with an eclectic style combining neo-Byzantine and Romanesque elements.

[12] "A Necessary Struggle: Protest Resolution on the VHUTEIN Dispute," *SA* 3 (1928), 6.

[13] Ibid. p. 4.

[We are] AGAINST ignoring the new social and existential phenomena in architecture,

AGAINST ignoring contemporary materials and constructive systems,

AGAINST going back to old forms of "national" architecture

AGAINST building in the "styles"

AGAINST an orientation toward "reactionary artistic old formulae"

AGAINST the hegemony of the most reactionary architects in the provincial cities and the republics of the union, i.e., where a struggle against the danger from the right in architecture is indispensable.

What most worried the document's signatories was a "tendency, increasingly evident in the whole country, toward a revival of the old forms of 'national' architecture (Figure 1.1) and toward the reintroduction of the 'styles.'"

Most strikingly, the resolution of the assembly "[called] on the party and other organizations leading the Cultural Revolution to take an interest in the problems of architecture, and to organize discussions on the contentious issue with a broad participation of party membership and the Soviet public opinion." The document concluded that only one thing could solve the crisis: to attract "young architectural forces that have grown and learned their trade in a new revolutionary society."[14]

The plea for party intervention indicates how unconscious many were at that time of the actual nature of Stalin's *perestrojka*.[15] The resolution was published in the press. New

Figure 1.1 LEFT: Baku, "Moresque" first electric train station, 1928 (Photographer unknown); RIGHT: Erevan, "Byzantine-like" administrative building, 1927. (National Museum of Architecture Erevan, Armenia)

---

[14] See "Protiv neprincipielnogo eklektizma" (Against Unprincipled Eclecticism), *SA* 3 (1928), 92.

[15] For the real measure of the Bolshevik-Soviet popular support throughout most of the 1930s, see Stephen Kotkin, *Magnetic Mountain: Stalinism as a Civilization* (Berkley, Los Angeles, London: University of California Press), 1995.

A Call for the Party to Defend Modern Architecture

protests flooded the editorial board of the *SA*. "The immense majority of the architectural community had already decried earlier the erection of the Central Telegraph by the engineer I. I. Rerberg—just two blocks from the Kremlin," the journal reported.[16] Other critics chastised Ivan Zholtovskij's (1867–1959), "Renaissance" Gosbank (state bank) in Moscow and his "obsolete" Palace of Friendship in Mahach-Kala (Dagestan).

Deaf to these protests, the jury published its verdict after the second round of the library contest. The scandal was now complete. Not only had the jury turned down the previous prizewinners—the Fridman, Fidman, and Markov architectural team—with their elegant modernist solution, rendered in a graphically innovative blue monochrome,[17] but, as the protesters saw it, they had rewarded the worst entry, the one by Shchuko (Figure 1.2).

His building's entry consisted of a peristyle of fourteen square columns with diminutive capitals, all veneered with black granite. The columns supported a massive attic of white marble sculpted like a Roman sarcophagus and bearing the name of Lenin.

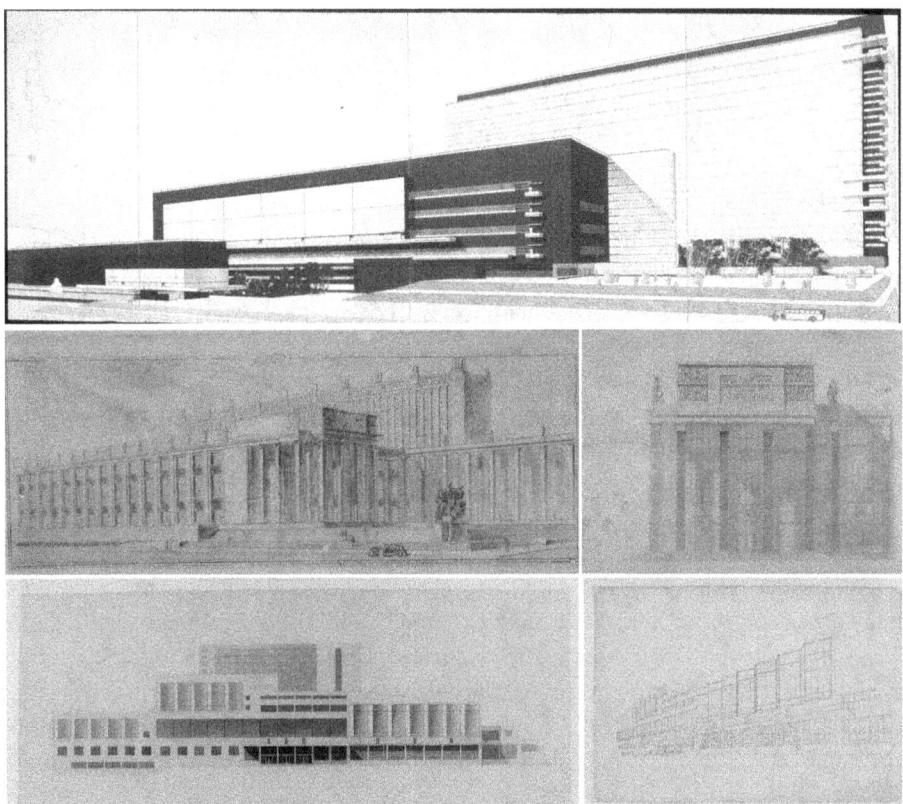

Figure 1.2 Lenin Library Competition: TOP: Fridman, Fidman, and Markov, First Prize. MIDDLE: V. Shchuko, Lenin Library, with Lenin's name on the "sarcophagus"-like pediment. BOTTOM: The Vesnin brothers' entry. (Courtesy Shchusev Museum of Architecture)

---

[16] Ibid. p. 2.
[17] *Stroitel'stvo Moskvy* 6 (1928), p. 3.

Soviet Architectural Avant-Gardes

Beyond the entrance hall, visitors were faced with monumental stairs framed by columns and classical sculptures.

In contrast to Shchuko's pompous and intimidating building, the Fridman, Markov, and Fidman design from the first round comprised three inviting, transparent library units, clearly conveying the message that they were repositories of knowledge accessible to all.

While forming small plazas and groves, the three buildings of the library were deployed in an ascending hierarchical sequence, away from the noisy boulevard that separated them from the Kremlin walls. With a touch of classicism, such as discreet cornices, the library aptly combined mainstream European modernism with some typical De Stijl devices that were inspired by J. J. Oud's or Walter Gropius's early work. Frozen in dynamic balance, the volumes were veneered with dark blue ceramic tiles and huge glass curtain walls. Alternating awnings and balconies along the building's edges gave the third, tallest structure—containing the bookstacks—a sense of refined elegance. Irregularly distributed balconies, recesses, and strip windows articulated its massive glass volume. A slender, elongated glass tower, streamlined in a Mendelsohnian fashion, contained stairs recalling Walter Gropius's in his 1914 Fagus Factory. The glass volume dramatically marked the main, ceremonial entrance, while acting as a lit billboard at night.

The smallest building, directly related to the street with an independent entrance, contained reading rooms for periodicals and a children's library. The central library structure, intended for research, projected a huge three-story prismatic bay window. Resembling a giant glass bookcase, the bay allowed optimal lighting to the main reading room while offering readers a commanding view of the Kremlin palaces and churches.

From the street, the bay allowed passersby an inviting view of its internal activity signifying open access to knowledge. The library's contrasting permeable and reflective abstract forms acted as a neutral urban link between eighteenth-century Moscow and the medieval Kremlin. Unlike Shchuko's artificially inflated verticality, accented by aimless giant orders, the first-place design in the first round had offered the simplicity and directness of large horizontal volumes. One spoke with provincial tiredness, the other with cosmopolitan modernity.

Joining the controversy that filled the pages of the professional magazines, the party daily *Pravda*,[18] the government daily *Izvestija*,[19] and the communist youth paper *Komsomolskaja Pravda*[20] (none yet fully under Stalin's spell) assailed the jury for selecting Shchuko. The criticism directed against the jury became ever bolder. Obviously reflecting the Moscow Party Committee's "Right" orientation,[21] *Stroitel'stvo Moskvy*, the official magazine of the City Hall, published a formal protest signed by the leading modernist

---

[18] *Pravda*, 15 VI 1928, p. 6.
[19] *Izvestija*, 13 VI. 1928, p. 5.
[20] *Komsomol'skaja Pravda*, 16 VI 1928, p. 1.
[21] See Catherine Merridale, *Moscow Politics and the Rise of Stalin: The Communist Party in the Capital, 1925–32* (London: Macmillan) 1990.

architectural societies—OSA (Society of Contemporary Architects) and ASNOVA (Association of New Architecture), which mutated into ARU in November 1928.[22]

The temperature rose when the editorial board of *Stroitel'stvo* published an open letter to the competition jury and to its president, the People's Commissar for Enlightenment, Anatolij Lunacharskij (1873–1933), saying: "Lunacharskij has to tell us why Shchuko was selected, and to explain to us why no young architects were invited. We will publish the answer in the next issue of the journal."[23] Lunacharskij never responded. The failure to answer, uncharacteristic of a man as highly cultivated and open minded as Lunacharskij, possibly indicates that the jury had retracted its first-round verdict, possibly under the pressure from Kaganovich who would soon be put in charge of the reconstruction of Moscow. However, what no one knew yet is that, as an early victim of Stalin's cultural revolution, Lunacharskij was about to be removed from his post as People's Commissar of Enlightenment, which he held eminently since 1918. Under the circumstances, the lame-duck commissar asked another member of the jury, actually the director of the old Lenin Library, Vladimir Nevskij, to respond in his stead. Nevskij's thirteen-page typewritten response was never published either.[24] The reason for that is easy to infer, given the political stakes at play behind the scenes. Still, the document presents some crucial insights into the early political pressures the architectural avant-garde was confronted with, while still holding the high grounds of their celebrity status.

Nevskij, an old Bolshevik who distinguished himself in the Civil War,[25] had no architectural expertise, nor was he able to understand what was wrong about the reintroduction of historicist architecture such as Shchuko had proposed. Classicism, after all, had long been associated in Russia with modernity. Therefore, paradoxically, eclecticism was not seen as "bourgeois"—a term Nevskij would rather associate with Le Corbusier. He wondered how could "the assemblage of glass cubes and prisms, championed by the young and middle-aged, produce a viable building, let alone a proletarian one." The fallacy of his argument was that he associated the general call for a new, modern, and therefore progressive architecture of his attackers in the *Izvestija*,[26] with simply the "young's lack of experience."

---

[22] Leading avant-garde architect and educator, Nikolaj Ladovskij (1881–1941) founded ARU (Associacija Arhitektorov-Urbanistov, or Association of Architects-Urbanists) in 1928, in response to the Five-Year Plan's huge program of urbanization. He produced many urban plans throughout the 1930s, including plans for the Magnitogorsk steel industry. In Nizhnij Novgorod, he built the automobile industry workers' housing. He was also the leader of the Rationalist school at the VHUTEMAS, and author of two Moscow Metro stations.

[23] *Stroitel'stvo Moskvy*, July 1929, p. 6. Lunacharskij was being removed from his post as People's Commissar, a fact the public still did not know.

[24] RGB archives (Russia State Library, former Lenin Library) op. 86 ed. hr. 1, pages 28 to 41, I owe this document to Mark-Eduard Akopjan, researcher at the Shchusev Museum of Architecture. The conference was presided by V. A. Kurts, Deputy president I. K. Luppol, Secretary V. N. Lazarev.

[25] "Nevskij" was his *nom de guerre*. My thanks to Mark-Eduard Akopjan for the information about Nevskij.

[26] Sunday, February 3, 1929 no. 28 (3564). The author of the article, Roman Jakovl'evich Higer, called for a new competition that would correct the failures of the MAO and the Narkompros. Higer, was an alumnus of the VHUTEMAS/VHUTEIN.

Given his obvious preference for Shchuko's entry—which fit Kaganovich's own— and comforted by the fact that at least it did not look "like a restaurant or a factory," Nevskij asserted, in his never published response, that he had worked closely with Shchuko to bring technical and functional aspects of his project to the "level of libraries [he] had visited in Europe." Therefore, he denigrated the young who thought that they "knew things better than anyone," while "pretending to be unimpeachable." After all, the ten projects that young architects presented in the open competition were, in his mind, simply "illiterate" (*negramotnie*). Modern architecture had nothing progressive per se.

As far as the current revived call for "proletarian architecture," he spelled out what no one dared to ask:

1. Where, when and who ever defined what was a communist or proletarian theory of architecture?
2. If it was defined, who among the "young" and the "middle-aged" formulated the foundation of such theory and practice?
3. On what grounds do the representatives of the "young" and the "middle-aged" consider themselves as irreproachable arbiters of Communist or proletarian architectural theory?

These sensible questions, coming from a person who, on the other hand, obviously was not quite getting it, may well have been one important reason the document was never given to the press. It clashed too visibly with VOPRA's mindless battle cries.

The prerevolutionary Shchuko, in his view, undeniably possessed the expertise younger architects did not. "While external aspects and façades may matter, it [was] a futile issue compared to the need of a properly functioning building." Obviously ignorant of the functionalist tenets of modern architecture, he inversed the principles: Modern architecture was all about the "façade," while historicist or eclectic architecture dealt with essence, that is, proper function. Such point of view did not prevent official attacks later in the 1930s from faulting "function" as all that allegedly mattered to modern architects.[27]

The Secret Creation of VOPRA: A Trojan Horse Amidst the Avant-Gardes

The actual response of Stalin's government to the appeals and protests in favor of modern architecture came two months after the event, with the launching of the All-Union

---

[27] Of course, this point of view can be disputed in cases where certain formalist exigences of modern architecture primed over rational considerations. The case in point was the machine room of the Dnieper Hydroelectric Plant (1927–1932) by the Vesnins (with N. Kolli, G. Orlov, and S. Andreevskij as co-designers). The engineer A. Dembovskija claimed about the project "All this colossal weight (120 tons on each column) is hung on the iron supports of the crane tracks underneath, increasing the weight; all for the sake of a fashionable motif of horizontal window." See Vladimir Paperny *Architecture in the Age of Stalin: Culture Two* (Cambridge: Cambridge University Press), 2002, p. 208.

A Call for the Party to Defend Modern Architecture

Society of Proletarian Architects (VOPRA) under Kaganovich's sponsorship.[28] Unlike the spontaneous Proletkult associations of writers or musicians (RAPP and RAPM respectively),[29] formed spontaneously in the mid-1920s, VOPRA was created "from above" primarily to undermine the authority of the architecture modernists. More than endorsing a principled position, VOPRA sought primarily to dictate the terms of the discourse, started with the Lenin Library dispute.[30]

The sudden and simultaneous surge in proletarian advocacy—indeed the first stage of Stalin's *perestrojka*—corresponded to an obvious signal the Central Committee gave the preexistent party organizations of the kind. Kaganovich's creation of VOPRA behind the scenes was part of the plan.

The new architectural group was a Trojan horse amidst autonomous architectural associations. Because it had the party apparatus behind it, even if secretly, VOPRA consolidated itself almost instantaneously throughout the key republics and centers of the Soviet Union, using a long-established party chain of command.[31] Within weeks, VOPRA branches sprouted in Armenia, Ukraine, Georgia, Leningrad, and Tomsk.[32] This was a feat that the forty Moscow members could not have achieved on their own in such a short time.[33] The Leningrad branch was created almost immediately after Moscow's, on September 27, 1929. Its stated task was in the first place to argue for a "proletarian

---

[28] A document of the Leningrad VOPRA branch dated 19. XII. 1930, states explicitly "Our Society (i.e., VOPRA) was established by the Central Committee" (*Наше общество (т.е. ВОПРА) учреждено ЦК Партии*)—in other words, by Kaganovich, Secretary General of the Central Committee. See Russian Academy of Science, "Communist Academy" papers, Fond 358, op. 1 ed. hr. 101, p. 3. This, however, was to remain secret, and a Leningrad VOPRA member was sanctioned for having aired it, and thus "embarrassed the party."

[29] Proletkult—a group of writers and artists assembled around a "proletarian cultural agenda" in the wake of the October Revolution that the Narkompros funded under Lunacharskij.

[30] As the RGALI documents show, the former members of VOPRA, now the party cell of the union meeting secretly, were in regular contact with Kaganovich, from the very beginning of the creation of the Union of Soviet Architects in 1932 and throughout the 1930s. "Perepiska s CK. Sekretny del Sojuza Arhitekrorov SSSR (Correspondence of the Secret Section of the Union of Soviet Architects with the Central Committee). Fond 674, Papka no. 5, 1/22, 1931–1936.

[31] Alex Weissberg's conversation with an arrested GPU officer who landed in his cell. The officer described the astonishing system Stalin had of instantly communicating his orders to the most far-flung regions. See Alex Weissberg *Conspiracy* of *Silence,* with a preface by Arthur Koestler (London: Hamish Hamilton), 1952, pp. 402–5.

[32] Zaslavskij—a leader of the Moscow VOPRA—sent letters to party organizations around the vast country urging them to open local VOPRA branches. Russian Academy of Science, "Communist Academy" Fond 358, op. 1 ed. hr. 101, p. 8.

[33] For example, in a May 20, 1930 letter to "Tov. Kuzmin," requesting the creation of a "VOPRA branch" in Tomsk, Zaslavskij recommends that *"Vesma neophodimo vsju rabotu po organizacii obshchestva soglasovat s mestnoj part. Organizaciej."* ("It is imperative that all issues regarding the work and the organization of the society [VOPRA] be done in agreement with the local party organization.") This clearly points to the fact that VOPRA was no other than a closely watched instrument of the party. Zaslavskij ends the letter saying that it is also indispensable that all the materials regarding the organization, orientation, and plans of the Tomsk branch be communicated speedily to Moscow, RAN archives, Fond 358, op. 1, ed. hr. 101. Kaganovich's first recorded advising (which was to continue throughout the decade, as RGALI papers show) appears in January 1930 among documents transferred to the SSA party cell after the 1932 closure of VOPRA. RGALI, Fond 674, op. 1, ed. hr. 1.

architecture," starting with the fight against "the unhealthy tendencies of the OSA (constructivism) and ASNOVA (formalism)."[34]

VOPRA's task therefore was to mobilize young Communist architects around the country to lead, as if "from below," the cultural revolution in architecture, "fighting for a proletarian concept"—indeed a poisoned apple. The first leaders included the Russian Arkadij Mordvinov (1896–1964) and the Armenians Karo Alabjan (1997–1959) (only four years younger than Kaganovich) and Gevorg Kochar (1901–1973). All, except for Mordvinov, who graduated at the school of engineering of the Moscow Technical University (MVTU), were alumni of the VHUTEMAS. They all were practicing modernists at least until 1932. By that time Mordvinov had already completed the Central Post Office in Harkov, in a fashionable "constructivist" manner, including a glazed corner of a tower topped with a monumental double-oriented clock.

Thirty-two-year-old Alabjan boasted several successful modern buildings in his native Erevan (Armenia) such as the Builders' Club; a Communal Housing for the Electro-Chemical Company, obviously derived from Le Corbusier's *Villas suspendues*; nicknamed *Shahmat* for its checkered façade; and the headquarters of the Geology Administration, in collaboration with his peers Kochar and Mazmajan—both leading figures in VOPRA. The group participated as a team with V. N. Simbircev in the 1931 competition for the Palace of Soviets, using a frankly constructivist language in their first version.[35]

Significantly, VOPRA immediately joined the protests against the results of the Lenin Library competition in favor of the Fridman project. Despite its advocacy of an imaginary "proletarian architecture," VOPRA's members were still practicing constructivist architecture. This changed on February 28, 1932, after the Construction Council of the Palace of Soviets (officially under Prime Commissar Molotov) rejected all the projects (including VOPRA's own constructivist entry) the jury had awarded. This was a signal to VOPRA communists to watch closely what would be the ultimate result of the Palace of Soviets' saga for a possible new direction. The architectural form ultimately never mattered per se. What counted was the ideological category attached to it, the ultimate goal being to discredit the targeted other—the authentic moderns.

The founding of VOPRA reflected the party's general effort to regain primacy in the political discourse.[36] Unlike the other modern architectural groups that numbered few Communists, if any, especially among their most prominent leaders, VOPRA was exclusively composed of young, recently graduated architects dedicated to the party,

---

[34] RAN, Fond 358, 1, ed. Hr. 43. Terehin, a Leningrad emissary, was excluded from the group a year later under the accusation of "political mistakes," such as claiming outside party ranks that the party was orchestrating the creation of VOPRA. By voicing this secret, Terehin had "embarrassed the party."

[35] For VOPRA project, see *Stroitel'stvo Moskvy*, January 1931. See also *Stroitel'stvo Moskvy* no. 8–9, 1930, competition for the Dnieprostroj House of Culture.

[36] About the authority crises of the Party at the end of the NEP period, significantly motivating the cultural revolution, see Sheila Fitzpatrick, ed. "Cultural Revolution as Class War" in Fitzpatrick, *Cultural Revolution in Russia: 1928–1931* (Bloomington: Indiana University Press), 1984. See also Robert C. Tucker *Stalin in Power: The Revolution from Above, 1928–1941* (New York and London: W. W. Norton & Company), 1990, p. 87.

some, like Alabjan since 1917. As such, their task, brewed by as high an instance as the Politburo, was to create a Moscow organization that would disseminate its branches to the most important cities of the Soviet Republics. The challenge was a fictitious "combat [against] bourgeois architectural groups," meaning the avant-garde. Such role was in complete consonance with the party's new "general line," that is, the "heightened struggle against the class enemy" as part of the cultural revolution.

VOPRA's Declaration

Soon after its creation, VOPRA published in the August 1929 issue of *Stroitel'stvo Moskvy*[37] its Declaration of Principle, in the name of the new "proletarian architecture" they were introducing. This document showed clearly that the issue at stake was not a call for the reintroduction of any form of historicist architecture. Quite to the contrary, any such attempt was called inadmissible and reactionary, the way the proponents of the "new architecture" in Western Europe would have had it.

The interest of the text, however, is that it prefigured fundamentally many of the fallacious arguments that were to be raised in the architectural debates down the next decade. Curiously, however, most of the political claims that were reused throughout the 1930s now described and applied to a radically different architecture in formal, structural, and technical terms than the mainstream architecture of the 1930s. This reinforced retrospectively the evidence that, from the outset, VOPRA had political, not professional, aims.

While it was clear what VOPRA was rejecting—in effect, the entire architectural production up to 1929—the group struggled to utter what "proletarian architecture" actually signified. This absence of theory was, among others, what distinguished VOPRA association from, for example, the 1925 proletarian literary group RAPP (Russian Association of Proletarian Writers). VOPRA had just a mandate. To mask this intellectual vacuum, VOPRA filled the proletarian discourse with phraseology and buzz words such as *dialectical materialism* that proletarian architecture supposedly reflected. Constructivism, and what they designated as "formalism" had, in their mind, all the attributes of modern, technically conscious, and rational architecture, but what it did not have was essentially some kind of "proletarian" veneer, an aura that would make it acceptable "to the masses." The absence of such arbitrary attribute made the work of the avant-garde "foreign," that is, an outgrowth of capitalism.

"Art" was another quality constructivism missed. The alleged rejection (*ostranenie*) of "art" in architecture meant "denying art to the proletariat." As far as formalism was concerned, it had adopted and deepened "constructivism's structural arbitrariness and abstract invention."[38] The very abstractness of modern architecture, i.e., its "plainness," was a sign of "capitalism's decay."

---

[37] VOPRA Declaration in *Stroitel'stvo Moskvy*, August 1929, p. 25.
[38] VOPRA Declaration, p. 26.

Without making it explicit, it was clear that VOPRA struggled to reconcile a recalcitrant dualism: adherence to modernism on the one hand, and the promotion of an incoherent political imperative on the other. VOPRA's members, trained by the avant-garde practitioners, understood what modern architecture had to be in order to be "modern and scientific," but stopped short of saying how to make it "proletarian." It was as if the term itself had magical properties whose mere evocation sufficed.

The aporia the discourse suffered from was most evident when considering "art" in architecture. Locked in an inextricable tautological circle, VOPRA, for example, simultaneously chastised the poetic dimension of Leonidovian architecture, while lamenting its "schematism devoid of art," as a clear sign of decadence.

As opposed to that, proletarian architecture—certainly hyper technical, rational, and objective—would bring back to architecture the art the formalists such as Leonidov had robbed it from. What "art" meant, however, remained equally undeclared. In fact, while rejecting eclecticism as the enemy, thanks to this ambiguous reference to "art," VOPRA declaration was leaving a door open, not necessarily consciously, to any future interpretations and, paradoxically, to the survival of modern architecture throughout the 1930s. The future reintroduction of ornament and any form and degree of classicist imagery remained a plausible if yet unuttered option. Kaganovich would later reassure the former VOPRA members, by then his party confidants in the centralized Union of Architects, that what really mattered was the "content." The sophistry of the argument notwithstanding, architecture could be legitimately a pastiche of any "national" or "classical" forms, as long as it carried a "socialist content." Even though that socialist content had to be proletarian, how this would be achieved architecturally remained in suspension to the very end, even when "proletarian" was replaced by a more embracing "socialist" realism, a term coined in August 1934 at the First Congress of Soviet Writers,[39] impossible to translate into architecture.

By September 1929, VOPRA was fully mobilized, first for subversive work against independent architectural movements, then against the VHUTEIN, and finally against the journal *SA*,[40] as discussed later.

The Final Verdict on the Lenin Library Competition

Between June 1929—following the waves of public protests—and January 1930, when Shchuko's project was imposed, the party devised ways under Kaganovich's secret supervision to derail the demands of the modernists and impose Shchuko's project for the Lenin Library. The need for such large-scale manipulative schemes, including the creation of VOPRA, demonstrates the exceptional authority the avant-garde still enjoyed by 1930.

---

[39] See, A. Zhdanov, M. Gorky, N. Buharin, K. Radek, A. Stetsky, *Problems of Soviet Literature: Reports and Speeches at the First Soviet Writers' Congress* (Moscow/Leningrad: Cooperative Publishing Society of Foreign Workers in the USSR), 1935. The term "proletarian literature" was still ubiquitously used at the congress.
[40] *SA* 4 (1928), pp. 109–10.

A Call for the Party to Defend Modern Architecture

On January 29, 1930, instead of allowing Nevskij to publish his twelve-page response (as Lunacharskij had asked him to do), the party decided instead to call for a consultative meeting (*soveshchanie*) "with—as the invitation stated—representatives of the Soviet public, aimed at changing the perception of the Lenin Library project" by Shchuko.[41] The "consultative meeting" had all the characteristics of a premeditated scheme. A free, spontaneous public debate was now to be replaced by an event with preordained conclusions. The presidium of the meeting included important party members, such as Nevskij himself who gave the introductory keynote. All the Leningrad invitees were known supporters of Shchuko, or else had a party task to impose Shchuko's project. For good measure, a few figures representing the avant-garde appeared on the list (such as Ginzburg's OSA, Nikolaj Ladovskij's ARU, and the VHUTEIN) among ninety invitees. All the media were summoned to witness a decision known in advance. Understanding the futility of such gathering, where the supporters of the Fridman or the Vesnins' projects were blatantly in the minority, no leading modernist bothered to come. The exceptions were Aleksandr and Leonid Vesnin, themselves contested participants of the invited competition.[42]

Even if a significant minority, not all Communist architects on the list supported Shchuko. Besides Fridman, a party member himself, some Moscow architectural theoreticians such as Maca (a party member active in the Communist Academy) did intervene, warning that it was "wrong to trample the march of the leftist architects who fight for a new proletarian art as our closest fellow travelers, because they are at the forfront of the new architectural thought."[43] He pointed out that "Shchuko's project, as an eclectic work, simply [lacked] any originality."

Also, clearly pointing to a behind-the-scenes orchestration of the meeting was the presence of Boris Iofan (1891–1981), who, virtually as Stalin's official architect, was never part of any architectural circle and rarely came to any event unless he was directly invited as a guest. Speaking immediately after Vesnin, who asked that Shchuko's project be abandoned because "the name of Lenin cannot be associated with the kind of eclecticism Shchuko presented us," Iofan insisted that "Shchuko's project [was] the best." He forcefully rejected "any association of leftist architectural trends with a proletarian ideology." As a talented architect who was about to design and build an exceptional, modern hospital near Moscow—the Barviha Sanatorium (discussed in the next chapter)—had been obviously delegated to pronounce those two sentences, as his party duty. Throughout the meeting he said no more.

The architect Orlov from Ginzburg's and Vesnin's OSA group derided the organizer's claim that such a small group present at the meeting could "stand for any kind of public opinion [...]. This kind of event would have required the presence of at least 2,000 people."[44]

---

[41] Archives RGB op. 120, ed. hr. 12, pp. 26–42. "Protocol." I thank Mark-Eduard Akopjan for this document.
[42] Fridman was the victor in the open competition, whereas the Vesnin project was competing with Shchuko's in the invited contest. In other words, there were at least three projects in the balance.
[43] RGB State Library (Lenin Library) archives, op.120, ed. hr. 12, pp. 26–42.
[44] Out of forty-two individuals invited and twenty organizations, including the press, only twenty persons came.

The last dean of the recently closed VHUTEIN, Pavel Novitskij argued that, while not excluding "the need to find a proletarian architecture properly speaking," for now "the most advanced architecture, that is, the architecture of the various leftist groups" was undeniably the closest to the proletariat, as the expression of a

> progressive architectural thought. The architectural ideology of Shchuko's project pertains to eclecticism—an attempt to fuse Renaissance principles with the architecture of the industrial age. As such it cannot fit a building that carries Lenin's name and reflects our times.

"Lenin" came repeatedly to the rescue of the avant-garde, a reference that would become anathema just a few years later.

Leonidov, who had not been invited, uttered the most candid and un-ceremonial remark, just before the meeting ended. A short exchange with the meeting organizer went like this:

> LEONIDOV: "I protest against the fact that the new generation of architects has been ignored, precisely the generation that is expected to build socialism [...]. I learned about this meeting only accidentally. But what I see here is not a public meeting, but a sort of family reunion."
>
> THE PRESIDENT: "Your claim about a 'family reunion' is absolutely unacceptable. We could not care less about your impressions. If you have something to propose, we will listen."
>
> LEONIDOV: "If someone cannot figure out what our task is supposed to be, he should drop out. To deal in our time with eclectic architecture is simply counterrevolutionary. Everything is old in Shchuko's project. [...] The old Bolshevik guard that has spoken here, is young no more, and has simply gone astray. What is clear to me is that the old men at this meeting are afraid to confront [the new generation's] socialist challenge."

Leonidov was left without response. The meeting ended with a long conclusion by Nevskij who complained that "a new library cannot wait for much longer. We have to have a place to put our books." He had worked with Shchuko to improve the latter's project, based on his experience with world libraries he himself had visited in Western Europe. Shchuko gave him full satisfaction in submitting to his demands. To the reproach that young architects were not given the opportunity to voice their opinion, he retorted that as early as 1927 he had approached the VHUTEIN with the suggestion that a Lenin Library be the subject of student thesis that year.[45] Finally, to conclude, he declared that the majority present at the meeting had spoken in favor of Shchuko's project and that no further discussion was needed.

---

[45] Leonidov had actually picked up the challenge for his final thesis, a work still commanding admiration today.

Eight months later, on September 30, 1930, the building of Shchuko's library was started. It took eight years to complete it. In 1935, five years into its construction, Nevskij was arrested and executed.[46]

By the time the Lenin Library was inaugurated in 1938, VOPRA members who had vehemently protested Shchuko's classicist project in 1929, had been long adorning their own buildings with classical columns, aping the architecture favored by Peter the Great.

The VANO: A First Step Towards a Centralized Union

Evidently enacting a strategic plan the party had defined, VOPRA promoted in April 1930 the creation of a confederated union of all architectural societies, the VANO, including a Moscow branch—the MO-VANO.[47] VOPRA's call for such a federation coincided with Kaganovich's rise to First Party Secretary of the Moscow Region—the Moscow Oblastnoj Komitet (OBKOM). As Moscow Communists, VOPRA members answered directly to him.

The idea of assembling the various movements into a federation was, in fact, first proposed by OSA's presidium early in 1929. Since this was not its initiative, VOPRA had rejected the plan.[48] The procedure exemplified the way VOPRA simultaneously undermined the independent organizations and tried to monopolize the architectural stage. This did not prevent VOPRA from sponsoring the VANO a year later—the first step toward a single architectural organization that would be easier to infiltrate and control.[49] However, unable to impose themselves on the other federated modernist groups, which were not keen to waste their time in VANO meetings, VOPRA reversed itself and began attacks against it.[50] Another more insidious problem was that members were expected to prepare reports about the activity of each confederated group. However, probably because VOPRA overlapped with an architectural party organization (whose meetings and membership were secret), VOPRA refused to comply.

---

[46] "Nevskij" was his *nom de guerre*. My thanks to Mark-Eduard Akopjan for the information, including about his arrest and death.

[47] VANO stood for Vsesojuznoe Arhitekturnoe Nauchnoe Obshchestvo, or All-Soviet Architectural Scientific Society created on August 27, 1930. RGALI, SSA Fond 674, op. 1, ed. hr.1.

[48] See "Let's Create a Federation," *SA* 3 (1929), p. 89. The documents also belie the current notion that VOPRA had refused to join VANO as Anatole Kopp claims in his *L'Architecture de la période stalinienne* (Grenoble: Presses Universitaires de Grenoble) 1978). Quite to the contrary, it was the first to join it as the RGALI archives, as SSA papers indicate.

[49] The various architectural associations gradually dissolved themselves in the course of the year as its members were joining VANO: VOGI on February 16; ASNOVA on April 11; MAO on April 14, followed by VOPRA and ARU. RGALI Fond 674, op. 1, ed. hr. 1

[50] RGALI Fond 674 op. 1 ed. hr. 2 (1) Meeting of 17 January 1931, Protokol 6. The complaint was that out of 21 members only three were active. The Vesnins and Ginzburg were regularly absent from the meetings.

The Assault on the Avant-Garde's Institutions

VOPRA's ultimate attacks on VANO notwithstanding, VOPRA architects used their VANO membership to claim the right to place some of their own members on *SA*'s editorial board. Probably following a behind-the-scenes top party directive, VOPRA's leader Alabjan pushed his way into the *SA*'s editorial board and managed to have *SA*'s neutral, professional name, *Contemporary Architecture,* changed into the ideologically charged *Revolucionaja Arhitektura (RA)*.

The new name obviously consonant with the unfolding of the cultural revolution, called for subscriptions on the back cover of *SA*'s last issue with a flashy design by Aleksej Gan. Yet, pointing to dishonest maneuvering, not a single issue of *RA* ever appeared.[51] By the end of the year, *SA* itself had folded. Like a virus implanted into a cell, VOPRA was gradually eroding and destroying the institutions of the avant-garde from within.

VOPRA, however, was not given an easy task. Not only were its members supposed to discredit architects, pedagogues, and critics of international repute, but also to challenge practitioners and theoreticians sincerely and creatively devoted to the revolution, both architectural and social. While in 1929 their declared architectural credo differed from VOPRA's only in the degree of authenticity and intellectual integrity, one crucial semantic distinction played more than a rhetorical role: while the modernists strived for a progressive architecture, the Stalinists claimed, as we saw, ascendancy over "proletarian architecture." That ideological distinction, vacuous as it may have been, gave VOPRA an aura of unchallenged righteousness. What was at stake was the head-on clash between the avant-gardes in architecture and the "vanguard of the proletariat" from which the party itself drew its legitimacy. Indeed, as hinted at earlier, the established practice of the Stalinist leadership was to stir issues at a grass-roots level in a prearranged fashion and then claim for themselves the "enthusiastic support of the masses."

The End of the VHUTEMAS / VHUTEIN: VOPRA's Striving for Control and Uniformity

The VHUTEMAS experimental school, which had been renamed the Higher Artistic and Technical Institute (VHUTEIN) in 1926, was closed at the end of the 1930 academic year, after ten years of creative, if turbulent existence.[52] The new pedagogical institution was the result of the merging of VHUTEIN's architecture section and the school of civil engineering of the MVTU. The school was christened as Arhitekturnij Stroitelnij Institut (ASI), or Architectural Building Institute.[53] Such fusion was bound to cause cultural

---

[51] *SA* 6 (1930), p. 10. Gan, a former anarchist, is believed to have died in a GULAG concentration camp around 1942.
[52] See Selim Han-Magomedov, *Vhutemas* (Paris: Edition du Regard), 1990
[53] In 1933 it was renamed Moscow Architectural Institute (Moskovskij Arhitekturnij Institut).

clashes. In the controversy that exploded, VOPRA chose, of course, to support the arguments hostile to the avant-garde. Ominously, VOPRA's members now claimed to be acting "in the name and by commission of the proletariat," something they certainly would not have allowed themselves to claim had they not a license to do so "from above." The commissioning from the "Proletariat" was actually a euphemism standing for "the representatives of the proletariat," that is, the leadership of the Bolshevik Party. In practical terms in this case, that was Kaganovich, if not Stalin.

One of the pretexts for closing the VHUTEIN included its supposed lack of technical instruction provided to the students, as they allegedly worked on "outlandish projects," incompatible with the needs of the country. A case in point was the lavishly designed Georgij Krutikov's futuristic thesis project of "Flying Cities" that surprisingly could be compared with today's space stations. The units of the cities were served by small space automobiles.

The criticism, of course, was fallacious, adding malice to ignorance. Technical soundness, the use of both new materials and structural systems were at the heart of the teaching of constructivists such as A. Vesnin and M. Ginzburg. This is exactly what they meant when speaking of a "scientific approach to design." The rector Novitskij argued judiciously, as he responded that allowing flights of fantasy was an indispensable ingredient to any well-conceived architectural education, beyond an indispensable technical instruction.[54]

As opposed to the critics' claims, the school actually prided itself with the production of furniture prototypes and other industrial design items, including textiles and clothing for factories. In its October 1929 issue, *Stroitel'stvo Moskvy* presented, over four pages, the most recently built furniture by the students of the VHUTEIN, including spectacular chairs as thesis work by B. Zemljanicyn and Rozhin-Mjagkij under Tatlin's and El Lissitzky's supervision, respectively.[55] The journal introduced the furniture under the heading "FURNITURE as a Contribution to the Socialist Reconstruction of the Byt"—a typical if untranslatable Russian word standing for "way of everyday living."

The motto was: "Builders, Learn the Living Ways of the Workers—your Clients." Industrial furniture designers at the school aimed at mass production in sync with the rapid industrialization dictated by the Five-Year Plan. The products were also intended for the standardized communal housing programs that OSA had been experimenting with since 1926. All the modular furniture was meant to be affordable, transformable, and standardized. They would have certainly competed favorably with any of the new metal and wood furniture regularly exhibited at the Paris "Salon d'Automne" in the 1920s and 1930s, that Charlotte Perriand, Pierre Chareau, René Herbst, and other artists-architects of the Union des Artistes Modernes (UAM) had championed.[56]

---

[54] *Stroitel'stvo Moskvy*, July 1929, pp. 12–13.
[55] See *Stroitel'stvo Moskvy*, October 1929, "Mebel' Fakulteta po Obrabotke Dereva i Metalla Vhuteina" [Furniture from the school designed in wood and metal), pp. 9–12.
[56] See Udovički-Selb, "*C´était dans l'Air du Temps,* Charlotte Perriand and the Popular Front," in Mary McLeod, *Charlotte Perriand: An Art of Living.* (New York: Abrams), 2004.

As mentioned, the pretext floated around was that the students were eager to learn "real architecture," that is, to get a sound traditional academic education. While Peter the Great had long achieved in Saint Petersburg such rapprochement to neoclassical European trends, nothing had been done of the kind in the "big village," as Le Corbusier had called Moscow when he saw it in 1929. Kaganovich's task was thus clearly set. While using "proletarian" rhetoric and the dialectics of "content and form," he situated himself at an intersection between Czar Peter I in terms of esthetics and Baron Haussmann regarding urban modernization. "Socialist" attributes attached to it, even if just verbally, gave the trend an a priori political legitimacy.

Next in line was OSA's journal. Once most of the avant-garde's formal institutions had been closed by the end of 1930, VOPRA members were gradually moved into strategic government positions. In December 1930, slightly more than a year into VOPRA's founding, Mordvinov was installed as head of the newly radicalized Commissariat of Enlightenment's IZO (Otdel Izobraziteľnyh Iskusstv Komakademija or Department of Fine Arts of the Communist Academy). This was the position Tatlin once held under Lunacharskij, recently removed from his position as People's Commissar of Enlightenment. Between August 1929, when it was created, and December 1930, VOPRA was on its way to hold a dominant position in the architectural discourse, as Kaganovich had planned.

The Central Committee's Indictment of the Workers' "House Communes"

Another major blow to the activities of the constructivists was the May 16, 1930 Central Committee's decree (*postanovlenie*), which essentially ended a four-year experimental activity in search of quality affordable housing.

Ginzburg's OSA, now under attack, had been designing and building new experimental dwelling types since 1926 for the state building industry—the Strojkom. Based on a few typological variants, OSA offered socially affordable and innovative housing models towards solving the acute housing crisis. The idea was that those lodgings would go primarily to the working classes but ended serving the heavy government bureaucracy ("grown out of the working class"), a bureaucracy whose tastes and expectations were highly conservative.

Ginzburg had asked two central questions: How to solve "the nightmare of shared apartments"—the scourge of Soviet living conditions for over three decades after the revolution; and pointedly, "could the quality of the housing be raised without reducing quantity?"[57] The most advanced solution was reached in Ginzburg's and Ignatij Milinis's[58] 1930 Narkomfin, which can arguably represent the ultimate achievement of constructivism in its most authentic form.[59] In Ginzburg's words, these were "experiments in new types

---

[57] *SA* 3 (1926).
[58] Ignatij Milinis (b. 1899) had been Ginzburg's student at the Vhutemas.
[59] See Danilo Udovički-Selb, ed. *The Narkomfin House: Moisej Ginzburg and Ignatij Milinis* (Austin /Berlin: O'Neil Ford/Wasmuth), 2015.

A Call for the Party to Defend Modern Architecture

of dwelling that [favored] spatial combinations ["montage"] of fully individualized lodging spaces, while socializing a series of other functions into common dining rooms, resting halls, children's daycares, nurseries, clubs and recreation units, laundering facilities and the like"[60] (Figure 1.3).

The 16th Party Congress, a congress where Stalin's grip on power was to be strengthened, if not completely secured, was scheduled to last from June 26 to July 13, 1930. As preparations for it were underway, on May 16 the Central Committee issued an alarming injunction regarding the *perestrojka* of "socialist settlements." The injunction stated:

> Along with the advance of the [reconstruction] of the socialist *byt*, certain unfounded, semi-fantastic and therefore harmful experiments are conducted by some comrades (Sabsovich,[61] in part Larin and others) who want to jump "in one leap" over the obstacles that stand on the road to the socialist reconstruction of the way of life, due on the one hand to the economic and cultural backwardness of the country, and on the other to the need at this particular moment to gather all the resources available for the rapid industrialization of the country [...].[62]

The document, largely exaggerating the facts, went on claiming that "utopian undertakings such as the abolition of the family and marriage, and separating the children from their parents in favor of collective rearing would represent an enormous waste of

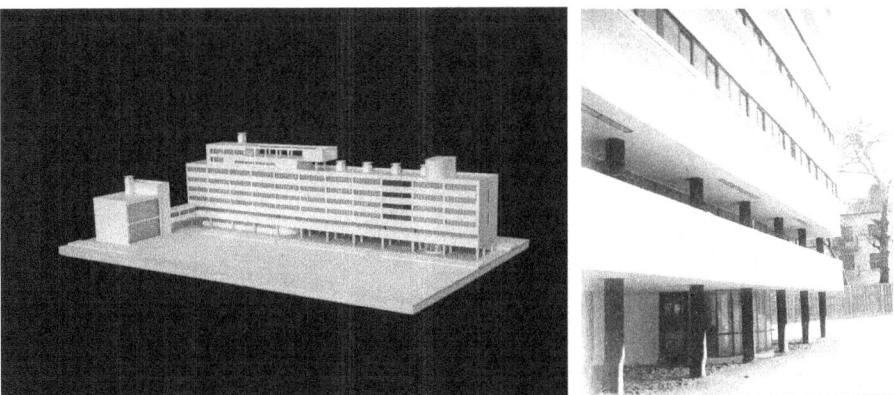

Figure 1.3 M. Ginzburg, Narkomfin Housing Model, and View of Northern Entrance. (Courtesy Shchusev Museum of Architecture)

---

[60] *SA* 4–5 (1926).
[61] Leonid Sabsovich was an economist and collaborator of Ginzburg's in *Sovremenaja Arhitektura*. In 1929 he sparked a debate about the future of Soviet cities that he published in *Planovoe Hozjastvo* (Planned Economy).
[62] See "On the Reconstruction of daily life (*byt*)" ["O Rabote po Perestrojke Byta"], published in *Pravda* on May 29, 1930, no. 145, and *Sovremenaja Arhitektura*. no. 1–2. 1930, p. 1.

27

available resources, and discredit severely the very idea of a socialist reconstruction of the way of life (*byt*)." The accused architects and planners were chastised for their "opportunism" and "far-leftist phraseology"—not an innocuous accusation if the architect happened to be a party member.

While the Central Committee's May 16 utterance appeared reasonable enough on first reading, its overstatements indicated an additional, undeclared motivation. At the start of his "revolution from above," the General Secretary, Stalin, was replacing the Leninist egalitarianism among party ranks (best represented in architecture by communal housing) with his own brand of class society.[63] Housing, nominally designed with the working class in mind, was now dispensed to the *nomenklatura*—mostly the employees of government commissariats. Unsurprisingly, the bureaucrats now aspired to traditional "bourgeois" dwelling comforts, preferably with rooms for servants. This was particularly true for the most privileged strata of the society—the secret police, the GPU and the NKVD. Granting good apartments, vacation resorts, and other privileges to the members of a ruling caste that also included a lesser number of selected scientists, writers and artists, heroic aviators, and a few designated factory heroes was one of the most salient ways Stalin held the system together, while vaunted as "Stalin's concern for the human person."[64] Furthermore, these dwellings and resorts were cynically presented, particularly abroad, as examples of living conditions of the working class in the Soviet Union. The 1939 Soviet Pavilion in New York astonished the public to such a degree, that the visitors' comments included numerous statements such as "I wish I could live in the Soviet Union" or "Long live Stalin" and other expressions of amazement about the life of the working class in Russia.[65] At the other end of the new class system stood its opposite, the "correctional" forced-labor camps whose expansion was just announced in the press on April 7, 1930 as another Central Committee Resolution. The "revolution from above" was gaining steam.

For good measure, following its May 16 injunction on housing, the Central Committee recommended to the government—the Council of People's Commissars (Soviet Narodnyh Komissarov, or SNK)—to establish "in a matter of fifteen days," regulations for the construction of workers' housing (laundry facilities, bathhouses, childcare facilities, factory kitchens, canteens, etc.)." In moving the issue into the hands of the government for expediency and "realism," the initiative in planning of workers' housing was, for all practical purposes, snapped away from the architects' hands into the bureaucratic swamp. Such a move stood just one step away from the withholding of all budgetary funds, except for the most barren housing necessities of industrial workers.

---

[63] For a powerful account on the rise of a new dominant, privileged class, see Robert C. Tucker, *Stalin in Power: The Revolution from Above, 1928–1941* (New York-London: W. W. Norton and Company), 1992, pp. 101–14.
[64] Under Lenin's egalitarian system, the party leadership could not have an income superior to a qualified factory floor worker.
[65] GARF Fond 5673, op. 1, del 23.

The End of *Sovremenaja Arhitektura*: Higer's Last Strike in Defense of Sanity

The journal *SA*, the standard bearer of constructivism, itself was subjected to a campaign of denigration beyond the case of Leonidov, one of its major contributors.

A series of attacks came the way of Roman Higer (1901–1985) targeting his essay: "About the Development of the Ideology of Constructivism in Contemporary Architecture," published in *SA* No. 3. 1928. In response to these attacks, Higer,[66] a second-generation constructivist architect and theorist—born the same year as Leonidov—published a long article, "Against Vulgarizers and Slanderers: A Few Clarifications to our Critics."[67] Higer continued:

> The work of these critics, who essentially copy each other, use a lot of words intended to "clarify" with pathetic unanimity the alleged theoretical mistakes and incorrect points of view of their opponent [read Higer]. They battle, in the majority of cases, with ghosts produced by fantasies of their authors. We find it completely superfluous to go into the details of our opponents' claims (despite their own many "sins" and "errors"). The controversy about functionalism in architecture has acquired in these articles such an abstract-philosophical form, that it could be easily turned into a general philosophical debate; while at the same time it rehashes topics that have already been vented in recent years in our Marxist literature. We certainly do not consider ourselves theoretically infallible, and we do not exclude the possibility of errors in our articles. But at the same time, we consider that any controversy makes sense only when the debaters operate with actual viewpoints. However, the articles that attack our positions go so far as to be almost unintelligible.

The fact that the texts all looked alike was a compelling indication that they were orchestrated from a single source; in the same way, later in the 1930s, the newspapers would be flooded with close to identical "outraged letters" coming from factory workers' orchestrated meetings condemning arrested "saboteurs and enemies of the people."

Still not aware of it, or pretending not to see it, Higer continued his response in order "to clarify" the journal's position "in the name of truth." He thus went on highlighting five fundamental points. He first addressed what he called the "dialectical evolution of culture," pointing out that their opponents lacked in "dialectical thinking," thus alluding, without mentioning it, to the Marxist epistemological method. "In their efforts to master a scientific and technological expediency," Higer claimed, "architects needed to rely on Western technology." Doing so, however, did not mean that they ignored the particularities

---

[66] Roman Jakovlevich Higer, a noted architectural critic and theorist. See S. O. Khan-Magomedov, *Arhitektura Sovetskogo Avangarda* (Moscow: Strojizdat), 1996, pp. 219, 382.
[67] In *SA* 4, 1930, pp. 10–12. Some of the journals cited were: *Pechat i Revolucija*, no. 9, 1929, "About the Roads of Development of Socialism," by Shalavin and Lamtsov, and "Functionalism is Not a Road" in *Isskustvo v Massy* no. 6, 1930, by Roshchin.

of the socialist edification. What was needed was "to take from Western technology the best and most valuable, and apply it to the needs of the proletariat," that is, "apply it to the specificities of our social tasks, and to the specificities of our Soviet way of life [...]. It should be clear," he continued, "to any literate person that what we are talking about here is the [dialectical] principle of the 'negation of the negation.' [...] If our opponents were not after controversies for controversies' sake [...] they would stop writing stupidities such as pretending that we are disseminating capitalist culture and quietly allowing capitalism to overcome socialism."

The second point dealt with "contradictions in architecture." Higer quoted his own article in which he ascertained that "the live dialectics of the architectural creation consist de facto in the resolution of a series of unavoidable contradictions [...] which, for a dialectical materialist, cannot be 'farfetched and abstract,' that is, [....] established a priori once and forever." He assailed the authors who quoted Lenin saying that "The human mind [naturally] does not [....] deal with what is old and frozen, but with live, dynamic conditions that grow into each other and transcend themselves [...]" because, "those who were citing Lenin did not realize, in their polemical blindness, that such a quote actually applied to themselves." He ended this point arguing that, by quoting Lenin his opponents only tried to mask the actual "metaphysical character" of their utterances.

From there, he turned to recurrent use of terms such as "subjective" and "objective" in human judgment and its political consequences, now applied to architecture. Higer noted the abundant use of it in his detractors' verbiage, pointing to the sterile, scholastic character of their arguments. Fourthly, Higer assailed the extraordinary misuse of alleged "mechanistic" thinking attributed to him, and quoted in his defense his own article:

> The real contemporary materialist teaching about reflexes [see Pavlov and Behterev], is that these have an effect, no doubt, on the so-called "higher" spheres of human psyche such as those related to art. They are all based on physiological, neurocerebral processes. From this scientific-materialist point of view, the artistic activity caused by conditioned reflexes derived from vital social "irritants," are physiological in nature, and therefore narrowly "utilitarian" [...] as is the case of all human essences, including our living spaces.[68]

"It is clear from the above," Higer insisted, "that there is not a single sentence here that could not be tested in a scientific laboratory." He went on displaying his familiarity with cognitive science as he defended another article he had written on formalism in *SA* 4, 1929. He redoubled his efforts to demonstrate that formalism too had a scientific basis in neurophysiology and called again on Pavlov whose experiments buttressed, as Bolsheviks thought, the Marxist theory on the socially conditioned features in humans.

Higer finally turned to architecture as a "visual art," in response to claims that the modernists had "expunged art" from architecture, and thus denied art to the proletariat.

---

[68] *SA* 4, 1930, p. 11.

Higer insisted that it was wrong to cultivate architecture as a "visual art" at a time when "we are seeking highly industrialized building technologies; when it has become imperative to devise new social types of buildings; to organize new forms of social housing; and plan new socialist settlements." He underscored the need to create an architecture that was "not based on style, but on science. An architecture where every single element is subjected to calculations, to prediction through planning and exact measuring." He emphasized that issues of "form" represented a complex problem related to the understanding of "art, which leads our efforts along the same principles as other spatial and planning endeavors [. . .]. However, we consider that it is useless to address form in architecture from the superficial point of view of 'purity' and 'stylistic authenticity.'" He finally came to the main point:

> Not "style," but a "socially correct and logically organized construction," respectful of each of its constituent parts, all of them pointing to the functional character of architecture. We definitely agree with our opponents when they say that "functionalism is not our style." Indeed—functionalism is not our style either. Because functionalism is a method, a method of thinking, a method of working that allows a gradual overcoming of the status of pseudo-science, liberated from the caprices of the so called "artist's inspiration" [. . .].

Then, referring to the revolution understood as a motor of history, Higer dramatically and prophetically declared with capital letters, "HISTORY WILL BYPASS THEM, RIDICULING THE DWARFS WHO THOUGHT THEY COULD STOP THE INEVITABLE."

In a postscript, Higer thought it necessary to address the cry "Death to art," launched, he interpreted, as a rallying call by artists and architects in the early 1920s. It was necessary, he thought, to counter VOPRA's malicious distortions of the call's meaning. He explained, to those who pretended not to know it, that such rallying salve referred exclusively and pointedly to "academic art."

The journal *SA* was closed a few months later. It was replaced with a new one, *Sovetskaja Arhitektura*, founded in early 1931 as the bureaucratic-sounding Organ of the Department of Housing at the Institute of Economy of the Communist Academy, under the editorship of Nikolaj Miljutin (1889–1942), world-known for his theoretical work on the Linear City, following the model of the Catalonian Soria y Mata. He had been recently demoted as People's Commissar of Finances, usually a preamble to arrest.[69]

---

[69] According to his daughter Katja Miljutina-Rappaport he slept with a gun under his pillow, ready to fight back. He also had a plan of escape as the roof was connected to a second stairwell at the opposite ends of the building. When the NKVD finally came, he played a bluff on them. He asserted that this was an identity mix-up pretending that there was another Miljutin in the neighborhood. He then grabbed the phone to call the Kremlin in "outrage." It worked. The officers of the NKVD left without him. (Interview with his daughter in New Jersey in June 2011.)

In a further erosion of the avant-garde's platform, Alabjan, the other VOPRA leader and ascending party star, took the position of deputy editor. From the old *SA* editorial board, only Ginzburg survived. Significantly, avant-garde artist Varvara Stepanova replaced Gan as the journal's designer, and largely adapted the original typesetting and design of her predecessor.

As *SA* was already closed since December 1930, Miljutin, the "Old Bolshevik" and now former People's Commissar, friend of Ginzburg's, rushed to publish an article about the communal housing policies in the first issue of his journal *Sovetskaja Arhitektura* in February 1931. He had designed and built his own penthouse on the Narkomfin's roof. It was a renewed effort to position himself approvingly in regards to the May 16 housing *postanovlenie* of the previous year—even as defending the fundamental idea of house communes.[70] Without mentioning the Narkomfin per se, he insisted that communal housing had a central role to play in the liberation of women from the indignities of household dependency. As an economist, he saw another advantage to such emancipation: it would propel women into the workforce with all the benefits this would represent for the country. He warned at the same time, judiciously echoing the May resolution, that any "radical leftist" speeding ahead of the country's possibilities to actually provide necessary communal restaurants, daycares, playgrounds, clubs and the like, could only discredit the idea of a new socialist way of daily life (*byt*). It was thus important to create building types of "transitional kind" that still offered the inhabitants the possibility to choose between traditional and innovative dwelling types. That was exactly what Ginzburg claimed to have achieved with his Narkomfin. Regardless, OSA's work came to a grinding stop as financing dried up.

By 1930, Kaganovich, now Stalin's right hand in the Politburo, had taken over all his duties, ready to defend the Stalinist line at the 16th Party Congress that opened on June 26, 1930. With his position as First Secretary of the Moscow Region Party, First Secretary of the Central Committee, and now full member in the Politburo, he secured a formidable power, only second to Stalin he served uncompromisingly with an iron fist and verbal and physical brutality. Having acquired a reputation for ruthlessness and blind obedience to Stalin while First Secretary of the Ukrainian Party, he had all the credentials Stalin needed for the final liquidation of the opposition in the Central Committee, that is, purging out all the early leaders of the October Revolution.

Kaganovich campaigned callously in the Central Committee against the "Rights" (*Pravie*) opposition, which resisted, in Buharin's words, to turning the country into a "police state." The Rights included Krupskaja, whose speech against forced collectivization sent Kaganovich around Moscow's party organizations in an effort of damage control.[71]

---

[70] N. Miljutin, "Fundamental Questions about the Building of Housing and the *Byt*," *Sovetskaja Arhitektura* no. 1–2, 1931. Most of the first dwellers of the Narkomfin, however were arrested over three years, and none returned. See op. cit. Vladimir Paperny, "Narkomfin narratives: Dreams and realities," in Udovički-Selb, Danilo, ed. *The Narkomfin House: Moisej Ginzburg and Ignatij Milinis* (Austin/Berlin: O'Neil Ford/Wasmuth), 2015, p. 20.
[71] Protocols of the Moscow Party Committee, Fond 17, op. 20, ed. hr. 209.

The attack against the Rights occurred first at the 29th Central Committee Plenum (the "Left" was all but defeated with Trotsky's exile), and then at the 16th Party Congress in June—the last congress to be dominated by the original leadership of the Soviet Union.[72] The violent move to oust this opposition marked the beginning of the general *chistka,* or cleansing of the party ranks.[73]

Even though in no way hostile to the social and political revolution per se, probably not even to the current cultural revolution in its ideal form, those who had carried modernism throughout the first decade of the revolution were now submitted incessantly to as vacuous ideological assaults as they were vociferous. This led the authentic architectural forces into continuous and exhaustive counter attacks.[74] Constructivists, rationalists, and suprematists were torn away from the original sources of their own architectural revolution—the tenets of the "formal method" of the Russian formalists— who theorized their work. They were compelled to claim that their current work had no connection with "early constructivism." The word itself, *formalism,* detached from its original meaning by the linguist Viktor Shklovskij that "form is the content of art" became anathema. Yet, in various ways, they managed to keep their trade alive to the end of the decade as argued later.

The Bauhaus in Moscow: Anomaly or Double Standard?

In what was only an apparent contradiction, given the systematic termination of all the avant-gardes' institutions in the previous year, in the summer of 1931 an exhibition of the Bauhaus opened in Moscow under Hannes Meyer's sponsorship—one year after the 16th Party Congress where both Stalin and Kaganovich further asserted their power, and a year before the imposition of single, centralized Unions in the field of the Arts. The manifest desire to maintain a link with European modern architectural institutions, such as the CIAM, was to characterize the Soviet attitude almost to the end of the decade. It was particularly important not to appear abroad as sidestepping from what was considered "progressive" in the West. The leadership, Kaganovich in the first place, knew that any visible official departure from modernist positions risked alienating a vast number of artists and intellectuals who supported the USSR.

Conversely, such potential poison had to be explained away internally. As Mordvinov increasingly imposed himself as an arbiter in architectural matters (he played a role in setting up the exhibition), *Sovetskaja Arhitektura,* which replaced *SA,* invited him for its first issue to write a review about the exhibition.[75] His article revealed the ambiguity the party architects, that is VOPRA, experienced in assessing constructivism and rationalism with the aim of undermining their practitioners; finding their own position regarding

---

[72] Even if long vanquished, in his paranoia, imaginary Trotskyites were Stalin's tenacious obsession and main reason of his anti-Bolshevik show trials.
[73] RGASPI Fond 81, op. 3, ed. hr. 4 p. 3.
[74] Op. cit. Hudson, pp. 101–18.
[75] See A. Mordvinov, "Bauhaus: k Vystavke v Moskve." *Sovetskaja Arhitektura* 1–2, 1931, pp. 8–11.

modern architecture; and defining a proletarian alternative. Unconsciously projecting his own contradictory position, the author claimed in terminological acrobatics that the Bauhaus

> reflects the ambiguities and contradictions in which art finds itself in capitalist Germany: it offers some elements of proletarian art in its relentless conflict with bourgeois ideology. However, suffice to look back at the development of bourgeois art in recent decades, to see, in essence, a tendency to evince any ideological content from art. Such rejection of art inevitably leads to the fetishization of abstract forms—that is, the "*Veshchism*,"[76] (*Sachlichkeit*), and technicism, while disallowing any place to art.

> As an example, Mordvinov cited—using a literary terminology later identified as "socialist" realism— "the rejection of any transcendent idea (*idejnost*); of any content, that is, of any subject matter (*sjuzhetnost*); or else of any description of the real world."

> The result is an extreme breakdown of painting into elementary forms and materials; Futurism into an expression of dynamics; cubism into the tectonics of objects; suprematism, into the abstraction of color values; constructivism, with its focus on the "faktura," [materiality] introducing natural materials while embracing the process of construction. This means the replacement of painting with production of things, the replacement of art with industrial technique—a logical road into the blind alley of art in a dying capitalism. [...] It is an art without perspective.

> While claiming that there was no way out of this blind alley, Mordvinov insisted that the only choice facing the artist was either the negation of art, or the return to the old bourgeois styles, at best "renovated through some instances of constructivism," by which he meant "neoclassicism," or "the negation of objectivity in art." Neither of these "could satisfy a true revolutionary artist." The Bauhaus was the expression of the latter trend.

Mordvinov actually saw two stages in the Bauhaus worth highlighting: "The formalist constructivism of Walter Gropius" and the "engineering / functionalist" trend of Hannes Meyer. He thus summarized: "The School of Walter Gropius estheticizes technology, while the School of Hannes Meyer denudes it by rejecting any aesthetics. The first strives to find new forms in architecture based on new technical means and materials from which he derives simple geometrical volumes. The second rejects formal problems, as its forms are derived from the function they play. The school of Walter Gropius absorbs the method of cubo-futurism and formalism, while Hannes Meyer replaces art with science and technology." To prove his point, he went into lengthy comparisons of the work of the

---

[76] In conjunction with German avant-gardists, El Lissitzky and Il'ja Ehrenburg founded in 1922 a short-lived journal *Veshch/Objet/Gegenstand* with a Neue Sachlichkeit bent.

two architects. Ultimately, Meyer's saving graces were that he dedicated himself to wholesome economical necessities for large consumption, and in that sense "he included the working masses." The social aspect of Meyer's work, Mordvinov went on, was not expressed so much in his architecture since "[...] the combative proletarian content of his yearnings [was] best represented in art-ideological propaganda expressed in posters, photomontages, design of magazines, books and brochures."

Following a lengthy discussion on what can never be achieved under capitalism, as opposed to what is accessible only in a country led by a Communist Party, Mordvinov asked: "So, what is in for us in Meyer's school? First it is the scientific aspect of his design method," which included functionalism. "Second [was] the rationalization of both design and production method, including standardization and typization." Third was education. "At the Bauhaus, students of all levels work with their professors at actually building their projects. Older students help the professors with training the younger." What he did not say is that, in fact, most of the Bauhaus teaching methods were comparable to those of the VHUTEMAS, if richer and more varied, he contributed to defeat. He went, nevertheless, as far as claiming that the Bauhaus pedagogical system "would work better in the Soviet Union than in a capitalist country, and it would be worth experimenting with it in all of our schools." The weakness of the German school was the lack of attention paid to the social-ideological content of architecture; its elimination of art; its mechanical aspect; and, finally, the reduction of the role of architecture to simple functions. This appeared to Mordvinov as an obstacle to the development "of an authentic proletarian architecture, based on a class content. The proletarian architecture unites technology and art in a dialectical embrace. We may only hope that Hannes Meyer will be able to overcome these weaknesses in the work that he will be performing under Soviet conditions." Once again, any critical analysis of such "proletarian architecture" was left up for the guessing, wrapped up in phraseology endowed with mythical accents. While there was no way Mordvinov could have said more, the advantage of such open-ended claims was that it could have, opportunely, multiple semantic incarnations. As Stalinization progressed, what was "proletarian" (later "socialist realist") represented whatever suited the political moment. In other words, a slippery definition of the kind that would not only allow, in the coming decade, all forms of arbitrary pronouncements and indictments, but conversely a considerable variety of architectural expressions, including the modern.

The Character Assassination of Ivan Leonidov, the Young Icon of the Avant-Gardes

Alabjan's and his fellow "proletarian architects" destructive campaign culminated with the introduction of the term *Leonidovshchina*—a word difficult to translate—*Leonidovism* missing the vocable's disparaging harshness. *Leonidovshchina* was thus to be used as a derogatory moniker VOPRA members associated with the talented and nonconformist, second-generation constructivist architect and his work. The term was part of the highly public campaign that erupted at the end of the year.

A member of OSA, Leonidov—the poet of constructivism—was by then widely recognized both in the USSR and abroad for his radically innovative designs. Leonidov, of peasant extraction, first studied the technique of icon painting in his village, prior to joining the VHUTEMAS with a passionate letter of intent in which he wrote candidly about his talent and burning fire for architecture.[77] As soon as he graduated under Aleksandr Vesnin with a thesis work that broke new frontiers in the discipline, he was both co-opted as a teacher at the VHUTEMAS and member of the editorship of the *SA* journal. He was as beloved by his students, as he was admired by his teachers. When Leonidov joined the faculty, A. Vesnin's entire studio moved into Leonidov's. After the first shock in hearing the news, Vesnin quickly regained his bearings and said with a smile, "That little devil!" The journal *SA* published every one of his later projects, including those, such as his 1930 Palace of Culture, that VOPRA had attacked so viciously. Orchestrated by Leonidov's older peer Mordvinov, this campaign against him marked the most acute moment of the dispute between architectural factions. If it ended tragically for Leonidov, the avant-gardes as such were far from being defeated.

The first attacks against Leonidov came, actually, from G. Kozelkov, one of VOPRA's early members. He took advantage of a public review of the recently completed competition for the Palace of Culture known as the ZIL—Zavody Imenni Lihachëva or "Lihachëv [Automobile] Factory" workers club,[78] located in the Moscow Proletarskij District. Addressing Leonidov's competition entry, Kozelkov accused Leonidov of no less than "sabotage."[79] The concept of sabotage (*vred*) was part of the nascent terminology Kaganovich and the other top Stalinist leaders were to use in the persecutions of the decade, among others to explain away the failures of their Five-Year Plans.[80] The harangue aimed at young Leonidov, who had graduated barely two years earlier with a Lenin Institute project that reinvented constructivism, became relentless. What bothered his accusers was Leonidov's inventive reinterpretation of the palace's competition program. He had rejected the idea of a monolithic building and devised a new concept: an open-air park where various activities, including sports, were dynamically scattered over the site, boasting a monumental glass pyramid in its center. The "sabotage" of a proletarian institution was his alleged disrespect for the program. His designs were consequently branded "a product of the West, a product of the bourgeoisie."

At the end of the malevolent diatribe, Leonidov answered with his usual candor, tinged with discreet irony: "I come from a working-class family. I could not possibly have become an architect of bourgeois extraction in eight or nine years spent in a school of

---

[77] On Leonidov cf. Andrei Gozak and Andrei Leonidov, *Ivan Leonidov: The Complete Work* (London, New York: Rizzoli), 1988 and *Ivan Leonidov:1902-19*, Alessandro De Magistris and Irina Korob'ina ed. (Milano: **Electa**architettura), 2009.

[78] The engineer Lihachëv founded and ran a vast automobile factory on American licenses since before the revolution.

[79] See Selim Omarovich Khan-Magomedov, "Ivan Leonidov, un architetto sovietico, 1902-1959," in *Ivan Leonidov, 1902–1959*, ed. Alessandro De Magistris and Irina Korobina (Milano: Mondadori Electa), 2009, p. 36.

[80] The concept of *vreditel'* (saboteur) was already established in the second trial of the "cultural revolution," staged against a group of engineers, supposedly members of an invented "Industrial Party."

architecture."⁸¹ Yet Leonidov's persecution had just started. In what appeared as a coordinated conspiracy Mordvinov orchestrated, articles and meetings relentlessly harassed the already towering figures among the architectural avant-gardes who were clearly poised to lead the Soviet architecture into next decades.

By fall 1930, a new meeting was called for at the ASI—the school that had replaced the VHUTEIN at the end of the spring semester that year. It was then and there that Mordvinov introduced his derogatory term. Along with the word "formalism," the former was to become shorthand for all that was to be rejected.

Leonidov was mercilessly derided where the fruits of previous campaigns had come to maturity. It was a barrage of invectives, mostly from the civil engineering students who had been already largely brainwashed through previous organized slanders in an atmosphere of fear. Those of the students, the ex-VHUTEIN students mainly, who disagreed, were clear that any defense of Leonidov would only lead to their own expulsion from the school. According to witnesses, Aleksandr Vesnin, who was present, helpless in the face of the moral lynching of his beloved "Vanĕchka," had tears in his eyes, unable to react to such an enormity with obvious official support.[82] Leonidov, who hardly ever used alcohol, spent the rest of the night inebriating himself.

But this was not enough. Mordvinov pushed further, now with an editorial in *Isskustvo v Massy* (Art to the Masses). His article, "Leonidovshchina i eë Vred" ("Leonidovism and Its Harm") sought to discredit both the rationalist and constructivist approaches to architecture. "Leonidovists"—according to Mordvinov—"represent(ed) the extreme formalistic wing in constructivism." Worse, "they synthesized all that [was] negative in formalism itself [...]."[83]

In the September–October 1930 issue[84]—one issue before the last, as the journal was to close abruptly in December—*SA* responded in measured but assertive terms with an editorial addressing the *ad hominem* attacks against Leonidov. While the journal prominently featured Leonidov's project for the Palace of Culture, it is worth quoting the response in some detail to help assess what was at stake at this juncture for the avant-gardes. In nuanced but cautious language, the editorial board declared:

> [...] The numerous reviews in the press, in University debates and other discussion venues were openly aimed at discrediting the project of I. Leonidov.
>
> The editorial board of *SA* is well aware of weaknesses of some of his projects: the lack of consideration for actual conditions, a disregard for the economic possibilities of the present day, along with some degree of estheticism. All of this is

---

[81] S. Gorskij, "Otrubite ej kryl'ja, in *Smena* no. 4, 1931, pp. 22–23, quoted in *Ivan Leonidov, 1902–1959*, ed. Alessandro De Magistris and Irina Korobina, p. 36.
[82] Ibid., p. 37.
[83] Arkadij Grigorevich Mordvinov, "Leonidovshchina i eë vred," *Iskusstvo v Massy* (Art to the Masses), in the column "Let Us Destroy a Foreign Ideology;" quoted in *Ivan Leonidov, 1902–1959*, ed. Alessandro De Magistris and Irina Korobina, p. 37. No. 12 (1930): 12–15.
[84] See, "Ot redaksii" *SA* no. 5 1930, pp. 2–4.

without doubt a manifest weakness of Leonidov's work. However, those who criticize Leonidov's work completely disregard what, from our point of view, represents as well an enormous value of his work. This project [the Palace of Culture] is, along with all its weaknesses, a work far more valuable than what his competitors have come up with. And this is because Leonidov approaches his projects as a socially minded architect, a deep-thinking architect, who addresses his task with clarity, while correcting [the program's] insufficiencies; at times rethinking it from scratch, but always aiming at what, from his point of view, can accelerate the reconstruction of daily life [*byt*] on socialist principles. It is understandable that in doing so he cannot avoid some mistakes leading to "exaggerations." I. Leonidov often makes mistakes by going "overboard." But no one is immune to such mistakes. In any case, they in no way can justify unprecedented slandering to which Leonidov has been lately exposed. Slandering against him only because he thinks by himself, because he thinks about architecture in his own way, in a new way [...].

The board added that it could also agree with some criticism such as the abstractness of Leonidov's projects, suffering from "schematism." "Regardless," the editorial pursued, "we consider his work to be of great value as an experimental and inquisitive endeavor. We forcefully protest the despicable treatment Leonidov has been subjected to." The editorial board also agreed that a tendency of the youngest generation of architects to "imitate Leonidov" had to be condemned, "like any other mechanical imitation."

Of course, what the editors of *SA* knew very well, without saying so, was that these widespread attacks were not spontaneous but orchestrated "from above." Mordvinov did not care. He was mandated to accomplish a party duty.

The long arm of Kaganovich directing the actions of VOPRA members from behind the scenes was further reflected in Mordvinov's December 20 official speech and proclamation in sixteen theses, titled "O Melkoburzhuaznom napravlenii v Arhitekture—Leonidovshchina" (About the Petit Bourgeois Current in Architecture—Leonidovism). The proclamation was sanctioned by the Commissariat of Enlightenment's IZO to which, as mentioned, Mordvinov was recently appointed. While generalizing the *Leonidovshchina* into a trend, Mordvinov referred to some recognizable details of Leonidov's projects without naming them. These were the occasional use of dirigibles (in his Magnitogorsk urban plan and the Palace of Culture competition entry) or delicate, if ineffable and idiosyncratic renderings that invited imagination in subtle ways. Mordvinov hatefully vilified the work of this rising genius of the architectural avant-garde's second generation. In what amounted to malevolence, he pointedly avoided projects that would have nullified his claims.

Mordvinov's resolution stated—one could hear Kaganovich speaking—that the current "exacerbated class struggle [had] to find its place in architecture as well." The campaign had acquired an official stamp with Mordvinov already speaking with the authority of a government and party official, barely a year into VOPRA's creation, clearly exposing VOPRA's nature. The stunning claim of the resolution that concluded the meeting was that "the *Leonidovshchina* in architecture is a reflection of the typical psychology of one part of the small bourgeoisie, which, unhappy with the Soviet reality, is turning to foreign and hostile positions to the proletarian edification; in so doing it is aligning itself with the class enemy of the proletariat." The claim could not have been more menacing under the "revived class struggle" Stalin had proclaimed.

Interestingly, however, the resolution started with an apparently measured and dispassionate claim. As a general stance, it proclaimed that architecture had to submit itself to the demands of modern science and technology, rationalization and mechanization of means that would, in itself, speed up the construction of socialism through the most economical means—a fundamental claim of the constructivists. "The architecture in the USSR," the resolution went on, "is not uniform [...]. It shows a variety of trends each with its own world-view [sic], its theory and method of work [...]. The basic trends are: eclecticism; formalism, constructivism and proletarian architecture. Among them, eclecticism represents the reactionary wing." Almost as if coming from a constructivist handbook, Mordvinov continued his assessment.

> Eclecticism is wrong because of the technique it uses, the lack of inventiveness [*rutina*], the pointed rejection of the new methods of construction and the use of new materials etc. Its predilection for "the old ways," its false feudal [sic] constructive elements (arches, vaults), its attraction to old ways of life, its resistance to collectivist life, restore and celebrate the architectural concepts proper to our class enemy; its embrace of the psycho-ideology of the bourgeoisie [...]. All of it translates into a reactionary trend that has to be rejected.[85]

"The Formalists and the Constructivists" the declaration went on, "represent the fellow travelers of the proletarian architecture." Still, "The 'fellow traveler' status of the formalists and the constructivists differed in the way they evolved. Part of them keeps the old positions, while others strive to embrace the proletarian ways." Although with a different terminology, one could clearly recognize Taut's speech here. The official character of the resolution gave a particular weight to such claims.

Most intriguing, however, was the apparent acceptance that in the Soviet Union there were "varying attitudes regarding the construction of socialism and understanding of its own tasks." This was still pronounced in a pre-totalitarian context, as Stalin would not fully assert his power before the 1934 17th Party Congress, as mentioned earlier. Quickly, however, came a warning. There was a "need to fight capitalist elements and [...] the class enemy." This meant, "a struggle against bourgeois and petit bourgeois phenomena in architecture, involving reactionary groups and those among the fellow travelers who tend to slip into camp of the enemy." This was the argument Kaganovich would carry to the end of the 1930's despite his own weakness for "false feudal" architecture. With such slippery threats, the door was open to uncertainty, fear, and stifling dependency.

---

[85] See *Sovetskaja Arhitektura* 1–2, 1931, p. 18.

Whereas the position regarding eclecticism in particular might have contradicted what would later emerge as Kaganovich's architectural predilection, the actual purpose of this resolution was the destruction of Leonidov as a nascent towering force in the architectural discourse of the early 1930s—a force which could have led the profession into the decade and beyond. Out of a total of sixteen theses of the resolution, twelve were violent invectives against Leonidov. He was to be the sacrificial lamb in VOPRA's crusade for a preponderant position in the architectural realm, that is, for the role of an unquestioned arbiter.[86]

Following this indictment by the People's Commissariat of Enlightenment (Narkompros), Leonidov was removed from his teaching position at the ASI. For three years, he experienced a psychological paralysis. He did not participate in any of several prestigious competitions that followed, beginning with the 1931 international competition for the Palace of Soviets. In 1934, as the competition for the Commissariat of Heavy Industry was underway, he finally gathered all his creative force for the best and possibly last project he ever produced under his name[87]—a project that is still influential today (Figure 1.4).

Figure 1.4 Ivan Leonidov 1934 NKTP competition entry. (Courtesy Shchusev Museum of Architecture)

---

[86] See *Ivan Leonidov, 1902–1959*, ed. Alessandro De Magistris and Irina Korobina, p. 45.
[87] Quoted in ibid. p. 59, "Igarka, la costruzione di una città nell' estremo nord dell' Unione Sovietica." Recently some of the Igarka buildings have been tentatively identified as Leonidov's. See Ekaterina A. Barabanova, "Igarka, la Costruzione di una Città nell'Estremo Nord dell'Unione Sovietica, in *Ivan Leonidov, 1902–1959*,

The campaign against Leonidov did not abate. He would actually be used as a scarecrow and scapegoat for most of the decade. Typical of the humiliations he was to endure was the 1931 article in the youth magazine *Smena*, published with the menacing title "Otrubite ej kryl'j a!" ("Cut off their wings!"). After visiting the ASI, the article's author wrote that the "wings of creativity of the followers of Leonidov should be severed because the Leonidovshchina is no less than a reactionary absurdity, an enemy the luxury of wondering into fantasy. We therefore declare a war to any 'abstract creative fantasy! Let us cut their wings!'"[88]

By 1934, Leonidov had disappeared from the 1932 list of delegates to the founding congress of the All-Soviet Association of Architects. He was essentially kept at an arm's length from any possibility to build, even as he became head of a design studio in the Moscow city planning authority in 1932,[89] after a year spent as a planner above the Arctic Circle in the town of Igarka.[90] It is most likely thanks to Ginzburg that he was able to join the Commissariat of Heavy Industry from 1934 until his mobilization to the front trenches at the start of the Second World War—where he was wounded two years later, and demobilized in 1943. His downgrading was so merciless that even El Lissitzky, now recycled into a Soviet propagandist, had beaten into the drum of Leonidov's denigration. Short of damning him for the dangerous sin of "formalism," Lissitzky criticized in *Arhitektura SSSR*[91] the young architect's 1934 competition entry as a mere "theatrical stage set." An outraged Leonidov remarked that this was just a competition project with a very short deadline at that. The only concession, if significant, Lissitzky made to Leonidov's unique project, still influential today, was that Leonidov was the sole competitor who had taken into consideration the urban context of the project—the Saint Basil spires, and the Bolshoi Theater. One of the smart approaches to the project is that he divided the humongous program of the building into three distinct towers, each different in shape and materials.

For the rest of his brief life—he died at 57—Leonidov kept sketching architectural fantasies on wooden tablets, using his early training as an iconographer. Many of the tablets included reminiscences of his 1934 competition entry, now rendered in a dream-like form. The only work he built was a monumental stairway Ginzburg invited him to build in the park of his 1938 Kislovodsk sanatorium, discussed in the next chapter. Under Ginzburg's protection, who died in 1945, he worked as an anonymous draftsman at the Commissariat of Heavy Industry—ironically, the commissariat of his failed 1934 competition. In the late

---

ed. Alessandro De Magistris and Irina Korob'ina, pp. 58–81. Ekaterina Barabanova speculates that Leonidov designed part of Igarka. She bases her claim on a formal analysis and the fact that Leonidov is known to have gone there as member of a team of architects in 1931. However, this may be contradicted by Ginzburg's and A. Vesnin's claims in February 1936 during an SSA meeting that Leonidov's burden with alleged "formalism" comes from the fact that he was never given the opportunity to build anything. See Chapter 5.

[88] Quoted in *Ivan Leonidov, 1902-1959,* ed. Alessandro De Magistris and Irina Korobina, p. 37.
[89] See A. Gozak and A. Leonidov *Ivan Leonidov* (London: Academy Editions), 1988, p. 31.
[90] Op. cit. *Ivan Leonidov:1902-19*, ed. Alessandro De Magistris and Irina Korob'ina.
[91] *Arhitektura SSSR,* October 10, 1934.

1940s he edited, along with the essayist David Arkin (1889–1957) and Viktor Vesnin a collection of books *The Architecture of the Cities of the USSR* published by the Academy of Architecture of the USSR. After Stalin's death, in the mid-1950s, students realized that the old man who was earning a living as an instructor of model-making in the basement of the Moscow school of architecture was actually the legendary Leonidov.

***

The partial victory of the cultural revolution over the architectural profession encouraged the architecture leadership to turn its subversive actions into a system.

Perceiving themselves as both agents and accelerators of history, Communists claimed that ultimately "history was on [their] side," regardless of possible mistakes or temporary setbacks. This exacerbated deterministic claim, allegedly derived from Marx, was reflected in a peculiar trans-historic, metaphysical conception of the party.

Secrecy added an aura to the imaginary "revived class struggle" against long-dismantled social fabric that Stalin launched in 1928 with his new party line. Such fiction opened wide the door to unchecked, arbitrary acts. Still, most modern architects, members of the party or not, often saw themselves throughout the 1930s as loyal supporters of the revolutionary cause and simultaneously as defenders of a compelling legacy of the previous decade.

CHAPTER 2
CONTINUITY AND RESISTANCE: DESIGNED BEFORE 1932, COMPLETED DOWN THE DECADE

On April 23, 1932, the Central Committee issued the fateful *Postanovlenie* "Ob Perestrojke LITHUDORG" (About the Reconstruction of Literary and Artistic Organizations), which targeted the independent art societies, including architecture—or what was left of the VANO federation discussed in the previous chapter. The latter was dissolved on July 11, and five days later *Izvestija* announced the creation of the All-Union of Soviet Architects (Sojuz Sovetskih Arhitektorov), the SSA. The by-laws of the new Union came from the Central Committee. The centralized association of architects replacing VANO was to be a single, overarching architectural organization the authorities could monitor easily thanks to a strong internal party organization (*partgruppa*) that the former associations did not have. Unlike what had been the case with VANO, the SSA by-laws excluded from its membership students, technicians collaborating with architects, and all other "lower categories" such as manual workers. Elitism was replacing former egalitarian openness and transparency.[1]

VOPRA was formally dissolved but reconstituted in the form of a party cell internal to the new association. In other words, the party was now omnipresent, if operating from behind the scenes. A compromise was achieved between the constructivists, represented by Viktor Vesnin and Ginzburg, and the leaders of the now defunct VOPRA, Mordvinov and Alabjan. Viktor Vesnin assumed the presidency of the SSA, while Alabjan became its executive secretary, his real power lying in the secret role the union's party cell would play over the coming years.[2]

That year also saw the outburst of a great famine, where, by all accounts, millions died of hunger. The famine was caused by a combination of ill-conceived forced collectivization of the land and massive confiscation of wheat as cash crop for the acquisition of machinery from the West which the accelerated industrialization imposed.

The first issue of the official journal of the Union of Architects, *Arhitektura SSSR*, appeared in July 1933. As the "organ of the SSA," and striving for uniformity and single

---

[1] SSA meetings of July 4, 1932 and July 20, 1932. *Stenogram* of meetings about the endorsement of the organization's by-laws; Viktor Vesnin's introductory note started with some drama: "Comrades, you certainly know why we met here today [...] The need for architectural uniformization has been felt for a while. The absence of unity had a negative influence on our work." RGALI 674, op. 1 ed. hr. 7 (1) p. 189 and pp. 144–47.

[2] RGALI, All-Union of Soviet Architects. Fond 674, op. 1 ed. hr. 6, July 1932. (Protokol soveshchanija rukovodjashchyh organov [...] v svijazy [...] Postanovlenija CK VKPb ot 23 Aprelja 1932) Protocol of the reunion of the leading organs in connection with the decree of the Central Committee of April 23, 1932 674. op. 1 ed. hr. pp. 1–75.

mindedness, it was to gradually supplant Miljutin's journal *Sovetskaja Arhitektura*, which nevertheless survived for two more years as Miljutin's fortune faded. It is to be stressed that the new journal, despite its unattractive appearance (even though signed by Lissitzky), published uninterruptedly modern and avant-garde architecture, domestic and foreign, to the end of the decade. This included essays by the leaders of constructivism and suprematism as will be discussed in the fourth chapter.

The former VOPRA leader Alabjan was finally installed as chief editor, as his career of a well-tuned apparatchik grew steadily. His role as party activist and Kaganovich's confidant was crowned in 1936 with his nomination (formally an election) to the Supreme Soviet—the country's presumed parliament—as the new constitution defined it. Referred to as "The Great Stalinian Constitution," it cynically included freedom of religion, speech, assembly, and the press. Significantly, the prominent leader of the avant-gardes, Viktor Vesnin, was also selected that year for the supreme legislative body, blurring facile categorizations.[3] It seemed that some sort of balance was sought after, which characterized Kaganovich's position, as discussed in chapters four and five.

None of the former editorial board members of either *SA* or *Sovetskaja Arhitektura* were invited to join the new journal. The vitality of the architectural avant-garde circles was such, however, that by July 20 the possibility of creating new ad hoc internal "creative units" was already raised. The fierce confrontations that preceded the dissolution of the *gruppirovke* during the cultural revolution[4] soon resumed in the SSA itself.

In this context, therefore the chapter considers—with the exception of Ginzburg's 1938 sanatorium in the Caucasus—buildings designed before the April 1932 decree but completed in the course of the decade without alterations.[5]

The gradual, if elusive, conceptualization of "socialist" realism that followed, represented often, if not exclusively, a spontaneous revival of entrenched conservative, academic art forms. These were, however, hardly more widespread than what had been the case in the 1920s, if the rise in general building activities is discounted. The prestige of Soviet modernism's leaders was so compelling—at least in the case of architects—that they rarely lost their positions. Exceptions were Ivan Leonidov and, six years later, Konstantin Mel'nikov. They were identified rhetorically with "formalism" and singled out as convenient negative models, not always without some embarrassment in the case of Mel'nikov. Already a legend by the end of the 1920s, he was the most productive of them all, with numerous workers' clubs, garages, housing, and markets—including the first modern building raised in the Soviet Union: the Mahorka pavilion at the 1923 Agricultural Exposition; and the most celebrated pavilion at the 1925 Paris Exposition of Decorative Arts, making him the epitome of an instant international celebrity.

---

[3] The first show trial against sixteen Bolshevik leaders the same year included Georgij Zinoviev—mostly remembered as the head of the Communist International (Komintern) and Lev Kamenev, longstanding Politburo member and Deputy Chair of the Government.
[4] Hugh Hudson, *Blue Prints and Blood: The Stalinization of Soviet Architecture, 1917–1937* (Princeton University Press), 1994.
[5] Towards the end of the decade, if mostly in the 1940s, it became fashionable to add "ornaments" to some completed constructivist work.

Continuity and Resistance

Leonidov, on the other hand, was the deepest and most inventive young constructivist of the second generation—far ahead of his time to his misfortune. He was never given the opportunity to build. Yet, according to Jerzy Soltan who worked with the Parisian master, he was "the only architect Le Corbusier feared."[6]

Institutional Position of the Avant-Gardes after 1932

The modernists remained visible in leading positions in most of the new Stalinist architectural institutions. Arrests were made, however, among the younger generation—all of them party members—often leaving the masters suspended in a vacuum.[7] Viktor Vesnin, one of the three brothers who led the constructivist movement with Moisej Ginzburg, became Secretary General of the All-Union of Soviet Architects from the moment the new organization was officially established.

Throughout the 1930s Ginzburg was in charge of a team planning sanatoria and rest homes in the Crimean Black Sea coastline as a top architect in the Commissariat for Heavy Industry. He played a central role in the Union of Architects as well. The leaders of the avant-garde led five out of twelve city architectural workshops (ARHPLAN) Kaganovich established in 1933, as discussed in Chapter 3. The heads of the ARHPLAN workshops included the independents Mel'nikov and Il'ja Golosov (1883-1945), the rationalist Nikolaj Ladovskij (1881-1941), and the constructivists Ginzburg and the Vesnins, each leading their own workshop. Ladovskij, the theoretically minded architect, former leading figure of the VHUTEMAS/VHUTEIN, and inventor of Russian architectural "rationalism," built little but was author of an important street-level Metro pavilion and an underground station in Moscow discussed in the next chapter.

It is important to reiterate, that the persecutions and trials—the "great party purges" or *chistkas*—were at the beginning primarily, if not exclusively, directed against old Bolsheviks and committed younger party members such as Gustav Klucis (1895-1938), one of the few avant-garde artists who contributed directly to the Russian Revolution and the Civil War. He was arrested in 1938, while boarding an airplane bound to New York, to work on the Soviet 1939 pavilion. He was just back from the Paris World's Fair where his photomontage at the entrance of the Soviet Pavilion featured a Stalin larger than life, towering above a congregation of diminutive citizens applauding his 1936 constitution. According to some sources, Klucis was shot immediately upon arrest, along with a group of one hundred other Latvian communists, on Stalin's direct orders.[8] A

---

[6] Jerzy Soltan (1913-2005), GSD visiting Professor of Architecture who had worked with Le Corbusier. Public lecture I attended in the mid-1980s.
[7] The better known were Aleksej Gan, Mihail Ohitovich, Solomon Lisagor, Markov, Lazar Rempel', Gustav Klucis, and Ja. Aleksandrov; as well as the celebrated theater director Vsevolod Mejerhold (collaborator of Ljubov Popova and A. Vesnin) all active members of the Bolshevik Party.
[8] About the arrest and execution of Klucis, see Margarita Tupitsyn, *Gustav Klutsis and Valentina Kulagina: Photography and Montage after Constructivism* (New York: Steidl and ICP), 2004. I owe to Jean-Louis Cohen the information that Klucis was executed along with one hundred Latvian communists.

specific cause for an arrest was never needed, it would be determined a posteriori. But a 1930 poster by Klucis that showed Stalin as a dark, looming figure in the background, half concealed behind Lenin's radiant face, may have singled him out. Worse, the poster was mentioning only Lenin. As an early Bolshevik revolutionary, Klucis had his own strong political motivations that were not derived from any devotion to Stalin, and so could turn against him. That made him dangerous a priori. Stalin's vengeance could take several years to materialize.

By contrast, none of the Vesnin brothers ever joined the party, nor did Ginzburg, Mel'nikov, or Leonidov. They were therefore much less vulnerable, even when mass arrests started as a way of obtaining unpaid labor to accelerate industrialization. They belonged to the category of *nepartijci*, or nonparty sympathizers, without a stake in the functioning of the regime itself. Among the most noted avant-garde architects who were *nepartijci*, besides Leonidov, only Konstantin Mel'nikov (1890–1974), the staunchly independent expressionist, was criticized by the regime. Subjected to growing public attacks for his alleged "formalism," he ceased to practice architecture altogether after 1937. For most of his long life thereafter, he lived quietly in the two interlocking cylinder house he had built for himself in the most prestigious part of central Moscow in 1927–1929. Like all top architects he had an official chauffeured car at his disposal.[9] After quitting architecture, he made a living as a painter, his first vocation. According to his son, the NKVD never disturbed or questioned him in the years that followed. He led an active social life hosting artists and musicians in the expansive salon of his idiosyncratic house.[10]

The Ambiguities of the Decade

Throughout the 1930s the Soviet establishment listened to the beat of two drummers. Architecture journals of the period illustrate this clearly, as *Stroitel'stvo Moskvy* could change its cover from conservative to modern depending on the architectural issue it addressed. Alabjan himself considered favorably the possibility of a CIAM congress in Moscow for 1935, as he prompted Kaganovich to support it.[11] At the same time, he fiercely combated the constructivists in party meetings, as discussed in Chapter 4. Despite recurrent attacks in the press against Le Corbusier regarding his 1934 Centrosojuz, invitations kept coming to him throughout the decade. On the occasion of his visit to Le Corbusier in spring 1935, Iofan urged him to come to the Soviet Union for a lecture series. The French architect responded positively on July 28, 1935.[12] These invitations could not have been extended without Kaganovich's agreement. In December 1935 Le

---

[9] RGALI, 674, op. 2, ed. hr. A total of thirty-five architects and engineers were entitled to a car.
[10] Author's interview with the architect's son Viktor Mel'nikov, himself a painter, May 2004. See also. Frederick Starr *Mel'nikov: Solo Architect in a Mass Society,* (Princeton: Princeton University Press), 1981.
[11] RGALI, Sekretarijat Orgokomiteta 674, op. 1, ed. hr. 2. See also Fondation Le Corbusier FLC, H2-5-266, 270.
[12] Paris, FLC H2-9-373, 3–4.

Corbusier was also invited to join the new All-Union Academy of Architecture (a graduate school) as a scientific correspondent. He accepted the invitation, while reminding his host about his distaste for "academies" as such.[13] In response, he received a sample of the journal *Arhitektura za Rubezhom* (*Architecture from Abroad*) (Figure 2.1), published by the academy in a surprisingly modern design, and boasting an imposing view of the Rockefeller Center on the cover on its 1935 second issue.[14] The journal was published from 1934 to 1937 when the academy itself was unraveled for imaginary "Trotskyite" sympathies, followed by several arrests.

Most intriguing was Kaganovich's actual support for the constructivists, as addressed in Chapter 4. Such ambiguous position regarding modern architecture was also evident in his attitude about the Metro stations he supervised.

However, despite their continuous efforts to woo CIAM to Moscow, it was the SSA officials who postponed the organization's fourth congress, to be held in Moscow in 1933. The belief that it was the CIAM that canceled the Moscow congress, supposedly in response to the 1932 Palace of Soviets international competition, and its alarming results was not exactly correct. This erroneous belief is apparently based in part on letters that

Figure 2.1 Journal *Arhitektura za Rubezhom* (*Architecture from Abroad*). (Photo by author)

---

[13] FLC I2-5-292.
[14] The pristine condition of the samples kept at the Lenin Library could be an indication that the journal fell into the category of publication that not all Soviet citizens were allowed to read.

Soviet Architectural Avant-Gardes

Cor van Eastern, Victor Bourgeois, and Siegfried Gideon wrote to Stalin on April 19, 1932, lamenting the antimodernist choice of Ivan Zholtovskij, Boris Iofan, and the American Hamilton. In their correspondence with Stalin, they did raise serious doubts about whether their congress could be held in Moscow under such circumstances. The CIRPAC, CIAM's executive body based in London, nevertheless continued making plans to hold its fifth and even sixth congress in Moscow, on Soviet insistence.[15] It was important for the Politburo and Stalin to be careful not to be perceived abroad as abandoning progressive positions when their international image was at stake.

As noted earlier, a double standard applied, regardless of their personal tastes and choices. In its effort to achieve control over the architectural culture of the country, the party's supreme authority had to cater to at least two audiences—the conservative domestic population (meaning the *nomenklatura*) and the progressive international *intelligentcija*, which supported the October Revolution and the modern art it had come to expect from the USSR.

Divergent Orientations at the Pinnacle of Power

The ambiguities and contradictions regarding the direction architecture was to take following the fateful April decree of the Central Committee on the curtailing of independent architectural associations were exacerbated as no architectural model or specific style ever followed the decree. Kaganovich specifically declared in a 1934 party meeting that "we are not going to determine a style by decree."[16] The disagreements about what constituted modernity in architecture complicated and, ultimately, enriched both the transition and the resistance to the never circumscribed "socialist" realism discussed in the Introduction and previous chapter.[17] If we judge by who were his favorite architects—such as Arkadij Langman (1886–1968), or Boris Iofan for that matter—it becomes evident that Stalin opted for the image of a modern American corporate architecture that Langman echoed in his own work. Stalin even sent Iofan to New York in 1934 (along with Shchuko and Gel'freih) to study the city's skyscrapers from close up (Figure 2.2). The influence of the Radio City building was immediately evident in the design change of the Palace of Soviets from the 1933 version close to Hamilton's, to the one that appeared after the trip in 1935 (see Figure 2.12).

The most recent ones, such as the Empire State Building, projected power and stability (even in name) that fascinated Stalin more than any a priori ideological stance, as he

---

[15] Letter of March 29, 1933, FLC I2-5-293. See also Mart Stam's mission to the CIRPAC from Moscow discussed later.
[16] See note 1.
[17] For an excellent and highly informative story about Soviet engagement with the American program of new skyscrapers and their connection to the conceptualization of the Palace of the Soviets, see Katherine Zubovich, dissertation "Moscow Monumental: Soviet Skyscrapers and Urban Life under High Stalinism," Chapter I, UC Berkley, 2016.

Figure 2.2 Boris Iofan, watercolor of the Rockefeller Center. (Private collection)

ignored the specific capitalist genealogy of skyscrapers. Unawares of what was at stake, at the 1937 congress in Moscow Frank Lloyd Wright reminded his audience mercilessly about the origins of skyscrapers. As discussed in the last chapter, he attacked the Palace of Soviets as an incongruous capitalist product "undeserving of the great Lenin." The well-known eight skyscrapers built under Stalin after the war were dispersed in a theatrical gesture at eight corners of the Soviet capital, absurdly uprooted from their actual raison d'être as a type.

In 1935 Langman completed a sober, unadorned, pristinely executed government building, the State Planning Committee, GOSPLAN (today the Russian Parliament or Duma) just across from Shchusev's Hotel Moskva of the same date (Figure 2.3).

Free of any ornament, entrusting its modernity to expensive materials and metal finishes in a Loosian way, the building's façade was characterized by a powerful rhythm of alternating vertical bands of window openings and blind vertical strips, recalling Albert Kahn's 1919–1922 General Motors Building in Detroit. Stalin saw the high-powered corporate gloss in Langman's architectural vocabulary as lending a modern edge to the Soviet capital. The high esteem this building commanded was expressed in Jurij Pimenov's 1937 famed canvas "New Moscow."

The painting focused on Langman's building in an obvious celebration of a certain American modernity, as imaginary skyscrapers loomed in the background in association

Figure 2.3 A. Langman GOSPLAN building, Moscow 1935. (Photo by author)

with a luxurious convertible car, driven casually by a woman just after the rain. The scene could have been located anywhere in New York or Chicago. The proximity of the Kremlin and the prominence given to Langman's building clearly indicated the significance Stalin attributed to the style—an ascetic style similar to his own persona: he wore buttoned-up soldiers' uniforms at all times and slept only a few hours a night on a narrow camp bed set by his desk, as a picture of his dacha office in Sochi testifies. Perceptible from the street, the window of his Kremlin office was known to be lit at any time—a sign of his omniscient presence.

In contrast, the residential and commercial quarters built under Kaganovich's control, just around the corner on Tverskaja Street (by then renamed Gorky Street), boasted nineteenth-century eclectic architecture (albeit restrained and elegant), by the former constructivist and VHUTEMAS alumnus, Andrej Burov (1900–1957). Mordvinov had some of his own luxury housing on the same street, further north, known as block A and B, Shchusev's Hotel Moskva itself, completed in 1936 and facing the Kremlin, was in a certain sense a synthesis of the two trends: a compromise between Stalin's and Kaganovich's preferred styles, with bands of round-headed windows and a wealth of cornices competing with stern, uninspired, contemporary banality. Its "American" character was immediately obvious to Frank Lloyd Wright, who declared at the congress to his bewildered hosts that the hotel was exactly what he had been fighting against all his life in the United States.[18] Shchusev designed it for dignitaries visiting Stalin who

---

[18] Frank Lloyd Wright "Architecture and Life in the USSR," in *Architectural Record,* October 1937, pp. 59–63.

would wait for their audience for weeks if not months.[19] The hotel became, despite its mediocrity and awkward urban setting, a historical and cultural icon.

Conversely, Kaganovich was open to historicism, as long as it could be claimed that it had a "socialist content."[20] The 1934 Red Army Theater Kaganovich commissioned from Alabjan was a case in point: Hammers and sickles adorned the pseudo-Composite capitals, while the column shafts' sections, like the plan of the building itself, were shaped as five-pointed stars, in keeping with the popular "architecture parlante" of the so-called French eighteenth-century "revolutionary" classicists. This peristyle was Alabjan's response to Kaganovich's expressed wish of introducing "our own order."[21] Whether the hammer and sickle and the star accounted for the "content" or not, the Red Army Theater was an incisive illustration of the architectural taste of the Politburo's second man. He allegedly watched Alabjan closely as the architect labored to fit a theater into a pentagram.

Kaganovich was not alone, of course, in embracing classical eclecticism in the name of modernity. Classicism in Russia was widely viewed as a progressive alternative to the entrenched Byzantine style that had been indefatigably recycled since the tenth century, when the northeastern Slavs adopted Christianity.[22] Lunacharskij's well-known claim about Greece's invention of democracy, whose architecture was therefore suitable to a proletarian state, amusingly pitted ancient Greece against the Byzantine.[23] Such specious claims were ultimately endorsed even by Hannes Meyer, involved after 1932 in the gigantic urbanization trend of the Soviet Union. He declared in 1933 "I became interested lately in classical architecture and ancient architecture in general, as I have discovered [...] the significance of the 'national expression' in socialist architecture."[24]

Renaissance revivals, nevertheless, were harshly criticized, even in the general press. As late as 1937, Palladian revivals were sardonically referred to as plagiarism. A Soviet cartoon in the satirical journal *Krokodil*, reproduced in the *Architectural Record* in 1937, showed Palladio dragging a Soviet architect to a police station, asking to arrest him because the only original feature in that architect's design was his signature—an obvious allusion to Ivan Zholtovskij's Inturist housing across from the Kremlin walls.

This no doubt complicated issues and was fodder for acerbic debates about the modernity fitting a people's revolution. The cartoon was a barely veiled accusation of the prerevolutionary Palladian expert Zholtovskij, and his popularly acclaimed 1934 Inturist elite housing facing the north walls of the Kremlin, as a take on the Palazzo del Capitaniato

---

[19] See Milovan Djilas *Conversations with Stalin* (London Rupert Hart-Davis) 1962. Djilas visited Stalin several times as a partisan leader during the Second World War and resided in the "Moskva" Hotel.
[20] Kaganovich was known for advocating what he called "National in Form, Socialist in Content" (if Stalin was probably the one who formulated it first). "Theoretical Fundaments in the Theory of Soviet Architecture," in *Sovetskaja Arhitektura* n. 6/ 1933, p.5.
[21] See Chapter 4.
[22] See Dmitrij Shvidkovskij, *Russian Architecture and the West* (New Haven and London: Yale University Press, 2007).
[23] Lunacharskij's conversation with VOPRA members in January 1932 RGALI, 674 op.14 ed.hr.p.32.
[24] Quoted in J. L. Cohen, M. De Michelis, M. Tafuri, eds., *URSS, 1917–1978: La ville, L'Architecture* (Paris: L'Equerre and Rome: Officina edizioni) 1979, p. 311.

Soviet Architectural Avant-Gardes

in Vicenza. Yet, despite the criticism of Renaissance revivals, Zholtovskij was emulated in the 1930s in what could be taken as a third direction in Soviet architecture of that decade. These styles represented the broad framework within which constructivist buildings, conceived before the April 1932 Central Committee decree, were completed in the course of the decade, populating the urban landscape of Soviet cities undisturbed.

The Vesnin Brothers' Lihachëv Palace of Culture, Part One: The Small Theater, 1931–1934

The 1930 competition for the Palace of Culture, which brought an abrupt and brutal end to both Leonidov's teaching and practicing career, had not, according to the jury, resulted in any fully convincing solution. Therefore, in 1931 the commission was passed on to the Vesnin brothers—a safe placement.[25]

The "ZIL" Palace of Culture of Moscow's Proletarskij district, addressed in the previous chapter, was among the last of the late 1920s workers' clubs attached to factories for the benefit of its employees. The workers' clubs were meant to offer organized leisure time, following the reduction of daily work from twelve to eight hours a day, in the wake of the revolution.

The palace was raised on the site of the seventeenth-century Simonov Monastery used as a burial site for the aristocracy since the early Middle Ages (Figure 2.4). The monastery was demolished in 1923. However, it was never completely destroyed, nor was the palace ever fully completed, as the large 4,000-seat theater was not built. Standing side by side the two could be read as a metaphor of the aborted histories of Russia.

Figure 2.4 Site of the Simonov Monastery (Courtesy Shchusev Museum of Architecture); and extant towers (Photo by author)

---

[25] See December 28, 1931 "Dogovor" (Contract) with the brothers and the MOSPS (Moscow Regional Council of Trade-Unions), signed on a April 15, 1931. State Museum of Architecture KP OF-6105/94.

Obviously, between the two dates, some discussion about the Vesnins' ideas took place. Numerous yellow tracing kept at the Shchusev Museum of Architecture, may have been part of those discussions.

Continuity and Resistance

The small 1,000-seat theater was inaugurated in 1934, that is, two years into the 1932 consolidation decree; it operated as a functional unit on its own.[26] A lavish plaza-like interior vestibule, adorned with a Lenin statue, was encased in a huge, double wall-to-wall, concave glass surface spanning two floors. As the Vesnins claimed in the *Arhitekturnaja Gazeta*, "The theater lobby is a large volume that joins the ground floor with the first floor [...]. We wanted people to really breath freely and easily in that lobby."[27]

The west sidewalls of the theater, allowing a glimpse of the Simonov Monastery's surviving tower, featured two powerful semi-cylindrical balconies, almost identical, if larger, to those Ginzburg had attached to the south façade of his 1930 Narkomfin.

The second part, started in 1935, was built over the next two years. Its inauguration was celebrated in December 1937 as a prominent constructivist work with not a single alteration, as argued in the next chapter.

At the same time as ZIL's small theater, Panteleimon Golosov (1882–1945)—the brother of the better known Il'ja Golosov—built from 1933 to 1935 the magnificent headquarters of the Moscow daily *Pravda*, somewhat disfigured today by punched-out air condition boxes. It combined typical constructivist wraparound balconies and mainstream modernist ribbon windows. In the center, indicating the stair system and main circulation areas branching into the offices, an entirely glazed surface over four floors, and projected forward—another constructivist feature—was stretched vertically between the entrance canopy and a fifth-floor balcony, which acted as a solid frame. Turning the corner, to the shorter side of the building, a dramatic glazed volume indicated the production and printing areas, intentionally transparent for a newspaper whose name means Truth. The insistence on large glazed volumes offering a view of the interior was reminiscent of the design strategy of the brother's Vesnin 1922 *Leningradskaja Pravda*. Without having been altered or redesigned after 1932, Golosov's powerful project was another clear testament to the early resistance of the avant-gardes (see Figure 2.6a).

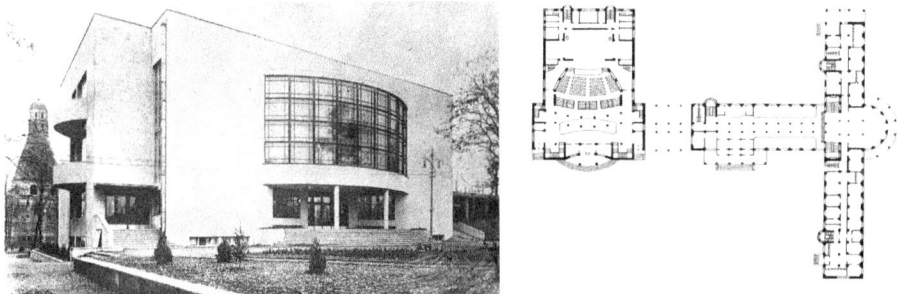

Figure 2.5 Small Theater completed in 1934 (remaining tower of Simonov Monastery in background); and plan of the entire Palace of Culture 1935–1937. (Courtesy Shchusev Museum of Architecture)

---

[26] See "Zakljuchenie" State Museum of Architecture KP OF-6105/95.
[27] *Arhitekturnaja Gazeta*, March 3, 1936.

Soviet Architectural Avant-Gardes

Figure 2.6 a) Panteleimon Golosov, *Pravda* headquarters in Moscow, built from 1933–1935 (LEFT: Courtesy Shchusev Museum of Architecture; RIGHT: Canadian Center for Architecture—gift of Howard Schickler and David Lafaille); b) Front façade. Photo Hannes Meyer. (Canadian Center for Architecture—gift of Howard Schickler and David Lafaille); c) Front entrance, detail. (Canadian Center for Architecture—gift of Howard Schickler and David Lafaille)

Continuity and Resistance

Panteleimon's brother Il'ja Panteleimon (as head of the Masterska N. 4), inaugurated a year later an imposing housing complex in Moscow (Figure 2.7). Dotted with obsessive multiplicity of dotted windows, the building recalled Le Corbusier's Moscow Centrosojuz, or for that matter, the work of the Italian Rationalist Adalberto Libera whose work was published in Moscow two years earlier.[28]

The Palace of Soviets: "American in Form, Socialist in Content"

Hardly a year after the fate of the Lenin Library was sealed and ground was broken for the theater of the ZIL automobile factory's Palace of Culture, a third major contest was announced: The International Competition for the Palace of Soviets.[29] With a series of four different competitions for the same program, from 1931 to 1933, the topic would dominate the entire decade, albeit only the foundations were ever built.

The first competition was held in two stages. A preliminary one was launched in February 1931. It was open to ten invited individual architects, including Boris Iofan and the Palladian expert Zholtovskij, along with four teams of avant-garde architects, grouped as competing VANO "brigades." These were Ladovskij's ASNOVA, founded in 1923;

Figure 2.7 LEFT: Il'ja Golosov, D. D. Bulgakov multi-purpose housing block, Moscow, 1936. (Courtesy Shchusev Museum of Architecture); RIGHT: Adalberto Libera, fragment of the Palazzo Del Littorio, Italian Pavilion, Brussels, 1935, published in L. I. Rempel's *Arhitektura Poslevoennoj Italii*, taken from 1934 German magazine. (Photographer unknown)

---

[28] See Ja. I. Rempel' *Arhitektura Poslevoennoj Italii* (Moscow: Academy of Architecture), 1935. The palace was prominently featured over the entire inner cover.
[29] See Yuya Suzuki. "Konkurs na dvorec sovetov 1930-x gg. v Moskve i mezhdunarodnij arkhitekturnyij kontekst." PhD dissertation, State Institute for the Study of Art, Moscow, 2014.

Ginzburg's OSA, created in 1926, and renamed by 1930 as SASS;[30] VOPRA that Kaganovich created in 1929, with Alabjan and Mordvinov at the helm; the ARU[31]—Association of Architects-Urbanists—Ladovskij founded in 1928 to take part in the ongoing debates about "socialist settlements."[32] The purpose of the first stage was to find a proper location for the palace and formulate its program. The chosen location required the demolition of the world's tallest Orthodox church, Christ the Saviour, built in the course of the nineteenth century to celebrate Russia's victory over Napoleon. The program was analogous to the unbuilt 1922 Palace of Labour (with the latter's presumed location on the Ohotnorjadskij square).

The 1931 palace was supposed to significantly transcend the role of a Soviet legislature—the Supreme Soviet. The published program demanded that the building be the focus of multiple cultural functions, assemblies, and mass parades, indicating emblematically the fusion of a legislative function with orchestrated mass activism as staged direct democracy. However, the essential and most telling difference was that the Palace of Soviets program demanded "monumentality" (already a favorite of the Lenin Library) and a hypertrophied square footage.[33]

On July 19, 1931, the *Izvestija* announced the second stage—now open to international competitors—with a deadline set for October 30. The submission date was ultimately extended to December 1, mostly due to the sudden September demand for an increased square footage. Given the nature of the request, it most probably indicated an outside political intervention.

Out of 160 competition proposals (twenty-four from abroad, of which eleven were from the United States) the jury allotted three ex-aequo prizes to Zholtovskij, Shchuko and Gelfreich,[34] one looking as a medieval fortress (Zholtovskij), and the other (Shchuko and Gelfreich) as the Doge Palace in Venice. In addition, the ex-aequo first-place award went to the young twenty-eight-year-old England-born American architect Hector O. Hamilton of East Orange. Despite his young age, and with only two years at the Cooper Union in New York, Hamilton was not a novice. Registered in New Jersey, he had already

---

[30] Sector of Architects of Socialist Construction (Sektor Arhitekorov Socialisticheskog Stroitel'stva, or SASS).
[31] Association of Revolutionary Urbanists (Associacija Revolucionyh Urbanistov).
[32] The topic of human settlements in a socialist country was the focus of vibrant debates that held the attention of the profession at the start of the First Five-Year Plan with its huge urbanization programs.
[33] The total square footage was increased in September from the initial 36,800 m² to 38,810 m².
[34] First prize (lower than "Grand Prize") was awarded ex-aequo to VOPRA members Karo Alabjan and Simbircev; to Zhukov and Chechulin; and to Dodica and Dushkin. Second prize went to two other Americans—Kastner and Stonorov.
 On the competition for the Palace of the Soviets and its prehistory see, among a substantial literature on the subject, Selim O. Khan-Magomedov, "K istorii vybora mesta dlja Dvorec Sovetov," in *Arhitektura i Stroitel'stvo Moskvy*, Jan. 1988, 21–23. See also a Central Committee Bulletin *Dvorec Sovetov*, 1931–32; *Il Palazzo dei Soviet 1931–1933*, Alberto Samonà, ed. (Rome: Officina Edizioni), 1976; N. S. Aratov, *El Palacio de los Soviet* (Montevideo: Pueblos Unidos) 1945, 2nd. edn; Peter Lizon, *The Palace of the Soviets: The Paradigm of Architecture in the USSR* (Colorado Springs: Three Continents Press), 1992. For the program, see "Programma proektirovanija Dvorca Sovetov SSSR v Moskve," in *Dvorec Sovetov: Vsesojuznyj Konkurs, 1932* (Moscow: SSA) 1933, pp. 123–29. See also *Stroitel'stvo Moskvy* 8, 1931, 8–10. Yuya Suzuki. "Konkurs na dvorec sovetov 1930-x gg. v Moskve i mezhdunarodnij arkhitekturnij kontekst." PhD dissertation, State Institute for the Study of Art,

designed some buildings in the United States and in Italy. He was, in addition, an employee of Albert Kahn.[35]

The prize given to Hamilton (Figure 2.8) clearly reflected the general Soviet fascination with the United States[36] as both the later intermediary 1933 and the 1935 (after Iofan's return from the United States) versions pointed to Hamilton's and other recent American achievements respectively, notably Raymond Hood's high-rise (see Figure 2.12).

Boris Iofan's project was among the awarded entries in the first open competition. Like most projects, it featured two halls of different sizes, separated by a plaza that boasted an obelisk topped with a symbolic statue of a worker (Figure 2.9).[37]

Figure 2.8 LEFT: Hamilton's winning entry (Private collection). RIGHT: Iofan's 1933 version of the Palace of Soviets before Iofan's trip to New York. (Courtesy Shchusev Museum of Architecture [Canadian Center for Architecture—gift of Howard Schickler and David Lafaille])

Moscow, 2014. Katherine Zubovich, "Moscow Monumental: Soviet Skyscrapers and Urban Life under High Stalinism," (UC Berkley), 2016.
[35] "The palace of Soviets," in *Architectural Forum,* March, 1932. Hector O. Hamilton https://en.wikipedia.org/wiki/Hector.Hamilton
[36] Two other American architects, Albert Kastner and Oscar Stonorov, shared the second prize. Of the 272 projects submitted, 14 were from the United States, including designs by Joseph Urban and Thomas Lamb, whose projects were retained along with Le Corbusier's, Perret's, Mendelsohn's, Gropius's, Pöelzig's and Brazini's. For a discussion of that "fascination," see Jean-Louis Cohen, "America: A Soviet Ideal," *AA Files* 5 (Jan. 1984), and his forthcoming book on *Amerikanizm in Soviet Russia*. See also Jean-Louis Cohen, *Building a new New World* (New Haven: Yale University Press), 2020, and the praise for the American city in David Arkin's preface to Lewis Mumford's *The Story of Utopias*. In their second letter to Stalin, the CIRPAC members compared Hamilton's project to an American corporate building, a church on the Hohenzollernplatz in Berlin, including department stores with "pseudo-Gothic appearance." Fondation Le Corbusier. (FLC), H2-5-266, 270.
[37] For an elaborate discussion of the multiple competitions for the Palace of the Soviets see Zubovich, doctoral dissertation.

Figure 2.9 B. Iofan winning entry in the first competition for the Palace of Soviets. (Courtesy Shchusev Museum of Architecture)

Nine additional international projects were highly praised, in particular the projects by Le Corbusier, Enrich Mendelsohn, Hans Poelzig, and Walter Gropius, with the jury's promise to take their proposals into consideration in further developments of the competition.[38]

With its task terminated, the jury submitted the results to high party authorities, that is, to the official "Construction Council." It is safe to assume that, from this point on, Kaganovich and Stalin himself were directly involved with the decisions about the project. Actually, Vjacheslav Molotov, head of the Soviet government, and one of the most hardline members of Stalin's Politburo, was the official chairman of that "Construction Council."[39]

On February 28, 1932, the verdict of the Construction Council was returned just two months before the Central Committee's fateful April 23 *Postanovlenie* ordering the dissolution of all the independent artistic associations. The Construction Council's demands and comments given in ten points were not only to determine the remaining two competition stages, but to define the final project approved for construction by 1937.

The secretive council assessed that "none of the entered projects [reflected] the grandeur of our socialist construction, and that no convincing solution was found in any of the submitted entries."[40]

Demanding a monumental, celebratory architectural and sculptural unit, the council insisted, first, that breaking the program into separate units (around the large and small auditorium, as most competitors had done), was unsatisfactory, and that the palace

---

[38] See Peter Lizon, *The Palace of the Soviets*, p. 100.
[39] Ibid. p.107.
[40] Construction Council, quoted in Lizon, p. 100.

should be assembled into "one single volume." Second, "no colonnades or other buildings disturbing the integrity of such volume were admissible"—a remark obviously pointing to Stalin, rather than Kaganovich.[41] "The single building should open squarely onto the front plaza, *privileging verticality over horizontality*" (author's emphasis). Further,

> A predominantly *low-rise composition* observed in many projects is *not desirable*. Competitors should consider a *bold, tall, many-storied* building, avoiding, however, any ecclesiastical appearance. [author's emphasis]

What was desirable, evidently, was a skyscraper. In the wake of the upcoming April 23 decree, it is worth noting, however, that no particular architectural style was requested, a point of view, as we will see later, that was consistent with Kaganovich's position. The text went on:

> The council could not find a project among submitted entries that would definitely express *monumentality*, simplicity, wholeness, or grace of architectural forms appropriate to the great goals of our socialist society. The committee does not want to *foresee* or *forecast any architectural style* but insists that the *palace should express the best results of modern*, as well as *classical architecture* by means of contemporary technology. [author's emphasis][42]

An ambiguous, not to say wavering stance regarding both "modern" and "classical" aspirations was evident, most probably reflecting the divergent expectations of Stalin and Kaganovich. Such ambivalence would linger to the end of the decade, the ultimate solution being an eclectic synthesis of both.

Overriding the jury's selection and expunging all foreign contributors, including Hamilton,[43] the council named twelve competitors, balancing conservatives and avant-garde proponents, that is, I. Golosov, Ladovskij, Ginzburg, and Lisagor, and, of course, the Vesnin brothers. The implicit withdrawal from the international character of the competition in favor of a domestic venue was reflected in the tenth and last statement: "The architects chosen to work on the final project shall be freed of all other tasks for three months during their search for a solution." They would also receive a "favorable financial remuneration."[44] All twelve domestic architects continued competing from March to July 1932. Five architects were retained to continue from August 1932 to February 1933. Only the Vesnins survived from among the moderns. The council

---

[41] The strange a priori rejection of "colonnades" might be another indication that this was Stalin's demand: No American skyscraper had any.
[42] Ibid. Lizon, p. 100.
[43] As solid American references were incorporated in the Moscow skyscraper to suit Stalin (as the 1933 version shows manifestly), the classicists Shchuko and Zholtovskij conveniently replaced Hamilton possibly to please Kaganovich.
[44] Lizon, p. 101, as the final point of the council's report.

announced further that the teams that would come up with the best solution would design the palace in a collaborative way—pointing again to inherent ambivalence.

On May 10, 1933 the council declared Iofan's project "as the principal scheme for the Palace of Soviets," while ambiguously allowing the inclusion of "the best elements of other schemes." These were Shchuko's and Zholtovskij's projects—very possibly Stalin's concession to Kaganovich.

For the first time the council explicitly demanded "a powerful sculpture of Lenin, rising to 50–75 meters" whereby the palace itself was to become "a pedestal for the figure of Lenin." Lenin thus replaced the "worker" featured in some of the 1931 projects, including Iofan's. This was a clear indication of an evolving ethos.

With Stalin's further interventions, now in personal contact with Iofan, the project kept growing heaven-bound in Iofan's architectural office (see Figure 2.10). The latter, which was also Iofan's apartment, was conveniently situated just across from the Kremlin on the right riverbank of the Moskova in an apartment complex Iofan had built for the high political bureaucracy.[45] Easily and securely accessible to Stalin, the latter pushed the building ever higher until it surpassed the Eiffel Tower.[46] The statue seemed, rather obviously, aimed as well at surpassing Bertholdi's Statue of Liberty in size and placement. The analogy was to reemerge explicitly in 1939 at the New York World's Fair.

The building's large conference room could seat fifteen thousand spectators, while the small could fit "only" six thousand. Pertaining already to the domain of science

Figure 2.10 Still echoing Hamilton's "Gothic" character, the Palace of Soviets starts growing heaven-bound, 1932. Fourth Round Competition. (Courtesy Shchusev Museum of Architecture [Canadian Center for Architecture, Gift of Howard Schickler and David Lafaille])

---

[45] I owe the information about the location of Iofan's architectural studio to Marija Kostjuk, a historian at the Shchusev Museum of Architecture, who is completing a book manuscript on Iofan.
[46] Sona Hoisington, "'Ever Higher': The Evolution of the Project for the Palace of Soviets," *Slavic Review* 62, no.1 (Spring 2003).

fiction, the building, so close to the river's banks, had slim chances to stand without sinking.

Iofan's version was definitely accepted on July 4, 1933. With the project now firmly in his hands, Iofan could squarely leave behind such references to the "Roman Mausolea" of a Zholtovskij, or the Venetian Doge's Palace by Shchuko and Gelfreich. He reverted to a modernity favored by Stalin, that is, the modernity of the latest American corporate skyscraper typology, epitomized by the Empire State Building and the Rockefeller Center in New York. Replacing the term "national" with "American," the Palace of Soviets was fast becoming "American in form and 'socialist' in content".

The string of competitions for the Palace of Soviets, as well as the unceasing further revisions of its design throughout the decade, exemplified the inherent contradictions in the Soviet struggle to redefine its architecture in terms of an elusive "socialist" realism, while anything termed as "proletarian" was fading away.

The outsized, ever higher pharaonic dimensions sought for the Palace of Soviets can be explained, in part, by a sense of enduring complex of inferiority even the Bolsheviks experienced in the face of the "West." The Old Bolshevik Party Secretary of Leningrad (then still Petrograd), Sergej Kirov, illustrated implicitly this point in 1922, on the occasion of the competition for the palace's predecessor, the Palace of Labor, as: "Architecturally, [the Palace of Labor] must show our friends and foes that we, 'semi-Asiatics,' whom they continue to look down upon, are capable of adorning this sinful earth with such works of great architecture as our enemies never dreamed of."[47]

***

The reassessment of the final versions of the Palace of Soviets (1934–1937), that hyper-Stalinist project of oppressive monumentality—never-built yet most visible symbol of Stalin's *perestrojka*—reveals striking affinities, not only with American corporate modernity, but even with Soviet avant-garde art of the 1920s.

By 1934, upon his return from New York, and now completely free from historicist impositions, Iofan radically changed his project by reintroducing what can be seen as both Hood's 1931 skyscraper and Malevich's early 1920s suprematist experiments, alluding to the latter's abstract "skyscrapers"—the *Arhitektony* (Figure 2.11).

Simultaneously, an attentive analysis of the 1934 version of the palace (the model exhibited in Paris) reveals equally significant references to Raymond Hood's (1881–1934) recently completed Rockefeller Center. This last version features sets of receding vertical slabs, repeated as ornaments in the palace's retreating rings of diminutive "Rockefeller Centers." (Figure 2.12). The existence of a dialog between Soviet Stalinist architecture and Hood's Manhattan skyscraper, is strikingly confirmed, by the latter's comparison with the 1940s high-rise luxury apartment on Novinskij boulevard (Figure 2.13).

Such features had already appeared in Hamilton's competition project in the assembly of vertical slabs seen in the small balustrade markers along the Moskova banks (see

---

[47] Kirov's speech to the First All-Union Congress of Soviets on December 30, 1922, S. M. Kirov, *Izabranye stat'i i rechi: 1912–1934* (Selected articles and speeches) (Moscow: Gosizdat), 1957, pp. 150–52.

Soviet Architectural Avant-Gardes

Figure 2.11 LEFT: Malevich, 1922; *Arhitektony* RIGHT: Detail of the 1935 version of the Palace the Soviets. (Courtesy Shchusev Museum of Architecture)

Figure 2.12 LEFT: Raymond Hood's Rockefeller Center, 1933 (Courtesy Library of Congress); RIGHT: Close-up of the 1935 version of the Palace (Courtesy Shchusev Museum)

Figure 2.13 Elite Moscow housing (Photo by author)

Figure 2.8). It is not to be excluded, however, that the palace's connections to the Rockefeller Center actually reveal Hood's own indebtedness to Malevich. A direct encounter between suprematism and the United States art scene occurred in 1927 in a New York City "Machine-Age Exposition."[48] The exhibition included works by Malevich and Lissitzky. Organized by Jane Heap of *The Little Review*, the exhibition re-contextualized "Russian constructivism (sic) into an American [environment]."[49] It is to be noted that Hood's Rockefeller Center marked a radical departure from his strikingly simplified building massing and detailing of his architecture which preceded his Rockefeller Center.[50] Regardless, Hood's New York skyscraper complex was an attraction repeatedly and lavishly featured in the Soviet professional press (see Figure 2.1).

As mentioned, Iofan had visited New York in the early 1930s and witnessed the completed Rockefeller Center (see Figure 2.12). References to the iconic Rockefeller Center (or, for that matter, to Malevich's *Arhitektony*), had already appeared in Iofan's entry in the 1934 competition for the Commissariat of Heavy Industry, a project that recalled both Hamilton's design strategy for the Palace of Soviets and the just-completed government building by Langman (Figure 2.14).[51]

Figure 2.14 LEFT: Langman, GOSPLAN Building, 1935 (Photo by author); RIGHT: Boris Iofan, Narkomtjazhprom (NKTP) competition entry, 1934. (Courtesy Shchusev Museum of Architecture)

---

[48] Barnaby Emmett Haran, "The Amerika Machine: Art and Technology between the USA and the USSR, 1926 to 1933" (PhD Thesis, University College London, 2008), 62.

[49] Ibid. p. 60. I am grateful to my graduate student Elijah Montez to have brought this exposition to my attention in his term paper for my seminar on Soviet avant-gardes.

[50] This was evidently the case of the design of the American Radiator Building (a descendent of the Chicago Tribune Building) to the New York Daily News Building of c. 1927.

[51] I base this assumption about Langman in part on an event recounted at the time as an anecdote about Stalin's impromptu visit to an exhibition of competition projects. Stalin, as the story goes, immediately asked, "Where is Langman?" Since the latter had not been awarded any prize, someone ran to Langman's entry and hung "First Prize" under it before Stalin reached the project. If the event itself is just anecdotic, the reference to Langman cannot be fortuitous.

In a world where the written word was too dangerous to print, oral anecdotes inevitably flourished. While not fully reliable, they necessarily reflected some core truth.

Soviet Architectural Avant-Gardes

If Iofan's palace retooled American modern corporate design for the needs of the Soviet state, it also exemplified the long-lasting impact of the 1920s Soviet architectural revolution. Although both the 1933 and 1934 renditions of the building seem at first sight to abjure everything the avant-garde stood for: abstraction, rigorous minimalism, and the rejection of axial symmetry, closer scrutiny reveals the project's hidden spirit of modernism. Juxtaposed with Kazimir Malevich's white "skyscrapers" (*Arhitektony*), Iofan's 1937 white gypsum model of the structure (now stored in the Moscow State Museum of Architecture) reveals the imprint that suprematism left on Soviet architecture. A blow-up of the 1937 model shows even more strikingly features of Malevich's variations on the theme of suprematist skyscrapers akin to the Rockefeller Center (see Figure 2.11).

Even though now symmetrical and mutually identical, the slabs of the little "Rockefeller Centers" (or Malevich's *Arhitektony*) were assembled in nervous multiple layers attached together as bundles to the main body of the skyscraper.

Malevich himself contributed to the convergence of suprematism and Stalinism. At the 1932 Leningrad exhibition "Soviet Artists in Recent Years,"[52] he placed a Lenin statue on top of a number of his suprematist skyscrapers exactly as Iofan would do two years later on the second version of his "suprematist" Palace of Soviets (Figure 2.15). Equally ephemeral, both Malevich's and Iofan's skyscrapers were involved in an analogous dream of transcendence.

Figure 2.15 Malevich's 1930 exhibition "Soviet Artists in the last 15 Years" at the Russian Museum in Leningrad, with Lenin's statue on top of some *Arhitektony*. (Photographer unknown, from Alberto Samonà, ed., *Il Palazzo dei Soviet 1931–1933* (Rome: Officina Edizioni), 1976)

---

[52] See Alberto Samonà ed. *Il Palazzo dei Soviets, 1931–1933* (Rome: Officina Edizioni), 1976, p. 36.

Continuity and Resistance

The Rest Homes and Sanatoria Movement: A Battlefield of Resistance, 1932–1938

The discourse on what constituted modern architecture in the light of European and United States architecture, as argued above, reverberated throughout the country in the example of a ubiquitous type: the sanatoria and rest homes.

Replacing the workers' clubs of the 1920s, the building of rest homes and sanatoria in the following decade offered some of the most interesting examples of competing modernities found in the rest of Europe, as well as enduring avant-garde resistance. Playing the role of Dachas the czar bestowed on the devoted nobility, the select access to rest homes stood for Stalin's vaunted "concern for the human person."

Boris Iofan's Sanatorium at Barviha, 1929–1936

In the midst of a stylistic tug of war between visions of Americanism, modernism, and historicism, with Karo Alabjan now firmly rooted in Kaganovich's predilection for eclecticism, such as their Red Army Theater, one of the most interesting modernist sanatoria was inaugurated in the resort of Barviha, some thirty kilometers from Moscow. It was built and reconstructed between 1929 and 1936 without any alteration of its original modernist features. Situated in a park, the hospital was an elite resort for members of the Central Committee and foreign Communist dignitaries.[53] The architect was again Boris Iofan (Figure 2.16).

Figure 2.16 RIGHT: Boris Iofan, Barviha exterior view of single rooms and apartments (Courtesy Shchusev Museum of Architecture); LEFT: Double-room apartments. (Courtesy Mariya Kostyuk)

---

[53] The famous Komintern leader Georgi Dimitrov, who defied the Nazis against trumped up trial for allegedly setting afire the Reichstag, died in Barviha in 1947. The Barviha sanatorium serves today as a medical facility of the Presidency of the Russian Federation, and it is mostly off limits to visitors.

Despite repeated attempts, I was unable to secure a permit to visit and photograph the building. I am grateful to Mariya Kostyuk, a researcher at the Shchusev Museum of Architecture writing on Iofan, for generously giving me the permission to use some of her own photographs taken *in situ*.

Soviet Architectural Avant-Gardes

The versatile architect was simultaneously busy with the Palace of Soviets and the 1934 entry to the Commissariat of Heavy Industry competition, while soon taking up the Soviet Pavilion in Paris—all crucial projects for the regime. Under Stalin's gaze, he worked in at least three different architectural languages: modernist (the Barviha Sanatorium), "socialist" realist (the Palace of Soviets) and the cosmopolitan style of the American "corporate architecture" (the Commissariat of Heavy Industry), while the Paris Pavilion embraced all three, as we will see later.

The Barviha first variant was completed by 1934. Its most innovative feature was a string of round rooms that eliminated any dark corner, thus maximizing insolation, essential for fighting tuberculosis. By 1936, however, the facility was reconstructed because the round rooms could not accommodate personal bathrooms, to the understandable displeasure of its privileged patients (Figure 2.17).[54]

To overcome the problem, the rooms were redesigned in a more conventional fashion, albeit forming an oblique comb, a superbly assembled set of rooms pointing like sunflowers to the sun. The slanted rooms with their bulbous windows gave the sanatorium its distinctive baroque appearance. In the course of the reconstruction of the rooms, Iofan never succumbed to any historicist embellishment. The windows and balconies kept the same form with their oblique axis, affording the sanatorium its memorable continuous wave of bubbly lumps as an innovative reinterpretation of the bay window.

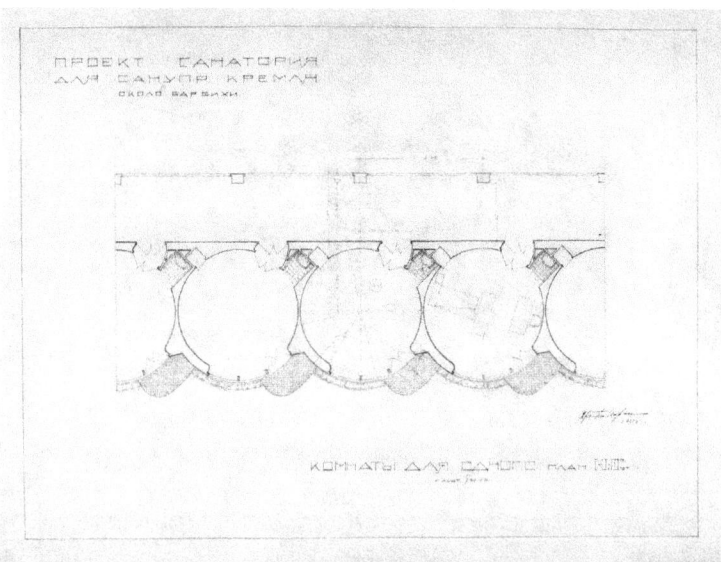

Figure 2.17 Barviha's initial round rooms. (Courtesy Shchusev Museum of Architecture)

---

[54] The reconstruction of Barviha's design process is based on the drawing archives of the Shchusev Museum of Architecture, July 2016.

Continuity and Resistance

The hospital's dynamic, asymmetrical, modernist plan of interlocked, jolting arms was rendered in a way close to the constructivist tradition of "editing," that is, juxtaposing or associating constitutive elements of a building such as, in this case, the assembly of serrated, and skewed individual rooms, or larger apartment facilities.[55] The simplicity of the building's whitewashed horizontal volumes contrasted lyrically with its dark, crystalline openings, rhythmically distributed along the façade. A powerful circular dining room and kitchen formed a joint connecting the three dormitory arms, where each façade represented a variant on the theme of bay windows "bursting from the modern box." The whole was exposed to contrasting tensile, white verticals of the surrounding birch woods.

The sanatorium's interior was no less intriguing (Figure 2.18). The furniture Iofan designed for the place paid homage to the modernist work of the 1920s. The restrained, thin tubular chairs, tables, and beds in the spacious and well-lit rooms owed their elegance as much to tough productivist aesthetics of the 1920s, as they did to Iofan's own experience with Italian modern design which he absorbed in Rome while a student.

Figure 2.18 Tubular furniture in the Barviha Sanatorium, 1936 (Courtesy Shchusev Museum of Architecture)

---

[55] It is to be noted that, however, by the mid-1930s "constructivism" loses its specificity and becomes essentially a descriptive catchall for "modern architecture" in general.

67

Soviet Architectural Avant-Gardes

The Voroshilov Sanatorium and Rest Home in Sochi, 1931–1934

In 1929, Miron Merzhanov (1895–1975), another architect who later built for Stalin (even as prison inmate in 1943[56]), won the first award for the rest home/sanatorium competition for the Red Army. The commissioner was the Army's People's Commissar and Politburo member Kliment Voroshilov (1881–1969). The building still carried his name at least until 2006 when this author visited the premises (Figure 2.19). If not necessarily constructivist, but highly modern in the sense of the European New Architecture, it displayed powerful, continuous floor-to-ceiling glazed surfaces, contrasting with an array of white geometrical circular and prismatic volumes, topped with huge verandas, shaded by white, striped awnings. The complex, accessed only by funicular from the Stalin highway, commanded a hillside overlooking the Black Sea.

Significantly, the modernist Voroshilov Sanatorium was the only building chosen to represent Soviet architecture in the Soviet Pavilion at the New York 1939 World's Fair in a strong statement in favor of progressive architecture.

The "Ordzhonikidze" Sanatorium in Kislovodsk, 1935–1938: Constructivism, "Far from Being Expunged"

By 1935, Ginzburg was leading a team of architects in the Crimea, as mentioned, with the task of transforming a huge area of 650 km² of the peninsula into an elite resort of rest homes and sanatoria. This work might have been an occasion for Ginzburg to test the "de-urbanist" theories he inherited from Mihail Ohitovich (1896–1937), his former collaborator and young sociologist whom the GPU executed two years after his arrest in 1935 as a "Trotskyite adventurist."

It was in this context that Ginzburg received the commission for the "Ordzhonikidze" sanatorium in Kislovodsk—a health spa known since ancient Rome—perched high up in the northern chains of the Caucasus. Architecturally the most intriguing, and semantically the most complex among the sanatoria, the all-but-forgotten "Ordzhonikidze"

Figure 2.19 The Voroshilov, 1934. Rest home in Sochi. (LEFT: Courtesy Shchusev Museum Of Architecture; RIGHT: Photos by author)

---

[56] Even imprisoned, he was able to continue designing and building from a position Solzhenitsyn would call the "First Circle" in reference to Dante's Inferno.

Figure 2.20 M. Ginzburg, Ordzhonikidze sanatorium, Kislovodsk. View of the eastern dormitory overlooking Leonidov's monumental stairs, and 1936 site model—comparable with 1933 Alvar Aalto Paimio Sanatorium. (Courtesy Shchusev Museum of Architecture)

was designed and built from 1935 to 1938. This was to be Ginzburg's most successful work since his 1930 Narkomfin (Figure 2.20).

Built for the People's Commissariat for the Heavy Industry, where Ginzburg was employed, the Ordzhonikidze was commissioned exclusively with top officials in mind.

Soviet Architectural Avant-Gardes

As Ginzburg wrote in his 1940 monograph about his sanatorium, "Comrade Sergo Ordzhonikidze[57] cared above all to create the best living conditions possible for the top leaders of the NKTP, crushed under the heavy duties of their tasks."[58] The rooms were conceived not only as sleeping facilities but included study spaces equipped with furniture that Leonidov designed specifically for the sanatorium (Figure 2.21).[59]

Three years into the April 1932 decree, the site model of the sanatorium, as published in Ginzburg's book, projected at the outset the image of a frankly constructivist assembly of buildings. Along with their corridor strip windows, reminiscent of Narkomfin's, the sanatorium units were set across the site in a dynamic, nonaxial guise. A circular therapy building, anchored the ensemble. Conceptually the composition was strikingly reminiscent of Aalto's Paimio Sanatorium's site, completed two years earlier and published in the *Architecture d'aujourd'hui* to which Ginzburg had unrestricted access.

In the sanatorium's park Leonidov displayed a replica of the balconies (Figure 2.22) from one of the three towers of his Heavy Industry Commissariat (NKTP) 1934 competition (see Chapter 1, Figure 1.4).

Nikolaj Kolli's Book Preface: Ginzburg's "Surviving Problems"

Two years after the completion of the sanatorium, Kolli—Le Corbusier's former Centrosojuz collaborator and only Soviet member of the CIAM—wrote an introduction to the 1940 monograph about the Kislovodsk sanatorium.[60] He conceded that Ginzburg's team "made a sincere effort to embrace the style of socialist realism [...]" guided by the "Stalinian concern for the human person" (*Stalinskaja zabota o cheloveke*), which meant,

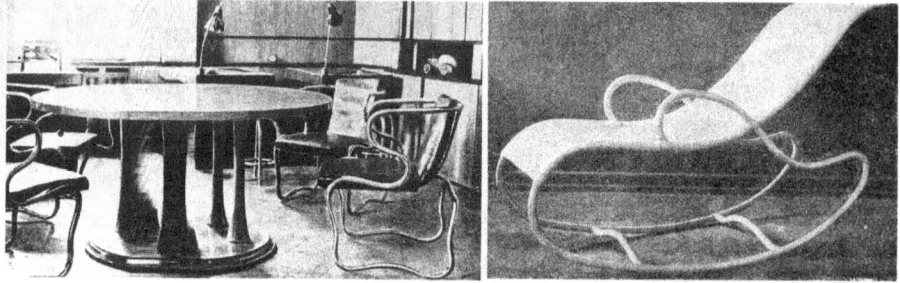

Figure 2.21 LEFT: Leonidov, chairs for the House of Pioneers, Moscow, 1934. RIGHT: Leonidov lounge chair for the sanatorium, 1938. (Photographers unknown)

---

[57] Sergo Ordzhonikidze, a moderate and good-natured Georgian and member of the Politburo, was the Commissar for the Heavy Industry and sponsor of Ginzburg's sanatorium in Kislovodsk. He was known to refuse immediately and publicly condemn the arrested members of his ministry and beyond.
[58] M. Ja. Ginzburg, *Arhitektura Sanatorija NKTP* (Moscow: Academy of Architecture, USSR), 1940, p. 9.
[59] M. Ja. Ginzburg, *Arhitektura Sanatorija NKTP* op. cit. p. 86
[60] M. Ja. Ginzburg, op. cit. p. 6.

Continuity and Resistance

Figure 2.22 LEFT: Leonidov's 1938 landscaping with replica of the balconies of one of the three towers of his 1934 NKTP competition entry (Photo by author). RIGHT: Leonidov's park amphitheater. (Photographer unknown)

according to Kolli, "the straightforward sincerity of expression, and insistence on an organic connection between form and content."[61]

Still, Kolli had second thoughts: Despite all the commendable efforts Ginzburg made to achieve the highest expression of "socialist" realism, his work was not entirely free of "formal schematism"—a term used to describe and discredit constructivism, that is modern architecture. Indeed, Kolli went on, "the treatment of the wall surfaces, the windows, the *loggias* and so on, clearly [echo] compositional devices of former constructivism with all its ascetic oversimplifications." In addition, one detects as well some residues of "functionalism." Contrived as it was, the criticism had a point: the building's architecture was highly indebted to the avant-garde. "Thanks, however," Kolli went on, "to positive self-criticism expressed in the book, the authors took on themselves the insufficiencies of their work." Significantly, Kolli concluded magnanimously, similar "surviving problems" pointing to constructivism *"are to be found, after all, in various degrees, throughout the architectural production of our days* [author's emphasis]." In other words, by 1939, when the introduction was written, modern architecture was still ubiquitous in the Soviet Union.

Moisej Ginzburg and "Socialist" Realism

By the time the book was published in 1940, it was not possible anymore to talk about constructivism, as discussed in the last chapter. While, on the other hand, "socialist" realism was still far from having acquired any concrete definition, it was still an open box

---

[61] Ibid. p. 27.

into which any architectural discourse could fit. Therefore, in the chapter "Problems of Socialist Realism,"[62] Ginzburg tried, over five pages of a fifty-two-page book, to make some sense of it, thus legitimize the stylistic choices he had made in his sanatorium. In other words, it was still a matter of conjecture. It also showed the degree to which Ginzburg continued to insist on maintaining his professional integrity, rather than force his architecture under any prescribed given. He did rather the opposite: force such elusive concept onto his own turf. Using carefully ironic double-talk, he wrote, "Our effort was to attain socialist realism, to whatever degree possible as a style. [In so doing] what we actually strived to achieve was an architectural expression fitting a sanatorium, that is, the essential, typological characteristics of a socialist sanatorium." In other words, he wanted "to establish what [would be] the principles of an institution that not only did not have a precedent but could not have possibly emerged in other historic periods, that is, under conditions of a capitalist society."

"Therefore," Ginzburg continued, "the characteristics of [socialist realism] are not supposed to be derived from some kind of 'generic' architectural precept but have to come out as much as possible from the organic specificities of a given building's function." This being established, Ginzburg spelled the methodology that guided his design in the spirit of what he referred to as "socialist" realism.

At the outset, he claimed to have taken into consideration "the great Stalinian concern for the human person"—the obliged mantra Kolli had already mentioned three times in his own short preface. By this Ginzburg meant essentially the need to pay attention to what an Alberti would have simply called *commoditas*. "Only such Stalinian concern, and only that, could lead to a correct solution," which consisted in, "caring about comfort; having an informed understanding of an organism such as a sanatorium; observing a functional relationship between the dormitory and the therapy buildings; and to take rigorously into consideration every detail," such as making sure that "all the rooms were oriented to the south."

Second, and no less important for a well-understood "socialist" realism, he thought, was "a truthful and sincere architectural expression"—a possible reference to John Ruskin's "Lamps of Architecture," a classic in the USSR. Such concern, he continued, led to a necessary "organic connection between form and content"—a possible allusion to Wright's functionalism. Ginzburg insisted, as he did about his 1930 Narkomfin, on the "growth" of the building as an organism in close association with its immediate realm.[63] The role of the architect was, in constructivist terms, to organically "montage" or assemble the structure rather than "build."[64] "Without these [features]," Ginzburg reiterated, "socialist realism [would] not be possible." Therefore, in the case of the Kislovodsk sanatorium, "we made every effort to carefully listen to the inner life of its organism, in

---

[62] Ibid. p. 27.
[63] At the Narkomfin, situated in a park, Ginzburg avoided cutting almost any tree, so that some appear on vintage images almost pressed against the building he raised on black pilotis to maintain a spatial continuity between the two sides of the park.
[64] In a certain sense, Wright's "organic" architecture appeared to some opponents of the "Bauhaus" architecture as a modernist alternative to what they called "*dom korobka*" ("box architecture").

order to give it an apt architectural expression." This meant, "that [the organism's] inner life would help us define a correct conception of the general site plan with all its particularities. This principle—deriving the form from its content—explained for example the "severe and rigorous architectural expression of the medical building," free of any frivolous ornamentation. In order to justify the modern aspect of the site plan and of the medical building in particular, Ginzburg declared that

> actually, the inner life also determined the essential concept of the general site plan and of all its specific features. The same way, the severe and introverted form of the medical building was derived from its inner organic structure, and thus had to remain simple and laconic. The functional content of the buildings determined their architectural features.

Thus, he seemed to say that form followed function. He emphasized further that an equally important trait of "socialist" realism was the yearning for simplicity of expression. He emphasized that such simplicity had nothing to do with scarcity and asceticism (the way modern architecture was criticized by its foes). "We made every effort to reach the most difficult form of simplicity, one that resulted from an in-depth distillation of forms." He insisted further that simplicity in architecture "has necessarily to be associated with two architectural qualities: plasticity of forms and forms that express organic qualities [...]. We achieved the plasticity of forms through the layering of wall surfaces, and the way we treated form itself [...]." While doing so, Ginzburg had constantly in mind the importance of "avoiding uncritical use of one or another historicist style" and rather seek "the most contemporary forms." His controlled language achieved heights of double-talk, the way his architecture expressed, as we will see, a subtle ability to thwart censorship with ironic stratagems.

"Conceding," he went on, "that it was of utmost importance to learn from the best of our [architectural] legacy, we were no less convinced, for the same reason, that socialist realism—*the style of our great epoch*—*has still to find its specific character and its proper forms*" (author's emphasis).

Expanding further on the meaning of the term "organic," as applied to his architecture, Ginzburg explained that, from his point of view, organic meant "having a clearly articulated beginning and an end; [differentiating] top and bottom; clearly defining each part of the organism with a beginning and an end;" all of which he claimed to have achieved in his sanatorium. As if musing on Gottfried Semper's typology, he insisted that "the ground floors of all the buildings [were] heavy and monumental, using dolomite stones, solidly anchored into the soil. All the buildings end with trellises and light covers, ultimately "dissolving into thin air"—incidentally a famous quote from Karl Marx's *Communist Manifesto* (Figure 2.23).

Other aspects pointing to the organic nature of the sanatorium buildings were the clear articulation of the structural system. "We pointedly avoided any [false] decorative features such as pilasters or the like." He then listed what comprised contemporary architecture. This entailed a rigorous architectural and historical analysis, showing, probably with

Figure 2.23 Eastern dormitory's roof mass "Dissolving into thin air" and trellised roof garden. (Photos by author)

Viollet-Le-Duc in mind, how inseparable were the orders from the stylistic expression of the time they belonged to. He thus pointed out boldly "to the *detrimental consequences of copying historic styles today,* and [in particular] *to the harm they* [caused] to *contemporary Soviet architecture* [author's emphasis]." Without saying so, he was actually recalling, throughout, some of the arguments he developed in his 1925 *Style and Epoch,* where he had written (in analogy with the organic character of the machine) about "the naked constructiveness of [the machine's] component organisms."[65] In so doing, he was in reality reconnecting with the theoretical origins of constructivism: Russian Formalism.

Then, turning once more to an obliged buzzword, Ginzburg noted, before ending the chapter, that "regardless of its simplicity, socialist realism is inseparable from the idea about our immensely *joyous life,* brilliant and fulfilling[66]—something that can be achieved through the union of architecture and art"—a "union" officially advocated since the early 1930s, yet nowhere to be found in his project. After discussing this trend in the case of his sanatorium, he ended evoking again "Stalin's concern for the human person without which," he claimed, "this sanatorium would not have been possible."[67] In this exercise of obliged abasement, he had managed to safeguard a modicum of dignity.

The Buildings

In Kislovodsk, like on the Black Sea of Crimea, Ginzburg supervised the overall work of a team of architects. Besides a site plan in the best tradition of modern urban planning, he was personally responsible for the eastern building, and the central, two-floor medical structure. Started in 1935, and completed in 1938, Kislovodsk's "Ordzhonikidze" Sanatorium overlooked an absorbing expanse of valleys and mountain ridges of the Northern Caucasus.

Acting as a hinge, the central, two-floor therapy building connected visually the six-floor western and eastern frontal dormitories (Figure 2.24). As Ginzburg wrote, "The whole

---

[65] M. Ginzburg *Style and Epoch* (Cambridge MA: MIT Press),1983, p. 121 (Translated by Anatole Senkevitch). Original published in Moscow, 1924.
[66] In her book *Hope Against Hope,* Nadezhda Mandelstam evoked repeatedly the obligation one had to evoke "the joyous life" of their time, whenever one was in presence of either friend or foe. *Hope Against Hope* (London: The Harvill Press), 1971.
[67] Ibid. p. 31.

composition should be immediately readable; while the attentive [visitor] should be able to gradually discover all its complexity." Ginzburg concluded, in a Corbusian allusion that, "the *optical symmetry* [author's emphasis] of the composition should give a sense of a unified whole, with great diversity in the details."[68] On further scrutiny, the first desired axial symmetry of the three buildings was soon broken by a north-wise extension to the western dormitory that reestablished a dynamic, modern compositional principle.

Complexity was the right term. At first sight, the "Ordzhonikidze" compound, and Ginzburg's eastern wing in particular, followed neither a constructivist nor any eclectic, historicist style. In search for a compromise that would avoid aping slavishly any assumed "socialist" realist banality, he reached out for a telling solution. For the immediately visible façade of his eastern dormitory, he aptly reinterpreted the Milanese "Novecento" style—an idiosyncratic, mannerist architectural expression that alluded to classical forms, but was outright modern and innovative in its own right.

Trained as an architect in Milan before the revolution, Ginzburg returned to Italy in 1935 as head of the Soviet delegation to the 13th International Congress of Architects in Rome where he could familiarize himself with the latest Italian trends. Since he was closely associated with the Italian architectural scene, he could not have missed such a provocative book as L. I. Rempel's *Arhitektura Poslevoennoj Italii* (*Post-War Architecture in Italy*).[69] Rempel' had already published in the architectural journal *Za Rubezhom* (*Beyond the Borders*) an essay on Adalberto Libera's Palazzo del Littorio—the Italian Pavilion in Brussels—a temple to fascism. His book came out in Moscow in 1935. While Giuseppe Terragni and his circle of rationalists were tellingly passed over, the book was richly illustrated with works by Marcello Piacentini, Mario Sironi, Antonio Carminati,

Figure 2.24 General panoramic view of the sanatorium (from the south), with the central therapy building acting as a pivot between the west (architect Vantangov) and the east (Ginzburg) front dormitories. (Photographer unknown)

---

[68] Ibid. p. 5.
[69] L. I. Rempel, *Arhitektura Poslevoennoj Italii* (Post-War Architecture in Italy) (Moscow: Academy of Architecture), 1935. The illustrations were mostly gleaned from German magazines.

Soviet Architectural Avant-Gardes

Adalberto Libera, and others, including Novecento architecture. The book emphasized that the Italians had successfully combined "constructivism" with traditional art.[70]

While taming its most extreme mannerism, and in a hide-and-seek game with the censor, Ginzburg chose the Novecento style for the immediately visible front façade, the one most likely to be photographed. Close to the method Michelangelo applied in the Laurentian Library, Ginzburg treated this façade as if carving and extracting from the mass of the wall the architectural features hidden, as it were, in its core (Figure 2.25).

The front façade of the building ended, on its western extremity, with loggias deeply excavated out from the building—thus allowing for a summer respite from a southern exposure. (In front of the loggias he projected small polygonal balconies to catch the sun

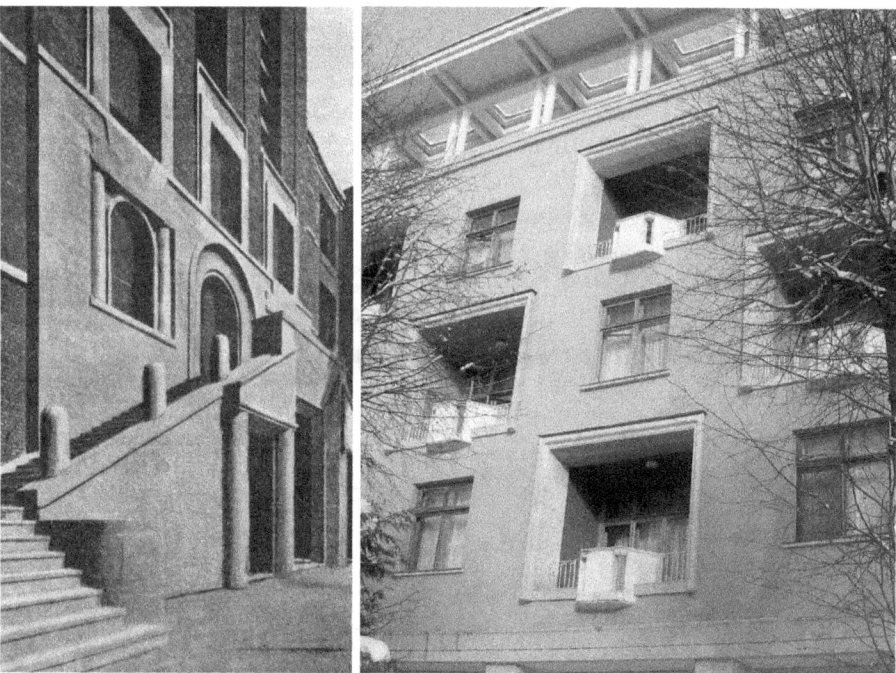

Figure 2.25 LEFT: Antonio Carminati, Camera del Lavoro, Milan, in "Novecento" Style (Rempel's *Arhitektura Poslevoennoj Italii*, taken from 1934 German magazine, photographer unknown); RIGHT: Kislovodsk Sanatorium Eastern Pavilion, using the same "carving" into the mass of the front façade wall—a design feature Michelangelo was first to use in his Laurential Library and later the Capitoline palaces in Rome. (Photo by author)

---

[70] To be on the safe side, the author warned at the outset that "Fascism and Nazism [were] not the same thing." Nevertheless the book was withdrawn from circulation a few months later as a "scandal," but Rempel himself was not arrested as believed thus far. As Russian scholar Anna Vlazemceva, who interviewed Rempel's daughter for her work on the relationship between the Soviet Union and fascist Italy reported to me, the actual reason for his arrest much later was that he had married Trotsky's former lover. The illustrations were mostly gleaned from German magazines.

in cooler days.)[71] Reinforcing the sense of "carving" (and "layering"), the projected loggia parapets were framed by two columns as if "sculpted out" from the wall to give further articulation to the whole (see Figure 2.26). The main part of the façade was a game of alternating windows and balconies displayed in checkered vertical rows recalling Le Corbusier's less sophisticated "Villas Suspendues": one central small balcony and two windows above and below it, followed next by the reverse: two balconies above and below with one window in the center (see Figure 2.25). All the buildings ended with roof gardens and pergolas that "dissolved in thin air," as he had done in all of his buildings since the 1926 Malaja Bronnaja Street Gosstrah Housing in central Moscow—this time as appropriate solariums for the patients afflicted with tuberculosis. This asymmetry, internal to the building, allowed for an overall symmetry with the other western building, where the loggias would serve visually as a connecting transition. But this was not all.

A "persistent visitor" (as the one Ginzburg invoked, and the present author followed) was in for a significant surprise. Whereas Ginzburg did introduce a version of the Novecento, this was true only for the main façades—those that would find their way into official magazines and journals. Never published or photographed, the less obvious side and back elevations of the buildings revealed fragments of Ginzburg's dialog with his own time: with his architecture of the 1920s, and with the architecture of other architects who had taken part, like himself, in the adventure of the *Temps nouveaux*.

While the ceremonial Novecento front façade appeared in the cited monograph with Kolli's preface, the less visible parts, as expected, were completely ignored.[72] In a sense, Ginzburg created a hidden grove of personal architectural mementos on the secluded

Figure 2.26 Deeply "carved" corner of the eastern building and C. E. Vantangov's more sober 1938 western building. (Photos by author)

---

[71] Initially, Ginzburg had planned collective balconies. However, as Ginzburg commented: "Comrade Ordzhonikidze thought such arrangement would be 'un-socialist' and therefore insisted that each room had its own terrace undisturbed by the neighbors." The reasoning must have looked strange to Ginzburg since he quoted the patron verbatim.

[72] Even after repeated research campaigns over the years, the Shchusev Museum of Architecture in Moscow did not yield any record of them—only the fronts.

side and back façades of the dormitories. In a dialog with a bygone era, his buildings suggested subtly Walter Gropius's Bauhaus dormitory, with the iconic balconies, reflected in the most recluse parts of the western building (Figure 2.27).

Somewhat more accessible, the flank of the eastern pavilion presented a glass curtain wall, as if a wink to Mies van der Rohe. But more to the point, Ginzburg attached jokingly to the glazed surface a "levitating" balcony directly reminiscent of Ladovskij's Rationalist antigravitational experiments, that is, to Leningrad's ASNOVA 1930–1931 kitchen factory featuring its own floating balcony (Figure 2.28). It could not be accidental.

The sculptural stairs and balconies on the western building (Figure 2.29), casting powerful shadows, invited memories of Le Corbusier's "volumes under the sun," and even, more strikingly, the interior "balcony" of his Villa La Roche.

The most direct allusion to the Modern Movement's principles, and to Le Corbusier's architecture in particular, were, of course, the flat roofs with their suspended gardens and innovative pergolas that dissolved the volumes open to the sky.

Finally, the central medical pavilion gave Ginzburg an opportunity for one last elusive daydream. Dedicated to cutting-edge technology and science, the building's program itself allowed Ginzburg to be unabashedly modern; he introduced a huge glazed cylinder for the central solarium and connected it to the luminous interior of the main therapeutic swimming pool boasting surprisingly early brutalist staircases (Figure 2.30).

Contrasting with the heavy stairway, which led to it, a scintillating double circular glass inner garden was delicately set in the core of the building celebrating modernity (Figure 2.31).

While describing his project, Ginzburg claimed that "the severe form of the medical pavilion, sternly closed upon itself, arose from the rigor of its function [...] which did not need any external embellishments and thus remained simple and 'laconic.'"

Figure 2.27 LEFT: Back of western building. (Photo by author); RIGHT: Gropius Bauhaus student dormitory. (Fragment, photo by author)

Figure 2.28 LEFT: Side of western building "levitating" balcony (Photo by author); RIGHT: Leningrad's ASNOVA (Ladovskij's rationalist school) Kitchen Factory (1930–1931), architects Barutchev, Gilter, Meerzon, and Rubanchik. (Photographer unknown)

Figure 2.29 LEFT: Secluded façade of western building (Photo by author); RIGHT: Villa La Roche interior. (Courtesy Artists Rights Society)

Figure 2.30 Brutalist stairs of the central medical facility. (Photos by author)

Soviet Architectural Avant-Gardes

"Laconic" was the buzzword for "modernist," the best that could be said about the otherwise vilified "box-like," "schematic," "ideologically unprincipled," or simply "foreign" architecture the Soviet avant-garde had championed. Behind the frontal, "official buildings" stood a number of characteristically Neue Sachlichkeit administrative edifices, not unconnected to a concept Lissitzky and the avant-gardes had already embraced in the early 1920s and divulged through their short-lived journal *Вещ/Gegenstand/Objet*.

This way, a clear sequence had been established from the "public" south façades with their Novecento forms, to the unofficial secluded avant-garde fronts, ending defiantly, further back to the north, with administrative units unapologetically "box-like," to the point of provocation (Figure 2.32).

***

When the Kislovodsk sanatorium opened, Stalin was ending his Second Five-Year Plan and concluding the most brutal purges and mass arrests of his career with a 1938 third

Figure 2.31 Double-glazed cylindrical inner garden in the core of the medical pavilion. (Photo by author)

Figure 2.32 Medical administrative buildings; administration and physicians' offices. (Photographer unknown)

major public show trial, and the execution by shooting of Buharin. By that time, Ginzburg had lost five close friends and collaborators, Ohitovich, Gan, Lisagor, Klucis, and soon the theater director Mejerhold, to incarceration and death, while millions were forced into labor camps. As if blindly separating the two—involvement with exuberant creativity and tragic personal experience—architects seemed to be living double lives.

CHAPTER 3
BUILDING MODERN ARCHITECTURE: "IN AN ATMOSPHERE OF GENUINE CREATIVITY," 1933-1939

The difficulty in agreeing what "socialist" realism ought to mean in architecture was compounded by, as previously mentioned, the divergent stylistic preferences of the party's top leadership, and of the professionals themselves. Such ambiguity opened a space for significant architectural experimentation and diversity, widened by the degree of tactical tolerance accorded to constructivist architecture virtually until the end of the decade. A point in case was the construction of the second major part of the Palace of Culture completed in 1937, five years after the April 1932 Central Committee dissolution decree. So were two striking garages Mel'nikov built between 1933 and 1936 as head of the Mossovet No 7 of the ARHPLAN.

The most important domestic project, one that occupied an entire post-1932 decade, was the Moscow "Metropoliten" whose first three lines were completed at vertiginous speeds. Significantly, they displayed an array of competing stylistic expressions, including a strong avant-garde presence. The feat was especially remarkable since absolutely no one in the country had any experience with building tunnels and stations for underground trains. A single exception was a Russian engineer who had worked on the Paris Métro since the turn of the century. Even Nikita Khrushchev, by then a high official in the Moscow administration, was called for help because he had been a miner before the revolution.[1] The competitions and the building of the three first lines took place in almost complete creative freedom, buoyed by an unprecedented enthusiasm of the architectural profession, as Moisej Ginzburg himself ascertained.

The second and third major projects of the decade were the Soviet pavilions in Paris (1937) and New York (1939) respectively. While the former, as will be discussed later in this chapter, relied singularly on suprematist precedents, the latter celebrated Americanism already detected in the ultimate design of the Palace of Soviets.

Cities that were especially receptive to constructivism, such as Novosibirsk in particular, but also Sverdlovsk, Rostov-na-Donu, Voronezh, and Baku, clearly testified to the degree modern architecture still had, up to 1939, a right of citizenship, despite the architecture party apparatchiks' concerted futile efforts to undermine it.

---

[1] Elena Zheludkova, "Predistorija Stroitel'stva Moskovskogo Metropolitena: Dorevolucionnye Proekty i Diskussii 1920-h Godov," in *Moskovskoe Metro Podzemnyj Pamjatnik Arhitektury*, ed. I. V. Chepkunova, M. A. Kostyuk, E. Ju. Zheludkova, (Moscow: Kuckovo Pole), 2016.

The Vesnin Brothers' Lihachëv Palace of Culture, Part Two: 1935–1937

On December, 1937, as Moscow's third show trial was underway, and Nikolaj Buharin was writing his last, tormented letter to Stalin from the damp cellars of the Lubjanka prison, begging him to spare him from a public trial and let him drink morphine rather than being shot[2]—the Vesnin brothers' elaborate constructivist Palace of Culture was inaugurated with fanfare.

A Felliniesque all-nighter included a masked ball starting at 11:00 p.m. with pulsing Tango dancing, a costume competition at midnight under fireworks, a waltz at 1:00 a.m., and classical concerts, peppered with jazz, throughout.

The evening began at 5:00 p.m. with a guided tour of the building's facilities, and a solemn address at 6:00 p.m., followed by artistic performances two hours later.

Next came "sound cinema" screenings, or else encounters with writers and poets reading their work. Astronomical observation of the firmament was offered to more scientifically inclined guests, but the latter could also engage in billiard tournaments or mass sing-along choruses. There was also the opportunity to listen to "Western music," or go to lectures on Stalin's brand-new constitution; or else, if in a patriotic mood, explore the concept of "motherland" in Russian art and literature. Finally, at 3:30 in the morning, a "grand carnival procession" would swing out and around the building under the tunes of popular music and swirling lights of blasting fireworks[3] (Figure 3.1).

The program of the celebratory soirée was put together in such a way as to reflect and activate the facilities of the building itself: a 1,000-seat theater; lecture rooms and workshops; a dancing hall and a 400,000-volume library; a concert hall and a game room. Fountains and palm trees graced a restaurant open to a large greenhouse garden. A coiled stair—recalling at first sight the Villa Savoye's own—accessed the rooftop telescope observatory (Figure 3.2).

The building's main, long front was articulated by six glazed vertical, irregularly spaced half cylinders, which recalled Gropius's glass cylinders of his 1914 Deutscher Werkbund model factory (Figure 3.3).

The treatment of the Vesnins' major constructivist work, completed as late as the end of 1937, both in the celebratory way it was inaugurated and the prominent advertisement it received in the mainstream press as an uncompromisingly modern building, pointed to a sense of unremarkable normalcy rather than provocation. Constructivism could still be treated as "one of" the legitimate expressions of the decade's architectural culture. This was no doubt due to Kaganovich's tolerant, if not outright supportive, attitude toward the constructivists, as will be discussed in the next chapter.

---

[2] See Karl Schlögel *Moscow, 1937* (Malden, MA: Polity), 2012, "Letter to Koba" p. 529.
[3] Shchusev Museum of Architecture archives, inauguration Program, KP OF-6105/104.

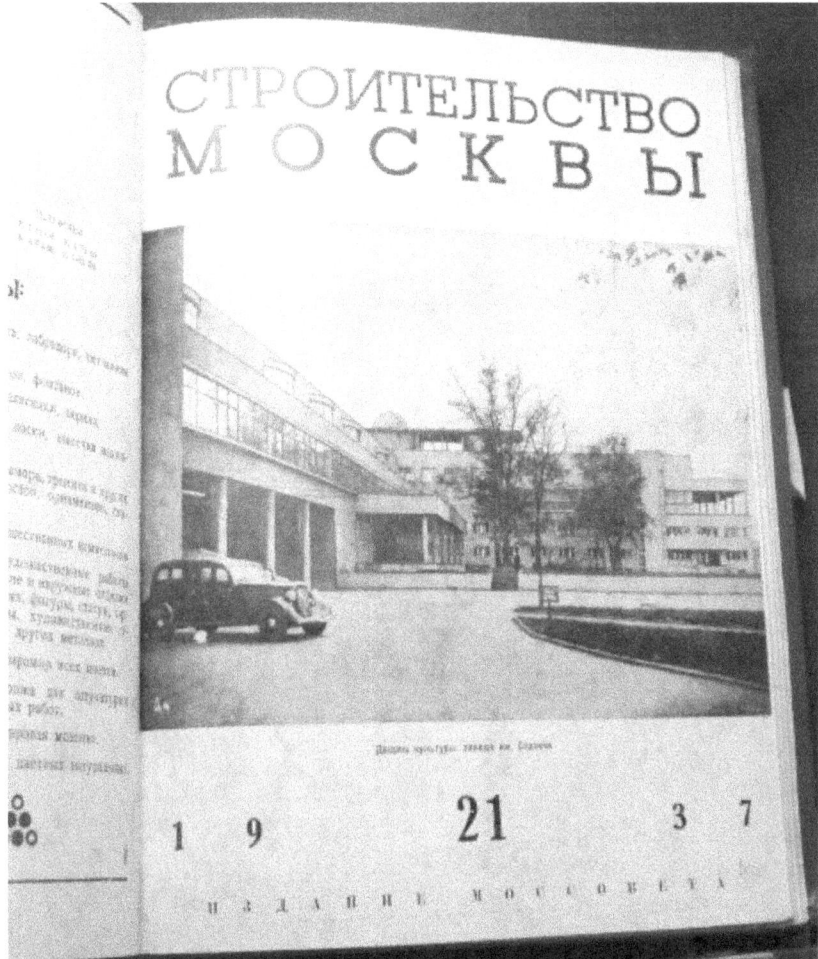

Figure 3.1 The second part of the ZIL Palace of Culture on the front page of *Stroitel'stvo Moskvy*, published upon completion, 1937.

Regarding the building's overall image, the use of pilotis at the three major entrances, as well as of a ribbon window from one end of the building to the other pointed obviously to Le Corbusier's influence, which the Vesnins always acknowledged. The access to the 1934 theater foyer established a short north-south axis, echoing a parallel one at the opposite end of the long east-west axis with its own round entrance (Figure 3.4).

A third, more ceremonial, centrally placed access to the building was attached to the long east-west axis, addressing the entire building. The overall assembly and articulation of masses denoted the Palace's dynamic constructivist constitution. The volumes parallel to the theater axis at the east end of the building were engaged in a play of verticals and horizontals, masses and voids, where pilotis alternately sank into or emerged from the building, revealing at a glimpse the nature of the building's structural system. An interplay of tectonic and stereotomic elements gave the building a sense of expressive rigor and wealth.

Soviet Architectural Avant-Gardes

Figure 3.2 Palace of Culture: Coiled stairs leading to observatory. (Photos Vladislav Ogay, 2016)

The Interior: "Unusual Integration of the Stairways and Galleries."

The uniqueness of the building, however, appeared in its virtually unknown and thus far unexplored interiors:[4] Waving forms flowed throughout the building's spaces in endless arrangements. Aleksandr Vesnin claimed in 1936, "Le Corbusier treated space in a new,

---

[4] Unfortunately, subjected recently to "renovation," the interior has been permanently disfigured.

Building Modern Architecture

Figure 3.3 Main entrance of the Palace of Culture with glass semi-cylinders above. (Photographer unknown, courtesy of Shchusev Museum of Architecture)

very interesting way [as] they interpenetrate each other. We have applied this principle of fluid space in the Palace of Culture"[5] (Figure 3.5). More than drawing from Le Corbusier, however, the wavy interiors seemed, rather, to anticipate Alvar Aalto's own wavy spaces.

Despite Vesnin's deference to Le Corbusier, to strengthen perhaps his own position, the Palace of Culture's interior features were yet untested at this scale in constructivist architecture, nor for that matter, in the European New Architecture up to 1930—European expressionism notwithstanding.

Indeed, as Vesnin continued, "the unusual integration of the stairways and galleries within the building's interior should, in our opinion, accentuate the open character of the space [...]." A powerful flying symphony of undulating stair parapets, mezzanines, bridges and passages represented a major innovation in both constructivist architecture and in the so-called "modern movement" with its pervasive orthogonality before the 1933 Plan Obus. The trend emerged explicitly for the first time in Aalto's interior of his 1939 Finnish Pavilion in New York, which echoed the architect's name—Aalto—meaning "wave."

---

[5] Selim Khan-Magomedov, *Alexandr Vesnin and Russian Constructivism* (London: Lund Humphries), 1986, p. 173.

Figure 3.4 LEFT: Palace of Culture eastern round entrance on east-west long axis; RIGHT: Revealing of the structural system, forming inner terraces. (Photos Vladislav Ogay, 2016)

Figure 3.5 Palace of Culture interior: A flying symphony of undulating forms. (Photos by author)

Aalto was exactly nineteen years old to the day when the Russian February Revolution toppled the Tsar, whose subject he had been until then. It is thus very likely that he had been taught Russian at school, making it easy for him to follow the developments of modern architecture in the USSR. Finland's and Russia's intertwined histories, as well as Finland's closeness to the Soviet Union and its architectural avant-gardes, were reasons why a "constructivist" movement in its own right flourished in Finland in the 1930s.[6] What is more, Aalto's Paimio Sanatorium (1929–1933) had a not immediately noticeable exterior elevator—today referred to as "landscape elevator"—attached to the western tip of the long dormitory arm—the way the Vesnin brothers had done it in their celebrated 1924 competition entry for the headquarters of the *Leningradskaja Pravda* (Leningrad *Pravda* newspaper offices). The project was prominently published two years later in the journal *SA*. Conversely, the Paimio site plan was most probably the source of Ginzburg's site plan of his Kislovodsk sanatorium, mentioned in the previous chapter. The probable place of the Russian avant-garde in Aalto's specific modernism, and vice versa, certainly calls for further exploration.

The condition of the small 1934 theater, which stood on its own, could have been the opportunity to change or adapt the rest of the project into some form of "socialist" realism, full three years before the entire building was completed. Numerous yellow-trace paper sketches actually show ornamental details applied to the building, that is, "art" being tentatively attached to the brothers' constructivist building.

The destination and date of these pencil sketches are not clear; they could have been responses to an outside pressure to introduce added ornaments on the façade. None of it, in any case, was retained in the final 1937 building. According to Selim Khan-Magomedov, "While many constructivist projects, being built in the late thirties, began to be 'enriched' with traditional details, the Vesnins remained faithful to their original concept. Alexandr Vesnin carefully watched the work progress and made no concessions."[7] The ubiquitous bulky and unmodern off-white marble veneer—ill-adapted to wavy, flowing spaces, which covered stairs, columns, parapets, and balustrades in a rather awkward way, may have been the sole "concession" the brothers made to historicism: the choice of "classical" materials[8] (Figure 3.6).

This suggestion is backed up by Kaganovich's call for the use of marble in a meeting of the architecture party on September 27, 1934, just about the time the second part of the Palace of Culture was started.

---

[6] The Artists' Association of Finland, and the University of Texas Art Museum, curated an exhibition on Finnish constructivism in 1979. It was organized under the sponsorship of the Finnish Ministry of Education, January 7– March 18, 1979.

See also Kirmo Mikkola, "Konstruktivismi Suomen Modernissa: Arkkitehtuurissa Kuvataiteesa ja Taideteollisuudessa" in *Muotja Rakenne* (Helsinki, Finland: Ateneumin Taidemuseo), 1981.

[7] Selim Khan-Magomedov, *Alexandr Vesnin and Russian Constructivism* (London: Lund Humphries), 1986, p. 173.

[8] RGALI, SSA, 674-2-7 (1). I am grateful for this intriguing observation to my graduate student, Elijah Montez—made spontaneously in the course of one of my seminars.

Soviet Architectural Avant-Gardes

Figure 3.6 Awkward marble veneering of curved surfaces. (Photos by author)

The modernity of both the building and the cover design of a magazine that had long moved away from the covers Lissitzky and other avant-garde graphic artists had once designed, were a strong indication regarding available choices (see Figure 3.1). The frankly modern look of the 1937 cover testified indeed to a conscious and concerted "will to modernity," emblematically expressed in the association of the building, the automobile, and the graphic design. It also contemporized modernism into the late 1930s.

The Moscow "Metropoliten," 1933–1941: A Case of "Outright Freedom of Invention"

The ideas and projects for an underground railway, intensely debated since the turn of the century, were interrupted with the onslaught of the Great War.[9]

After 1917, Shchusev and Zholtovskij, who ultimately did not take part in the project—revived the idea of a subway, along with burgeoning plans for the reconstruction

---

[9] Elena Zheludkova, "Predistorija Stroitel'stva Moskovskogo Metropolitena: Dorevolucionnye Proekty i Diskussii 1920-h Godov," in op. cit. *Moskovskoe Metro Podzemnyj Pamjatnik Arhitektury,* I.V. Chepkunova, M. A. Kostyuk, E. Ju. Zheludkova, ed. (Moscow: Svjaz Epoh), 2016.

of Moscow. By 1923 City Hall (the Mossovet) created a sub-section for the Moscow transit department, the MGZhD (Moscow City Government Railways), exclusively dedicated to the planning of the Metro.[10] The department soon undertook negotiations with the German AEG and Siemens-Bauunion, while experts were sent around the world to study extant subways. By 1926 the Moscow project got the name "Metropoliten" after the Paris Métro. The overall project was confided to S. N. Rozanov who had been a leading figure in the expansion of the Parisian underground since 1906.

The launching of the First Five-Year Plan, aimed at an accelerated industrialization, brought subway plans to the forefront of priorities under the GOSPLAN, the government planning committee. More precisely, while forced industrialization was meant to catch up with the United States, the metro was aimed at surpassing it.

On June 15, 1931, one year after the 16th Party Congress that gave Stalin an increased hold on power, the Central Committee revived the Metro project, while calling for vertiginous speeds for its completion.[11] For the project to succeed, Rozanov, recently thrown in jail for dubious financial mismanagement, had to be released as he was the only engineer in the country who had serious expertise in building subways.[12] No prescribed style was called for. Each station was to be a world in itself; whereas no one had a clue about what a Metro station was—modernists or classicists alike. In a place of rising crude totalitarianism, the building of the metro suddenly surged as a land of unclaimed freedom. There was one and only demand: to make it the most beautiful in the world—in two years.

The First Line, 1933–1935

Just two years after the architectural and artistic projects were started, the first line of thirteen stations, thirty-five meters deep, opened on May 15, 1935, in a great city celebration that included Stalin's first radio broadcast speech. Two months later, on July 10, the New Moscow Plan was also ready.[13] The construction of the stations, over and below grade, involved an elite cadre of architects, artists, and sculptors of the most diverse artistic persuasions, age, education, and schools of thought inherited from the previous decade. This included old academics and young modernists who responded with a wide span of stylistic concepts, as Kravec had exhorted them to do, calling for unseen "new architectural expressions." Neither were the vocal demands for "proletarian architecture" ever heard, nor was any hint of "socialist" realism ever invoked.

Unlike the case of the Lenin Library, large numbers of young architects were invited, while classicists like Zholtovskij or Shchuko recused themselves.[14] An overall official

---

[10] Josette Bouvard, *Le Métro de Moscou: La construction d'un mythe soviétique,* (Paris: Sextant), 2005, p. 30.
[11] The building of the Metro was classified "Udarnoe stroitel'stvo"— "a shock building site," by a decree of the government (SOVNARKOM) on October 13, 1931, Decree number 1034.
[12] Zhedulkova op. cit. p. 20.
[13] The story of massive urbanization of the country has been broached convincingly elsewhere, and I will be concentrating on the architectural developments.
[14] Alessandro De Magistris and Anna Petrova, "Sintez Iskusstv v Moskovskom Metropolitene: Polistilizm Stalinskoj Neoklasiki," in op. cit. *Moskovskoe Metro*, p 46.

demand was that the underground stations be considered as "palaces for the people" and to strive for "a critical apprehension of the architectural legacy."[15]

Architects were organized in twelve workshops (*masterskie*), as discussed in the next chapter.[16] Avant-garde masters headed five of them at the City of Moscow Metroproekt, including the Vesnins, Ladovskij, Mel'nikov, Ginzburg, and I. Golosov—all working mostly with young architects. Each *masterska* was expected to present a core concept of the station to be designed, subject to the approval of the group's leader. A jury decided about the best entries from the twelve *masterskie*.

Twenty-nine-year-old Aleksej Dushkin (1904–1977) designed two of the most successful modern underground stations for the first and second lines respectively. Those two stations, the 1935 Kropotnitskaja and the 1938 Majakovskaja were emblematic of the decade's pursuit of architectural modernity: the comparison between the above-ground pavilion by architect Kravec and the underground hall of the same station by Dushkin testify to the diversity and extreme stylistic contrasts carried out in the Metro stations from 1935 to 1944: The first, a take on a Palladian Serliana, the second a spectacular architectural innovation, beaming with modernist white abstractness (Figure 3.7).

Dushkin's first station, Kropotnitckaja (formerly Dvorec Sovetov), had been intended as an underground antechamber to the future Palace of Soviets. The design was confided to him, even though he had graduated just the previous year; but he had won as a team member one of the first prizes for the Palace of Soviets in 1931 while still in school.

The space was defined by a three-spanned system of reinforced concrete columns, four of which at the center of the platform featured a different section—from polygonal to square, leaving a sense of ambiguity, but also clearly articulating the space. The novelty of the proposal was the use of girder-less, flower-shaped concrete supports, lit by powerful concealed sources of light—an outright innovation in illumination systems.[17] The masked lights splashed the capitals from below giving a sense of weightlessness: the capitals seemed to be resting on a flood of light, in consonance with the avant-garde's antigravitational experiments.

Facing initial skepticism regarding his lighting system,[18] Dushkin ultimately prevailed after demonstrating his point with mock plaster capitals. The pentagram-shaped capitals projected onto the ceiling were emblematic of the five-pointed Red Star of the Third International—an appropriate "architecture parlante," in Claude Nicolas Ledoux's terms—at the threshold of the Palace of Soviets.[19] The columns and their lit capitals, as Dushkin remarked, were actually "lotus flowers" that could be related in form to ancient Egypt's orders, but not without causing him some political problems. Was he alluding to despotic absolutism at the threshold of the Palace of Soviets? In his defense he rejected any ideological

---

[15] *Arhitektura SSSR*, September–October, 1933, p. 25.
[16] Irina Chepkunova "Tri Podhoda k Projektirovaniju Metro: 1930e gody" in op. cit. *Moskovskoe Metro*, p. 43.
[17] Dushkin, *Moskovskoe Metro*, op. cit. p. 137.
[18] See memoires of his wife N. O. Dushkina, *Zhizn' Arhitektora Dushkina: Kniga Vospominanij, 1904–1977*, (Moscow), 2004.
[19] Claude Nicolas Ledoux, whose architecture was referred to as "revolutionary classicism," was well known to Russian architects. See David Arkin 'Gabriel' i Ledoux, 'Problemy Arhitektury: Sbornik Materialolov' 1 (Moscow) 1936, pp. 117–40.

Building Modern Architecture

Figure 3.7 White abstractness: A. Dushkin underground station "Dvorec Sovetov," renamed today as Kropotnickaja. (Courtesy Shchusev Museum of Architecture)

implication, highlighting an innovative technical and architectural reinterpretation of the columns of Luxor. What may have been on his mind, if only intuitively, was the rich symbolism of the lotus flower. Spanning cultures from China to Egypt and Europe, the lotus was a symbol of universal significance, associated with spiritual awakening or enlightenment. In this sense the blossoming of the lotus could allude to the revolution born, like lotuses, from mud, that is, from backward Russia into pristine floating flowers of socialism.

The lotuses, which could be also experienced as frozen fountains of light, softly filling the space in an ascending movement, gave an uplifting sensation to the passengers, as the underground ceiling, suffused with soft light, seemed to dissolve. Dushkin was in fact applying the lessons of Ladovskij's rationalist method, which dealt with the psychological effects of architecture on the user, here counteracting the otherwise oppressive sensation of being located deep underground.

The light gray columns, lifting the white capitals pressed against the white slabs above, themselves applied to the white ceiling, seemed to recall in subtle ways the white on white suprematist compositions of a 1918 Malevich (Figure 3.8). He was to repeat this evocation of Malevich in his second station by using his Black Square on the floor of Majakovskaja station, as Alessandro De Magistris has suggested.[20]

---

[20] See Alessandro De Magistris and Anna Petrova "Sintez Iskusstv v Moskovskom Metropolitene: Polistilizm Stalinskoj Neoklassiki" [Synthesis of the Arts in the Moscow Metropoliten: Polystylism of the Stalinian Neoclassicism] in *Moskovskoe Metro* op. cit., pp. 46–49.

Soviet Architectural Avant-Gardes

Figure 3.8 LEFT: Kropotnickaja Station (Courtesy Shchusev Museum of Architecture); RIGHT: Malevich, Kazimir (1878–1935). Suprematist Composition: White on White. 1918. Oil on canvas, 31 1/4 x 31 1/4" (79.4 x 79.4 cm). 1935 Acquisition confirmed in 1999 by agreement with the Estate of Kazimir Malevich and made possible with funds from the Mrs. John Hay Whitney Bequest (by exchange). The Museum of Modern Art. (Digital Image ©The Museum of Modern Art/Licensed by SCALA/Art Resource, NY)

Dushkin was involved in an incident that could have ended tragically. As he was walking home after dark, he was stopped by police agents who arrested him for not carrying his identification papers. The interrogation in the Lubjanka NKVD premises was clearly set to identify him as a spy or worse. He vehemently denied it all, to no avail. This was the start of a journey of no return had he not been saved by no other than the British Foreign Affairs minister Anthony Eden. The visiting minister was shown Dushkin's station and, fascinated, asked Kaganovich for the privilege of meeting the architect. Nowhere to be found, Dushkin was ultimately discovered at the Lubjanka, and yanked away *in extremis* from the grinding, all-powerful jaws of the secret police.[21] Dushkin received several Stalin awards for his station.

The Second Line, 1935–1937

As a designer at the Metroproekt, Dushkin also built the Majakovskaja station (Figure 3.9) for the second Metro line that opened on May 20, 1937—as the great Moscow show trials and mass arrests accelerated. While the design of the Palace of Soviets represented

---

[21] In her memoires, his wife, N. O. Dushkina, *Zhizn' Arhitektora Dushkina: Kniga Vospominanij, 1904–1977*, (Moscow), 2004, relates his arrest by the NKVD. At the opening ceremony, Kaganovich congratulated Dushkin, and referred to his wrongful arrest. Quoted by Mariya Kostyuk, "Kropotnitskaja" in op. cit. Metro Exhibition catalogue, p. 94, 2016.

Building Modern Architecture

Figure 3.9 A. Dushkin, Majakovskaja, 1938. Lighting system and the Black Square. (Photos by author)

an exploration into novel lighting systems, conspiring with modern flowing white spaces; the equally experimental Majakovskaja, the arcaded gallery notwithstanding, was a study in steel structures furnished by the new Magnitogorsk industry that flourished as Stalin's Second Five-Year Plan was coming to a close. Engineers R. A. Sheinfains and Je. M. Grinzaid designed the steel structure expressive of the constructivist spirit of its inner core (Figure 3.10). Excavated at a depth of thirty-four meters, the station's steel posts and beams were used for the first time to carry oval arches transversally and longitudinally, as if in a shallow station, implying a technological feat.

These light steel structures replaced effectively the excavated bulky rock supports of the more conventional stations. Relentlessly seeking light and homogenous spaces as in his Dvorec Sovetov station, the steel structure allowed Dushkin to articulate the three naves into a sophisticated single space, floating as it were, within the tunnel. To symbolically acknowledge the concealed steel posts set in the core of the structural system, he veneered the arches with brilliant stainless-steel bracings of both longitudinal and transversal loops, amounting to another architectural innovation: the use of exposed corrugated stainless steel for decorative purposes. Exactly at the same time, in Paris, the sculptor Vera Muhina was stunning the world with her giant sculpture on the Soviet Pavilion, using that same rust-free steel for the first time in art.

The visible ventilation shafts, introduced ornamentally around the rim of the station's vaults, alternating with light fixtures, appeared along the steel veneers, as a discreet nod to the machine aesthetics. Pointing to a constructivist device, the incongruous association

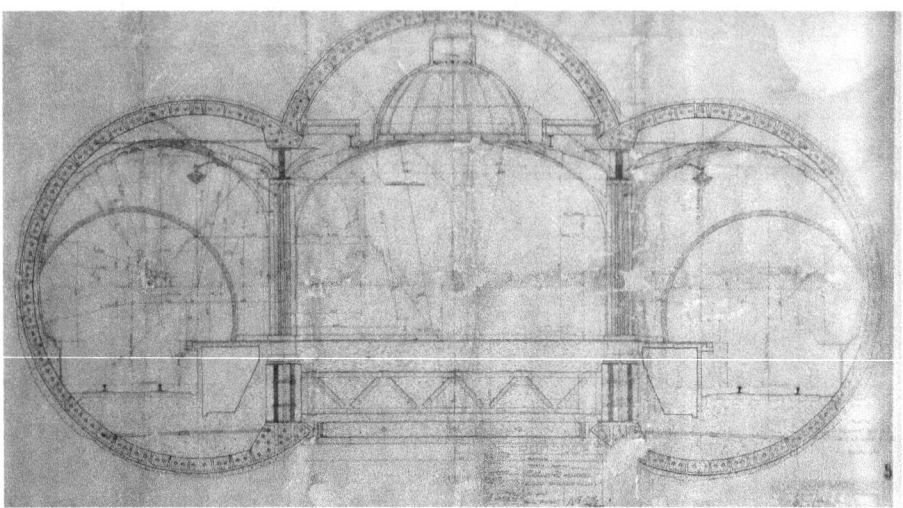

Figure 3.10 Section of Majakovskaja showing steel structural system, a technological feat "floating" within the tunnel, by R. A. Sheinfains and Je. M. Grinzaid. (Courtesy Shchusev Museum of Architecture)

of steel as an industrial material with a venerable marble veneer of the columns and the floors, Dushkin created an effect of "estrangement" (*ostranenie*), in keeping with the formalist method of "semantic displacements."[22] In addition, Malevich's "black squares," deployed over the floor of the central nave (see Figure 3.9), further asserted emblematic connections with the work of the suprematist avant-garde.[23] The fact that black and red squares alternated on the station's floor does not diminish, but actually reinforces the claim. In 1922 El Lissitzky, Malevich's suprematist follower, published a children's story about the fate of a black and red square—*Dva Kvadrata* (Two Squares), which came to Earth from outer space. The black crushes while the red survives.[24] Beyond political allusions, Black and Red were ubiquitous colors of the avant-gardes.

On the other hand, it is interesting to note the significant difference there was between Dushkin's competition entry and the actual built project of the underground station. The competition perspectival image was markedly conservative with its ribbed ceiling, including allusions to large artwork on the vaults, and checkered floors—a trademark of the very official postmodern "Red Classicist," Ivan Fomin (Figure 3.11).

---

[22] About the avant-garde's indebtedness to the theory of the Russian Formalists, see Manfredo Tafuri "Avanguardia e Formalismo, Fra la NEP ed il Primo Piano Quinquenale." in *La Ville L'Architecture: URSS, 1917–1978*, ed. L. L. Cohen, M. De Michelis, M. Tafuri (L'Equerre / Officina Edizioni), 1985.

[23] Op. cit. De Magistris, *Moskovskoe Metro*, p. 46. Black and Red were, after all, distinctive colors of the avant-garde.

[24] See El Lissitzky *Dva Kvadrata* (Berlin), 1920 (the story of *Two Squares*—the squares of suprematism).

Building Modern Architecture

Figure 3.11 Dushkin's competition entry for Majakovskaja. Note the importance given to murals on the ceiling and ornamented vaults, none of which survives in the built station. (Courtesy Shchusev Museum of Architecture)

It is almost certain that the conservative competition renderings were calculated for an easier win as use of such stratagems were not uncommon in the 1930s. Once the commission was in hand, all the intricate coffering was cleaned into pure abstract vault surfaces, undisturbed by ornaments, but for Malevich's squares of nonfigurative art.

Mosaics by Aleksandr Deineka, the celebrated "realist," were meant to decorate the oval domes. Further distancing himself from the competition entry (where he had implied large surfaces for art on the vaults), Dushkin managed to keep them to a minimum by limiting the mosaics to the domes' small oculi. Obviously uncomfortable with the official trend of the "union of the arts" encroaching upon architecture's integrity (he had managed to avoid any added "art" at the Dvorec Sovetov) he kept Deineka at arm's length. Depicting floating people in a Chagall manner—the tiny mosaics, actually representing diving athletes—could be detected only when one stood directly under the dome, as if, amusingly, looking through a periscope to the open sky. The photographs of the station, taken from any angle, convincingly show how a cunning stratagem saved the architecture's modernist purity unobstructed by any "socialist" realist ingredient. In his memoirs, however, using a subterfuge, Dushkin claimed that the invisible mosaics, concealed by the spatial disposition of the vaults, were a "mistake."[25]

---

[25] See De Magistris in op. cit. *Moskovskoe Metro*, p. 49.

It seems difficult not to raise doubts about the veracity of such a claim, coming from an architect of his stature with a proven ability to masterfully control space.[26] He had to know the mosaics would not be apparent, unless standing directly under them, and improbably looking straight up in a busy Metro station. Dushkin's predilection for wholesome architecture was again clearly expressed, like at the Dvorec Sovetov station, keeping any concession to added realist art to a token minimum, invisible if possible.

For Dushkin, light was an essential ingredient of architecture. At the Majakovskaja, he introduced four qualities of illuminations: concealed, reflected, modulated, and exposed. He reinterpreted his Dvorec Sovetov concealed lights, which now at the Majakovskaja, rather than dramatically "burning" the substructure, only brushed lightly the vaults in broad smooth vertical strokes. The indirect sources of light were framed by subtly modulated clefts echoing the corrugated metal. The rim of each dome displayed sixteen lecterns reminiscent of Louis Sullivan's own. Tiny hammer and sickles, alternating with five-pointed stars, were amusingly stamped in between the lamps. Large fixtures, suspended from the ceiling, ran along the actual train platforms, their shine reflected from the stainless-steel veneers of the arches.

Other Metro stations and their architects

Nikolaj Ladovskij, one of the leading figures of the avant-garde, known for his self-branded "rationalist" teaching at the VHUTEMAS/VHUTEIN, was given two stations on the first line: one underground—the Lubjanka, formerly Dzherzhinskaja, and the other, a surface entry pavilion of the Krasnye Vorota, opened on May 15, 1935.

Both were explicitly intended to awaken and act upon the psyche of the passengers through the effect of the "spatial unconscious produced by discreet optical and kinetic sensations."[27] The exterior pavilion of the Krasnaja Vorota, assembled (or "montaged") in a constructivist manner, was a bundle of telescoped cylindrical arches that acted in two opposite directions: while descending into the station, the diminishing "kinetic" arches gave the passengers a sensation of being absorbed into the underground in a downward movement; vice versa, when exiting, the travelers experienced the opposite movement: they were "eased'" onto the surrounding Krasnovorotskaja square by rising arches that framed an expanding view (Figure 3.12).

The Dzherzhinskaja underground Metro station was built without the usual vast central access nave due to geological complexities (Figure 3.13).[28] Like the London Underground, it featured only a single, closed cylindrical "tube" encompassing the train platform and the rail tracks. This condition gave Ladovskij the opportunity to intervene

---

[26] See Dushkin's train station in Sochi, its intricate spatial deployments over a difficult site, dating from the early 1950s.
[27] See Alla G. Vronskaya "Composing Form, Constructing the Unconscious: Empiriocriticism and Nikolai Ladovskii's 'Psychoanalytical Method' of architecture at Vkhutemas," in John Shannon Hendrix and Lorens Eyan Holm *Architecture and the Unconscious* (Hamhan: Ashgate), 2016.
[28] Op. cit. *Moskovskoe Metro*, p. 106.

Figure 3.12 Nikolaj Ladovskij, Krasnaja Vorota Metro entrance. (Courtesy Shchusev Museum of Architecture)

in the perception of the cramped space with sophisticated optical (and psychological) effects. To visually increase the space, he illuminated with modern continuous light bands the pylon side, while leaving in the shadow the opposite wall of the cylinder thus emphasizing perceived depth. The other optical device acting on the psyche was to interrupt rhythmically, at irregular intervals, the gray recessed marble veneer of the pylon with protruding bands of white marble slabs that connected the two opposite walls as emphatically pulsating circles found three years later in Ukrainian-born Sonia Delaunay's 1938 painting "Rhythm," evoking virtual movement.[29] To a certain extent, like Ladovskij's rationalism, orphism, a post-cubist movement that started around 1914 (in the wake of Guillaume Apollinaire's coining of the word), included concerns with expressing sensation, and relied on form and color to communicate meaning. Besides further contributing to the expanse of the cylinder itself, Ladovskij's irregular spacing of the bands circling the platform and the train tracks created a sense of nervous rhythmic pulsation and unsettling speed in the way sound propagates.

The constructivist Nikolaj Kolli (1894–1966), a member of the Academy of Architecture, who, under pressure, started distancing himself from constructivism, was the author of the Kirovskaja station street entrance pavilion—today Chistye Prudy. The

---

[29] Sonia Delaunay, born Sarah Ilinitchna Stern, from Ukraine, created *c*. 1914 a post-cubist movement, Orphism, with her husband Robert Delaunay. Her and Ladovskij's work appear to have been a matter of parallel interest, as no direct connection seems to have existed.

Soviet Architectural Avant-Gardes

Figure 3.13 Ladovskij, Dzherzhinskaja station, 1935. (Courtesy Alessandro De Magistris)

Figure 3.14 Chistye Prudy, František Sammer (Nikolaj Kolli's Workshop), 1937 (Courtesy Shchusev Museum of Architecture)

Czech architect František Sammer who worked with Kolli was the author of the underground station (Figure 3.14).[30] While the underground spaces were designed in a rigorously abstract modern style, albeit with the obliged marble veneering, Kolli's entrance pavilion was a combination of simplified orders and mainstream 1930s European architecture with ubiquitous round window openings, fashionable in Europe in the 1930s. This eclectical pavilion obviously drew from a French modernized academicism, commonly published in Soviet magazines, notably *Arhitektura SSSR* and *Za Rubezhom*.

***

The end of the Second Five-Year Plan and the twentieth anniversary of the revolution in 1937 called for visible accomplishments, whether fictitious or not. A mix of terror, sacrifice, and heroism, but also spectacular achievements, cemented Stalin's myth. Among these achievements were the two Moscow subway lines, completed, as we saw, at staggering speeds under Kaganovich's command. For most of the second half of the decade, with three Metro lines built by 1941, moderns and conservatives competed feverishly in building the best stations—glittery underground salons that made New York's subway look "like a sewer," in Wright's own words.[31]

Admittedly, cynicism notwithstanding, Kaganovich had a point when he asked in his memoirs, "Where do you see here, bourgeois gentlemen, [...] the destruction of the personality, the destruction of creativity, the destruction of art?"[32]

The works resumed in 1943 when modernism was finally defeated, as the Vesnin brothers' tacky monument to the Battle of Stalingrad testified.

The 1937 Soviet Pavilion in Paris: A Dream of Transcendence

Kaganovich's preference for historicism, versus Stalin's interest in American mainstream corporate modern, was clearly visible in the 1937 Paris Pavilion. The triangulation of Stalin, Kaganovich, and Malevich resulted in a virtual tug of war between visions of socialism, modernism, and eclecticism for the future of Soviet architecture, which lasted to the end of the decade. Indeed, in a meeting in 1934 with the party members of the Union of Architects, Kaganovich had recommended moderation towards the constructivists because they were still building all over the country.[33] This plurality of approaches to architectural modernity allowed the constructivists to hold their ground throughout the decade.[34] The Soviet Pavilion in Paris expressed all three.

---

[30] See Viteslav Procháska, "Architetti Cecoslovacchi in URSS negli Anni Trenta," in ed. Ciucci, et al. *Socialismo, città, Architettura URSS 1917-1937: Il contributo degli architetti europei* (Rome: Officina Edizioni) 1972.
[31] F. L. Wright, "Architecture and Life in the USSR," *Architectural Record* (October 1937), vol. 82, no. 4, p. 61.
[32] Quoted in Alessandro De Magistris, "Synthesis of Art in the Moscow Metropoliten: The Polystylism of the Stalinian Neoclassicism," in op. cit. *Moskovskoe Metro,* p. 46. See Lazar Kaganovich, *Pamjatnye Zapiski* (Moscow: Vagrius), 1996.
[33] Moscow, RGALI, SSA, Party Protocol, Fond 674, op. 2 ed. hr. 7 (1), p. 47.
[34] September 27, 1934 party meeting with Kaganovich. RGALI, SSA, Protocol 674, op. 2 ed. hr. 7 (1), p. 47.

Soviet Architectural Avant-Gardes

Figure 3.15 View of night spectacles at the 1937 Paris world's fair. German (left,) and Soviet (right) pavilions framed by the Eiffel Tower in flames. (Personal collection. Photographer unknown)

Commanding the retrofitted Trocadéro's majestic esplanade, the pavilion faced the German in a memorable gesture across the central axis of the Paris "International Exposition of the Arts and Technology in Modern Life" (Figure 3.15).

The images published in the USSR, however, prudently censored the view of the vast concourse by cropping away the German Pavilion. Those acquainted with that memorable panorama could have experienced, at first sight, the distinct feeling that Hitler's Pavilion had been spirited away. Following suit, the present passage will focus solely on the Soviet half of the concourse as it appeared in the Soviet press at the time.[35]

Upon his return from Moscow and Paris, Frank Lloyd Wright visited the Soviet Pavilion which he celebrated for its "low, extended, and suitable base for the dramatically realistic sculpture it carries." He regarded Iofan's pavilion as "the most dramatic and successful exhibition building at the Paris fair [...]. Here, on the whole, is a master architect's conception that walks away with the Paris fair."[36]

At night, when it reached its full potential, the pavilion turned into a comet dragging a tail of brilliant streaks with its glittery ribbon windows "sliding" along multiple receding

---

[35] For a discussion of both pavilions, see Danilo Udovički-Selb, "Facing Hitler's Pavilion: The Uses of Modernity in the Soviet Pavilion at the 1937 Paris World's Exhibition," in *Journal of Contemporary History* Special Edition (*JCH*), Vol. 47, no. 1, Jan. 2012.
[36] F. L. Wright, "Architecture and Life in the USSR," p. 61.

cornices (Figure 3.16). Swirling lights from the Eiffel Tower were reflected off the pavilion's polished Samarkand marble. Formed as a majestic pedestal, the pavilion carried a vigorous forward thrusting couple: a "Male Factory Worker" ("Rabotnik") and a "Female Collective-Farm Worker" ("Kolhoznica"), designed by Vera Muhina, a Paris art graduate.

Significantly, Muhina's sculptural composition espoused in profile, now in a "realistic" mode, El Lissitzky's 1920 new design for Malevich's cubo-futurist "Victory over the Sun," first played in 1913. The implied reference to Lissitzky's work of the early 1920s clearly pointed to the persistence of the avant-garde's spirit in the imaginaries of Soviet artists, even if a shift had occurred from the artistic avant-garde to a "political vanguard."

The credo Bolsheviks derived from a form of extreme historic determinism led, ultimately, to its Stalinian version—"according to which universal reason is objectivized in the guise of inexorable laws of historical progress."[37] With determination, Muhina's sculpture pointed to just that. It is, therefore, no accident that, at night, the visual means Iofan and Muhina chose to represent such promise also evoked strikingly the messianic call of the allegorical shooting star that led the Kings to the Savior's cradle. In other words, having gained control over history, Muhina's "star" pointed to the path humanity was called to take (see Figure 3.16).

Modernism's Resistance and Survival: A Synthesis

Addressing one of the fair's preferred themes, the so-called "union of the arts," in vogue in the 1930s both in France and the USSR, Iofan attempted to develop "a composition based on a synthesis of architecture and sculpture." Ribbon windows under flexible cornices and the assemblage of volumes engaged in a dynamic tension of multiple, sliding and layered prismatic masses, including low and stretched "prairie"-like engagement with the ground, clearly recalled Wright's early architecture. Loosely resembling a hand carrying a flaming torch, Iofan's structure could be viewed as a skillful compression of multiple architectural experiments—futurism and cubism, neoplasticism, and, most notably, Malevich's suprematism itself, albeit all of it assembled along axial symmetries.

Iofan was actually explicit about his suprematist references even more than those found in the Palace of Soviets. Not only was the pavilion itself an assembly of vertical sliding slabs recalling Malevich's sculptures; Iofan invited a suprematist artist and disciple of Malevich, Nikolaj Suetin,[38] to prominently line up a series of majestic white *Arhitektony* on both sides of the pavilion's monumental central stairs (Figure 3.17).

As late as 1937, two years after Malevich's death, such progenies of his *Arhitektony* pointed to the tenacity and depth of the Soviet modernist legacy. Far from dead, modernity (the American skyscraper) and modernism (Soviet avant-garde) remained alive for a long time in the imaginaries of Soviet architects.

---

[37] Slavoj Žižek "The Two Totalitarianisms," in *LRB*, vol. 27 No. 6, March 17, 2005.
[38] Suetin also worked on the 1939 Soviet Pavilion in New York.

Soviet Architectural Avant-Gardes

Figure 3.16 TOP: "The Comet" pointing to the transcendent path of humanity (Personal collection); BOTTOM: El Lissitzky theater set for Malevich's "Victory over the Sun." (Photographer unknown)

Already suprematist in character, the early renderings of the pavilion reaffirmed formal concerns comparable to two of Iofan's preceding projects, the 1934 version of his Palace of Soviets and his competition entry for the Commissariat of Heavy Industry, as suggested in the previous chapter.

Building Modern Architecture

Figure 3.17 LEFT: Malevich's Solo Arhitekton; MIDDLE: View of central stairs, framed by N. Suetin's Suprematist sculptures (Private collection); RIGHT: Iofan's early "Suprematist" sketches for the Soviet Pavilion in Paris. (Courtesy Shchusev Museum of Architecture)

The "Rockefeller skyscrapers," as it were, assembled in the ultimate model of the Palace were direct replicas of the Soviet Pavilion in Paris, which had been in the works since the end of 1935 when the Soviet Union accepted an invitation to participate in the fair. It is telling that a photograph of the pavilion published in *Arhitektura SSSR*—taken from a low oblique angle—cropped out the statue, obviously pointing to the structure's affinities with its American model. With the Rockefeller Center detectable in all three projects, Iofan created an American trilogy celebrating Stalin's power.

This complex architectural fusion in which political power controlled contradictory, if not outright incompatible architectural programs was part of the strategy of the new Stalinist leadership to consolidate its position on the international scene and simultaneously legitimize its image with the leftist movements that had sided or sympathized with the Bolshevik Revolution. Stalin also considered it important to convince the world that he had no designs for spreading the Bolshevik Revolution.[39] A characteristic example, incidentally, was the same issue of *Stroitel'stvo Moskvy* (January 1937) in the holdings of the Lenin Library and the one found in the Washington Library of Congress. The former's cover boasted a portrait of Stalin pasted over a red flag with its golden hammer and sickle and the project of the Palace of the Soviets in the background; the latter, rendered in blue monochrome only, just showed the Palace of Soviets above a faint silhouette of the Kremlin. In other words, the version sent to Washington conveyed a competition of skyscrapers rather than a contest of ideologies. The Soviet Union was simply catching up with the United States.[40]

---

[39] See 1929 Stalin's conversation with an American businessman, as an unofficial envoy of the US government. Stalin claimed that the idea of the expansion of Bolshevism belonged to Trotsky he had defeated, see Stalin, *Collected Works* [J. Stalin, *Sochinenija* (Moscow: Institut Marksa-Engel'sa-Lenina Pri TsK VKPB(b), Tom X, 1946–52].

[40] The 1937 Paris Expo coincided with the rule of the Popular Front government in France, dominated by the socialists. The Soviets felt they could safely display a dramatic hammer and sickle carried by a male industrial worker and a Kolhoz woman by Muhina, using the pavilion as a pedestal.

The survival of a significant residue among artists of a genuine devotion to the enduring myths of the revolution and a pervasive belief that they still could share a common ideal of revolutionary transcendence with a metaphysically conceived party is too often overlooked in the assessments of the period.[41] It is precisely the survival of such faith, so palpable in the Soviet Pavilion that accounted for much of the acclaim the pavilion received abroad, even as a hybrid between vanguard and reaction, cynicism and candor.

Still striving to partake in the quest for modernity, albeit transfigured by a growing retrograde cultural environment set towards what Jeffrey Herf would call "reactionary modernism," the new architectural trend reflected the enduring fascination with its American models. Prophesying that it would catch up with this major leader of modernity, the specific models sought after were primarily those in which the increasingly self-confident Soviet state recognized the reassuring image of its newly established social order. At the same time, the progressive architects' surviving devotion to the revolution—a belief so evident in the pavilion's contradictions as a modernist interpretation of a rigid totalitarian regime—was still powerful enough to elicit admiration even, as we saw it, from such staunch modernists as Wright. Although Soviet architects were clear that the efforts towards an ill-defined "socialist" realism was antithetical to their creative ideals, now supposedly sacrificed to the "masses," the transcendental essence attributed to the party seemed to reconcile the chasm.

***

Following the immense success of his Paris Pavilion, Iofan had resisted taking part in the New York competition, allegedly for being too busy working on the Palace of Soviets. He argued that "correctly representing our Soviet Union abroad meant too much of a responsibility, while soliciting an enormous energy."[42] The true, underlying question was how to repeat the Paris triumph without actually repeating himself.

Iofan finally relinquished when, in his words, the idea of creating a separate tower topped with a worker came to mind. This idea, in fact, stemmed from his early competition for the Palace of Soviets where a statue of a worker stood on top of an obelisk commanding a plaza framed by an arcade and two separate meeting halls (see Chapter 2, Figure 2.9). He was given a second chance to revive a previously winning project, yet ultimately rejected. Inevitably, the overwhelming Paris setting with its powerful propylea, and hemicycle of Laprade's "Pavillion de la Paix" with its obelisk were clearly on his mind as well. The resulting project was a combination of both (Figure 3.18).

Like the Trocadéro, the horseshoe-shaped galleries, with both extremities acting as ponderous, vertically layered propylea recalled those of the Palais de Chaillot. The

---

[41] The epitome of a significant misunderstanding of the psychological and ethical state of mind of most Communists (in particular among the Bolshevik leadership but also among "nonparty" members) is the interpretation of Buharin's last letter to Stalin, prior to his execution. Arch Getty and Oleg Naumov, *The Road to Terror: Stalin and the Self-destruction of the Bolsheviks, 1932–1939*, (New Haven and London: Yale University Press), 1999.

[42] A 1972 interview with Iofan, conducted by Vjacheslav Andreev, and quoted in the Exhibition catalogue ed. Irina Korobyna and Aleksandr Rappaport, *Paviliony SSSR na Mezhdunarodnyh Vistavkah*, (Moscow: Museum of Architecture), 2013, p. 132.

Figure 3.18 LEFT: 1939 New York Pavilion (New York World's Fair 1939–1940 records, Manuscripts and Archives Division, The New York Public Library); RIGHT: 1937 Exposition Palais De Chaillot by Jacques Carlu with Laprade's "Pavillion De La Paix" and its obelisk. (Private collection)

pavilion's semicircular gallery obviously echoed Albert Laprade's "Pavillion de la Paix" with its obelisk Iofan had witnessed at the 1937 Paris International Exposition. While American corporate modernity was implicit, the competition guidelines had found it necessary to warn the competitors against any constructivist temptations. The guidelines demanded explicitly that "the pavilion project be in no way based on the simplified forms of constructivism."[43] While the warning in itself reflected the official position in this respect by 1938, the need to raise it only proved, a contrario, that such possibility existed at the end of the decade. It was telling that the only architectural work represented in the pavilion was the modernist Voroshilov sanatorium (see Chapter 2, Figure 2.19).

Constructivism at Large: The Case of Novosibirsk, 1933–1936; Sverdlovsk, 1933–1939; Rostov-na-Donu, 1934; Voronezh, 1934; Baku 1929–1938; Kujbyshev (Samara), 1936

The vitality Soviet architecture demonstrated abroad could not have been sustained without an analogous presence in the country at large. If Moscow had avant-garde leaders of world stature capable of producing iconic architectural works such as the ZIL Palace of Culture, other cities enjoyed sophisticated architecture by exceptional progressive practitioners (often trained in Moscow) whose work has rarely reached world anthologies. The intense urbanization, called for in the first two Five-Year Plans, demanded all but provincial epigones. A number of VHUTEMAS graduates left Moscow for those cities.

---

[43] GARF Fond 5673, Op. 1 del 23, pp. 67–69.

Soviet Architectural Avant-Gardes

While the leading avant-garde "rationalist" Nikolaj Ladovskij was taking an active part in the planning of new industrial cities in the first half of the decade; and while Moisej Ginzburg was planning in the Crimea to the end, numerous constructivist buildings dotted the entire country, started before April 1932 but completed at different times throughout the decade without modifications—some as late as 1939. While taking both into consideration, this section of the chapter, however, primarily points to modern architecture designed and built after that date.

A few cities such as Novosibirsk (South-West Siberia); Sverdlovsk (Yekaterinburg before 1924 and after 1991) located east of the Urals; and Samara (Kujbyshev) in South-Western Russia in the Kujbyshevskaja region, bordering with today's independent Kazakhstan, had all been particularly receptive to progressive modern architecture of the highest quality, as they grew rapidly under the first two Five-Year Plans of Stalin's industrialization campaigns.

Novosibirsk

This South-Siberian city, straddling the vast, languorous Ob river, was fueled in the nineteenth century by the arrival of the Trans-Siberian Railway. As a frontier city, it also benefited significantly from the Five-Year Plans. The presence of many noted modern architects such as Boris A. Gordeev, Sergej Turgenev, and Dmitrij Agaev, made it possible for constructivist architecture to maintain a fighting presence virtually throughout the decade. Still a number of modern buildings were, ultimately, to be "ornamented," mostly in the post-war 1940s.

Novosibirsk had a new urban plan that the GIPROGOR planning institute developed as early as 1928,[44] with contributions from Aleksandr Vlasov, a VHUTEMAS alumnus, and from Ernst May's alternative plan in 1931. The work completed in the course of the 1930s generally reflected the CIAM principles, not in the least due to the numerous Western European modern planners, notably the Germans, working in the USSR. A strongly established modern architecture, far away from Moscow, allowed an extended survival of modernity.

Institutions 1933–1935

The most important work in Novosibirsk was the Regional Executive Committee Oblispolkom (Oblastnij Ispolitel'nij Komitet) on Krasnij Prospekt (Figure 3.19) by classmate architects Boris A. Gordeev (1903–1943) and Sergej Turgenev (1902–1975)—completed in 1933. Trained as a constructivist, Boris Gordeev was an architect of notable talent, who continued designing and building modern structures in Novosibirsk throughout most of the 1930s, as addressed in this chapter.

While it resembled, at first sight, the Moscow Commissariat of Agriculture by Shchusev, what immediately struck the observer was the incomparable subtlety of the details and formal articulation missing in Shchusev's eclectic work. It has been compared convincingly

---

[44] See I. V. Nevzgodin, *Konstrutivizm v Arhitekture Novosibirska* (Novosibirsk), 2013, pp. 43–44.

Figure 3.19 Novosibirsk, Regional Government architect, Boris A. Gordeev completed in 1933. (Courtesy Balandin Museum of Siberian Architectural History of NSUADA. Architecture of Novosibirsk. Avant-Garde)

with Erich Mendelsohn's Schocken department stores.[45] A powerful projection of a half-cylinder, taut like a sail, and lifted two floors above ground on a pair of pilotis made the building memorable. Even though a ubiquitous part of the constructivist vocabulary, the uniqueness of such a cylinder was that, rather than connecting obliquely the two arms of the building as a hinge—the way I. Golosov would have done—it simply acted as a projected extension of just one of the building's arms, the other arm abutting directly into the first.

Despite its volume, continuous ribbon windows alleviated the mass of the tower-like half-cylinder with delicate sophistication. The curved windows were framed below and above by neutral dark gray bands, themselves bordered by thin white strings. The horizontal strips also divided the windows at mid-height of each floor, while every second string was extended through the whole length of the side façade. Tiny verticals of the window frames, in turn, rhythmically sectioned the glazed bands—all of it coordinated in a convincing constructivist montage.

The side façade encompassing the cylinder boasted another glass volume projected off its surface as a fully glazed prism, extended over several floors. A similar, albeit much smaller, and electrically operated glass volume, appeared, two years later, on Terragni's Casa del Fascio in Como, as both Italians and Soviets keenly observed each other's creations. Gordeev's giant glass prism seemed to have slid down the façade, completely uncovering and reinforcing the perception of the top floor as the building's continuous

---

[45] Ibid., p. 198.

pinnacle, while stopping at mid-level of the second floor to form an awning above the side entrance. A different disposition of the last floor windows, without the white string cutting them at mid-height, acted as an end cap of the cylinder. The same was done with the last floor of the side façade: What were four separate windows on a typical floor were now assembled two by two, again clearly defining the upper end of the building from the rest.

Significantly, the two façades, meeting at a right angle, were not replicas of each other. They actually acted as opposites. What was restrained in one was expressive in the other. The projected glass prism on the side façade became on the main a two-dimensional glazed surface, as if absorbed into the building. Further, the flat, inert surface of one became a powerful projection of balconies of the other. Emphasizing the contrast between the two façades, one had windows flush with the wall, while the other, smaller windows, were sunken into the wall's mass. The cast shadows these indentations created, further enriched the difference between analogous but not identical façades. The same narrative was interpreted in two different ways.

Projected balconies, set symmetrically on both sides of the vertical glass curtain, counteracted the "absorption" of the "prism" into the building. A generous canopy completed this arrangement of the main façade, clearly indicating where the main entrance was. Finally, to sum up this constructivist game, the building was judiciously rendered in two shades of gray that brought it all harmoniously into a single compositional scheme. The building was so powerful in itself that no one dared to add any ornament to it when this was becoming a trend by the end of the decade.

Another institution that celebrated its completion two years after the Oblispolkom was the General Direction of the West-Siberian Railroad for the Tomsk Region. This massive building by architect Arkadij. N. Shirjaev (1908–1954) was part of a typology that boasted a massive semi-cylinder, flanked with two prismatic volumes, used as a type for both institutions and housing. The Railroad Administration was an important late modern building, executed and preserved with no alteration (Figure 3.20).

Figure 3.20 Architects Vengerov and A. Shiraev Administration of the West-Siberian Railroads – Tomsk Region. LEFT: Competition entry, 1933 (?). The actual Façade can be noticed behind the grid of the columns; RIGHT: Completed building 1935. (Courtesy Balandin Museum of Siberian Architectural History of NSUADA. Architecture of Novosibirsk. Avant-Garde)

It is worth noting that the competition entry for this building looked much more conservative than what was actually built. This was not a single case, as we already saw another example in Aleksej Dushkin's Majakovskaja Metro station (see Figure 3.11) opposing a conservative competition entry to a bare modern white volume. The submitted entry boasted huge orders without capitals forming a grid visibly covering in the background what was to become the actual built façade behind the historicist screen. It is evident that in the 1930s architects, sensing the increasingly retrograde environment, or simply to please a conservative jury, considered it safer to avoid alarming anyone with entries that were too extreme, especially when, in addition, the jury's roster included non-architects and representatives of various administrations. The Railroad Administration building was a significant case in point.

Housing, 1933–1939 A number of remarkable modern apartment buildings were also raised in Novosibirsk, by leading modernist architect Dmitrij Ageev, born in 1902, the same year as Leonidov.

Ageev, whose death seems to be unknown—a possible indication that he disappeared in the torment of the Terror—collaborated with one-year-younger Boris Gordeev, on another significant housing completed in 1933—the Kuzbassugol (Figure 3.21). The latter was a cooperative housing for the coal mining employees. The primary strategy here was to play with a variety of assembled volumes (or "montaged" as Ginzburg

Figure 3.21 Novosibirsk, 1933 Kuzbassugol Coal Mining Workers, by architects. B. Gordeev and Dmitrij Ageev. (Courtesy Balandin Museum of Siberian Architectural History of NSUADA. Architecture of Novosibirsk. Avant-Garde)

would have it) of different sizes and configurations, detracting from any sense of "boxlike" appearance. Alternating horizontal light and dark strips of the balconies and between windows, added a sense of material sophistication that further challenged the "box."

Curiously, only the smaller block had the windows framed in black. Recessed windows reinforced the synergy with the projecting wraparound corner balconies. Other smaller but highly effective architectural devices—such as the white metal parapets of the balconies, framed above and below with white tensile metal bars—simultaneously eroding and energizing the mass. A third volume was a wraparound staircase container. This time, it embraced the main architectural body vertically and over the roof, thus counteracting dynamically the balconies' horizontals. The main body of these interconnected volumes of projected white balcony-like glazed blocks, acting as small winter gardens, recalled those Ginzburg designed in 1927 for the Malaja Bronnaja Street Gosstrah apartments in Moscow.

A year later, in 1935, S. P. Turgenev, N. V. Nikitin, and Gordeev himself inaugurated another apartment building that closely reflected constructivist features of the previous decade, including balconies wrapped around the corners of the building; insistence on glazed corners, ribbon windows, and the ubiquitous double clock crowning the tower's top.

Deeper into the decade (1934–1938), Gordeev and Turgenev completed a "Housing for Artists," a sober building with an elaborate cornice crowning the edifice—a possible concession to the times or else as a way of restraining the brutalism of the whole (Figure 3.22). Interestingly, the photography of the building (possibly by the architects themselves) was slanted in the avant-garde manner of a Rodchenko, inviting a constructivist reading.

A 1936 apartment block by the same architects had an entirely glazed stairway, splitting the huge building into two equal volumes and projected forward, off the façade, as if squeezed out by the two abutting sides (Figure 3.23). Glass volumes projecting beyond the façade clearly pointed to Gordeev's style. The extremities of the main façade were framed by a system of balconies that were not wrapped around the corner as expected, but created a frame. It was a question of proportions, which Gordeev controlled masterfully. It is obvious that, in this case, corner wraparound balconies would appear too feeble given the mass of the building that they would be supposed to "contain"; rather, Gordeev added an identical series of balconies at both ends of the façade, framing it independently. Not immediately perceptible was the subtle variation between the fenestration of the first two floors and the rest of the seven levels. The difference in height of the windows of the two lower floors—the first row of windows looking stretched—established a clear difference between the more ceremonial band above the ground and the rest of the floors.

Upon turning the corner, however, the full constructivist features came to the fore again with its wrap-around balconies, including another identical "squeezed" vertical glass of the staircase projected off the façade. The latter had an added monumental glazed surface over two floors indicating the location for social activities of the cooperative. This time the corners with wrap-around balconies were inverted (see Figure 3.23, left image, bottom right), thus creating a novel spatial opportunity for the

Building Modern Architecture

Figure 3.22 Gordeev and Turgenev Housing For Artists 1934–1939. Note the slanted composition of the photo, an echo of Rodchenko's style. (Courtesy Balandin Museum of Siberian Architectural History of NSUADA. Architecture of Novosibirsk. Avant-Garde)

apartments with their deeply recessed terraces. This complex building was raised for the OGPU—the political police.

A number of buildings by Gordeev, however, such as his 1934 constructivist apartment building for the employees of the Sibzoloto (Siberian gold industry) were "decorated" over in 1948 with applied bas-reliefs. In general, it seems that such additions were implemented mostly on housing buildings whose residents belonged to the rising privileged class of the bureaucratic establishment in a quest for decorum.

Finally, worth noting, was an idiosyncratic university building completed in 1938—a chemistry and technology college by architect A. I. Bobrov. It's rather unique, an entirely

113

Soviet Architectural Avant-Gardes

Figure 3.23 Two views of B. Gordeev's Housing Project, "Dom-Kombinat"—polyvalent housing building with restaurant and community services for the OGPU members, 1936. LEFT: side façade; RIGHT: main entrance volumes and courts. (Courtesy Balandin Museum of Siberian Architectural History of NSUADA. Architecture of Novosibirsk. Avant-Garde)

glazed round tower over five floors was attached to a plain four floor prismatic main body. Balconies protruding from each floor, at the juncture between the glass tower and the prismatic block, helped articulate the two. A projecting and winding, partially independent ground floor, also entirely glazed and wrapped around the tower's base, acted as a plinth to the entire building.[46]

Sverdlovsk (Ekaterinburg) Housing, 1933–1939

The most important urban event in Sverdlovsk—an eighteenth-century city east of the Urals on the Eurasian continent, which, like Novosibirsk, was on the pathway of accelerated industrialization—was the construction of the huge residential compound, lodging the NKVD secret police. The architects were I. P. Antonov and V. D. Sokolov. The compound was endearingly named (to some) "Gorodok Ckekistov" (Chekists' Townlet) after the name of the first Soviet political police, the Cheka, established under Lenin.

A gated compound started in 1931 and completed in 1939, implementing a similar design strategy as Novosibirsk's railway administration, the Gorodok with its serrated disposition of dwelling blocks, included all possible commercial facilities (luxurious for Soviet standards at the time) with exclusive food stores, daycares, laundry services, restaurants, and cultural amenities (Figure 3.24 a–c).

In other terms, the compound was the epitome of a realized house-commune at a grand scale, serving the most privileged segment of Soviet society. It was built over some eight years from 1931 to the end of the decade with twelve residential buildings of six floors each, partially attached to each other creating lively "Bauhaus"-style serrated slabs with slanted roofs and polygonal bay-windows. The main cylindrical apartment building for single individuals reached ten floors, ending with colosseum-like square windows. The compound was completed in 1939 without any modifications. It is notable that this

---

[46] The only extant photograph, owned by the Novosibirsk "Oktjabarskij" Museum is of too low resolution to be publishable.

Building Modern Architecture

Figure 3.24 a) Sverdlovsk (Ekaterinburg) "Gorodok Chekistov" housing for the NKVD (Secret Police), Administration Building 1931–1939 (Courtesy Vitaly Sumin, Deputy Director SOKM History Museum, Ekaterinburg/Sverdlovsk); b) Sverdlovsk (Ekaterinburg) "Gorodok Chekistov" model and view of single employees housing, 1931–1939 (Courtesy Shchusev Museum of Architecture); c) Sverdlovsk (Ekaterinburg) "Gorodok Chekistov" housing for NKVD families, 1931–1939 (Courtesy Vitaly Sumin, Deputy Director SOKM History Museum, Ekaterinburg/Sverdlovsk); d) Sverdlovsk (Ekaterinburg) "Gorodok Chekistov," general view and model, 1931–1939. (Courtesy Shchusev Museum of Architecture)

Soviet Architectural Avant-Gardes

was not the only case of constructivist buildings raised, even late in the decade, for the secret police, in a certain sense reinforcing the notion that there was no official opprobrium against it, as discussed further in the next chapter.

Rostov-na-Donu

Among the highlights of Rostov-na-Donu, a city straddling the vast Don river that flows languorously into the landlocked Azov Sea,[47] was a hotel by Armenian architects I. E. Cherkesjan and H. H. Chalkushjan, completed in 1934. The hotel stood partially on pilotis and displayed a vast floor-to-ceiling glazed surface of its restaurant on the second floor, the entire building flanked on both sides of the corners with semi-cylindrical glazed window towers. The sculptural relief on top of the façade was a concession to fashionable "unity of the arts" (Figure 3.25).

The architects made a concession to the current infatuation with the "synthesis of the arts" as they added a bas-relief on the main façade "like a postage stamp on a letter," as Moisej Ginzburg once remarked sardonically.[48]

A major avenue, Budennovskij Prospekt, was rhythmically flanked by five multi-storied residential buildings, each boasting characteristic constructivist balconies wrapping around the four corners. The double-height ground floors displayed fully

Figure 3.25 Hotel in Rostov-na-Donu by Armenian architects I. E. Cherkesjan and H. H. Chalkushjan, today "Marins Park Hotel," 1934. (Photographer unknown)

---

[47] See the epic novel *Tyhij Don* (translated as *Quiet flows the Don*) by M. Sholokhov.
[48] M. Ginzburg, "The Creative Tasks Ahead of us," in *Arhitektura SSSR*, 2, 1934, pp. 63–69.

Building Modern Architecture

Figure 3.26 Apartment blocks on Budemovskij Prospekt, built between 1928 and 1936 with no alterations. (Photographer unknown)

Figure 3.27 "Utjuzhok" building, City Utilities Administration in Voronezh, 1934, by architects Popov and Shaman. (Photographer unknown)

glazed convenience stores that alleviated the mass of the building, seemingly suspended above the ground. Started in 1928, the series was completed, undisturbed, by 1936. They were slightly "corrected" with ornaments only between 1948 and 1949[49] (Figure 3.26).

Voronezh

The City Utilities Administration and Retail in Voronezh, a town midway between Moscow and the North Caucasus, was the work of the talented A. I. Popov-Shaman and completed in 1934.[50] The building, situated on Nizami Plaza, called "Utjuzhok," deftly combined offices, retail, housing, and a vast sunlit reception hall open to the city through nine large windows controlling the intersection of two major arteries (Figure 3.27). It was completely gutted by bombs during the Second World War, and promptly rebuilt by 1950 without any additions or modifications.

The main cylindrical corner recalled those of Novosibirsk and Sverdlovsk. There were, however, significant differences. As opposed to the two previous ascetic and rational buildings, the Voronezh building presented a rich variety of glazed bands announcing to the exterior its multiple functions: the plinth of a high basement for retail; the vast openings above establishing a dynamic dialogue with the city; two bands of more discrete, introspective office windows; and finally, on top of the semi-cylinder, a light band of ribbon windows forming a delicate crystal crown. The whole was articulated by powerful, if hierarchically disposed, verticals and horizontals. An outwardly projecting, dominant staircase fed the circular volume, while acting as a visual hinge between the administrative and housing units of the building. At the opposite end, a second staircase served the apartments themselves. Slightly set off from the plan of the façade, it gave the building a formal conclusion. In the same vein, the external wall of the main staircase was frankly projected from the building's façade, somewhat in Gordeev's style, if less sophisticated; it folded over the roof at a right angle to allow for two narrow, vertical glazed bands on the sides to draft additional modulated light onto the landings. All these subtle moves came, of course, to their full effect at night.

Baku

The 1934 Baku (Azerbaijan) news agency on the landlocked Caspian Sea by S. Pen, was designed before the 1932 decree, but built two years after with no modifications. It appeared as the exact opposite of the one in Voronezh. It celebrated an expressionist constructivism unique in its kind. The wavy effect of the round balconies, wrapping around the stairwell, or more exactly, the wavy shadows cast off the balconies, was produced by the change in width of the balconies themselves. The device created an

---

[49] Rostov is also known for its modern theater, intentionally reminiscent of a tractor, pre-revolutionary architects Shchuko and Gelfreich won against the Vesnins in a 1930 competition and completed in 1935.
[50] Voronezh was the city where Osip and Nadezhda Mandelstam were first exiled from Moscow, before Osip was finally arrested. Cf. Nadezhda Mandelstam, *Hope Against Hope*, (London: The Harvill Press), 1999.

Building Modern Architecture

Figure 3.28 Newspaper agency in Baku, Azerbaijan, architect S. Pen, 1929–1934. (Photographer unknown)

ambiguous reading of the stairwell shaft. With its trademark pilotis, continuous large windows with white curtains behind them, and its expressionist stairwell and balconies, it could be said that the building simultaneously reverberated amusingly the work of Gropius, Le Corbusier, and Mendelsohn (Figure 3.28).

Kujbyshev

The city of Kujbyshev's most memorable architectural work was a pristine housing complex the architects Matveev and Bosin inaugurated as late as 1936. Enveloping a landscaped park, the low-rise buildings were characterized by highly emphasized stairwell verticals. Like a tree, the stairs held apartments on both sides of the "trunk," which, as tree branches, dissolved, as it were, into light, glazed corner balconies, giving a sense of movement and grace, further articulated by colored versus white surfaces.

***

This brief survey of provincial cities indicates that a well-established modern architecture in general since the 1920s managed to survive the onslaught of conservative mediocrity, with various degrees of success, for most of the 1930s. Additions and embellishments were applied primarily, as mentioned, after the Second World War when historicist eclecticism finally triumphed. This, apparently, concerned in the first place the housing whose elite users were likely to complain about "boxy" architecture. They were the presumed "masses" who disliked any modern expression while privileging kitsch. However, it is important to stress, as will be discussed in the last two chapters, that the April 23, 1932 decree did not carry any provision either against modern architecture, or, even less, a prescribed new style.

Modernity as a Standard

In February 1935, a Central Committee and Soviet Government joint decree called for developing standardized types of high school establishments. The move resulted in various models. The most intriguing among them, because of its frank modernity—including pilotis and corner widows—was Fridman's standard school for Moscow, completed *c*. 1938 (Figure 3.29).[51] In other words, rather than favoring a historicist or eclectic style, in 1936 the government opted for modernity as a standard. The author was the same Fridman who was a competitor in the Lenin Library contest (see Chapter 1). Having long adopted classicist revival, he logically concluded that a historicist typology would hardly fit the type, pointing again to the flexibility in the stylistic options.

Figure 3.29 Standard High School Building in Moscow by architect D. Fridman. 1936 (Photographer unknown)

---

[51] See A. I. Aksel'rod *Arhitektura Strany Sovetov: Shkoly* (Moscow: Academy of Architecture of the USSR), 1948, pp. 11 ff.

Mel'nikov's Last Project, 1936

While Mel'nikov was still lauded for his work, if increasingly reprimanded for his "messy" ARHPLAN workshop handling; as well as for the perceived "formalism" of some of his projects (even in the view of avant-garde architects such as Ginzburg)—as discussed in the last chapter—he completed his best project of the decade (see Figure 3.30). Designed in 1934, and inaugurated in 1936, the building is still in use today. It was a garage for the Planning State Agency (GOSPLAN) in the outskirts of Moscow. As always, unique in its

Figure 3.30 Konstantin Mel'nikov, GOSPLAN garage, Moscow, 1934–1936. (Courtesy Shchusev Museum of Architecture)

kind, it was a humorous addition to the "architecture parlante," echoing his 1934 Narkomtjazhprom or NKTP. The project's huge circular self-standing window alluded to a car wheel, thus differing radically from the equally giant circular window of his 1934 "Inturist" garage, flush with the wall. The theme was again the machine, that is, now, the automobile.

With fluid baroque forms, Mel'nikov articulated five elements of a car: Besides the monumental wheel—as the most attractive feature of the project—surface standing with its glazed surface quite explicitly standing in for a giant car headlight—witness the conic vault extended behind the glazed opening. Below, as if holding the wheel, were curved and layered concrete strips, alluding to car shock absorbers, while the tall office building recalled an automobile radiator—ubiquitous in cars of the 1930s. Finally, the exceptionally long and thin chimney, tightly connected to the wheel, stood perhaps for the car's exhaust pipe, despite its square section.

This was to be Mel'nikov's last project, before he withdrew from public view, secluded in his two-cylinder house, where he painted and hosted artists for decades to come.

***

The chapter has attempted to include a wide range of most diverse building types. They all spoke, in various degrees, about the modern architecture, often markedly cosmopolitan, that was created during the 1930s—well after the April 23, 1932 decree on the dissolution of independent artistic associations. An effort was made as well to broaden the discourse beyond the two most quoted centers such as Moscow and Leningrad. The next two chapters will address the cultural and political circumstances under which it was all possible, highlighting the debates in the professional media and secret party meetings, on the one hand, and on the other, casting full light, for the first time, on the single most important event of the decade—the 1937 First Congress of Soviet Architects.

CHAPTER 4
THE SHAPING OF ARCHITECTURE IDEOLOGY WITHIN THE STALINIST PROJECT: UNREACHABLE "PROLETARIAN" ARCHITECTURE YIELDS TO UNATTAINABLE "SOCIALIST"

Emblematic of the slowness of the efforts to Stalinize architecture, that is, to explain it in terms of an elusive "socialist" realism were the repeated postponements of the First Congress of the Union of Soviet Architects from 1933 to 1937. The reason for the delays hinged on the difficulties that the Union's communist leadership experienced in imposing their will, not only on the masters of the architectural avant-garde, but also on the youngest generation of architects, including the young communists. What is significant, however, is that the demands for abandoning modern architecture were not coming from either the Central Committee or the Politburo, at least until February 1936. Still uncertain whether matters were truly under control, the party group (the former VOPRA) kept postponing the date with increased anxiety, including outright panic as the jubilee year 1937 approached, and could not be bypassed. The dictates of the party kept falling short of convincing the leadership of the SSA to stop advocating constructivism, while struggling to impose their policy even to the Komsomol architects (the communist youth). The latter did not see the point of abandoning modernism in exchange for an architecture that the SSA party leaders themselves struggled to define or demonstrate.

For the same reason, early on, the authorities asked the CIAM to delay the Moscow meeting scheduled for 1933. The SSA's party organization sustained a desire to host such a congress, while dismissing CIAM's modernism at home, points to the complexity of the architectural politics started in 1928 with Stalin's Cultural Revolution. The efforts to curtail constructivism over the decade used three vehicles: The new journals such as *Arhitekturnaja Gazeta*; the enforced exercises of "self criticism" at the "Creative Consultations" (Tvorcheskie Soveshchanija) within the SSA; and the secret actions of the SSA party cell. So, the actual turning point was not the April 23, 1932 Central Committee as thought thus far, but February 1936 when the growing general political repression started taking aim pointedly at modern architecture. By the 1937 Congress of Architecture, constructivism had become anathema. Still, it took two more years to finally silence the proponents of the so-called "boxy architecture" on the building sites. The stratagem, like we saw Ginzburg doing in Kislovodsk, was to call "socialist" realism whatever you built, or else, winning competitions on conservative images, and then building what was your actual intent.

Soviet Architectural Avant-Gardes

Arhitektura SSSR, an Open Forum

The other new journal, *Arhitektura SSSR*,[1] "Organ of the Union of Soviet Architects," with its uninspiring bureaucratic look, contrasted unfavorably against the deeply innovative typeset and layout that once so powerfully graced the Vesnins' and Ginzburg's *Sovremenaja Arhitektura (SA)* or Ladovskij's *ASNOVA*. Soon, Leonidov proposed that the journal be redesigned, but, unsurprisingly, met with Mordvinov's disagreement.[2] The first issue of *Arhitektura SSSR*, appeared in July 1933, while Miljutin was theorizing the variants of Soviet modern architecture in his own journal *Sovetskaja Arhitektura*, where he called for the adaptation of the existing trends, never for their rejection.

The design of the *Arhitektura SSSR* was entrusted to Lissitzky, the point being, possibly, to have an internationally recognized name from the avant-gardes, while erasing any visual continuity with their former publications. Titles and captions were, after all, translated into French, aiming obviously to an international audience. This was consistent in an almost emblematic way with the political ambiguities of the 1930s.

The fierce confrontations that preceded the dissolution of the *grupirovkie* in 1928–1930, soon resumed within the SSA itself.[3] Official clamors against their perpetuation, however, were raised only at the start of 1936, when the political situation in the country was taking a sharp turn into generalized repression. The move to close the revived architectural groupings was decided at an "Expanded Consultation" of the Leningrad SSA administration as late as the end of December 1935.[4]

Modern architecture never left the pages of *Arhitektura SSSR*, either domestic or foreign. Created in the wake of the April 23, 1932 Central Committee Decree, the journal maintained a connection to the avant-gardes virtually to the end of the decade. Either through showcasing the work of individual architects; thematic discussions or autobiographical evocations; retrospectives and essays by the very leaders of constructivism, rationalism, or suprematism; even including Leonidov's projects or regular reviews of current modern architecture in Europe, the journal afforded a critical presence.

One of the last reverberations of a modern thinking about architecture in *Arhitektura SSSR* was Moisej Ginzburg's essay "The Organic in Architecture and in Nature,"[5] echoed his concept of constructivism, albeit without mentioning it, published as late as September 1939. In the essay, Ginzburg debated the meaning of organic architecture in opposition to "classical." Smartly taking advantage of the lack of definition of "socialist"

---

[1] The initiator of the new journal was Arkin, the VOKS Secretary. He presented a plan of publication on May 5, 1933. RGALI, SSA. 674, op. 1 ed. hr. 7 (1). Arkin, a relatively progressive figure, clearly left his mark on the publication.

[2] (November 2, 1934) RGALI, SSA, 674, op. 1 ed. hr. 9.

[3] See Alessandro De Magistris, "Il dibattito architectonico degli anni '30–'50 nelle pagine di *Arhitektura SSSR*," in *Casabella* 602, 13 pp. 46–53.

[4] "Against the *Grupirovshchiny*, for the consolidation of All Forces of the Architectural Front!" in the *Gazeta* No. 71, December 22, 1935.

[5] *Arhitektura SSSR*, no. 9. 1939, pp. 76–80.

realism, he filled the void with his own thinking about architecture, by simply avoiding the use of condemned terms, as we will see Ginzburg doing in his 1940s book on the Kislovodsk "Ordzhonikidze" sanatorium below.

Arhitektura SSSR tried to present itself as a neutral, detached medium, open to all that was called "architecture" on the professional scene of the country and abroad. Starting with 1936, however, it turned increasingly militant with intrinsic bias in the ideological and political sense. It would even include regular reporting on the show trials or else harangues against presumed "saboteurs" or "enemies of the people" in its very editorials, while Stalin's name was regularly printed in red.

As the decade progressed, the rubric on the so-called "architectural legacy" was gradually inflated through a growing effort to address "the critical assimilation of the architectural heritage," as an undeclared new direction. Two concepts recurred obsessively—"formalism" and "eclecticism"—at times almost as a ritual expiation. Still, excellent critics and theoreticians such as D. Arkin, R. Higer, L. Lissitzky, N. Miljutin, and a few others, regularly broached these and other related issues intelligently, if at times with perceptible self-control.

Even so, Le Corbusier's Centrosojuz—now Commissariat of Light Industry (Narkomlegprom)—received a prominent space in two articles, one by Arkin and the other by Kolli in the same October 1938 issue.[6] Leonidov's project for an open-air theater and restaurant as part of the reconstruction of the Moscow Hermitage was featured prominently over an entire page, with detailed descriptive comments in the second issue of *Arhitektura SSSR*.[7] Leonidov's 1934 Narkomtjazhprom competition entry was also displayed, even though shunning its most original aspects.

The new journal was to be published monthly. A long, unsigned foundational editorial, most likely Alabjan's, appeared characteristically under the heading: "Our Tasks Ahead."[8] There was no hint about "proletarian architecture" anymore, as if the same Alabjan had never invoked it so adamantly just three years earlier, while the avant-garde's institutions were being demolished one by one in its name. The concept was now moving to an equally unspecified "socialist architecture," the ideological reference of a word being apparently more important than its actual meaning. Typically, what was to be rejected was always made more explicit than what it was supposed to be replaced with. The editorial was no exception. It lamented, at the outset, the low quality of the average Soviet architectural production, ruled by the "boxy pseudo-architecture, devoid of any art"—a reference that would become a buzzword against modern architecture, surprisingly analogous to the way French reactionary architectural criticism evoked contemporaneously the *pan-bétonisme intégral*. The other extreme was the never explicated "formalism." It was to be used down the 1930s in incantatory fashion. Kaganovich, who certainly had read the draft of the editorial for the first issue of a new

---

[6] *Arhitektura SSSR*, no. 10, 1938, N. Kolli "Dom Narkomlegproma," pp. 27–34. D. Arkin, "Dom na ulice Kirova," pp. 34–36.
[7] *Arhitektura SSSR*, no. 2, August 1933, p. 15.
[8] *Arhitektura SSSR*, no. 1, July 1933, p. 1.

official journal, had a more nuanced point of view. He claimed that "architecture should express its purpose"[9]—an ambiguous position standing between the eighteenth-century "architecture parlante" and the "form that follows function." In this sense, he had criticized Leonidov's Narkomtjazhprom competition entry for giving its assembly hall the form "of a cauldron."[10]

More significantly, Alabjan evoked with insistence the celebrity status "Soviet architecture enjoyed in the world"—the work of the avant-gardes obviously—as he called for it to:

> strengthen [*ukrepit'*] the future close association [*svijaza*] with the progressive [*peredovymij*], revolutionary architectural trends and thoughts in the West [sic]. Doing so should be one of the most important tasks of the Union of Soviet Architects [author's emphasis].

It is not impossible that these surprising statements, especially the way they were worded ("revolutionary architecture"—under capitalism?), aimed also at the foreign progressive architects working in the USSR; but it is equally obvious that no specific "official style" was ever called for. If anything, Alabjan was strongly critical of "eclecticism, historicism and false Renaissance revivals"—whatever "false" may have meant. The editorial thus emphasized:

> Soviet architecture has to reject decisively any attempt to revert to bourgeois eclecticism—to the lifeless restoration of old historical styles, under the pretext of caring for "problems of legacy"—instead of embracing creatively an architecture rich in new ideas.

Soviet architecture, the text insisted, had to embrace instead "socialist values [...] rich in ideas and art." Not to be discounted was the difference that was made between what the journal called "*primitivnie psevdo racionalnie 'dom-korobki'*"—or primitive pseudo-rational "box-houses"—and authentically modern architecture—an architecture, which, in the worst of cases, was classified as "functionalist" for being overly concerned with "function" to the detriment of "art."[11] To undertake this journey, Soviet architecture had to discard any "formalist recipes, and their numerous approaches." The stance clearly showed the difficulty the journal met in coming up with any sensible definition of "socialist architecture," not unlike the previous "proletarian."

Yet, almost by accident, Alabjan seemed to have hit the "philosopher's stone" as he concluded: "in the struggle for the creative growth of Soviet architecture, an enormous

---

[9] RGALI Protocol of party meeting 674. Op. 1 ed. hr. 8 (1), p. 34.
[10] Ibid. p. 35.
[11] Generally, in the first half of the 1930s, the concept incorporated what was contemporaneously called in France the "Union des Arts": the addition of frescoes, statuary and bas-reliefs as with the two Paris Museums of Modern Art (1934–1937).

significance lies in the *critical assimilation of the architectural heritage* [author's emphasis]." Here was, expressed in a nutshell, the theme of the ritual "self-critical" confessions that were to follow to the end of the decade under the heading "Tvorcheskaja Diskussija" (Creative Discussion). Simply put, without any a priori style being imposed. What was at stake was an attempt at engineering the creative act itself.

The second issue of *Arhitektura SSSR*[12] largely confirmed that stance. Under the title "Architecture in the Struggle for Quality"—the quality of the creative process—the anonymous editorial aimed at the "reconstruction" of Moscow and the appropriate means for achieving it through the city's "architectural heritage."[13]

What was remarkable, however, was that, more than a year after the April 1932 dissolution, far from ignoring, let alone rejecting, modernism, the second issue of the journal displayed a series of constructivist buildings under construction in Moscow. Beyond foreign reports, which included extensively Le Corbusier's Centrosojuz on Mjasnitckaja Street and Jaromir Krejcar's inspiring, modern sanatorium in Teplice outside Prague, the Soviet Union was represented by the rousing modern competition entry for the Moscow House of Books by B. M. Velikovskij (with P. P. Antonov and A. A. Zhuralev) on Orlikov Lane. The versatile Shchusev received a prominent place with his Moscow Agriculture Commissariat designed in his constructivist manner, analogous to, if far less refined than Gordeev's Oblispolkom in Novosibirsk. His Hotel Moskva facing the Kremlin, however, presented an assumed "Americanist" style, that is, a dull, modernized classicism without orders. Unlike his agriculture commissariat, which boasted a prominent place on the journal's pages, the hotel was embarrassingly under covered, if still impossible to be bypassed. Shown to him in 1937, Wright declared, as mentioned earlier, to the inevitable embarrassment of his hosts, that this was exactly the kind of architecture he had fought against all his life in the United States.[14] He visited the building with Shchusev in person.

The September–October 1933 double issue of the journal reinforced the notion that there had been no explicit break with the 1920s. The entire section dedicated to architecture proper (the journal featured various rubrics for contemporary production, retrospectives, history, theory, art, and technology) was a commented retrospective of the Vesnin brothers' most significant work, including the 1922–1923 design for a Palace of Labor , which heralded constructivism in architecture; the pristine 1924 competition entry for the *Leningradskaja Pravda*—the "Billboard Building"; the failed Lenin Library project; the 1927 Moscow Mostorg Department Store; the still incomplete theater section of the ZIL Palace of Culture (see Chapter 2); and the modernist 1933 Defense Complex project for Moscow. Still, a certain reticence towards their work transpired as the term *constructivism* was never mentioned. All of their work was referred to as "functionalist,"

---

[12] *Arhitektura SSSR*, No. 2, August, 1933.
[13] While reading concurrently the minutes of the Politburo meetings, one is stunned by the ongoing discussions, mixing at the same meeting, "potato winter storage," "Our relationship with Great Britain," and the adoption of new *lozungi* (slogans) to be hung in the streets. RGASPI Fond 17 op 20 del 316 Feb–Dec 1930.
[14] F. L. Wright, "Architecture and Life in the USSR," *Architectural Record* (October 1937), vol. 82, no. 4, p. 61.

that is, an architecture where allegedly all that mattered was function, without concern for "aesthetics"—aesthetics understood as an a posteriori application of "art," rather than its "organic" integration, as the Vesnins and Ginzburg were soon to criticize on the journal's pages.

While the overall eminence of the opus of the brothers was highly praised, classifying it as "functionalist" was an opening for an implicit attack on their supposed embrace of "barren geometrical volumes," that is, their alleged "fetishism of the 'box.'" What was missing in their work, according to the unsigned editorial was, again, a touch of "art." Vague as it still was, a critical slant regarding the architecture of the 1920s was taking shape.

The 1935 May issue of *Arhitektura SSSR*[15] introduced yet another rubric: autobiographies of select "Masters." Moisej Ginzburg was the first invitee. His testimony was a unique occasion for the reader to witness, from within, the intimate struggle of a classically trained architect who was to become a leading world modernist. Ginzburg admitted that he tried to fit creatively into the challenges of a revolution. Choosing to highlight his past struggle with classicism, Ginzburg implicitly condemned the current state of affairs where "classical architecture" seemed to be again the *plat du jour*. Ginzburg astutely emphasized that his career "started with the 1917 Revolution," as he had just graduated from the Politécnico di Milano. He went on: "My personal growth evolved, in sync with the development of our Soviet land. The first period, between 1917 and 1921, was for me a time of internal struggle, trying to overcome the classicist education I received in Italy." In other words, it was thanks to the revolution that he had been able to overcome the hurdle of classicism, and engage on the path of the "New Architecture." Had he not done so, he would have been, he claimed, "torn away from the revolution" along with all the progress the latter implied. For Ginzburg, as he admitted, this had been a hard-won transformation. He was also saying implicitly that insistence on classicism was counterrevolutionary, to whomever wanted to hear.

Next came the 1921–1925 period, a time of accumulation of new knowledge, that is, the realization of new technical and social tasks an architect had to embrace in order to respond to the demands of a new client: the masses. These were, in his words, "the levers" that helped him rise up to the task. He also noted, modestly, how the successes of foreign masters in the West and America—such as Wright, Loos, and Le Corbusier—showed him the path to follow. He then listed the work he did during that period, which included the competition for the Palace of Labor (1922). At this stage, he was still, unlike the Vesnins, far from a properly modern language, albeit having drifted away from classicism. Interestingly, the Vesnins' entry for this same competition heralded the beginning of constructivism in architecture, manifestly under the influence of the Russian Formalists. They were awarded a third prize. Finally came the elegant Gosstrah Housing on Malaja Bronnaja Alley (1927)—his first real breakthrough into constructivism.

---

[15] *Arhitektura SSSR*, No. 5, 1935, pp. 8–12.

The third period was 1925–1932, during which he founded with the brothers Vesnin, Aleksej Gan,[16] and a few others—referring with a touch of sarcasm—"the well-known Soviet Movement—the so-called 'constructivism.'" Curiously, he did not mention either his OSA group, or his journal *SA*.

Among the collaborators he quoted for the period after 1933, glaring was the absence of Mihail Ohitovich, whom he could not mention. The latter had introduced Ginzburg in 1930 to the theory of disurbanism that Ginzburg endorsed with enthusiasm. Arrested in early 1935, Ohitovich is believed to have been shot as a "Trotskyite adventurist," almost immediately after his arrest.[17] Unable to mention Ohitovich, Ginzburg's discussion about town planning from that period remained amputated. He actually said very little of significance about his very active contribution to the theory of urban planning from 1930 to 1932.

Mordvinov, the ideologue apparatchik, had his own autobiographical essay published in the same issue, possibly to keep some kind of balance the journal had to care about.

Following the journal's established practice of publishing echoes from European developments in modern architecture, D. Arkin had an essay on Loos in December.[18] Two years later Le Corbusier's Mundaneum was greeted briefly, albeit over an entire page, and termed a "significant project."[19]

In August of the same year,[20] *Arhitektura SSSR* opened its pages to Miljutin[21] (see Chapter 1). It was a long theoretical piece on "constructivism" and "functionalism." Obviously with Ginzburg's 1925 *Style and Epoch* in mind, he claimed, "The machine appears as the origin and the culmination of constructivism."[22] Not exactly accurate with the terms he used, and historic precedents he quoted, Miljutin saw "constructivism as a trend [and a style] that originated in France with Le Corbusier, who, as its apostle [...], declared openly, to the point of cynicism, 'either constructivist architecture or revolution,' in order to attract the bourgeoisie to his architecture."

Beyond this approximate (and comic) ideologized history, toward the end of his essay Miljutin raised more interesting questions regarding the place and role of "constructivism-functionalism" under Soviet conditions. He insisted pointedly: "The

---

[16] Aleksej Gan (1893–1942), a prominent avant-garde artist, the first to respond to join the revolutionary government. He published a constructivist manifesto in 1922, in collaboration with artists Varvara Stepanova (1894–1958) and her husband Aleksandr Rodchenko (1891–1956). Gan designed the journal *SA* from its foundation in 1926 to 1930 when it was closed. He died in 1942 in a Soviet labor camp where he was sent for his anarchist past.

[17] "Trotskyite Adventurist" was *Pravda*'s title about his arrest. See also S. O. Khan-Magomedov, *Mihail Ohitovich*, Series Fond "Tvorcy Avangarda," 2009. About the tragic moments that unfolded in the last instances preceding his brutal arrest see Hugh Hudson, *Blue Prints and Blood: The Stalinization of Soviet Architecture, 1917–1937* (Princeton University Press), 1994.

[18] *Arhitektura SSSR*, No. 6, 1933, p. 15–16

[19] *Arhitektura SSSR*, No. 5, 1935, p. 56.

[20] *Arhitektura SSSR*, No. 8, 1935.

[21] About Miljutin, see Chapter 2.

[22] N. A. Miljutin, "Constructivism and Functionalism: An Essay Towards the Understanding of the Twentieth Century Architectural Movements," in *Arhitektura SSSR*, No. 8, 1935, pp. 5–10.

criticism of constructivism-functionalism [...] should not mean an outright rejection of all of its aspects [...] since the style is also the reflection of a number of achievements mandating their introduction into Soviet architecture. These are the parts of the trend that belong to an organic expression of industrialization and technical progress." In other words, by 1935 the avant-garde still had its cautious public defenders coming from within the Soviet government itself.

Five months later, Higer, now the journal's main architecture critic, had a celebratory essay on the avant-gardes, under the fitting title (not without a hint of wistfulness) "The Architecture of the Revolutionary Years."[23] Central to the article was the Vesnins' Palace of Culture, still under construction. This was the second time in less than a year that the journal reviewed the unfinished building, giving the reader a sense of extended time by making this highly anticipated constructivist masterpiece part of the current architectural discourse. The other project lavishly praised was Ginzburg's Narkomfin.[24]

The journal included on equal footing the overall architectural production regardless of the style, from modernists to classicists, but pointedly favored the avant-grades, even though with comments often tainted with ideological overtones and disclaimers for balance. In a sense, this reflected the sustained fluid ambiguity of the journal's architectural position to last at least up to 1939.

Despite an inevitable a priori political bias that mostly characterized the anonymous editorials—and, beyond restrictions and self-censorship, with essays such as I. Vercman's discussion on "Hegel and Architecture"[25] (1936) or Higer's, Arkin's, Ladovskij's,[26] Miljutin's, and Ginzburg's substantial theoretical discussions—the journal maintained a serious intellectual discourse.

As Miljutin's *Sovetskaja Arhitektura* folded the same year, the September 1934 issue of *Arhitektura SSSR*[27] published, under the title "The Masters of the Young Architecture," the profile of four architects: Leonidov with a minor design for the reconstruction of Tverskaja Boulevard (renamed "Gorky" after the writer's death), and even an image of his Palace of Culture that Mordvinov had vilified in 1930. Next to Leonidov was the avant-gardist Mihail Barshch's (1904–1976) planetarium, an icon of the second generation of constructivists (disfigured in recent years). The reviewer was Higer, who had defended Leonidov against his detractors in one of the last *SA* issues in 1930 as discussed in Chapter 1. Higer accurately detected the suprematist character of Leonidov's designs, finding them extremely attractive graphically, but inoperative architecturally. He praised nevertheless the concept of his Palace of Culture—a field with various cultural amenities, including a glass pyramid—all dynamically distributed over a landscaped park.[28] The other two "young architects" were Aleksandr Vlasov, a former constructivist, with a neo-Renaissance university building in Leningrad, a change of direction Higer called,

---

[23] *Arhitektura SSSR*, No. 11, 1935, p. 65–69.
[24] *Arhitektura SSSR*, No. 5, 1935.
[25] *Arhitektura SSSR*, No. 6, 1936 pp. 65–71.
[26] N. A. Ladovskij, "The Foundations of my Creative Work" in *Arhitektura SSSR*, No. 9, 1934, pp. 14–15.
[27] *Arhitektura SSSR* No. 9, September 1934, pp. 33–35.).
[28] See Chapter 1.

curiously, a "change in form, but not in essence." The fourth architect was Mihail Sinijavskij (1895–1979) who collaborated with Barshch on the planetarium. His was a modernized eclectic "House of the Specialists," on Gorkij Boulevard. Of the four, only Barshch's modernist project was built.

Still, while calling Leonidov a "sublime architect," Higer characterized his work as one belonging "to the extreme wing of our constructivism, that is, to the extremes of the powerful approach to art in the best tradition of the journal *Lef*"—a broad association of avant-garde leftist writers, critics, designers, and photographers, edited by Osip Brik and Vladimir Majakovskij.[29]

Featuring together four young architects, two constructivists, an "eclectic" and a newly minted "classicist," the journal projected itself as an open tribune for all the movements representing the Soviet architectural moment among the second generation. A manifest attention was paid to constructivism, if not always referring to it by name.

Leonidov reemerged with his entry to the 1934 competition for the Commissariat of Heavy Industry (Narkomtjazhprom) (see Chapter 1, Figure 1.4) on Red Square that Lissitzky sadly called "not much more than a stage set,"[30] even if acknowledging that Leonidov's project was the only one that took into consideration the architectural context—from the Saint Basil church in front of it, to the Bolshoi theater behind it. In presenting his project (each author discussed his own work), Leonidov pointed to the fact that, until then, Saint Basil and the Kremlin acted as an architectural center of Moscow. The new monumental ensemble was going to change that. In other words, Leonidov saw his project as an outgrowth of the extant historical structures, a sensible response to the call for the valorization of "architectural legacies."

In the same critical essay that he was invited to write about the Narkomtjazhprom competition projects, Lissitzky bluntly called Mel'nikov's project "dense with provincial bad taste." These assessments, justified or not, obviously belonged to a very different category than what Alabjan and his likes had been pursuing—thus pointing to the presence of a panoply of critical genres to be found in *Arhitektura SSSR*.

"Socialist Realism not yet Revealed": The Metaphysics of a Genre

With the January 1935 issue, the journal started yet another rubric dedicated to the "Masters of Architecture," mixing generations and stylistic denominations. Mel'nikov was featured first,[31] with Higer again as a reviewer. The projects included Mel'nikov's famous 1925 Soviet Pavilion in Paris; his Frunze Workers' Club (1927); the Kauchuk (1928); Rusakov (1929); and Svoboda (1930) among his most successful. His private, two

---

[29] The *LEF* (Levy Front Iskusstv or The Left Front of the Arts) had two runs: 1923–1925 as *LEF* and 1927–1929 as Novyj LEF. Rodchenko designed most of the journal's covers.
[30] *Arhitektura SSSR*, No. 10, 1934, p. 5. The projects the journal published included, besides Leonidov's and Mel'nikov's, were: I. Golosov's, the Vesnin brothers', Ginzburg's, Mel'nikov's, I. Fomin's, D. Fridman's and Fidman's.
[31] *Arhitektura SSSR*, No. 1, January 1935, pp. 31–35.

Figure 4.1 Konstantin Mel'nikov, Competition Entry for the Commissariat of Heavy Industry (NKTP), 1934. (Courtesy Shchusev Museum of Architecture)

interlocking cylinder house was also featured, and again, so was his extravagant entry to the Narkomtjazhprom (see Figure 4.1).

Higer evaluated the "Mel'nikov phenomenon" saying:

> The very name "Mel'nikov"—whom we call an innovator par excellence—sounds lordly, although not always quite reasonably. Regardless, we tend—whatever the domain of man's activity—to lionize the creators of new forms and their methods of work.[32]

After comparing his method of composition to Picasso's analytical process, as well as to Kandinsky's and to the futurist poet Velimir Hlebnikov's and Malevich's,

---

[32] Ibid. p. 30.

Higer claimed, perhaps with Cézanne in mind, that Mel'nikov would turn "every architectural thought into geometric assemblies, with his surprising Martian architectures."

Calling Mel'nikov's architectures "Martian" could seem strange. In fact, Higer most certainly had in mind the Jakov Protazanov film *Aelita Queen of Mars* (1924), whose stage sets on Mars by avant-garde artists Aleksandra Ekster and Isaac Rabinovich, served as a laboratory of forms for the architectural modernists, and more specifically for Mel'nikov's Paris Pavilion.[33] Towards the end of his essay, however, as he tackled the question of the grandomania of Mel'nikov's Narkomtjazhprom "dwarfing anything Ledoux may have imagined,"[34] he rightfully concluded that Mel'nikov had gone overboard. He put it mildly, however, claiming that "the fantastic line of development of his creative process had reached its ultimate expression. [...] There is no doubt that Mel'nikov is unique for his inventive architectural talent [...] one that merits admiration." But, what Higer felt compelled to ask was crucial:

> To what extent do these formalist dynamics fit the general trends of Soviet architecture? One does not see in it any element of socialist realism. Does Mel'nikov need to forget about his creative individualism? [...] Not at all! It would be terrible if something of the like happened. It would be sad if Soviet architecture were to deprive itself from the originality of Mel'nikov's creative talent. Socialist realism in architecture does not mean, after all, the resuscitation of the Parthenon, or of the baths of Caracalla, or else, of the Palazzo Pitti.[35]

Evidently uncertain about what "socialist" realism was or ought to be, he again, like other critics, defined it by what it was not.[36] He reasonably thought that Mel'nikov should show more "creative self-discipline," adding that "such creative self-discipline would strike a balance between what is buildable and what are just the author's inventive possibilities." To conclude, Higer had finally to admit that "in truth, *the content of socialist realism in architecture is not yet quite revealed*" [author's emphasis]. The nebulous character of the concept pointed apparently to a metaphysical realm in need of "revelation." In other words, defying logic, Higer failed to see in Mel'nikov's project "any element" of something that, actually, was not yet quite revealed.

---

[33] The tower made of triangles standing in front of Mel'nikov's Pavilion is evidently inspired by the film's tower of transparent collapsible triangles serving as an observatory that allows Martians to watch sceneries on Earth.

[34] He probably had in mind the work of Etienne-Louis Boullée rather than Ledoux's.

[35] Ibid. p. 32.

[36] In the *Great Soviet Encyclopedia*, published in Moscow between 1926 and 1947, the entry "Socialist" Realism makes no mention of architecture, as opposed to literature (two-thirds of the entry), painting, sculpture and even music ("The music has to be joyful and optimistic"), pp. 239–47.
To consult unaltered volumes of that encyclopedia, one has to seek the copy of the Library of Congress. Since it took twenty years to be completed, early entries such as "Buharin" have been censored by gluing the incriminating pages together. Since the renovation of the library a few years ago, that historic encyclopedia unfortunately has been removed without trace.

He struggled over two more paragraphs trying to point to what "realism" *was not,* in a breathless exercise in casuistry. As he contradicted himself from one sentence to another, the conclusion seemed to be that the "revelation" would still have to wait.

The intractable point was brought up at a party meeting the same month. A discussant noted that "socialist realism was brought to us from another artistic field. It did not spring from architecture [...] It's been taken from literature [...] and has not been yet deciphered [sic] in architecture, *but any party member can feel it instinctively*"[37] (author's emphasis)—a tentative discourse that boarded with religious mysticism that met Higer's "revelation." At the same party meeting, someone complained reasonably, "Here we are, saying that our architecture has to express socialism. That's very nice, but nobody says how is that architecture supposed to look like."

Arhitekturnaja Gazeta: Organ of the "Orgkomitet"

An "Orgkomitet" (or Orgkom), responsible for the organization of the congress, was composed in 1933 of a dozen of members whose names the SSA leadership had presented for approval to the Central Committee. The initially selected members were all top representatives of the avant-gardes, including: David Arkin, the architectural essayist and critic, Head of the VOKS (Government agency for foreign cultural exchanges); Viktor Vesnin (the more politically savvy of the three brothers); M. Ginzburg; I. Leonidov; N. Ladovskij; and Mihail Barhin (1906–1988), author of the *Izvestija* (headquarters in Moscow's Pushkin square). By April 25, 1935, however, a new, increasingly conservative Orgkomitet was installed, which included: V. Vesnin as Secretary; A. Shchusev (a protégé of Khrushchev's); M. Barhin; Ivan Fomin (1872–1936)—the so-called "Red Classicist"; B. Iofan; Mihail Krjukov (1884–1944), Rector of the Academy of Architecture; N. Kolli; M. Ginzburg; Leonid Chernishev (1881–1963); Ja. Aleksandrov; Ivan Maca (1894–1974), architectural historian; D. Arkin; Aleksandr Vlasov (1900–1962); Abram Zaslavskij (1892–1962); I. Zholtovskij; and K. Alabjan. The government published the names of the Orgkomitet and installed thirty-two-year-old Ja. Aleksandrov as the Committee's Secretary. The latter was also Vice-Rector of the Academy of Architecture founded in 1933. When Stalin decided in 1936 to disband the Academy as a nest of "Trotskyites," Aleksandrov was arrested and executed.[38]

The Organization Committee had a publishing organ, the *Arhitekturnaja Gazeta,* which, somewhat oddly, appeared every five days. While acting as an official journal for general consumption, *Arhitekturnaja Gazeta* was a debate forum aimed at the upcoming Congress. The magazine filtered the internal debates, even as the modernists had an unrestricted access to it. The first issue on December 30, 1934, just days after Sergej Kirov's assassination, displayed on the front page a centrally placed editorial titled "Let us Create an Architecture Worthy of the Great Era of Socialism." It was flanked on both sides with a portrait of Stalin and Kaganovich, on the left and the right of the page

---

[37] RGALI, SSA, 674, op. 2 ed. hr. 8, pp. 131–44. Meeting held on October 22, 1934.
[38] 1936. RGALI, SSA Protocol 674, op. 2 ed. hr. 7.

respectively. The column under Stalin featured well-wishers for the success of the magazine including A. Enukidze, president of the Academy of Science and Ja. Aleksandrov. More interestingly, under Kaganovich's portrait on the right column, were the responses of solicited world architects (contacted on December 11, 1934 by telegrams). The first was Frank Lloyd Wright who expressed "the hope that the Soviet architects will be successful in bringing to their country an original organic architecture. I hope that a group of young Soviet architects will join my school in Taliesin to contribute together to the progress of architecture."[39] An enthusiastic Arkin, Secretary of the VOKS, who had dispatched the solicitations, answered Wright in English (unpublished). The tone and substance of the letter grants a full quotation:

My Dear Mr. Wright,

Let me thank you from all my heart for those pleasant words of welcome you so kindly sent us on the occasion of the publication of the first issue of our *Architectural Paper*. I have already had an opportunity to tell you how greatly our architects appreciate your works and what a great regard we all have for you.

We are mailing you issue of our new magazine, containing the text of your charming telegram and we sincerely hope that in the future you will kindly continue to collaborate.[40]

Auguste Perret sent a long letter where he emphasized that "architecture [was] a collective art par excellence [...] one that proves most clearly the Marxist doctrine." But he also warned: "While socialism is the gravedigger of capitalism, it is also its inheritor." He concluded: "I wish you fraternally, dear comrades, a heartfelt success. All [the journal's] collaborators are, without any doubt, fighters for the great cause whose triumph fills me with joy."[41] Francis Jourdain compared favorably the conditions of architecture under socialism as opposed to capitalism; Karl Moser was introduced very approximately as "one of the founders of the CIRPAC, that is, as they call it—'The International Association for the New Architecture.'" Moser hoped that the new magazine would adopt a program fitting the principles of the European Neues Bauen; "a group of Danish socialist architects" was next.[42] Jaromir Krejcar's and J. J. Oud's letters were ignored. Krejcar, leader of the Czechoslovakian Union of Socialist Architects (and author of the remarkable 1937 Czechoslovakian Pavilion in Paris), promised to bring a "large delegation" to the congress, while Oud sent in German a substantial three-page skeptical, even polemical response regarding his concerns about the fate of Soviet architecture. He emphasized that, without knowing "what the policy of the magazine would be," (he was prompted only by a telegram, which put him "in a very difficult position"), he could not

---

[39] RGALI 674, op. 1 ed. hr. 8.
[40] RGALI VOKS papers 674, op. 1 ed. hr. 14.
[41] Quoted in the *Gazeta*, December 12, 1934, RGALI 674 op. 1 ed. 8.
[42] See the first issue of the *Arhitekturnaja Gazeta* No. 1 Moscow, December 30, 1934, p. 1. Krejcar announced a large delegation to the congress.

take a stance vis-à-vis the new publication. "It is difficult to ascertain what is today the leading line of Soviet architecture." He ended saying that if the magazine was to endeavor its efforts to "reclaim an architecture that would be both contemporary regarding construction and contemporary in its aesthetic expression [which seems not to be the case anymore in Russia], then I would say in the introduction to the first issue of your magazine that I welcome it with all my heart."[43] Le Corbusier was apparently avoided, possibly due to the public controversy regarding his just completed Centrosojuz.

The invitation, sent in the form of sketchy telegrams to specific architects soliciting their support of the *Gazeta*, seemed to be primarily one of the tests the Soviets used to gage the attitude the major world architects had versus the Soviet Union, especially after the debacle of the Palace of Soviets.

The magazine's first editorial referred to Soviet modern architecture, highlighting that "our constructivists fought correctly for the implementation of contemporary building systems and materials, but in so doing they impoverished the arsenal of means and forms used in architectural craftsmanship."[44] This could be overcome by paying more attention to architecture's "historical legacy." With that, the journal's editors laid down the central issue of the decade's discourses: "architecture should not exist in a historic and contextual void." The controversy would take place primarily in *Gazeta*'s regular rubric, titled "Pre-Congress Discussion Tribune."

Other discussion vehicles on the topic were the regular SSA's "Creative meetings" (Tvorcheskie Soveshchanija) about the place of history in contemporary architectural expression. These consultations would ultimately become a platform aimed at recuperating the younger modern-oriented architects—the so-called "former constructivists"—through prescribed "creative self-criticism."[45] The difficulty of such "reeducation" (which attempted to include the avant-garde's leaders themselves) forced the congress—initially scheduled for the fall 1933—to be postponed six times.[46] It was finally to start on June 15, 1937.

"Liberated Creation"

One year after Kaganovich had created the twelve Moscow architectural workshops (the ARHPLAN Masterskie)—almost half of which were headed by the leaders of the avant-

---

[43] RGALI, VOKS, 674 op. 1 ed. hr. 14.
[44] Op. cit., p. 1.
[45] For a rich and elaborate discussion of the debates about the meaning of the Soviet "Historic Legacy" as a productive concept, see the dissertation by Richard Anderson, "The Future of History: The Cultural Politics of Soviet Architecture, 1928–1941," Columbia University, 2010.
[46] First scheduled for fall 1933, the congress was moved to a year later. On September 26, 1935 it was rescheduled to March 1, 1936; on March 11, 1936, alleging the need to give time to the architects to study the new constitution, it was moved to November 15 of the same year; and finally, in April 1937 it was moved to June 15, 1937 when the congress finally took place. RGALI, SSA, 674 op. 2 ed. hr. 4. This situation was particularly embarrassing since each deadline was officially published in the *Pravda* by Molotov, the Prime Commissar of the SNK (Government).

gardes—see previous chapter—the journal launched a survey calling on their respective principals. The question was to assess the value of the new ARHPLAN system.

The responses of twelve Masterskie leaders, including Mel'nikov, Ladovskij, Shchusev, Kolli, Krutjikov, the Vesnins, Ginzburg, and others, were critically affirmative. Ginzburg, who never minced his words, responded with a bold heading, "Liberated Creation."[47] Its significance calls for a longer quote of Ginzburg's actual words, which clearly convey sincerity that always characterized his public utterances. He forcefully praised the new system.

> The work of the architect and the results of the Mossovet's Masterskie have reached *enviable social and creative heights*. Instead of the messy work that described *all previous years of architectural production*, we have achieved an atmosphere of *genuine creativity* [author's emphasis]. This resulted in the first place in a heightened demand from the architect; second it changed the character of the designer's relationship to the commissioner. The prerevolutionary attitude toward design as a sort of idiosyncratic "merchandise," which the client had to pay as an honorarium, survived in the first years after the revolution.
>
> Now, with the new design institutions, and the socialized demand for projects, all understand that a design is the result of an artistic creation, which is not valued in monetary terms. This means that the project is not supposed to please the subjective taste of this or that client, but rather to reflect the objective needs of our city planning, that is, the architectural needs of our environment.

Most significantly, he went as far as comparing favorably the Masterska n. 3 he was responsible for in the ARHPLAN system with his own defunct OSA, "which I am identified with, and have worked successfully with under the State Strojkom, planning the southern shore of the Crimea."[48] Ginzburg's only complaint was the rigid separation between the Masterskie, so that an artificial gap was created between planning and architectural design. He overcame this difficulty by establishing an informal "productive relationship" with the Masterska n. 8 lead by the Vesnins. The two complemented each other to mutual benefit.

In other words, he had recreated the positive aspects of his former OSA, while taking advantage of "new creative possibilities" offered by the new system. This was, actually, the beginning of a de facto reinstatement of a "*gruppirovka*" such as existed before the April 1932 dissolution. This and other informal working groups lasted, to the architecture party's chagrin, for most of the decade.[49]

The optimistic description Ginzburg gave of the new system was certainly reflected in the way the underground Metro was built. The competitive independence of the various Mossovet workshops, with no other client but the public interest, resulted in the clearest

---

[47] See *Arhitektura SSSR*, No. 9, September 1934, pp. 15–16.
[48] Orgkomitet Protocol, 647, op. 2 ed. hr. 66, pp. 158ob. p. 159.
[49] The issue was raised repeatedly in meetings up to the start of the congress.

case of avant-garde survival and revival in the 1930s. Under the inexorable growth of a totalitarian police state, architecture miraculously preserved its freedom—for a while.

On August 27, 1935, two years into the founding the ARHPLAN, a frustrated Alabjan sent a letter to its presidium, with his opinion about the leaders of the Masterskie. Several leaders " had not been up to the task." These included "Mel'nikov, Ladovskij, and a few others." Among those who, in Alabjan's view, had performed well were, not surprisingly, "Vlasov, Chechulin, Mordvinov, Gol'ts, and their likes." All of them had adopted some form of reactionary eclecticism. Still, Alabjan was not critical of Ginzburg's and the Vesnins' Masterskie. They were in some ways still untouchable.

The Enduring Principles of the Constructivists: A Reconsideration

Back in February 1934 *Arhitektura SSSR*[50] had opened its pages to V. Vesnin, A. Vesnin, (Leonid had recently died), and Ginzburg under the journal's rubric "Creative Tribune." This was a text of particular importance, even if it inevitably rehearsed some self-evident claims. The aim was to set up clearly the principles the leaders of the avant-garde defended, two years after the fateful 1932 dissolution decree. The essay came on the heels of endless debates that populated the meetings of the union, and those of the party, in search of a "uniquely Soviet" architecture, accessible to the proletariat. Five months later, at their own congress, the writers were to come up with a new literary genre they would christen "socialist" realism.[51] The SSA party cell, which always operated through secret meetings, but considered itself to be the proletariat's historically legitimized leader, desperately tried to give an architectural definition of "socialist" realism. It never happened.[52] More to the point was the search for ways to soften and transcend "plain and boxy constructivism," or else, how to turn the pumpkin into a carriage.

The two Vesnins and Ginzburg, therefore, started their article in *Arhitektura SSSR* with the remark that:

> It's been a very long time since we spoke about architecture. In the meanwhile, a string of critics—the so-called "former functionalists"—managed, under the guise of "self-criticism" of their own "former" ideology to attribute to us a wealth of sins and transgressions with a very cavalier attitude.

The avant-garde leaders went on claiming that much had changed in their own position regarding architecture. They were therefore going to raise some essential

---

[50] *Arhitektura SSSR*, No. 2, 1934, pp. 63–69.
[51] See *Problems of Soviet Literature: Reports and Speeches at the First Soviet Writers Congress* ed. H. G. Scott, with Speeches by A. Zhdanov, Maxim Gorky, N. Bukharin, K. Radek, A, Stetsky (Moscow-Leningrad: Cooperative Publishing Society of Foreign Workers in the USSR) 1935.
[52] In fact, as we shall see, at the congress Alabjan improvised, *en désespoir de cause*, the Soviet Pavilion in Paris as the epitome of the style.

theoretical points, starting with the much-vaunted "assimilation of the historical legacy." But they first had to ask: "Which legacy? No one ever raised that question."

With a touch of sarcasm, they asked if the legacy their critics had in mind was the "Islamic legacy, Chinese, Japanese, or Indian perhaps?" And went on citing the multitude of other possible legacies where European history was concerned. "Gothic maybe?" they asked sardonically.

Without saying it, there was obviously a problem as the only "legacy" in Russia were the Byzantine-derived churches or traditional izbas, the former not exactly suited to socialism, while the latter already considerably exploited before the revolution.

Then, in inevitably didactic terms, they turned to the thirty-year-long development of the European New Architecture (Neue Bauen), which was directly connected, they claimed, to the current architectural situation in Russia. They had an alternative to propose; if legacy was to be considered, one should take into consideration the entire history of architecture, "from the primitive hut to the stratospheric balloons" of their own day, insisting that this approach should not be limited to architecture proper, but to include all of the great cultural and artistic achievements in history.

They submitted further that, obviously, what was usually understood without being said was that the "legacy" in question was the "so-called classical Greco-Italian architecture." They thus turned to the nineteenth century, "the century of science" when the incongruence between "classical architecture" and progressive scientific and technical achievements of the time became evident—"thus the wakeup call of the American Frank Lloyd Wright, the Austrian Loos, the German Gropius, the French Le Corbusier, and the Dutch Oud." However, they went on astutely, "due to the social condition capitalism imposed on Europe and America [they no doubt had in mind the Great Depression], further evolution of the New Architecture got itself into a dead end."

That modern architecture had run itself into a "blind alley in capitalist countries" due to capitalism's limitations, and that it could be developed further only in socialist Russia. If an astute a subterfuge, it did not convince many. During a party meeting someone derided the stance, by asking, "Are we supposed to believe that Le Corbusier is a martyr of capitalism?" Another interpretation of Vesnin's claim, was raised by the same discussant: "Le Corbusier gave us a formula about how to integrate historic and cultural data into a contemporary expression. So why try to reinvent the wheel?"[53]

To successfully deal with this "dead end," the essay's authors proposed that two essential conditions be satisfied: first, to raise the cultural level of the architect; and, second, to understand the "mechanics" through which architecture is generated. If the first part were accomplished, the educated architect would know how to understand what were the particular circumstances, political, economic, and otherwise that led to specific architectural solutions in the past. "For example," they proceeded, "if we compare the Athenian Acropolis to the gardens of Versailles or to the Shah-i-Zinda in Samarkand, we may want to understand why and how did each specific solution come about."

---

[53] RGALI, Party Protocol, 674, op. 2, ed. hr. 8, p. 128.

The authors then undertook an elaborate analysis of the lessons an architect would need to have in mind while seeking new, contemporary responses, which was not the same as copying the forms. At this juncture, probably to satisfy the expected "self-criticism,"[54] but more so to further press their point, they admitted that this kind of methodology had been insufficiently used in their own Masterskie over the last ten years, obviously drafting an uninterrupted line of design and research from 1925 to 1935—as if there had never been any April 23, 1932. First, they did not deny the paramount need to take to heart the historical precedents as useful lessons for contemporary architecture, and see how it would contribute to "proletarian architecture," taking as an analogy the way Marx derived materialist philosophy from Hegel's idealist system. It thus mattered to take into account what were the "endless necessities and demands of many millions of proletarians and farm laborers." The three constructivists, however, insisted that those could not be "primitive fulfillments of needs." What was necessary was to find and build a "new organism," sanctioned socially as a precondition of what could be called "a new architectural organism."

Second, the authors insisted on the role of science and technology, of new inventions and discoveries that created a powerful environment of their day. Architecture had the chance to go through untold transformations. It was thus clear that the stratospheric probes and the conquest of the Arctic, remote as they may appear, exerted an indubitable influence on the building trades.

They went on listing specific new technical and technological innovations directly applicable to architecture, "which could not be ignored." They pointed to the fact that in ancient Greece or in the Renaissance, architects were always abreast with the latest scientific knowledge. They went on citing Vitruvius, Alberti, Da Vinci, and others. They maintained that classical architecture reached such a level of perfection, because it was practiced, among others, by the cultural avant-garde of their time. "Today, of course, our task has to be posited differently. It is evident that we cannot keep in mind all the scientific achievements of our day [...]. So, an adapted methodology has to be found, to balance correctly current social needs with the possibility of fulfilling them architecturally." This should require a method that would allow "a full deployment of the architect's creative forces, and at the same time be open to the complexities and enrichments current circumstances [could] provide."[55]

So, the method in their view, should not be built on contradictions, but on the "organic" fusion between the goal, the means, and the architectural form; between the content and the form, calling it a "creative functional method." Having defined the method, they turned to "the creative tasks ahead of us."

They introduced the concept of type, that is, "type understood as a continuous refinement of the social demand [...] since well-understood typization is one of the

---

[54] Self-criticism was encoded in the Stalinist ethics as a way, not unlike religious "confession" practices, to stay in line with the party dominant claim of the moment, that is, to "regain the party's confidence." The practice spilled into the general behavior of other organizations.
[55] RGALI, Party Protocol, 674, op. 2, ed. hr. 8, p. 63.

most interesting social and architectural tasks, whose solution is the closest there is to the new proletarian architecture."

This stance reflected exactly the work Ginzburg had undertaken in 1926, while intensely involved in refining and building house-communes for mass production, such as the Narkomfin on Moscow's Novinskij boulevard. The research and practice, as we remember from the first chapter, was abruptly terminated by a Central Committee decree in 1930, followed by the closure of his own journal *SA*. In 1934, Ginzburg was publishing, at Gosstroizdat press, his seminal book *Zhilishche* (*Abode*), which reminisced and summed up the results of five years of experimenting with dwelling types around the country. The main challenge was how to achieve mass production without lowering the architectural quality.

The article further pointed to the importance of treating the issue in a holistic manner. This would help understand the interconnectedness between architectural elements, through distillation of ideas, that is, where one architectural solution would replace another through dialectical interaction. This, they claimed, was not possible in the West with such levels of complexity.

As they continued listing what was impossible to achieve "in the West," one remains wondering if they could have been unaware of ongoing large-scale urban experiments in social democratic countries; or if that was just a smart subterfuge used preemptively to protect their position from being dismissed a priori as "bourgeois."[56] This might have explained why their essay was, surprisingly, resuscitating the category of "proletarian architecture," long fallen into disuse as a programmatic battle cry.

They concluded highlighting what they saw as a comparative advantage of the Soviet Union where, besides "the large-scale building campaigns specific to our country, and the absence of private developers and private landowners," made the whole difference.

The next issue at stake was the "synthesis of architecture," that is, the union of architecture and nature on one hand, and art on the other. This encompassed the need to know when architecture complements nature and when it contradicts it. They listed different cases in point, addressing in particular the role of color. Ginzburg, who had been closely studying the psychological effects of color on the users of his Narkomfin, in collaboration with Bauhaus pedagogue Hinnerk Scheper, was certainly the prime contributor to this segment of the text.[57] From there, the article engaged in a long discussion of color and its transformative effects on space.

Finally they addressed the "synthesis of art and architecture." They rejected the way it was usually understood in Russia "as an addition to the building, of a bas-relief or a sculpture, like a postal stamp on a letter." Such approach was to be rejected. "The synthesis of architecture and art," they stated, "presupposes very difficult interactions between the artist and the architect, which may not always be possible."

---

[56] In a speech to the Central Committee, Kaganovich derided the Vienna Karl Marx Hoff for being heated with stoves, while the Soviet workers, he claimed, enjoyed central heating.
[57] See Alla G. Vronskaya "Invisible Colors: The Narkomfin House-Painting Experiment." In *Narkomfin, Moisej J. Ginzburg, Ignatij F. Milinis*, O'NFM_6, ed. Danilo Udovički (Austin/Berlin, Tubingen: Center for American Architecture and Design/Ernst Wasmuth Verlag) 2016.

They suggested that such synthesis could be found most easily in historic architecture. They smartly took as an example the medieval Palazzo della Signoria and Michelangelo's David set in front of it. This association "contrasted the pristine whiteness of one with the dark ruggedness of the other." Given the accidental juxtaposition of the two, made independently in different eras, and in the absence of any a priori organic connections, what the authors were saying implicitly was that well-understood architecture should be self-sufficient, and that any synthesis with sculpture could happen authentically only a posteriori, not without deepening the understanding of both in the process. While not saying it explicitly, they had just touched on the essence of the constructivist method, one that distinguished their modern architecture from the West European. This was of course the principle of "estrangement" (*ostranenie*) that sought an "excess of meaning" in the association of contrasting semantic series, as posited by the Russian formalists, best exemplified in the new Soviet cinema.[58] This is why, when speaking about his Narkomfin, Ginzburg used the term "montage," while rejecting explicitly the word "building."

After bringing up other examples, including Pallas Athena on the Acropolis, as well as the triangular tympanum of the Parthenon, they concluded that a synthesis couldn't be achieved by filling empty places on an architectural work. The correct response was to seek intersections between two independent creative lines that reinforced each other through contrast.

Continuing their slalom between the voluntarist, artificial obstacles the current discourse on historicism imposed, they finally reached their last point:

How to value the architect's creative range.

> This issue demands in the first place a sense of measure. In our country, however, these questions are understood in an elementary way: how to get in more sculptures, how to achieve greater bombast, how to pack it with more angles. One should not forget for a single instant that wise creative restraint is one of the most valuable and precious characteristics of the artist (of course avoiding asceticism, skimpiness).

The parentheses above were needed here to ward off any association with "boxy architecture," an expedient term used ubiquitously to denigrate modern architecture.

> This wise creative restraint is the attribute of the best architectural monuments of our and past epochs. But, of course, one has to understand that our Soviet architecture emerged when we were poor to the extreme."

The country was richer now, allowing for a greater field of opportunities and more sophisticated design, warning however that here too a measure had to be found, wisely balancing the economic and the artistic.

---

[58] See the early films of Sergej Eisenstein, or even more to the point, Dziga Vertov's films such as "Man with a Movie Camera" (1929).

Evidently, these concluding remarks were a final effort to protect themselves from numerous lurking Scylla and Charybdis of the current uncertain architectural climate, while they tried to convey the essence of their modernist credo, without provoking immediate rejection or negative characterization.

The SSA Party Cell vs. the Avant-Gardes: "An Uphill Battle"

As revealed at the party meeting of February 8, 1934—close to two years after the April 23, 1932 decree—the All-Soviet Union of Architects (the SSA) existed beyond Moscow only in name.[59] This considerably complicated the preparation of the congress. The situation was no better among the ranks of communists around the country, prompting the Moscow Department of Culture and Propagation of Leninism to undertake an inquiry from Georgia to Armenia, to Siberia, the Urals, and Leningrad.[60]

The findings were devastating. At times, the local party organization did not even know for sure how many members they had, while interpersonal relationships were called "unhealthy." The excuse was: "Well, in Moscow you have Kaganovich." Reporting from Baku, Mordvinov mentioned that even party *chistkas* (cleansings or arrests) of the party ranks had been taking place. It is difficult to know if chaos prompted the *chistkas*, or if the *chistkas* were actually the cause of the chaos—probably both.

In Moscow, matters were hobbling no less. The constant postponements of the congress created an embarrassing situation since each term was officially scheduled and rescheduled in the form of government decrees, which the Prime People's Commissar and Politburo member Vjacheslav Molotov, published in the press.

On top of regularly corresponding with Alabjan—his man from the old VOPRA he helped create in 1929—Kaganovich would even get involved in the SSA party meetings. This was the case of the September 27, 1934 meeting.[61] In his speech to the members he went over the topics and papers to be presented at the congress. What was at stake was the recalcitrant "mobilization of the public opinion of architects," that is, the serious difficulties the *partgruppa* (the party cell) experienced in conjuring not only the avant-garde's leaders into cooperation, but even the communists themselves.

There was a concern that only the constructivists would speak at the congress, or else that only the "leaders" (the communists) would be taking the floor, while the nonparty people would remain silent, a cause for major embarrassment in both cases. And, if no communists were to speak at the congress, as Kaganovich noted, that would considerably decrease the significance of the event.[62]

More importantly, in his address Kaganovich further recommended that, if party members were to criticize the constructivists at the congress, they should do it with

---

[59] RGALI, SSA, Party Protocol, Fond 674, op. 2 ed. hr. 7.
[60] "Otdel Kultury i Propagandy Leninizma: Kratkaja Zapiska o Soveshchanija s Svjazi Sezda Arhitektorov" Moscow, October 21, 1934, pp. 56–59. 647, op. 2 ed. hr. 11.
[61] RGALI, SSA, Party Protocol 674, op. 2ed. hr. 7 (1), pp. 47–50.
[62] RGALI, SSA, Party Protocol, 674, op. 2 ed. hr. 7 (1), p. 48.

moderation, because "the constructivists have housed millions around the country, and will build for millions more." Remarkably, he claimed: "We should not limit ourselves to one single approach to architecture. *We are not going to determine a style by decree* [author's emphasis], but we still should fight against nudism in architecture,"[63] which he also called "nihilism."

Beyond that, whether architects would use orders or not, he insisted, the decision belonged to them. "We should not make a fetish out of the orders." At the same time, somewhat contradicting himself, he suggested that "we have to create our own type of order." This was obviously what Alabjan attempted to do for the Red Army Theater with his pseudo-Corinthian orders, branded with hammers and sickles and columns shaped as five-pointed stars in section. "Architecture," Kaganovich went on, "should be simple but not simplistic." This was a significant distinction in Kaganovich's utterances: Modernism was not banned per se. What was offensive was "vulgar schematism." In other words, he dismissed "box-like architecture," but not, a priori, more complex constructivism.[64] Rather, Kaganovich would add, "like classicism: grandiose in its simplicity. Baroque should be rejected. We need basic, decent homes. [...] The task of the day is to build structures that are literate, simple, and beautiful." The constructivists could have hardly disagreed, but for a stumbling detail: what did "beautiful" mean, and who would have the power of verdict? In the case of the Metro stations, as we saw it, Kaganovich was consistent: he left it to the architects, and pluralism thrived.[65]

Stalin's man faced the Communist leadership of the SSA with remarkable flexibility. He seemed evidently more open-minded than the very architects he was addressing—the leadership at least.

At the same time, ambiguities abounded. So, among the topics he inanely considered "necessary" at the congress, was "to launch a debate on specific architectural details such as 'the column,' 'the pilaster,' 'the ceiling,' 'the cornice,'" further revealing his personal taste in architecture. Introducing marble was also recommended.[66] And finally, some Marxism would not hurt: a paper on the "dialectical evolution of styles" was advisable. Ignorance and pragmatism laced with limitless power were ominous ingredients, despite good intentions.

Beyond his buoyancy, Kaganovich wisely recommended the members not to get carried away by too much optimism.[67] They could not expect to replicate the triumphs of the recent writers' congress, "where we have Bolsheviks of Maxim Gorkij's stature.[68] Unlike the case with the writers, we do not have prestigious architects who are also party

---

[63] RGALI, SSA, 674, op. 2 ed. hr. 7 (1). p. 49.
[64] At this point, constructivist and "modern architecture" were conflated.
[65] Indicative of his own openness is that he took the visiting Anthony Eden to the most rigorously abstract and monochromatic subway station by the young Dushkin as discussed in the previous chapter.
[66] This probably explains why the brothers Vesnin covered the wavy, liquid interior of the Palace of Culture with awkward segments of marble—an obvious afterthought that granted the Vesnins' architecture a place in the pantheon of "Soviet" architecture.
[67] RGALI, SSA, 674, op. 2 ed. hr. 7 (1).
[68] Kaganovich also listed Panferov, [Aleksandr] Fadeev (1901–1956) and Serafimovich (1863–1949).

members. [...] Besides, he went on, the Marxist literature is much poorer on architecture than on other disciplines."[69]

Alabjan, however, had his own agenda. No doubt piqued by Kaganovich's remark, if he was not a "prestigious communist architect," he might achieve prestige by other means. His stance did not differ significantly from the times of VOPRA, where the issue was less about architecture than about the preponderance in the field. The privileged political position he created for himself thereafter would help. Architecture per se was not his prime concern.

At the November 4 joint party meeting (with Ukrainian and Leningrad delegates),[70] he admitted that *"reining in the constructivists will be an uphill battle [...]. For the moment we are [just] dealing with generalities [...]. Everybody is working well, but the struggle ahead will be tough."*

Toward the end of 1934 (document not dated), Alabjan produced what were supposed to be excerpts from Kaganovich's plans for the event:

"Regarding the issue of style, what is necessary is to engage a serious research into its origins, and its nature. *We are not against classicism, but we reject its fetishization* [author's emphasis]. We have to ground ourselves on socialist realism, which rejects copying or reproducing forms. *We have to criticize the constructivists, but we have to insist on their positive sides* [author's emphasis]."

In conclusion, the typical paper needed to have:

One: A historic overview.

Two: Our Marxist approach to the criticism of philistinism.

Three: Address to which degree we should apply a historic style in our architecture, followed finally, by five to eight principled positions.[71]

Obviously going beyond Kaganovich's recommendations, what Alabjan wanted to prevent at all costs were dissonant statements and unexpected controversial outbursts at the congress because, as he put it in a nutshell: "The constructivists want to come out as an offended side."[72]

He finished haltingly: "The struggle will be difficult, but we should not fear it. We just need to counterbalance them. We need, as Communists, to be able to counter them." And finally, he had to reconcile himself with the fact that "the preparation of the congress is obviously a great challenge." The stakes were high, as Alabjan concluded: "The coming Congress of architects is of enormous importance for the Central Committee, and for

---

[69] RGALI, SSA, 674, op. 2 ed. hr. 7 (1), p. 30.
[70] RGALI, 674, op. 2 ed. hr. 1. Party meeting, November 4, 1934, with delegates from Ukraine and Leningrad party organizations.
[71] RGALI, SSA, Partgruppa 674 op. 2 ed. hr. 11 pp. 66–68, Fall 1934.
[72] RGALI 674, op. 2 ed. hr. 1. Party meeting, November 4, 1934.

Kaganovich personally. [...] The architects, members of the Communist Party, bear a huge responsibility for setting it up. To do so, it is important to have a consensus about ways to draw-in the large masses of nonparty architects." This was actually an implicit admission that architects at large still adhered to modern architecture. Fearing "uncontrolled outpouring" of support for constructivism—a very real possibility—he added, "It is our duty to be vigilant about each of their speeches."[73] There was a danger that the leaders of the avant-garde and their supporters, could predictably electrify architects from all over the country.

That rank-and-file architects were still adepts of modern architecture in their vast majority was soon to be revealed at the Congress.

The alternative that the SSA party cell tried to impose, in an act of pure voluntarism, was an unconvincing, ideologized, and ill-articulated architectural program, grounded in an undefined "cultural and historical legacy." A way to overcome it was to keep organizing the mentioned "tvorcheskie soveshchanija" or "creative counselling" that in practice resulted in brainwashing sessions of skeptics under the guise of "self-criticism." Ironically, the proponents of such amorphous architectural concepts, tinged with historicism, were themselves unable to say what such architecture would be, beyond vacuous phraseology.[74]

Following suit, a Ukrainian delegate announced that they would have "a paper on the tasks Soviet architects should perform," a demand for "unity" being paramount. This unity should, actually, be "the red thread traversing all of the papers at the congress." He also warned meekly that it would be a problem to have one paper devoted exclusively to the issue of unity, since "doing so would leave the impression that we actually do not have that unity, or else that unity is difficult to achieve," which actually was the case, to his misfortune.

The bête noire at all the party meetings were, relentlessly, the modernists. As Alabjan remarked, "The group around Ginzburg, Vesnin and Shchusev evidently wants to turn the congress into a platform for the dissemination of their own architectural views, to turn the congress into a meeting of their various factions. We cannot allow this." And he went on offering some unfortunate examples of the recalcitrant constructivists. Aleksandr Vesnin, for example was "against allowing government economic organizations to influence the projects, as he deems them incompetent." In other words, "they do not want the proletarian state to have an influence on the growth and development of architecture. [...] Ginzburg, for his part," Alabjan continued, "considers that the main topic of the Congress should be treated by several speakers. He wants to distract the attention from delving into our current concerns, and transform it into a stage for the dissemination of his own ideas. We already spoke with them about these issues, and they formally recognized their errors; but the tendency to form a separate block persists."

The conundrum of the situation was, on the other hand, that the avant-garde masters could not be simply ignored. "*We cannot just reject this group* [author's emphasis]." It was

---

[73] Each speech meant for the congress, had to be sent a month in advance, and scrutinized by the Orgkomitet.
[74] RGALI, 674, op. 2 ed. hr. 8, p. 131.

therefore imperative to compel them "to work with us immediately, through our sustained efforts." Alabjan knew very well that the avant-garde had still a significant influence among the members of the profession; and that any openly articulated argument against the Party's wishes would be massively supported. As a delegate from the Ukraine put it in the same party meeting, "We need unity in the implementation of a socialist style, framed ideologically by socialist realism." He did not elaborate.

The obvious problem was, as it transpired from the discussions, that, again, no one, its proponents included, quite knew what that "realism" was supposed to be. Nor, as was explicitly admitted at the December 19 joint meeting with Komsomol' representatives, what was the meaning of the vaunted "historic legacy"; let alone "what that eclecticism [was] supposed to be," as an attendant to the meeting remarked. Another member exclaimed: "We are speaking in favor of a 'cultural legacy' whose meaning we still have not figured out ourselves [*my sami eshchoj ne razobralis*]."[75] The evident absurdity of the situation, for all to see at the party meeting, did not facilitate Alabjan's pernicious efforts.

Alabjan was clear that this was also a widespread sentiment among the Komsomols, that is, the new generation of Communist architects. The attachment to modern architecture was tenacious and had no logical reason to be otherwise. Evidently, the nebulous alternative was professed for reasons other than the interest of architecture itself.

With Kaganovich looming over him, Alabjan went on critiquing the party organizations around the country, whose members did not consider that taking an active part in the preparation of the congress was their party duty—"a task that should always be on the mind of a Bolshevik."[76] His political career hinged on the success of the congress, meaning a dull, uneventful display of endless consonant monologues. The secretary of the Orgkomitet, Aleksandrov, and a party leader on par with Alabjan, protested that this "separatist group" (allegedly supported by Ginzburg, Andrej Burov,[77] and A. Vesnin), complained that, "*Soviet architecture was being eaten away by a gangrene* [author's emphasis]."[78] He pretended that such claim was not "fortuitous," as he tried to confront it to the treacherous grounds of Stalin's "Revolution from Above." In keeping with Stalin's fictitious class struggle, Aleksandrov held that "architecture is [also] a field of class struggle. The enemy tries to undermine our system with whatever means available, while hiding behind various colors. Burov is a typical chameleon, while others quietly conceal their subversive work."[79]

---

[75] Party meeting November 19, 1934. RGALI, 674, op. 1 ed. hr. 8 (1), pp. 23–107.
[76] December 7, 1934 SSA Party meeting. RGALI, 674, op. 1 ed. hr. 8 (1), pp. 2–18ob.
[77] Andrej Burov, of Leonidov's generation, was a brilliant constructivist architect who worked on stage sets for Eisenstein's *The General Line*. He ultimately adapted his architecture to the new demand, as he built several significant housing projects in downtown Moscow. Ambitious, he appears on every picture of Le Corbusier in Moscow. He was also known for his advocacy of architecture in public speeches, a rarity among Soviet architects, according to Khan-Magomedov.
See Khan-Magomedov, *Andrej Burov*. Series *Tvorci Avangarda* (Moscow), 2012.
[78] RGALI 674, op. 1 ed. hr. 8 (1), pp. 2–18ob.
[79] RGALI 674, op. 1 ed. hr. 2 (1).

The incessant Party meetings, between 1934 and early 1937, dealing, as we saw, for the most part with the preparation of the Congress, were devoted to ways of convincing the leading modernists to abandon their cause.

Yet obviously, the constructivist leaders were not the union's party leadership sole concern. Much more serious was the passive resistance of the rank-and-file party members who simply were not there to help. This specifically concerned the Komsomols. As one discussant at the October joint meeting with the Communist youth declared, "Whether a Kolli will join us or not, is not such an issue. We know he will. I am much more worried about the passivity of the party members; they do not come to the meetings of the union; when you ask them for help, they all have an excuse to avoid it. Besides, our communists do absolutely nothing to raise the young cadres."[80]

Alarmed, another discussant recounted that some Komsomol members reported to their workshop masters all that was said about the masters in secret party meetings. No less bewildering was to learn that in Fridman's Masterska, the nonparty members had the upper hand over the communists. The latter did not play a leading role even in theoretical discussions about Marxism. "And yet, here we are, supposed to be the vanguard, to play a leading role and be theoretically well-prepared [...]. Comrades, Lazar Mojseevich [i.e., Kaganovich] and Aleksandrov have to equip us in concrete ways for us to be actual leaders in our professional struggle."[81] The absurdity and artificiality of the assumed struggle of the "vanguard" could not have been revealed in more comic and infantile ways.

The younger generation's attachment, party members or not, to its avant-garde leaders, was only logical. They were architects before anything else, and many had been educated by masters of Aleksandr Vesnin's stature. As young party members and architects they were clear that what was being forced onto them was "counterrevolutionary," as Leonidov uttered it at some point in public. Such perception was voiced at ordinary party meetings as well. Alabjan and his likes would triumph at the congress if they succeeded in leveling everyone's speech into mindless mechanical responses, as a wild animal tamer would do. This was, in addition, even out of step with Kaganovich's pragmatic call for spontaneous diversity, but the only way to achieve preponderance and power.

On October 22, 1934,[82] at yet another party meeting, Aleksandrov distributed a list of tasks to be accomplished; the speakers expanded on them in support or disagreement. The persistent issue was how to formulate the new "Soviet" architectural program, and more importantly, how to bend the avant-garde masters into accepting this yet undefined, artificially produced, and purely voluntarist trend, marred in vicious circles.

As in VOPRA times, when the main topic was the never-explained "proletarian" architecture, what was now more important than finding a viable definition for it was simply to silence any discord. The avant-garde resisted. Its force was in their intelligently articulated credo, their unassailable reputation in Russia and abroad, and in particular,

---

[80] RGALI 674, op. 2 ed. hr. 2 (1).
[81] RGALI 674, op. 2 ed. hr. 8.
[82] RGALI, Party Protocol 674, op. 2 ed. hr. 8, p. 131.

because the avant-garde still commanded the most important Masterskie. Therefore, they had not only a considerable control over the architectural production, but attracted the best among the younger generation. That force was translated most visibly in the campaign for the Metropoliten, as seen in the previous chapter.

As a party member at the October 22, 1934 meeting emphasized, "The party has reminded us[83] that we had started limping because we have forgotten what is of essence. We are engaged in a historic undertaking in our struggle against the constructivists. [In their own defense] the latter are beginning to use a 'radical-left' (*levizm'*) phraseology."[84] "They say, 'Here are your Shchusevs and your Fomins[85] with their dark hallways, and unfit restrooms.' They assume the stance of a Demosthenes, a stance such as 'Haven't we warned you?' Then they charge back with their 'functionalism,' which they claim to be serving the working class."[86]

Gradually, the term "socialist" realism, which had replaced "proletarian architecture," was now becoming simply "Soviet architecture," a less demanding categorization, but also one that reflected a Soviet Union that had become a one directional, cemented establishment away from the revolution. This only moderately ideological and apparently fluid designation made things seemingly easier, while actually masking the opposite: a more hermetic, unassailable position, fitting the growing totalitarian environment.

As another speaker observed, some of the old masters, such as Shchusev, were beginning to join them. "So are Kolli and Ginzburg, but with them we have a different situation: They are changing their attitude only in words; their orthodoxy stands in the way of their transformation. They cannot get rid of their prophetic demagoguery. We have to help them;[87] and make sure to snatch them away from the camp of our opponents."

While most architects spontaneously rejected what they called "eclecticism," not all present at meetings were unequivocally in favor of using classicism as a "cultural legacy." One of the attendants of the next December 19, 1934 meeting[88] challenged Aleksandrov's adamant dedication to classicism with an insightful logic: "Comrade Aleksandrov tells us that classicism is the best response to, and the most consonant one with, our times. I disagree with that. Is it really necessary to emphasize that classicism is part of the superstructure of a slave-bound society? This style proved to be a strong, interesting, and serious architectural trend. But we need to put some limits to such legacy, or else we easily can find ourselves in the company of rather reactionary circles." In addition, he was disturbed that so little if anything, was said about "what is new today. *What did our own*

---

[83] "The party," as in this case, was referred to as if a metaphysical entity, dwelling in a sphere of its own separate from the membership.
[84] In existent in English the best translation for the term is the French *gauchisme*. The term is derived from Lenin's 1920 *Left-Wing Communism: An Infantile Disease*.
[85] I. Fomin attracted the sympathies of the Stalinists with his variations on the theme of neoclassicist revivals. One of his most representative architectures was his entry to the Narkomtjazhprom competition and the Mossovet building in Moscow.
[86] RGALI, 674, op. 2-8, ed. hr. 134.
[87] RGALI, 674-2-8, p. 135. The infantilization of people (or "the masses") was one of the essential social mobiles of Stalinism.
[88] RGALI, 674, op. 2 ed. hr. 8. p. 136.

era bring us?"[89] He stopped short from uttering the only possible response, of which he was no doubt perfectly conscious.

A year later, the situation had not improved, each side having apparently grown entrenched in their own position. In one of the numerous exchanges with Kaganovich, on September 15, 1935, just before departing for the 13th International Congress of Architects in Rome,[90] Alabjan wrote a three-page letter to Kaganovich about the union's latest unsuccessful "Creative Consultation."[91] The main question debated concerned the direction Soviet architectural production was to take, that is, what "creative method" was to be adopted.

He lamented that, even though the debates lasted for three days, the results were "hardly satisfying." He highlighted the various ways the modernists resisted being pressured into the mold of conformity the union's party organization hoped to achieve. This meant engaging in "criticism and self-criticism" exercises the party used to undermine the individual's intellectual integrity, ultimately fostering infantile dependency. The scheme was having persons admit mindlessly that their past ways had been a mistake that had to be amended *hinc et nunc*.

Three points of view transpired, as Alabjan tried to summarize: The first group was "straight out of Zholtovskij's school": Gol'c, Kozhin, and Krjukov—the pure classicists. Alabjan referred to their embrace of classical architecture as "formalism," possibly because it represented a formal transposition or "mechanical" coopting of classical forms, without subjecting them to "creative" interventions. This position was "in direct contradiction with the 'essence of our aspirations.'" Alabjan was, actually, stunned that the group could "declare openly" that classical architecture was their "method of creation," which could hardly be "socialist."[92] Burov and Vlasov, both VHUTEIN graduates, were quoted as having moved away from such formalism, as their architecture was becoming less "estheticized."

The second group, which included Fridman, appeared as "unprincipled," yet it adamantly refused any criticism. "Fridman's architectural amplitude encompasses anything from 'Americanism' to pure 'classical architecture.'" Fridman defended his veering to classicism by claiming, to Alabjan's outrage, that such was, "as far as [he] could tell, the current direction of Soviet architecture." Even if such state of matters was manifestly visible, one was not supposed to notice.

---

[89] RGALI, 674, op. 2 ed. hr. 8 p. 69.
[90] The 13th Rome International Congress of Architects took place from September 22 to September 28, 1935. On August 27, 1935 the Soviet delegation comprised, K. Alabjan, V. A. Vesnin, T. A. Shchusev, N. Kolli, D. Arkin, S. E. Chernishev, Vlasov, N. B. Burov, Aleksandrov, Mordvinov, Fomin, Al'esin and the Rector of the Academy of Architecture, M. B. Krjukov. In a letter to Kaganovich on August 8, 1935, Alabjan discussed possible topics for the Rome congress and an overall strategy. In an undated letter, probably August 1935, citing a decision of the country's leadership, Alabjan requested that black suits be promptly tailored for each of them "for official events." RGALI, SSA, 674, op. 2 ed. hr.7.
[91] RGALI 674, op. 2 ed. hr. 11 pp. 9–11.
[92] In defense of historicism, a speaker went as far as quoting Engels who "after all loved classical and Gothic architecture."

The Shaping of Architecture Ideology within the Stalinist Project

Finally, the third group was the group critical of both historicism and eclecticism. But, as Alabjan lamented, they never showed up at the meetings. These were the constructivists "who, evidently decided not to take any active part in the current struggles and politics." Somewhat contradicting himself, Alabjan found that most members decidedly rejected "formalism" (something Kaganovich needed to hear). In any case, Zholtovskij's Masterska was by now, according to Alabjan, virtually disbanded. Notably, the modernists still maintained a prestige the historicists were losing.

Apparently adept to scholastic thinking, Alabjan concluded with two points. First, that one could sense that a "noticeable inaction reigns among architects," especially after the period of great excitement the metro construction had provoked. "Architects now hardly care about problems of Soviet Architecture.'" Second, reverting once more to the most recalcitrant issue, he wrote: "An important number of architects does not believe in criticism and self-criticism." Many saw it as a "crusade," "a nuisance," even "a horror," in Alabjan's words. He finally admitted (noting that the same situation was found at the Academy of Architecture), "at the eve of the congress, we are facing concerns of the first order: How to organize a concrete, competent architectural critique. This is what we have now to devote our utmost attention to."

Having cleared his slate, he left for Rome.[93]

A Call for Constructivism to be the Future of Soviet Architecture

On November 27, 1935, Ginzburg, who was one of the leaders of the Soviet delegation to Rome's 13th International Congress of Architects (selected by the government), published upon his return to Moscow an essay to the regular rubric of the *Arhitekturnaja Gazeta*—the "Pre-Congress Debate Tribune"— the ambitious essay titled no less than "The Tasks of Soviet Architecture."[94] His vast critical article was published over a full folio of the journal. He advocated boldly not only for the perpetuation of constructivism as such, but for it to become the future of Soviet architecture. For a long time, or at least until January 1936, the magazine was a lively platform for architectural discussions, albeit principally an unsuccessful vehicle for the reining in of the recalcitrant modernists. The latter, of course, also used the venue for the defense and the propagation of their own positions. Almost four years after the fateful April 1932 decree on the centralization of artistic institutions, and in response to the mounting pressure on the modernists from the platform of an imaginary "socialist" realism, the aim of the essay was to once and for all define what constructivism was; what had been its evolution; and the crucial role it was bound to play in the future.

---

[93] It is interesting to note that Soviet architects did not respond to the invitation to join a Rome meeting of architects *L'Architecture d'aujourd'hui* organized in 1933, nor did they come to the one held in Prague in 1935. RGALI, 674, op. 1ed. hr. 8.

[94] M. Ginzburg, "The tasks of Soviet Architecture" in *Arhitekturnaja Gazeta* No. 66, November 27, 1935, p. 4.

Ginzburg stated: "Constructivism as an artistic genre with its own ideology," and according to Ginzburg, "undoubtedly represented a progressive phase in the development of the Soviet Union before the reconstruction." His implicit argument was that those who identified constructivist architecture with boxy, crude, and unattractive architecture, should also take into consideration the poverty of the country in its early years, "which had nothing to do with its deeper meaning and intent. [...] Today, when the needs and possibilities of the laboring classes have reached a significantly higher level, the previous ideology and practice does not fully meet the tasks of the architect anymore." Constructivist architecture had to adapt to a more complex demand. In other words, he noted astutely that modern architecture now had a chance "to become closer to socialist realism, that is, to a truly socialist architecture." In other words, constructivism not only could be understood as socialist, but had a major role to play in the future to the benefit of the country.

The avant-garde leader remarked however that, unfortunately, "the epigones of constructivism have now quite speedily distanced themselves from a school that does not bring either laurels or recognition anymore. They have, actually, abandoned it. They have abandoned what they never fully understood in the first place. For some, constructivism was a creative force, while for others it was just a Soviet style that was not only easy to abandon, but was now also safe to drop." What manifestly transpired from Ginzburg's stance is that the current gradual changes in the architectural culture of the country away from avant-garde architecture were less the consequence of specific demands from the political centers, than the abandoning of what was now perceived as socially less valorized. In other words the demand for modern architecture was phasing out.

He asserted, however, with determination that much of the "constructivism of the past has not lost its value and should, therefore be preserved at all costs [...] and pursued with determination." Those values, he insisted, could be summarized into three essential points:

- The struggle for a new social type in Soviet architecture;
- The struggle for the inclusion in the practice of the architect all of the world's scientific and technological achievements;
- The struggle for the synthesis of form and function as a standard for design quality, without neglecting, in each case, the creativity of the individual, i.e., the individual's "I."

In other words, despite his diplomatic approach and conciliatory tone, he obviously had not changed a single iota to what had always been his understanding of constructivism as a brand of rational, modern, progressive architecture. Far from having to be abandoned, constructivism had to be developed further. He warned that, unfortunately, current architecture was heading in the opposite direction. Having in mind the overall rising of historicism and eclecticism, he noted wearily: "Today the majority of our architects is opting for a fundamentally wrong way in addressing the architectural production." What was at stake, he declared presciently, was "the very survival or death of Soviet architecture."[95]

Regarding the much-debated "historic legacy," he took the example of Shakespeare's tragedies, which "do not interest us so much for the description of the life and mores of their time, as for the emotions and passions that still speak to us because they belong to timeless human concerns. In the same way, we are interested not in the form of historic architecture but in the emotions that underpin it." He elaborated his point using as an example the project he was working on for the Kislovodsk sanatorium, and the way he chose the forms and materials to reflect its natural context and historical precedents.

Thus, reaching the crucial and most difficult point he asked: "What do we expect from a socialist architecture? We still do not know with certainty. But what would be its general traits?" Again, avoiding utopian projections, he focused on what they were *not* supposed to be, that is, "an a priori rubberstamping of any kind of dogma that would act to the detriment of the unique, the new, the unexpected, the unprecedented." In other words, he demanded freedom of expression.

Faced with an imponderable, Ginzburg concluded with a romantic-like description of the creative process. He evidently did so to counter the absurdity of sanctimonious ready-mades imposed to the individual creator from the outside, laced with "self-criticism." This calls for a fuller citation:

> In order to comply with such tasks, the architect has to be highly motivated and inspired. Inertia in the design process, when an architect grabs a pencil with an empty head, should be banned. The architect has to go through a period of creative incubation when thoughts, ideas, images swell, from an initial amorphous and indistinct vision into a chaos of colliding ideas and images that fill the [architect's] entire consciousness, giving him no solace. [...] This condition overwhelms him with such a fiery force that the pencil in his hand draws ceaselessly in an effort to relieve the enormous pressure.
>
> At that point the pencil starts moving fast and obediently in the architect's hand. It sums up all that complex incubation, while helping the crystallization of crisp and well-rounded forms. Till then, in so far as the architect did not go through that complex process, or has not taught himself how to think, how to conceive and depict an authentic work, he will be unable to create a genuine socialist architecture, which is to perform the tasks that stand before him, leading to a happy life, the life of the new Man in a socialist society.

In other words, what Ginzburg was getting at is that there was no a priori conflict between authentic, creative constructivism and socialist realism. A well-understood constructivism, developed under improved material conditions of the country, that is, a modern, progressive architecture should be the future of Soviet architecture.

---

[95] This claim echoed an earlier Vesnin remark that "Soviet Architecture [was] being eaten by a gangrene" as reported by Ja. Aleksandrov, in the party meeting, of November 4, 1934.

A Central Committee Meeting on Construction Policies: Kaganovich Concurs with Ginzburg

Less than two weeks later, the Central Committee held, from December 10 to December 14 a conference on "Building and Construction Policies of the Country."[96] This included housing, industry, and railroads. With Ordzhonikidze, the People's Commissar of Heavy Industry presiding, most of the complete Politburo was present—but for Stalin. In addition, a long list of some 350 engineers, factory directors, and builders were in attendance. Two architects invited to present papers were the Academician Aleksej Shchusev and Moisej Ginzburg as Director of the Central Administration of the Industrial and Building Trades.

A narcissistic Shchusev, disdainful of anybody's position but his own, and now concurring opportunistically with the center of power, was finally able to take revenge over the constructivists whom he now branded unashamedly as "epigones of the West." This was an obvious derision of Ginzburg's earlier claims about the "epigones of constructivism" that Shchusev knew included him. His speech, "The Roads to Soviet Architecture," was published in the *Gazeta*.[97] He essentially complained that, no matter the "success" of his Hotel Moskva, the building trade was still "dominated by artisanal methods." [Here Molotov interjected sarcastically, drawing a general laughter—"but paid for handsomely!"].[98]

In his remarks, Kaganovich referred approvingly to Ginzburg's speech about the virtues of "typization," while ignoring Shchusev's. This reinforced the image of Kaganovich's critical acceptance of constructivism, as expressed in party meetings discussed earlier.[99] With an accent on industrialization, typization, mechanization, and education ("formation of new cadres"), both Kaganovich and Ginzburg formulated the future tasks in four analogous points.

Suddenly, as Kaganovich was spelling his points, Stalin irrupted into the hall as a deus ex machina, in complete disregard for the speaker he was interrupting. In an obviously calculated theatrical coup, he basked in the thunderous standing ovations he provoked with repeated "Hurrahs!" and vocal shouts of "Long live comrade Stalin!"

As the audience eventually calmed down, Kaganovich concluded his speech.

***

The December 1935 preliminary consultations with experts were to serve as informative background material for a plenary meeting of the Central Committee itself, planned for February 1936.[100] Starting with early January 1936, however, *Pravda* began publishing a

---

[96] *Arhitekturnaja Gazeta*, No. 70. December 17, 1935. p. 3.
[97] A. Shchusev, "The Roads of Soviet Architecture," in *Arhitekturnaja Gazeta* No. 70, November 17, 1935.
[98] Ibid, p. 1.
[99] See *Arhitekturnaja Gazeta*, No. 71, December 22, 1935, p. 12.
[100] See *Pravda* No. 42 (6648), p. 1–2, February 12, 1936 "About the Improvement of the Building Works and the Reduction of Costs." The Plenary meeting, including the SNK (government) was held on February 10 and 11.

series of symptomatic articles that attacked the *dom korobki* (box houses) and "formalism." *Pravda* being the "Organ of the Central Committee," such articles (often directly commissioned) always reflected ongoing internal debates gauged for the public. Not unrelated to the upcoming congress of architects, it was clear that the centers of power were coming up with a concerted stance on "socialist" realism in architecture: an official rejection of modern architecture was evoked for the first time. These 1936 ominous signs heralded the actual turning point in the fate of Soviet architecture. Nevertheless, Ginzburg and the two surviving Vesnins, as we shall see, were still ready to fight.

CHAPTER 5
THE IMPROBABLE MARCH TO THE CONGRESS: "SOVIET ARCHITECTURE EATEN BY A GANGRENE"

The Union of Soviet Architects party cell of course did not miss Ginzburg's determined essay published in the *Gazeta* two weeks earlier.[1] Quite to the contrary. With the political situation in the country worsening by the day, exacerbated in late December 1935 by the opening of Zinoviev's and Kamenev's second indictment—now elevated to a "Trotskyite-Zinovietvite Terrorist Center" (also known as the "Trial of the Sixteen")—the totalitarian police state was rapidly moving to its peak performance. While *Arhitektura SSSR* published editorials maligning "saboteurs" (vreditel'i), "enemies of the people," and calling for the reinforcement of the "vigilance against the class enemy," the *Gazeta* published regularly the entire proceedings of the trumped-up Moscow trials against old Bolshevik leaders, from Zinoviev to Buharin.

As the congress approached, that is, as the memorial year 1937 appeared gradually as a year that would be impossible to bypass, Aleksandrov, the Secretary of the Orgkomitet, became increasingly aggressive, leaving Kaganovich's recommendations of relative tolerance for the constructivists far behind. With an obviously final deadline for the congress that could no longer be changed, the architecture party leadership scrambled to have its options firmly in hand.

However, it took two full months for Alabjan's party cell to determine how to react to Ginzburg's article—with the NKVD now looming unpredictably above everyone. The party cell finally published its response to Ginzburg in the same "Pre-Congress Discussion Tribune" on January 28, 1936. Constructivism, now synonymous with the entire modern architecture, was attacked frontally for the first time, while the modernists were now called "former constructivists" across the board. The response was a collectively concocted article that Lidija Komarova was asked to sign.[2] The text was titled somewhat sarcastically, "Triada Konstruktivizma" to echo Ginzburg's three-point definition of the constructivist quest. Calling Ginzburg's piece the "most consequential statement published thus far in *Gazeta*'s rubric," alias Komarova remarked: "The architectural youth, which had shared the principles of constructivism in the past [...], received the essay with particular concern, as they had now reassessed their 'erroneous views,'" while submitting them now to fierce criticism.

---

[1] *Arhitekturnaja Gazeta* 66, November 27, 1935, p. 3.
[2] See Aleksandr Vesnin's claims at the Orgkomitet Plenum meeting of February 13, 1936, RGALI 674, op. 2 ed. hre.12, p. 1–9. Komarova, an alumna of the VHUTEMAS/VHUTEIN of Leonidov's generation, designed for her 1927 thesis, a party building that has been compared to the Wright's Guggenheim Museum for its spiraling shape of an inverted cone. Her mother was a Soviet diplomat in India.

Then, in a dishonest rhetorical inversion, Komarova was made to claim that, after all, "Ginzburg himself declared that neither the ideology nor the practice of constructivism [were] what they used to be," meaning supposedly that they could no longer solve the needs of the present day. Thus, constructivism had to go.[3]

The author(s) of the article remarked, however, that Ginzburg was obviously avoiding an "honest self-criticism of the role constructivism played in the past, and the harm it caused to the development of a truly socialist architecture." In other words, he was defending a "long discredited" position. Worse, Ginzburg attributed to constructivism all of the remarkable successes of Soviet architecture, while "ignoring the enormous role the party played in the creation of an authentic socialist architecture, buttressed by a *clear and coherent idea* [sic!]" [author's emphasis]. The pretense of something existing stood for the absence of it.

Ginzburg's sin was to treat constructivism as an "unconditional fact [...] as a progressive architecture in need of further development." The party group, instead, far from expecting to build upon the existing achievements of constructivism, as Ginzburg proposed, "wants it abolished to allow the development of an entirely new architecture." Such claim vividly contradicted Kaganovich's earlier statements in party meetings—an indication of a major shift behind the scenes. Since, the article went on, the constructivists did not devise a "clear and cohesive new idea" about socialist architecture—and far from it—all that Ginzburg did was to "parade baseless metaphysics"—a perfect quid pro quo reversal.

While the SSA Party leaders found themselves in apparent discrepancy with the pragmatic position Kaganovich had advocated, the brutality of such statements struck as entirely new. That constructivism had to be "abolished"—while not long before Kaganovich had recommended their "cautious criticism" at the congress, even allowing for future "millions of housing projects" on their watch—seemed to indicate that by early 1936 something new was happening in the background, apparently unrecorded.[4] This was most certainly the explanation for the two-month delay in responding to Ginzburg's article. With anybody now being a potential victim of the state terror—party members in the first place—a new degree of rising mindlessness under permanently "revived class vigilance" could be a further explication. The GPU and its executive branch, the NKVD, had now risen above the party, above the Central Committee, and had become accountable exclusively to Stalin in person. There were no intermediaries.

The *Gazeta* published—on the same page as the "Triada Konstruktivizma"— an essay by Solomon Lisagor (1998–1937), Ginzburg's close collaborator and former student, intended as a rebuke to the earlier superficial and inaccurate article by Shchusev.[5] A guileful sycophant, about whom Alabjan once said he had an "anti-Soviet way of looking at you," Shchusev had introduced his article saying in a most hypocritical way:

---

[3] RGALI 672, op. 2 ed. hr. 2, pp. 23–29.
[4] To begin understanding what happened would at best entail a search among the Central Committee and Politburo papers.
[5] Op. cit. A. Shchusev, "The Roads of Soviet Architecture," *Arhitekturnaja Gazeta* no. 70, December 17, 1935, p. 3.

The victory of Socialism in our country, and the Stalinian idea of love and care for the human person; the amazing efforts to raise productivity through the implementation of the Stahanovite method [...] will help the material conditions needed to the development of architecture.

Shchusev castigated the constructivists for having allegedly imposed a monopoly over the schools, and destroyed the *kultura masterstva*, that is, a culture of authentic professionalism.[6] This had resulted, according to Shchusev, in an "insufficient preparedness of the young generation." He went as far as claiming that the work of the leaders of the constructivist movement had mainly produced "paper architecture." A claim easily dismissed if only by looking at Malevich's performance in the 1920s, let alone the rich constructivist production of the 1930s around the vast country. At the same time, Shchusev claimed that there was nothing wrong with "eclecticism, which should not be feared."

Lisagor, a party member, was primarily prodded (a probable provocation) by his superiors' request to "raise the quality" of the texts *Gazeta* was publishing.[7] He thought Shchusev's vacuous article was a fitting occasion.

His essay was, therefore a response to Shchusev who had also referred to Ginzburg's article, lamenting about the "epigones of constructivism," who had "never understood its essence." Bluntly, Shchusev reused the phrase to, in turn, accuse the constructivists for being "the epigones of the West"—a damning and dangerous claim under the circumstances. He was obviously taking revenge against the weakened modernists, who did not spare him in the past for what they saw as his "chameleon-like" opportunistic architecture and posture.

In a beautifully crafted and intelligently argued essay to which, by his own admission, he had dedicated an inordinate amount of time and effort,[8] Lisagor, a MVTU graduate and Leonidov's elder, had drafted, in six conceptual units, an inspired argument in favor of constructivism. While making repeated efforts to express his respect "for the Master" (Shchusev), Lisagor pointed to the latter's cavalier attitude toward constructivism. He lamented that Shchusev had made "no effort towards a serious analysis of the constructivist concept"—while claiming that a "full ten years of Soviet architecture" was simply "false architecture." He went on:

> Soviet constructivism was born with the revolution, as an active supporter of October, as an active revolutionary architectural movement, which accepted the worldview of the proletarian state, and undertook a fight never seen before against the old architectural school of the former regime [...].

---

[6] The claim was false because the leading force of the VHUTEMAS were Ladovskij's rationalists. As mentioned, the students had the option of studying with classicists as well, such as Zholtovskij. As is natural, students flocked to modernists, that is, to constructivists and rationalists. Among the 'independent" modernists, students could choose from, were figures such as Mel'nikov ("Independent") or Golosov, a master in using classical forms through a modern expression (cf. the Moscow Zuev workers club).

[7] Stenogram of the SSA Orgkomitet, February 13, 1936, RGALI 674 op. 2, ed. hr. 12, p. 201. Lisagor was also responsible for the NARKOMFIN's sister housing on the Gogol'evskij Boulevard in Moscow. He lived next to Leonidov in one of the apartments.

[8] RGALI 674 op. 2, ed. hr. 12, p. 202.

Soviet constructivism, formulated scientifically, Lisagor went on, the tasks that the era demanded, and the technical means needed to achieve it. Besides, "Is it right to forget [as Shchusev did] the issues of housing construction, the planning of cities, the workers clubs and theaters, the questions of economics and standardization, and so on?"

While admitting that errors and downturns occurred, Lisagor pointed to the ultimate injustice it would represent to let it all go down the drain, and worse, to accept, as Shchusev was claiming, that "constructivism did not contribute in any significant way to the development of the architectural thought." The younger architect tried to disprove such stance by further quoting a number of achievements, such as the hydroelectric dam on the Dnieper, or the Palace of Culture that was to open in 1937—both by the Vesnins.

Yet Lisagor did not think that constructivism was a "socialist style" either. Despite all of its achievements, modern architecture did not "encompass yet the entire architectural production" of the country. But, in his view, constructivism possessed all the artistic ingredients that would one day allow it to become a "truly socialist architecture." For now, he agreed with Ginzburg's claim that constructivism would fully benefit from the material growth of the Soviet Union.[9] The last part of his essay addressed Shchusev's appalling praise of eclecticism.

Further, Lisagor "categorically protested" Shchusev's claim that the constructivists failed to contribute "in any significant way" to the education of new cadres, overlooking any serious discussion about the successes of the schools. He quoted a number of graduates, now important architects, who all came out of the VHUTEMAS/VHUTEIN, including "among many, many others architects such as Alabjan, Leonidov and Ivan Nikolaev."[10]

Lisagor further evoked the association of the school with such figures as Ljubov Popova, A. A. Vesnin, Vsevolod Mejerhold, in theater; Aleksandr Rodchenko, Aleksej Favorski, Vladimir Tatlin, Aristarh Lentulov, in the arts; and Vladimir Majakovskij, Vasilij Kamenskij, in literature—all of which Shchusev ignored. This evocation felt suddenly like a breath of fresh air from a bygone era, amidst the current "gangrene devouring Soviet architecture." Was it a dream?

While Lisagor was treading closer onto thin ice, he noted, "There were problems, but does this mean that the school had to be closed?" And decidedly moving forward one more step onto the cracking ice, he answered: "Of course not." As it was soon to appear, this last step proved to be a fatal one.

When Lisagor opened the *Gazeta* with his essay on January 28, he was stunned. His original title "A Response to Aleksej Shchusev" had been changed into "Constructivism and Eclecticism," which significantly modified the essay's scope and meaning. The title was obviously changed *in extremis*, behind Lisagor's back, because he had checked the final copy, just before it went into printing: the original title was still there.[11] Who changed it?

---

[9] Ibid. Ginzburg, *Arhitekturnaja Gazeta*, no. 66, November 27, 1935, p. 3.

[10] Ivan Nikolaev (1901–1979) who graduated from the VHUTEMAS in 1925. was, among others, the author of a superb Moscow Communal Housing of the Textile Institute (1929), recently restored, housing two thousand students.

[11] Stenogramma of the SSA Orgkomitet, February 13, 1936, RGALI 674 op. 2 ed. hr. 12 p. 201.

True enough, only four days later, an extensive and violently venomous rebuke signed by Genrih Ljudvig—a professor at the Military Academy, who also wrote for architectural journals—appeared in the magazine's next issue.[12] The change of title greatly served Ljudvig's response. Given the short time at hand, it was as if Ljudvig, or a "Ljudvig," had had the opportunity to read the manuscript ahead of time and start concocting his response before Lisagor's article even came out of the press. This way the response was ready for publication in the very next issue, that is, just four days later.[13]

There is little doubt that, in those days of growing repression, Lisagor's text had set an alarm, possibly with the NKVD on the lookout for convenient victims in the ongoing manufacturing of the Trotskyite "Trial of the Sixteen."

Such a forceful praise of the previous period, that is, one preceding Stalin's Reconstruction, could easily be construed as a "Trotskyite harangue" in the way Ohitovich became a "Trotskyite adventurist" for coming up with arguments about the historical legacy of Soviet architecture that differed from Stalin's.[14] Actually, Lisagor went even further by questioning the opportunity for the party to close a school that championed a "proletarian worldview." This was a goldmine for the NKVD, which could concoct a damning "case" against a disoriented victim. Yet this was not all.

Ljudvig's entire article, unconscionably sardonic, represented a defense of Shchusev—an architect of newfound prestige—with a vicious *ad hominem* denigration of Lisagor's position. By extension, the latter consisted in belittling the modernists in general. Therefore the principal fault of the constructivists, with their "highly self-assured" personae, was that they supposedly "dealt exclusively with technical and structural issues," devoid of "any idea, driven by artistic intent." The scandal was that Lisagor dared to "openly defend constructivism," a style derived from the "German postwar pessimism, having nothing in common, it goes without saying, with our joyful and happy reality." "Joyful and happy reality" was a phrase people were expected to utter profusely in public, in praise of the "great Stalin era," as Nadezhda Mandelstam described it in her book *Hope Against Hope*. Without anything to do with Lisagor's arguments, Ljudvig asked rhetorically, "Why is it that Lisagor claims that any architecture in capitalist countries [was] capitalist and that everything produced under socialism [was] socialist? Why such a degree of primitive mechanical thinking?"[15] "Mechanical" stood in opposition to "dialectical." Ljudvig did not apparently remember that this was exactly what Kaganovich claimed, namely that cities became socialist by virtue of being built in a socialist country.

Lisagor had never written such a puerile nonsense. The subtext was, of course, that Lisagor was incapable of higher, "dialectical thinking." The absence of such thinking was

---

[12] G. M. Ljudvig "Sistema izvrashchenija faktov ili: kak 'razoruzhajutsja byvshie konstruktivisty." (A system of inversion of facts: or how do former Constructivists disarm." In *Arhitekturnaja Gazeta,* no. 79, February 3, 1936.

[13] The magazine was published on the 3rd, 8th, 12th, 16th, 22nd, and 27th of each month.

[14] Ohitovich grounded this heritage in Russian peasant tradition, while Stalin saw it as an outgrowth of the historical action of the proletariat.

[15] "Mechanical" stood in opposition to "dialectical." Ljudvig did not apparently remember that this was exactly what Kaganovich claimed, namely that cities became socialist by virtue of being in a socialist country.

evident in the raw, "mechanical" character of constructivism itself. In other words, "constructivism was nothing else than a mechanical,[16] that is, literal transposition of Western architecture." Such arbitrary qualification allowed Ljudvig further to buttress his claim by reminding the reader of Le Corbusier's own concept of *machine à habiter*.

Contradicting himself, Ljudvig, who had denied the presence of any idea in the constructivist movement, suddenly assigned his victim "the role of a mediator of worldviews saturated with ideas foreign to us." He ridiculed Lisagor's claim that constructivism was born with the revolution, "while we know that there was no constructivist architecture before 1924." In fact, the first specifically constructivist project in architecture was the 1922 competition entry of the Vesnin brothers for the Palace of Labor (third prize). But much of it was in gestation, beginning with Tatlin's 1919 Tower, a quintessential constructivist work. So was, if closer to suprematism, Altman's decoration of Petrograd for the first anniversary of the revolution.

Ljudvig reproached Lisagor for only formally evoking "errors," and did not hesitate to mention the case of Ohitovich's "erroneous theories of disurbanism." The point was simply to relate Lisagor, a collaborator of Ginzburg's, to a man, also a former Ginzburg collaborator, recently executed as a "Trotskyite adventurist." The NKVD was building its fictitious "network" following only Stalin's verbal instructions. There were never any written orders.[17]

Worst of all, Lisagor was accused, with improbable bad faith, of defending the VHUTEMAS, "a school *condemned by the Central Committee of our party*"[author's emphasis]. "How was it possible to reach such a monstrous lack of criticism, such a monstrous trampling with facts?" There is no doubt that this school "where the constructivists called for the 'Death to art!'" as Ljudvig proceeded "produced a number of talented masters."

> But this was not the merit of the school's constructivists—quite to the contrary—it was due to the fact that the most talented students were able to survive constructivism by completing their education outside of the school. Regular students were deeply damaged by the constructivists [...] in their factory of cripples.

Nothing so violently false and uttered in such bad faith had ever been heard in party meetings—another sign of an ongoing radical reversal "from above," led, no doubt at this point, by the GPU itself.

Whoever was the real author of this text, it cynically ended with a quote from Lisagor. "He does not understand that the words he uses speaking about Zholtovskij's

---

[16] In the way "mechanical" was used, the word had a dual meaning: mechanical (literal) copying of a style and the "machine character" (dry and uninspired, artless) of constructivism. Thus a constructivist could be, by extension, called pejoratively a "mechanist," i.e., guilty of "mechanism."

[17] See op. cit. Alex Weissberg, *Conspiracy of Silence* (London: Hamish Hamilton), 1952.

school—namely that 'all such architectural trends [Renaissance revivals] are doomed, that the growth of our society has condemned'—are, actually, words fully and entirely applicable to himself [Lisagor] as well."

The Secretariat of the Orgkomitet met ten days later on February 13, 1936.[18] One of the topics was Lisagor's case. By then Aleksandrov was already referring to the constructivists as "the former."[19] He used the platform of the Orgkomitet to claim that it was easy to demonstrate that the constructivist theories were responsible "for all that *uproshchenstvo* [simplism] that got implanted all over our country [...]. If constructivism was propagated, it is not just because it [came] from people who were once part of the same camp, but it would be easy to demonstrate that they emanate from one single [reconstituted] *gruppirovka*." He manifestly had in mind the Ginzburg-Vesnins tandem.

Indeed, as we saw earlier, in Ginzburg's declaration about the ARHPLAN, the twelve Moscow workshops Kaganovich created were not impermeable, and given the weight the avant-garde carried in the system, collaboration among them developed spontaneously. Now, as the political tide was changing radically, back on December 22, 1935, *Gazeta* had published a vitriolic report from an expanded meeting of the SSA administration, under the military-style title "Against the *Gruppirovshchiny:* A Call for the Consolidation of All the Forces on the Architectural Front."[20] The fact is that new, spontaneous groups had been largely ignored until then, but no more. With the rise of state terror and the great Moscow trials underway, the noose was rapidly tightening on everyone, notably on unsuspecting Aleksandrov himself (albeit the probable author of "Ljudvig's" and "Komarova's" articles)—something he would have to deal with some eight months later when the time came for his own arrest.[21]

The opprobrium that Mordvinov had cast on Leonidov six years earlier was now magnified to engulf the entire avant-garde. The main culprit was, in Aleksandrov's view, "'our architectural school,' which damaged its students [...] because, as you probably remember [...] our Central Committee ascertained that the school ignored artistic values;[22] and this found its way into our architectural practice."[23] This inaccurate claim about the Central Committee, mentioned verbatim in Ljudvig's article where "*our* Central Committee," appears in both articles, is a probable indication that the true author of the articles Ljudvig and Komarova were forced to sign as a proof of allegiance to "the Party," was actually Aleksandrov himself.

---

[18] RGALI 674 op. 2, ed. hr. 12. pp. 154–224, February 13, 1936.
[19] Protocol of the Orgkomitet meeting on January 26, 1936. RGALI 674/2/p. 191.
[20] "Protiv grupirovshchiny, za konsolidaciju vseh sil arhiteknurnogo fronta" in *Arhitekturnaja Gazeta*, no. 71, December 22, 1935, p. 3.
[21] Aleksandrov's last signature on an official document appears on September 8, 1936. He was arrested the next day.
[22] This inaccurate claim about the Central Committee, mentioned verbatim in Ljudvig's article where "*our* Central Committee," appears in both articles, is a probable indication that the true author of the article Ljudvig signed was actually Aleksandrov himself.
[23] Secretariat Plenum meeting, February 13, 1936 RGALI 674 op. 2, ed. hr. 12. p. 160.

At the SSA meeting, Aleksandrov even threatened with "more blood spilling" as there was no "serious battle without blood-letting."[24] The paroxysm in debunking modernism had reached its peak.

Turkenidze, another party leader, who denigrated the VHUTEMAS, went as far as bringing Leonidov as the best example of the school's poor performance. Criteria and values were set upside down. Indignant, Leonidov responded: "Comrade Turkenidze declared that the VHUTEMAS damaged Leonidov, and I declare that it's Mordvinov and Turkenidze who crippled me."[25]

At some point, an exasperated Ginzburg warned that "if the tone of this discussion was not to change," he would refuse to show up at the congress and stop writing for the *Gazeta*. The threat was not to be taken lightly, as the absence of an avant-garde leader of Ginzburg's stature would have been a major embarrassment.

Alabjan, far more politically astute, tried a conciliatory stance and praised "our school," reprimanding Turkenidze for denigrating it.[26] "It is an error to claim that the school harmed us. Our school played a great role in our Soviet architecture. You make a serious mistake when you say that it damaged us."

Alabjan went on reminding the audience of actual expectations. "I consider that our task in these discussions is the following: We are expected to consider the most important issues of the present day." Hinting at the latest policies of the party, he added, "We cannot but tackle the questions that the party and the Sovnarkom [the government] placed before us." This meant that it was "imperative to go against the trash that burdens our architecture, and embrace the new trends" involving the entire society.

At this point Aleksandr Vesnin stood up to address Komarova's and Ljudvig's articles he characterized as "unacceptable both in tone and content." "Moisej Jakovlevich [Ginzburg] wrote, I would say, a very substantial article, with a very serious attitude regarding self-criticism." He pointed out that a disavowal of constructivism—a pure and simple rejection—would be mindless since constructivism had positive aspects, which needed to be emphasized and developed further. Vesnin went over all three points: further development of housing types; engaging new technological developments; and third, concern for the correct relationship between form and content—"all indispensable per se [. . .]. Yet what was Komarova's response? She referred to it as a 'Triada' with obvious sarcastic intent."

Regarding typology, he reminded her about the initiative the constructivists had in 1927 for an open, "comradely" competition, seeking the best in housing type. He was outraged that Komarova who took part in it could now pretend to ignore it. True, he did not believe that Komarova wrote the article on her own, but she signed it—therefore she

---

[24] RGALI,SSA Protocol 674 op. 2, ed. hr. 12, p. 157ob. An expression also referred to in Hugh Hudson *Blue Prints and Blood: The Stalinization of Soviet Architecture, 1917–1937* (Princeton University Press), 1994.
[25] RGALI ibid. p. 154. About Mordvinov's moral lynching of Leonidov, see Chapter 1.
[26] RGALI ibid. p.62. It was not difficult, however, to remember Alabjan's own attacks on the school when he advocated its closing as a VOPRA leader, which meant the Central Committee, i.e., Kaganovich. See Chapter 1.

had to own it. "She [had] been part of the entire history of constructivism,"[27] and it was "incomprehensible that someone could be as dishonorable into negating it all."

Then he turned to Aleksandrov. "And you, Aleksandr Jakovlevich, you too seem to know little about it. After all you too, I would say, seem to be a novice in the matter; you confuse things quite impossibly [...]. You confuse 'Krasin's box' with nascent constructivism.[28] That one was our enemy; we fought against Krasin. [...] You gave in to provocations!" As the room burst into laughter, Aleksandrov interjected: "So, we should blame Krasin?" Vesnin responded: "No, you, and the likes of you, do not know one thing from another, and just keep uttering nonsense."

The second point, the one about the valorization of technology, Vesnin continued, "was somehow eclipsed." He looked for it, but to no avail. Immediately after the indecent attribution to the constructivists of a harmful bourgeois ideology (which is supposed to be so self-evident, that it requires no proof), comes the third point, about form and content: the issue seemed perfectly clear—she did not even say if the point was good or bad. She just got to that point declaring: yes, form and content exist; she does not deny it. But what is the content?—Well, she claims that it is just "a naked utilitarian function." A. Vesnin called it another lie. "We always had in mind the artistic expression, and that can be demonstrated." He had recently published an article—an approach to the application of dialectical materialism to the design process, where the issue of form and content was addressed. And, again, "Komarova knew about that."[29]

After further dwelling on a few other absurd statements in (allegedly) Komarova's article, he pointed out her bias for not including Ginzburg's work in Tiflis (Tbilisi) where he had introduced slightly classicizing features as in Kislovodsk.

Vesnin then moved to Ljudvig. It was significant here that, as Vesnin emphasized insistently, the article was clearly written by someone other than Ljudvig. None of it could fit with the "decent man" he knew. Vesnin insisted that he really had a hard time speaking about the article, while he knew Ljudvig to be an honest and goodhearted person, who was also a former constructivist, and should know better. "It is evident," Vesnin went on, "that the main point here was to discredit Lisagor and constructivism. The claim that Lisagor has been turning facts upside down is nonsense." He had read the text carefully and found just the opposite: Ljudvig was the one distorting facts. Vesnin was particularly irritated by the claims that art instruction and architectural history were neglected at the VHUTEMAS, while imputing to the constructivists the slogan "Death to art!"—an outright nonsense. He went over his years at the VHUTEMAS/VHUTEIN and finally at the ASI, which replaced it, reminding those who wanted to hear about his constant efforts to maintain art in a prominent place in all the schools' curricula where he taught.

---

[27] Komarova was part of the first generation of students at the VHUTEMAS, born like Leonidov in 1902. She was member of the party, and had not much choice but accept to sign falsely the article.
[28] German Borisovich Krasin (1871–1947) was a conservative engineer who opposed modern architecture, but was responsible for some nondescript cubic buildings for Gidrofor, a Moscow hydro energy station. http://www.famhist.ru/famhist/klasson/002bded4.htm
[29] A.Vesnin and V. Vesnin, *Arhitekturnaja Gazeta* no. 20, April 8, 1935, p. 6.

He concluded saying that such methods of argumentation were unacceptable, even if confrontation was necessary. And he added: "True, you can reproach me for not fitting the current trend, but that's how it is. [...] We all stand on the same front; we all are Soviet architects with a common platform. At the same time each architect has the right to defend his own position, a position he deems to be correct; and each architect has to do it honestly. If he is shown to be wrong, he has to concede. The debates at the congress could only gain from it." He was still speaking from a platform of normalcy, while the boat was sinking irrevocably.

Then came Lisagor's turn to speak. He had offended Shchusev and some people in the audience had reprimanded him for his lack of "sensitivity and tact" toward the master.

Lisagor got up heavily. He spoke haltingly, with rising emotion, often speaking incoherently. He was one of those, he said, who were approached at a recent Orgkomitet meeting with the request to raise and sharpen the intellectual level of the discussions in the *Gazeta*. He had to admit a "secret..." He had spent three weeks, mostly at night after work, to come up with the essay in question: "I wrote it quite in good faith." He considered Shchusev to be a great master, having worked with him in the past. "I appreciated his sharp wit, his energy, his humor," and considered that he should be approached with the respect that is due to a master. "But does this mean that any criticism should be precluded?" He had addressed Shchusev in a straightforward manner, in ways no one had done before.

He moved to Ljudvig's article, which "distressed [him] deeply." Then, without transition, he resumed lauding Shchusev, while finding strange the way Shchusev was speaking lately; the faulty theoretical position in his article quite disturbed him, especially what he had to say about eclecticism. He regretted that Shchusev had left the room, but he stood by what he had written about him.

He turned to Komarova's claim that the party in the past only "tolerated the constructivists" but was now bound to cutting short their existence. Calling himself "a former constructivist," he went on shifting subjects disjointedly, hardly finishing his sentences. He chastised himself for not having been more critical of constructivism. "Is criticism necessary? Yes, it is."

Then, after a few more sentences, moving unpredictably from one issue to another, he suddenly declared: "I cannot stand it anymore! I have to say it all, to declare it all sincerely, from the beginning to the end." Unsolicited, in a mindless act of "self-criticism," he exposed his most vulnerable side. "There is in my biography a big dark page: I have once been expelled from the party.[30] [...] So, I cannot take offense at anyone who would impose on me whatever vigilance [...]. They would be right to do so [...] But does that mean that if I work in public view; and if the Orgkomitet is watching me, and I did not give any cause for concern [...] as my article testifies [...] that would be an outright disparaging learning [*vrednaja ucheba*].[31] My article is telling the truth. It is authentic. But was it necessary to ruin a person [*grobit' cheloveka*] from start to end? [...] If I was a

---

[30] Ohitovich had also experienced expulsion from the party: an open door to charges of "Trotskyism," against a destabilized, guilt-ridden arrested victim.
[31] It was not clear what he intended to say.

class enemy, who did bad things, had a noxious effect on society, then this would be right [*pravilno*]. But on what grounds?" He rejected Ljudvig's "unacceptable" article. Changing the title was wrong. [Someone in the audience shouted, "Yes, it is wrong!"]. Even Alabjan agreed.

Lisagor went on and on this way for three more typewritten, distraught pages.

Did Lisagor drink himself into this state of confusion—following an NKVD knock at his door in the dead of the night—a Moscow February night? Was he just stricken with panic?

Whatever the case, a fortnight later, they came to take him away.[32]

The Central Committee's Intervention

As tensions mounted, on February 20, *Pravda* published a short article, enigmatically signed in capital letters as "ARHITEKTOR," the way a medieval mason would refer to a mythical Vitruvius.[33] The article, titled "Cacophony in Architecture," could have been by Kaganovich himself, or by his order. It claimed:

> In the last few years, Soviet architecture went through great changes along the road of the creative perestrojka in the struggle for a high artistic and technical quality of construction. That struggle demanded in the first place the overcoming of the *vulgar* simplism of a corrupted style of Soviet architecture. [author's emphasis][34]

If not Kaganovich in person, there was little doubt, given the current practice, that it was published with an official imprimatur. The editorial addressed some six Moscow buildings as exemplars of what should be condemned. This included "pomposity," "mechanical reproduction of sixteenth-century Renaissance style," the arbitrary "combination of various styles," and a major debunking of two of Mel'nikov's buildings, notably his (unbuilt) 1934 Narkomtjazhprom competition entry with its two exterior stairs of pharaonic dimensions, directly connecting the street to the tenth floor (see. Chapter 4, Figure 4.1).

One third of the pamphlet assailed Mel'nikov's architecture, which was characterized as a pursuit of "form for form's sake." Mel'nikov's sole goal, the "ARHITEKTOR's" article declared, was "flashy originality" at all costs. Le Corbusier's Moscow Centrosojuz (by then reclaimed as Narkomlegprom—Commissariat of Light Industry) was highlighted as an architecture that cared only about "exposed structure" and "display of materials"—a curious remark since no structure is apparent from the outside. In other words, it was a

---

[32] He was never to be seen again. An anonymous friend of his had the courage to save his belongings, photographs in the first place, now kept in the Canadian Center for Architecture.

[33] *Pravda*, February 20, 1936, p. 4. See also Alessandro De Magistris "Il Dibattito Achitettonico degli Anni '30-'50 nelle pagine di *Architettura SSSR*," in *Casabella* no. 602, year LVII.

[34] *Pravda*, February 20, 1936.

"conglomerate of concrete, steel and glass," that Hannes Meyer's seemed to echo in his own characterization of the building as an "orgy of concrete and glass."[35] What was reproached to its "epigones" was the "poverty of expression" that ultimately turned their architecture into "military barracks."

Two points were to be highlighted in this carefully drafted text that seemingly reflected Kaganovich's position, held all along in party meetings. While, as we saw, the SSA party leaders rejected "simplism" (*uproshchenstvo*) as such, which, in their view, encompassed *all* of modern architecture in the USSR, *Pravda*'s text used a significant modifier by attacking only "*vulgar* simplism" [author's emphasis]—the infamous "box architecture." This seemed to allow tacitly for some more "sophisticated" constructivism. In this sense, it was indicative that, while the pamphlet went over several well-identified Moscow buildings, "constructivism" was not exemplified by a single case, even though a major one was about to be completed—the Palace of Culture by the Vesnins (see Chapter 3). This could further confirm that Kaganovich did not disapprove of *all* of "constructivism," as he had made it clear in late 1934, the year that coincided with the completion of the first part of that palace—the small theater. It is easy to assume that, without a higher authorization—Kaganovich?—the construction of the second, major part would not have been allowed to proceed. Instead, the building was celebrated with fanfare in December 1937, almost two years after the *Pravda* pamphlet came out.

Albeit not referred to explicitly, what one could deduce from the text, the new "socialist" architecture was supposed to be "top vigilant" and "rigorous."

Alabjan immediately called for a party meeting, as articles of this kind required. The text was read aloud, and commented ritually. In addition, two evenings at the Moscow Architectural Institute (MARHI)—the new school of architecture—were dedicated to the discussion of this short but dense text. "The crowd overflowed the hall."[36] While the *Pravda* article gained, reportedly, massive support among students and professors, a collaborator of Mel'nikov's, architect M. V. Kurochkin, a minor constructivist architect, courageously took his defense, targeting *Pravda*'s article as "incompetent," possibly unaware where the article was coming from. Mordvinov again took the opportunity to basely attack Leonidov along with Mel'nikov, both as "petit-bourgeois innovators."[37] Arkin deceptively claimed that "this article, actually, did not address any particular architect, but rather all that is offensive in our architectural production." He had to protect his privileged position as head of the VOKS.

All summed up, this was the first time, if still somewhat ambiguously and anonymously, that the highest party instances had intervened directly into prescribing what Soviet architecture was supposed to be, or at least what it was not to be—close to four years after the April 23, 1932 decree.

---

[35] Quoted in J. L. Cohen, M. De Michelis, M. Tafuri, eds., *URSS, 1917–1978: La ville, L'Architecture* (Paris: L'Equerre and Rome: Officina edizioni) 1979, p. 311.

[36] "Cacophony in Architecture: A debate at the Moscow Architecture Institute." Signed "G. G." In *Arhitekturnaja Gazeta*, No. 84, February 28, 1936, p. 1.

[37] *Arhitekturnaja Gazeta*, February 28, 1936.

All-Moscow Assembly of Architects: Twilight of the Moderns

Given the new circumstances, and in a major effort to dramatize the flurry of official directives published in *Pravda* throughout the month, a full Assembly (*Sobranie*) of Moscow Architects was convened for February 25, 26, and 27, 1936.[38] The way Alabjan put it in his keynote address at the assembly clearly indicated some serious consultations with Kaganovich had taken place: "*Pravda* has raised in the face of our entire society what should be the correct creative attitude of the architects."[39] Alabjan was finally coming to his own.

Two new topics were introduced in Alabjan's speech, the first obviously coming straight from Kaganovich, that is, the issue of "'the national expression' in architecture [...] which has been quite insufficiently treated thus far;" as well as the question of "the synthesis of the arts." He claimed those to be an essential way of creating a genuine "Soviet architecture."[40]

Alabjan then took on the two designated "formalists," Mel'nikov and Leonidov, "as the best illustration of what was wrong with 'formalism.'" A long tirade followed, essentially denigrating all of Mel'nikov's achievements—avoiding mention, of course, of the 1925 Soviet Pavilion that had represented the USSR to the world. Dutifully echoing the *Pravda* pamphlet, he asserted: "All that [Mel'nikov] cares about is to create an architecture never seen before." An example was his Rusakov workers' club and theater, with its three huge exploded cantilevered auditoriums that, according to Alabjan, "made spectators fear the hall would collapse under their weight." This was clear proof that Mel'nikov had "no concern for people [...] he just cared about his exhibitionist ego."

More cynical was Alabjan's attack on Leonidov "who never built anything" but persisted in his "mistaken ways." He dissected a minor, irrelevant competition entry for a Kolhoz club, as a characteristic example of formalism, published in *Arhitektura SSSR*. Candidly, Leonidov just protested that he "had always been a 'constructivist' and thus could not be a 'formalist.'" In any normal circumstances, his 1934 Red Square competition entry could have been celebrated as having actually pushed constructivism beyond the *dom korobka*, the "box house" (see Chapter 1, Figure 1.4). But of course, the goal was entirely different in its dishonesty. Modern, innovative architecture had to be destroyed whatever name was attached to it.

The clear indication that the modernists had begun to capitulate, even though still within rational limits, is that Ginzburg accepted to bury Mel'nikov and sacrifice Leonidov—both again for their "formalism." Still he did nuance his judgment: He claimed that each of them presented a different kind of formalism.[41]

---

[38] *Pravda*, March 1, 1936 "Na Sobranii Moskovskyh Arhitektorov" (At the assembly of Moscow Architects).
[39] K. Alabjan, "Against Formalism, Reductionism, Eclecticism," in *Arhitekturnaja Gazeta*, No. 84, February 28, 1936, p. 1–3. It's noteworthy that constructivism was not attacked frontally.
[40] Alabjan, "Against Formalism, Simplism, Eclecticism!" *Arhitekturnaja Gazeta*, no. 84, February 28, 1936, pp. 1–3.
[41] Moisej Ginzburg's speech at the Moscow Assembly, in *Arhitekturnaja Gazeta*, no. 84, February 28, 1936.

As for himself, Ginzburg stood his ground. He insisted that he "was not ashamed of his past work, quite to the contrary [he] was proud of it [...] because that was the product of Soviet creativity [*dejstvitel'nost*]. [...] Now, however, it [was] time to go forward; we have new arms, new forces, new possibilities at hand. We want to move forward to meet new triumphs."

Turning again to Leonidov, he claimed that Leonidov's great misfortune was that he had not yet built anything. He recommended to the younger architect to "make an effort, to be more careful with his work"—a possible double-talk. "Our responsibility towards Leonidov, is to tell him one more time: Leonidov, you have to understand that"— obviously, urging him to realize that times had changed.

While Ginzburg himself did start "adapting" his own work in Tbilisi and Kislovodsk, principled Leonidov refused to do so to the very end of his brief life.[42] Amidst the derision that Mordvinov had started six years earlier and had sustained over the decade with the malicious support of others, Leonidov, the poet, recalled Baudelaire's albatross:

Banished to ground in the midst of hootings,
His wings, those of a giant, hindered him from walking.[43]

In his own speech, Alexandr Vesnin returned to the issue of the unity of "form and content,"[44] where form was admittedly derived from content; and therefore "the new content of our life requires new forms." He was thus uttering implicitly a forward-looking modern architecture. This also indicated, and he probably would not have denied it, that he had capitulated from the theoretical origins specific to constructivism that set it so advantageously over the Western "New Architecture," notably the one professed at the Bauhaus. He was leaving behind the early linguistic concepts of the Russian formalists of the OPOJAZ who had fueled so effectively the brothers' architecture—from his theatrical work with Ljubov Popova, the Palace of Labor competition entry, to the *Leningradskaja Pravda* of the early 1920s. The design method had reached its zenith with Ginzburg's own 1930 Narkomfin—a housing project he had not "built," he insisted, but "montaged" (see Chapter 1, Figure 1.3). While Viktor Shklovskij had claimed that "form is the content of art," Vesnin had now reverted to the so-called modern movement's position that "form followed function." In his speech, Vesnin now advocated "the need to study the architecture of the past, which teaches us the laws of 'form making'—a way of reconciling his architecture with the new discourse about the "legacy of the past." He sought to reinforce his stance with quoting "Engels's dialectical method of the passage from the old into the new." Starting with the well-worn Parthenon, he ended with Le Corbusier's way of treating space as a sound example of how a given space would morph into a new one.

Vesnin, however, resiliently and dauntlessly did not seem to be ready to make any further compromise. Unlike Ginzburg, he refused any blanket judgments regarding

---

[42] He died alone in a staircase of a heart attack in 1959, at age 57.
[43] "Exilé sur le sol au milieu des huées, Ses ailes de géant l'empêchent de marcher." Charles Baudelaire *L'Albatros*, from *Fleurs du mal* (Translation by Eli Siegel (Definition Press), 1968
[44] See A. and V. Vesnin "Forma i soderzhanie," in *Arhitecturnaja Gazeta*, no. 20, April 8, 1935, p. 6.

Mel'nikov's alleged formalism. He conceded that such reproach could be addressed to some of Mel'nikov's buildings, primarily his 1934 Narkomtjazhprom entry with its unlikely stairs. But he invited his audience to recall examples such as Mel'nikov's Mahorka Pavilion at the 1923 Agricultural Exposition or his 1925 Soviet Pavilion in Paris, which "by no means could be regarded as 'formalist.'"

Furthermore, unlike Ginzburg, Vesnin refused to accept that Leonidov be treated as a "formalist." His unchanged position regarding the work of his former student was in keeping with the one the *SA* had articulated in defense of his Palace of Culture, back in 1929.[45]

That part of Vesnin's address, however, was censored in the *Gazeta*. Vesnin's text was replaced by an anonymous comment to the effect that "here Vesnin expressed reservations regarding Leonidov's work [...] but he refused to condemn him as a formalist." Before the intrusive censor allowed Vesnin's authentic narrative to be resumed, he inserted a warning that by doing so, that is, "by defending Leonidov's evidently wrong and harmful work, Vesnin [was] doing a very bad disservice to Leonidov."

Then, the *Gazeta* censor allowed Vesnin to resume his own speech: "We endeavor in searching for new forms. One has to derive them from life itself. But content is not only a utilitarian function, ideology plays a role as well."

After discussing the strength and failures of the brothers' own Narkomtjazhprom, he returned to the Parthenon to celebrate its "simplicity imbued with meaning." To this Mordvinov interjected provocatively: "You mean like Le Corbusier on Miasnitckaja Street?"

"Yes, you can include Le Corbusier's Miasnitckaja. I consider that Le Corbusier's work is on par with the work of a Brunelleschi." He went on: "A number of achievements of constructivism remain true to this day."

"Which ones?" interjected Zaslavskij, a party leader, and former student at the VHUTEMAS.

"First of all, the organic character of its architecture. We set for ourselves the goal of finding forms derived from the function, the materials and the construction." He ascertained that this point has withstood, "but what has to be developed further includes ideological dimensions, for thus far, the purely utilitarian had been prevailing." What was left to do was "an assiduous search for 'a new social type.'" It would be "developed into adequate forms, while fighting against eclecticism at all cost." He was obviously finding nuanced arguments that would satisfy his audience, and thus safeguard further deployment of progressive architecture.

Mordvinov asked: "And what is to be gained with that?"

Zaslavskij interjected instead: "And what is to be rejected?"

Vesnin replied, "What is left is to fight for is the introduction of the latest achievements in building technology."

---

[45] See Chapter 1. Minutes of the meeting, RGALI, SSA 674, op. 2, ed. hr. 11 (2).

Exposed to incessant hostile interruptions of his speech, Vesnin made an unexpected self-immolating retreat: "There was an inclination of ours toward oversimplifying the issue of function. In the process of designing, we did not pay sufficient attention to issues of art. All the time we considered that a correct organization of the function would give us the right architectural solution."

Here again Arkin interjected sarcastically, "What functions well, looks good, right?"

Vesnin replied, "Exactly. In this respect we were erring." After a few more self-inflicted wounds, he concluded:

> I still think that form has to be derived from function, but not automatically. One needs to approach [the design] from several points of view simultaneously. [...] It's true that in our journal we never called for the 'death of art,' but we still weren't sufficiently adamant in the fight against such tendencies. [...] Everything that has been said here about "socialist" realism, that is, that architecture has to be saturated ideologically, grandiose, and so on, is perfectly true and indispensable. But what we consider to be most important in "socialist" realism is to penetrate life itself and work on it, and to remember that the architect is the organizer of life, a conscious builder of socialism (...) In that sense we are actively embracing socialist realism.[46]

Mordvinov was elated.

Leonidov had his chance to speak at the assembly but what the *Gazeta* published was heavily censored, with entire crucial passages rendered just with one tendentious interpretation. Or, instead of abstracting the author's text, the censor replaced it, again, with his own comments and arguments. These amputations appeared only in the speeches of the two modernists who had refrained from disavowing their creeds—Leonidov and A. Vesnin.

Leonidov began by a bold ascertainment, turning *Pravda*'s criticism to his own advantage: "The timeliness of the signals [sic] that came from the *Pravda* is clear: our architecture is un-controversially sick of many illnesses." The cavalier reference to *Pravda*'s official article as "signals," was as brazen and refreshing as was his implicit use of the problematic buildings the paper criticized as so many arguments in favor of his own censure. He agreed with *Pravda*.

"I am festooned with a number of 'isms.' I am both a constructivist and a formalist and a 'schematist,' and so forth. [...] As a matter of fact, I have always been a constructivist; have worked with a group of constructivists."

At this point the censor intervened in the *Gazeta* report of his article: "By rejecting to be called a formalist, Comrade Leonidov continues to obstinately defend his formalist positions. The huge confusion, Com. Leonidov makes, has to do with his method of creation."

Leonidov: "The way the architect works—and first of all the way the artist works—does not allow definite norms such as: Today I got a beautiful plan; tomorrow I came up

---

[46] A. Vesnin's speech, *Arhitekturnaja Gazeta*, no. 84, February 28, 1936, p. 3.

with a beautiful façade for that plan, or the other way around. That old song of the radical formalists has long been debunked!"

The censor: "Insisting on his much reviled old Narkomtjazhprom, Leonidov admits that it has a degree of schematism, but he justifies it by arguing that 'the project had a very short deadline,' and the like. In other words, he fails to submit this project to any serious criticism."

If the assembly was to seal the fate of Leonidov, Daniil Fridman's speech—author of the intriguing housing and retail complex in Ivanovo[47] (with an Aalto sensibility for materiality and form)—epitomized the self-immolation of a constructivist. His "self-criticism," tinged with apparent dementia, was the fate of many talented epigones of the avant-gardes.

> Since the very beginning of the revolution, my comrades and I, we were infatuated with formalism. Looking at my projects of that period makes it clear that the author was obsessed with a purely formalist idea, and aspired exclusively to fill this form with content. [...]

He chastised himself for obdurately seeking dynamic compositions, "even where unnecessary"; avoiding symmetry at all costs. "We did not dwell on it for a long time ["Just ten years!" someone in the audience shouted]. "We rejected it stoutly," he resumed, further debasing himself. "We understood that if we were to continue on that road, that approach would not let us advance, it would preclude us from reaching a valuable project." Or, rather, closer to the truth, if he had persevered on that road, he would have simply jeopardized a well-rewarded, lucrative career. His decision epitomized the fate of many a modernist. He went as far as debunking his own two Metro stations by emphasizing that he understood a new era had arrived, and that the modernist aspects of some stations, above and underground were up for oblivion.

Basely, if pragmatically, he concluded: "The party and the government have presented us with enormous tasks. We are expected to come up with hundreds of thousands of buildings; to create a powerful base for a booming industry."

The French modernist André Lurçat was also in the audience and spoke briefly. He tried to lend support to his hosts of many years by wrapping up the issues in a deceitful rhetoric.[48] "The simplest definition of formalism," he said, "was an edifice void of content." But he warned that there were two kinds of "formalisms"—the academic one and the one "derived from constructivism. Academic formalism deals with dead material." He illustrated his point by quoting Viollet-le-Duc's well-known stance on formalism. The second case stemmed from what he claimed sententiously, and echoing Bruno Taut, to be "a usual occurrence with the constructivists: to either engage the form or the structure,

---

[47] He was also the author of the smart Lenin Library, discussed in the first chapter, and the standard school type discussed in Chapter 2.

[48] On his dealings with the USSR, see Jean-Louis Cohen, *André (1894–1970): L'autocritique d'un Moderne*, (Paris-Liège: IFA-Madraga), 1995, pp. 177–209.

which [was] a wrong way to approach design." Trying to cajole his hosts without overly compromising himself, he found nothing more substantial as a response to both than evoking "socialist" realism as a solution—without elaborating.

Adhering to the dogmatic Marxist Theory of Reflection, according to which architecture and art directly "reflect" social conditions,[49] he concluded didactically that "good architecture" was the one that reflected "a feeling for the human subject"— obviously alluding to Stalin's obliged *zabota o cheloveke*.

***

At the three-day February 1936 assembly of Moscow architects, the bottom line appeared, as an official speaker declared at the assembly, that "our task can be summarized as the need for a sweeping adoption of 'socialist' realism in all the arts."[50] The reason was that, so far, "there had been no serious work done about it in architecture. As a result, what we've got is a kind of housing units made of mutually unrelated boxes, which under no circumstances could be a matter of pride—and this is something Ginzburg would never admit." To this, an irate Vesnin interjected: "And what does Ginzburg have to do with that?!"

It was clear that matters had taken a definitive turn into silencing the modernist discourse no matter what. It meant also the final branding of Leonidov as an irrelevant architect, despite his highly inspired project for the Narkomtjazhprom, which was anything but "boxy architecture."

Leonidov's name was to disappear from the list of delegates to the congress. He made a living thanks to an anonymous job position—ironically at the Narkomtjazhprom— most certainly thanks to Ginzburg's high position in that Commissariat. As Germany invaded the country in June 1941, he was sent to the first front lines.[51]

Whereas constructivism was never to be mentioned again in the *Gazeta*, from February 1936 to the start of the congress in June 1937, formalism-bashing was carried out with eight articles, including Iofan's own,[52] in an expiatory ritual.

---

[49] Such concept, was first challenged after the war in Eastern Europe by Hungarian anthropological Marxist György Lukács (1885–1971).
[50] Minutes of the assembly RGALI, SSA 674 op. 2, ed. hr. 11 (2).
[51] In the trenches, Leonidov wrote a poem exposed to the first lines of the front:

From behind the horizon, the rising sun spreads the gold of its rays.
Wrapping the earth with warmth and light.
We stood in the trenches.
The front line.
The review of the artillery was over.
Some battalions launched the attack.
Whistle of bullets, thunder of mortars, heavy roar of tanks [...]

[author's translation].
The second part of the poem is the moving conversation with the peasant soldier next to him in the trenches. The poem was part of the 2002 Shchusev Museum of Architecture exhibition dedicated to Leonidov's hundredth birthday at which, equally centenary, Lidija Komarova spoke.
[52] B. Iofan, "Itogi i Uroki o Formalizme i Estetiki," *Arhitekturnaja Gazeta*, no. 93, December 4, 1936.

Aleksandrov's last signature on an official document appeared seven months later, on September 8, 1936.[53] He was arrested the next day and replaced the day after,[54] as if nothing had happened; as if he had never existed. He was branded as a "Trotskyite enemy and double dealer," the way the NKVD prompted Alabjan to write.[55] What Alabjan probably did not need to do is offer three additional names of people "who could say more about Aleksandrov," as noted in his response to the NKVD.[56] Those people could not but be arrested themselves.

Selecting Foreign Guests to the Congress

One of the serious undertakings in organizing the congress was how to establish who among the foreigners should be invited. To do so, the Soviets needed to determine who were the foes and who the friends among the European and US architects.

The VOKS—the previously mentioned Institute for the Relations with Foreign Cultural Organizations and Individuals—was the gate to be used imperatively in both directions of any correspondence. Help would, of course, be requested as well from the Soviet embassies around the world, which, in constant quest for friendly support, had their own ready-made lists. Early on, a witty device was found for world-renowned architects: to give them the opportunity to publish in *Arhitektura SSSR*. They were solicited to describe their design methodology. The response would appear under the heading "*Kak ja Rabotaju*" ("The Way I Work").

Among the first to be contacted was Frank Lloyd Wright, who, besides being a top world architect, had the advantage of being an American. *Arhitektura SSSR* solicited Wright's interview in December 1933.[57] His response was published in February 1934.[58]

> To show how the wheels go around in the creative mind of an architect is none other than creation itself. But to answer your questions as may be: The solution of every problem is contained within itself. Its plan, form, and character are determined by the nature of the site, the nature of the materials used, the nature of the system using them, the nature of the life concerned and the purpose of the building itself. And always a determining factor is the nature of the architect himself.

---

[53] RGALI, SSA 2-12 (2).
[54] From September 10, 1936 on, instead of Aleksandrov, letters are signed by one A. V. Laslo. Aleksandrov was expelled from the party on October 22, 1936. RGALI, SSA 674 op. 2, ed. hr. 12 (2), p. 85.
[55] RGALI, SSA 674 op. 2, ed. hr. 12.
[56] This arrest was part of the violent repression of the Academy of Architecture that engulfed Aleksandrov, its Deputy Rector.
[57] AVERY Drawings MSS 2401. 136. December 7, 1933.
[58] *Arhitektura SSSR*, 2, 1934 pp. 70–71. Hans Schmidt who was working in the USSR, and J. J. Oud preceded him; both in the 1, 1933 issue *Arhitektura SSSR*.

And then came the crucial point, which interested the Soviets most: The issue of classicism. Wright's response to Soviet architectural authorities was that:

> the only way classical or modern architecture can be helpful to us is to study that quality in them, which made them serviceable or beautiful in their day and be informed by that quality in them. As ready-made forms they can be only harmful to us.

There were two other points that sensibly touched the ongoing debates among Soviet architects: The question of "composition" in architecture (related to classicism) and its methods of design, to which the architect responded unambiguously that "in organic architecture, composition as such is dead."[59]

The second issue was about the so-called "synthesis in architecture," that is, the interaction between sculpture, art, and architecture. The answer was that these were to be used with moderation, if not completely banned. In a thoroughly studied and full-fledged architectural project, those were unnecessary. With such a response, he weighed in the balance with the Soviet modernists.

Wright's research on affordable housing, resulting in what was to become by 1936 the Usonian Housing Project, certainly solidified the relationship between Wright and the Soviets. Wright, in fact, had been entertaining sustained friendly contacts with the USSR through other venues.[60] He had repeatedly expressed his sympathies for the Soviet Union and the revolution throughout the 1930s. His first direct contact with the Soviet Union was an interview *Pravda* had solicited in October 1932, with a second one that followed a year later. What interested *Pravda* in the 1932 interview was "[his] opinion about the position of the intellectuals in the United States in connection with the economic crisis."

Wright responded:

> The present economic crisis has practically eliminated our profession, such as it was. It was a capitalistic prostitute. [...] In the epoch now painfully closing, disguised as "economic depression," architecture was only a bad form of surface decoration: landlord bait for tenants [...] capital will only spend money to make money, and there is no more to be made in the old building way. [...] I view the U.S.S.R. as a heroic endeavor to establish more honest human values in a social state than any existing before. Its heroism and devotion—and its plight too—move me deeply. Russia is a great hope. But I fear that pseudo-machine worship used to defeat pseudo-capitalism may become inverted capitalism in Russia itself and again prostitute the man to the machine. [...] Individuality is a precious asset of the human race where, free from willfully exaggerated personality, it stands upon a common basis fair to all.[61]

---

[59] This text is the author's translation from the published Russian version.
[60] AVERY Drawings MSS 2401.135, 136 and 160, 200–205, and MSS 2401. 569.
[61] AVERY Drawings, MSS 2401.135.

The following year *Pravda* editors "wished to acquaint their readers more thoroughly with the changes wrought in the life of the intellectuals during the last year" followed by a new list of questions.[62] Wright answered: "Little visible change in the life or the attitude toward life of the intelligenzia (sic) of the United States is evident. No clear thinking is possible to them. They are all the hapless beneficiaries of a success-system they have never clearly understood, but a system that worked miracles for them while they slept. The hardships of the last three years have left them confused but not without hope that more miracles will come to pass in their behalf. They are willing to wait for them to happen." He compared capitalism to a "gambling game," and that gamblers were hard to cure. "Everybody in this country prefers the gamblers' chance at a great fortune to the slower growth of a personal fortune," adding, "The capacity for rebellion has grown small, and the present ideals of success are making it smaller every day. [...] No radical measures have been undertaken in the New Deal."

Wright's musing about the Soviet Union, was not without bringing him some trouble at home. He was accused, among others, in an editorial of the *Racine Journal* of ignoring the "red menace."[63] Deriding obsessions of that kind, which included the "yellow menace," Wright replied in a long "Letter to the Editor" that "yes, a part-time resident of Racine—appreciating the privilege—I realize that telling the truth concerning the Russian struggle for freedom lays me 'liable' sure. [...] I pride myself on citizenship in a free country. I believe no one could fairly question my loyalty, nor doubt my service. The value of my contribution to American culture is a matter of record around the world." In his letter he quoted "the tenet in Russia's constitution" he appreciated most in particular: "*From every man according to his ability—to every man according to his contribution.*"[64]

His correspondents were Arkin, before and after the congress,[65] and Alabjan in 1939 whom Wright invited to visit Taliesin, while at the New York world's exhibition.[66] During

---

[62] The two interviews were given through an elaborate *Pravda* questionnaire, first in 1932 and a October 19, 1933 letter from Moissaje J. Olgin, the American correspondent to *Pravda* over three pages. Columbia University, AVERY Drawings, MSS 2401.135.
Izvestija, AVERY MSS 2401.203 Wright edited his two pages response over six versions. The final version was dated October 25, 1933.
[63] AVERY, MSS 2401.204.
[64] AVERY, MSS 2401.205.
[65] AVERY, A076A08. "My dear Alabjan and my dear Arkin, We have read your brotherly letters with appreciation and affection. Our hearts went out to you long ago in this horrible human conflagration. We feel we have done so little, and are enraged that our country was so late in realizing your strength and importance. [...]"
AVERY U030C7, Arkin to Wright, August 2, 1937 "Dear Mr. Wright [...] All our Moscow friends still look back with pleasure on their meetings and discussions with you. We hope that Olga Ivanovna and you retain good memories of Moscow, of our architects, our discussions, and our friendship. Your film has been sent, shipped from Moscow on the July 31, addressed to the USSR Embassy [...]. At the same time, we have sent you, under separate cover, all tour drawings and plans. The latter had been exhibited in Moscow. [...] We hope that our friendship, which began long before our Moscow meetings, will continue and grow strong, even though the oceans separate us." [Signed D. Arkin].
[66] AVERY A059D01.

the Second World War,[67] he responded to Iofan's appeal for support, and got involved with the Russian War Relief in New York, accepting to take part in a meeting organized at Madison Square Garden on October 27, 1941.[68] His having known and befriended Iofan appeared as a valuable asset at that meeting.

Prompted by a letter from the CIRPAC, in 1934[69] Alabjan wrote to Kaganovich to obtain his consent for a CIAM fifth meeting to be held in Moscow in 1935, as a follow-up to the Athens congress.[70] He detailed the history of the CIAM (he calls it "CIRPAC") and past plans since 1933 to hold the fourth congress in Moscow (postponed because Moscow was not yet ready to host them).

Obviously eager to get a positive answer, Alabjan referred to the "CIRPAC" as a "leftist organization" of architects with sympathies toward the USSR. Alabjan went on: "Having in mind the profound perestroika taking place in the field of [Soviet] architecture—an image distorted by Western reactionary architectural critics—I think that it would be particularly appropriate to bring them to Moscow, where we would be able to show them [the actual situation]." He also added that such congress would bring to Moscow "the most formidable forces (*krupneishie sili*)" of world architecture that are keenly interested in the achievements of our architecture. Such contacts could prove to be of practical interest to us."

As Russians had been assiduously trying, since 1932, to bring the CIAM to hold their own congress in Moscow, the Union of Soviet Architects delegated Mart Stam (the Dutch collaborator of El Lissitzky on the suprematist Horizontal Skyscrapers, and author of one of the best housing models at the 1927 Stuttgart Weissenhofsiedlung exhibition under Ludwig Mies van der Rohe's sponsorship) to London to personally contact the CIRPAC on the issue. A comic "spy" story ensued that alerted Scotland Yard, the Soviet embassy in London, the Soviet Foreign Affairs in Moscow and the VOKS.[71] Upon arrival from Leningrad on the *Rykov* steamer in May 1934, Stam was arrested while entering Great Britain; from there he was sent *manu militari* out to Holland.

Meanwhile, the Soviet embassy was telegraphing the Soviet People's Commissariat for Foreign Affairs, asking if they knew who was "that Marvin Stam," a Dutch citizen, who

---

[67] AVERY R039D04, 10/24/1941; AVERY R039C01, "Yes, my dear Iofan: We take our stand together against fascist barbarian; but let our stand be against all forms of 'barbarism.' The time is now. War itself is the foremost barbarism. Just as there is no just war, so there is no necessary war. [...] The people do not want to make war but rulers see no other way. [...] If civilization continues to function under Rulers, the civilization is doomed because Rulers can mean only war. [...] I will remember the celebration in Moscow of the Russian aviators." [In English]

[68] AVERY, R039A05, Letter to Wright from Joseph Losey, Executive Chairman, Russian War Relief, October 14, 1941.

[69] The letter suggested a meeting be held in Moscow in 1934. It also mentioned the annals and other documents. The signatories were Sert, Weissman (Yugoslavia), Gropius, Moser, Ljubetkin (London), Kaufman, Sirkus, Elena Sirkus (Warsaw), Merkelbach (Amsterdam), Le Corbusier, Giedion, Hazen Siss (Montreal), Arthur Korn (Berlin), V. Bourgeois, Beken (Amsterdam). RGALI, SSA, 674 op. 2, ed. hr. 11.

[70] Letter not dated, RGALI, SSA, 674 op. 2, ed. hr. 7 p. 70, 70ob, 71. Alabjan's letter also quoted all the previous activities of the CIAM, since it was founded.

[71] Confidential letter addressed to Alabjan from the Soviet Foreign Affairs Commissariat dated July 17, 1934. RGALI, VOKS, 617 op. 1, ed. hr. 8, p. 76.

pretended that the SSA had mandated him to contact an "international organization of architects" in London. Alerted through VOKS, Alabjan explained it away.[72]

If realized, such meeting would have certainly been an important political hit for the Soviets; but for the CIAM it would have meant allowing to be duped for a second time. The Soviets nevertheless did send a delegation to London in the late fall that year, but actually to attend the commemoration of the hundredth anniversary of the Royal Institute of British Architects.[73] What the Soviets presented there as the "latest achievements" of their "perestrojka in architecture," might have pleased the conservative institute (Alabjan was named their honorary correspondent). Despite the Palace of Soviets "Americanized" version and its new suprematist accents, it was enough of a warning about the apparently dominant architectural trend in the Soviet Union.

Before the questionnaires had been addressed to Wright and to European architects between 1932 and 1933, VOKS itself had solicited the prestigious foreign practitioners, who had taken part in the Palace of Soviets competition, to comment on the results. It was probably another way of establishing lists, moved, perhaps, by a degree of undeclared unease regarding the competition's inglorious outcome. After all, all the architectural luminaries of the world had been rejected. Wright had not taken part in the competition.

Lurçat himself offered a list of names to his hosts.

On request, Pierre Vago, the main editor of *L'Architecture d'aujourd'hui,* helped Arkin's VOKS, in December 1935, with a list of architects he divided between *Modernes, Jeunes,* and *Officiels.* Glaringly missing from Vago's list was Francis Jourdain who actually did go and spoke at the congress in the name of the large French delegation. The most important Paris art critics were also included. Vago did not have to mention Lurçat since he was working in the USSR on and off since 1934, but cited Le Corbusier. The latter was invited only some three weeks prior to the start of the congress possibly hoping he would not come—which is indeed what happened.[74] By now Wright had completely supplanted Le Corbusier in Soviet sympathies. The other, more likely reason for a late invitation was that two months before the deadline, the party still felt it was not ready to hold the event.[75] Yet it could not be moved, as mentioned, for the sixth time in a jubilee year such as 1937.[76]

***

---

[72] RGALI, VOKS, Alabjan's response, 674 op. 8, ed. hr. 8.
[73] RGALI, SSA, 674 2-2 (1) Letter to Kaganovich with names of the proposed members of the delegation. Kolli as Head, Alabjan, Aleksandrov Haji-Hasumov (Leningrad), Malozemov (Ukraine), Arkin and Zaslavskij. The letter was signed: Shchusev, Kolli, Krjukov, Alabjan.
[74] Letter of invitation Alabjan, Shchusev, and Viktor Vesnin signed jointly in Moscow on May 10, 1937. Fondation Le Corbusier, P5 11, T2 18.
[75] The issue was raised at a party meeting on March 5, 1937. RGALI, SSA 674 op. 28, ed. hr. 15.
[76] The full list of architects invited was as follows:

> FRANCE: Auguste Perret, Tony Garnier, Emile Magrot, Le Corbusier, Fressinet, Beaudouin, Lods, Pontremoli, Pierre Vago, Francis Jourdain, Georges Pingusson, Pierre Jeanneret. BELGIUM: Van-de-Velde, Arthur Verveck, ENGLAND: Persey Thomas, Sir Raymond Envin, Sir Jan MacAnister, Williams Ellis. HOLLAND: J. J. Oud, Willie La Croix, Van Eesteren. DENMARK: Eduard Geydberg. SWEDEN: Owen Markelius, Gunar Asplund. NORWAY Garand Hels. ITALY: Marcello Piacentini, Giovanonni, Del Debbio, Alberto Calza-Bini. CZECHOSLOVAKIA: Jurij Kroha, Karel Teige, Pavel Janek, Jan Vanek, Prof. Jože Gočar, Krejcar was not on the list. GERMANY: Walter Gropius, Erich Mendelsohn.

Soviet Architectural Avant-Gardes

On December 11, 1932 Alabjan wrote to the Central Committee as Secretary of the new Union of Soviet Architects. He declared that the Union had started to prepare the First Congress of Architects, to be held four months later, in March 1933.[77] Five years later it was still not ready. He had been far from prepared for the resistance the avant-gardes were to oppose to abandoning modern architecture.

Two months before the last set up for the congress, the *gruppirovke*— informal associations among architects that had reappeared around mutual interests and sensibilities—still represented a threat to the uniform ideological view that, by then, was expected to have pervaded the profession. Given such uncertainties, all the papers to be presented at the congress, as mentioned earlier, were to be sent to the SSA administration at least sixty days before the event.

The pervasive discomfort with the indeterminacy of what was to replace modern architecture was palpable even among communists. Party leaders, such as Bumazhnij, were criticized at the March 5, 1937 party meeting for having addressed exclusively organizational issues in their prepared congress papers, omitting the problem of *gruppirovke* and the "creative life" of the profession, that is, issues that were supposed to address new, yet still undefined, stylistic orientations. By now, a general direction was supposed to have been adopted uniformly: to reject "classical" historicism, "eclecticism," constructivism, and formalism. Yet no paper had considered what the profession's future tasks were to be in specific terms. At the same time, it was obvious that the issue could not be avoided at the congress—an embarrassing conundrum. Worse, two months preceding the great event, it was still not clear with certainty what was the general mood amongst the profession's practitioners at large.[78] The question was raised with anxiety at the same March meeting, as "the architectural masses" appeared to have been consistently hostile to SSA's party orientation.

Another party leader, the more hardline Turkinidze—who had crucified Leonidov just two years earlier—observed that the party should "get a sense about the kind of thinking various architectural circles harbor around the country; what kind of work do they do? [...] Do they resist party directives? [...] so we could know *in advance* what kind of opposition we are going to face at the congress [author's emphasis]." Turkinidze insisted: "We have to follow the tasks Lazar Moiseevich [Kaganovich] has set before us regarding the congress. The responsibility for this falls on us, the communists." By "tasks" he meant "the rationalization of the building process, the quality of the designs, typization, industrialization, standardization, but also the fight against denuded architecture [*Uproshchenstvo* or simplism]." Some attendees were reprimanded for panicking. As one of the speakers noted, "panic will lead us nowhere." The palpable fear was that once the "weaknesses" were to be pointed out at the congress, "we the communist leaders will be made responsible for all the faults." Turkenidze pointed out further: "If we are going to

---

[77] RGALI 674, op. 2, ed. hr. 2(1), pp. 10, 10 b, 11. RGALI, SSA 674, op.2, ed. hr. 47, p.20.
[78] Stenogram of the SSA party meeting presided by Alabjan Party Protocol, 674-2-28-2 pp. 2 to 4ob.

advocate 'socialist' realism, and not show how to do it, that is, what should that 'Soviet Style' actually be, they will tell us: well, show it to us in practice [*na dele*]. [...] I fear that we will be able only to talk about niceties, without being able to say how to achieve them." In other words, those most responsible for the implementation of "socialist" realism were at a loss, even by 1937, what would that kind of architecture be.

The situation was unchanged two months before the congress (and four years after it had been initially scheduled). Those most responsible for suffocating the avant-gardes were still unclear about what they would replace it with. They sensed very well that "the masses" (the architects at large) that the party was supposed to "lead" resisted such leadership, as the revival of the *grupirovkie* testified. Nevertheless, as Alabjan pointed out optimistically at the meeting, "some cracks in the balance of power" with the "creative *grupirovkie*" were beginning to appear: "An increased number of departures from constructivist and formalist positions." Still, what was not clear at all was *where* they were all heading. Looking around at the built environment, many, such as Daniil Fridman, one of the most creative avant-garde architects of the second generation, simply opted, as we saw, for time-tested values: neoclassical architecture—a choice by default. Someone at the meeting even suggested reasonably: "After all, maybe we are simply not ready yet"; and indeed the date of the congress was postponed by another month—from May to June.

The Congress

On June 17, 1937, while the terror under Stalin was at its peak, the congress was inaugurated with fanfare in the Kolonnij Hall of the Dom Sojuzov—a 1766 neo-Palladian building by architect M. F. Kazakov (1738–1812). The building was raised as a Nobility Assembly (Blagorodnoe Sobranie), i.e., a Moscow outpost of the Saint Petersburg Imperial Court on the Bolshaja Dimitrovka Street, in the vicinity of the Bolshoi Theater.

The members of the presidium, whose president rotated daily, were announced in front of five hundred delegates from around the country and the world (see Figure 5.1).[79] The entire Politburo was named honorary sponsor, causing frenetic applauses and repeated resounding hoorays as the name of each member was solemnly read to the delight of the audience. Stalin's name, read last for more effect, was greeted with thunderous salutes and extended applauses no one dared to stop.[80]

Telegrams from factory workers saluting the congress from the most distant points of the Union, resembling each other almost verbatim, were dutifully read aloud. The content of such telegrams was always coordinated and composed from a single source, bestowing

---

[79] The Presidium members were N. Kolli, V. Vesnin, I. Golovko, N. Bulganin, President of the Moscow Soviet, B. Iofan, V. Shchuko, A. Shchusev, I. Chernyshev.
[80] Usually, when present, Stalin would give a sign to the audience to stop the applauses, or else he would join the clapping in appreciation, so his stopping to clap was a sign to the audience that all was fine.

Figure 5.1 *Arhitekturnaja Gazeta* with Alabjan's Keynote Speech. Photo: Presidium Members (LEFT to RIGHT): N. Kolli, V. Vesnin, I. Golovko, N. Bulganin, President Of The Moscow Soviet, B. Iofan, V. Shchuko, A. Shchusev, I. Chernyshev.

them a surreal sense of unanimity. A choir of young pioneers, uniformed in white shirts graced with red scarves, sang patriotic hymns.

The following day, a particularly emotional announcement held everybody's breath: a group of heroic aviators, V. P. Chlakov, G. F. Bajdukov, and A. V. Beljakov, was to attempt on June 18, "to fly to America over the North Pole without landing."[81] There was also some significant excitement on the other side of the pole, especially in Portland where the aviators were expected to land after sixty-three hours and ten minutes of uninterrupted flight over nine thousand kilometers.[82] *Pravda* reported from its New York desk: "In the United States they are getting ready to greet the *letchiki* [pilots]." (See Figure 5.2.) The article lauded the Americans for, as one had to admit, putting all their meteorological instruments at the pilots' disposal, and keeping constantly in touch with them, as they

---

[81] For an overview of Soviet engagement in the North Pole see John McCannon. "To Storm the Arctic: Soviet Polar Exploration and Public Visions of Nature in the USSR, 1932–1939." *Cultural Geographies* 2, no. 1 (1995): 15–31.

[82] *Pravda,* June 19, p. 3. See also, https://www.rbth.com/history/328994-stalins-route-soviet-pilots-us-north-pole

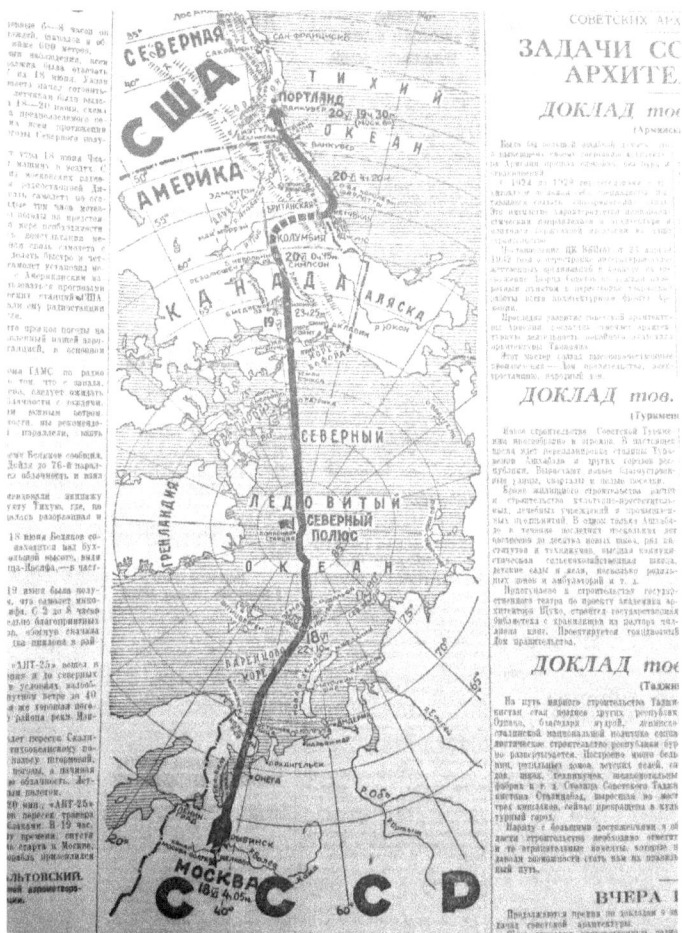

Figure 5.2 *Pravda:* The tracing of the route the Soviet aviators flew from the USSR to Portland, United States, June 1937. (Author's scan)

approached the border. President Roosevelt greeted them later personally in the Oval Office. News of their position and radiogram messages were announced daily at the congress.[83] Wright was to write later, in 1943, to Alabjan and Arkin, "I will remember the celebration in Moscow of the Russian aviators' first flight over the pole to America. What a big time that was and how it thrilled us all. It was more significant I think than we realized then. As a matter of fact, all frontiers are much less important now. Nationalism is fading since it became the enemy of all nations."

---

[83] AVERY Drawings MSS 2401.

This kind of mix of patriotic and technological exploits of the "New Soviet Man" Stalin carefully nurtured, along with relentless, ever-expanding news about arrests and trials of spies, saboteurs, and traitors of the motherland that filled the media was a combustible that carried the day, every day. It drowned the scourge of shared, overcrowded apartments and endless queues for daily necessities, including the uncertainty about who would be arrested next.[84] Intense hopes that these were needed sacrifices leading to the *lendemains qui chantent*,[85] kept the momentum going.

Alabjan gave the keynote address to the assembly, following the morning opening session. He spoke as the grand arbiter of Soviet architecture, dispensing lectures right and left, including to his former professors—world-renowned architects. He posed himself distinctly above the "crowd," as an untouchable repository of architectural wisdom.

He first pointed to what seemed to him to be a fact: that architecture had a privileged position in Soviet society. Nowhere in the world did it face so many demands and such challenging perspectives. He compared this condition to the situation in the West where architecture faced a serious crisis due to the capitalist depression. He took no less than a Frank Lloyd Wright to support his stance, quoting him twice in his speech "As the famous American architect wrote a few years ago: 'The economic crisis [in the United States] has put on the line our profession. In our era [he went on quoting Wright], which is now nearing its end, architecture is only about nasty forms of decoration [...] as the accumulated capital now satisfies itself with fakeness.'" That what Wright was lamenting about resembled singularly what the growing practice in the USSR was, did not cross his mind. He praised the achievements of Soviet urbanism under Kaganovich's leadership and the transformation of Moscow into a socialist megacity. He referred disdainfully to the "petit-bourgeois theories of disurbanism," which had been flatly rejected"[86]—a public slap on the face of Ginzburg, who would risk considerably, given that his "mentor" on the subject, Ohitovich, had been executed two years earlier.

Alabjan further complained about the continued presence of formalism in Soviet architecture, including other creative genres he deemed erroneous. Significantly, he mentioned that *surviving instances of constructivism were still to be found around the country* and/or appeared in competitions. He specifically quoted the Vesnin brothers' recent buildings, such as their entry to the Narkomtjazhprom (Commissariat of Heavy Industry), as well as Ginzburg's Izvestija proposal, which according to him still suffered from "schematism" and "abstraction."

---

[84] The members of the former bourgeoisie, however, especially the technical intelligentsia, felt safe. The NKVD had no use of them as "'Trotskyite adventurists." Author's 2002 interview with Marina X, from a family of engineers, and a civil engineer herself. Her grandfather contributed to the building of the Trans-Siberian Railway in the nineteenth century; while her uncle, Vladimir Petrovich Skryl'nikov was solicited in 1934 to explain why the concrete poured into the foundations of the Palace of Soviets kept sinking inexorably—response: "too close to the river banks."

[85] From Gabriel Péri's, last letter before being executed by the Nazis as a prominent French Communist, journalist and Resistant.

[86] RGALI, 674, op. 2 ed. hr. 30, pp. 20–69.

He censured the work of Mel'nikov "in the last six or seven years," taking as an example his workers' club Kommuna as "lacking in the most minimal comfort," and went on dissecting the "awkwardness" of the building starting with its vestibule. He claimed that everything was subjected to the primacy of the façade, as the "Stalinian concern for the human person" was shunned away—a rather heavy claim not devoid of serious threat.

"At the Moscow Conference of Architects,[87] Viktor Aleksandrovich Vesnin," Alabjan went on, "pointed out correctly to the negative aspect of some architects emulating, for instance, the reborn classicist Vlasov. Yet in this rebuke he was talking from the position of constructivism [...]. This group had to shed their wrong orientation, and work assiduously on themselves to change their erroneous beliefs. This entails strength and courage." What he reproached to Vlasov was the latter's embrace of classicism. In general, Alabjan insisted on rejecting those who, according to him, preached steadily the study of classical architecture. Ubiquitous eclecticism appeared as the consequence of a "low mastery of the trade, insufficient culture, but also a lack of principled understanding of Soviet architecture. In such cases, even the individual talent of the architect does not save him from gross mistakes." He attacked those architects who mechanically mix "Western and Eastern architecture," ending with a purely decorative architecture with no concern for the natural and urban context. He named a few architects guilty of such mistakes, including the author of the government headquarters in Tbilisi "that hides the most beautiful view on the David mount." The influence of such problematic works was reflected in the student projects. The response to it was "socialist" realism that distinguished itself with its "simplicity and veracity." Such artistic "straightforwardness" could be achieved through the professional mastery of the trade having "nothing to do with simplism." This entailed the ability to balance content and form. "Such architecture is an inalienable part of our era, with its concerns for the aspirations of the popular masses."

Echoing Kaganovich who maintained that a style could not be determined by decree, Alabjan insisted that "socialist" realism could not be subjected to any external norms and canons. "Imposed strictures and limitations are alien to it. In fact," Alabjan proceeded in a textbook voluntarist argument, "the method of socialist realism opens unlimited creative possibilities and emulations to the architect." Significantly, nevertheless, Alabjan pointed to the Soviet Pavilion in Paris as "very instructive." He correctly brought it to bear with the same author's Palace of Soviets.

These claims introduced a significant moment. It was the first time that the elusive "socialist" realism was referred to concretely. It brought to an apparent resolution all the uncertain debates and voluntarist intimations of the decade. "Socialist" realism therefore represented an open-ended formation that could include, as we have seen,[88] modern

---

[87] See *Arhitekturnaja Gazeta*, no. 70. December 17, 1935, p. 3.
[88] See chapter 3.

architecture and art, suprematism and constructivism, corporate American architecture and Wrightian accents, as long as it was monumental, ideologically adorned, and axially organized.

Another reference was added, as Alabjan concluded: "The fundamental character of Soviet architecture is derived from Stalin's concern for the human person. The Moscow Metropoliten represents the best example of it. The party requested from the builders that each station be a work of art so that the people who would use them would experience a moment of joy. The Moscow Metro is not a simple utilitarian enterprise, like is the case of the Paris Métro. Our government did not have in mind profit. The intention was to serve the public with the most beautiful architectural work possible."

Toward the end of his speech, Alabjan addressed the importance of the industrialization of architecture, insisting on the help they were receiving from "American and West-European masters, some of whom are here, honoring our congress." This provoked a long, standing applause.

As the applauses calmed down, Alabjan made another interesting remark: "We can learn a lot from the leading French masters, such as Auguste Perret who developed a sophisticated use of concrete, notably precast concrete." Was Perret's form of classicism cast in concrete, simple and pure?; what Alabjan had in mind when describing the "simplicity" of "socialist" realism?

Were these apparent contradictions between chastising the constructivists for their alleged foreign influence and the declared enthusiasm regarding "the Western masters from whom we can learn a lot?" Was the inclusion of Wright revealing, not only a double standard, but a repressed inferiority complex? Hadn't the Soviet avant-gardes been in many instances even superior to the Western "New Architecture"? It would have been difficult at the time to find "in the West," as complex and intelligent a building as was Ginzburg's 1930 Narkomfin. Ambiguous reflections were to appear some twenty years later in Le Corbusier's work, or even later in the Smithsons' "streets in the sky"—the latter precisely born out of the criticism of CIAM's shortcomings.

"We, Soviet architects," he concluded, as if oblivious of what he just said, "we have to increase our struggle against bourgeois theories and theorists, against the idealistic understanding of the architectural creation, against open and hidden formalism." And, *in fine*, the best and safest way to achieve all of this was, according to Alabjan, to "tighten our ranks around the Central Committee of our party and around our leader, teacher, friend, and comrade Stalin; and always watch our mistakes and be ready to correct them promptly."

The first session of the SSA congress was adjourned to the next morning.

***

Nikolaj Kolli was the second speaker in the morning session of the second day, following Shchusev's insignificant talk, calling Soviet architects, it is to be noted, to take stock from "America and Europe."[89]

---

[89] RGALI, 674 op. 2 ed. hr. 31 p. 1–25.

Kolli's topic—"The Tasks of Soviet Architecture"[90]—differed substantially from his essay published in the *Gazeta* on January 3, 1936. In his speech, a converted Kolli declared (betraying himself and his former modernist companions, whom he now referred to as "they") that after a brief flirtation with neoclassicism immediately after the revolution, "the center of creative architectural life moved to the schools of art and civil engineering, all the way to the end of the 1920s." Rewriting history, and without even mentioning the VHUTEMAS in name, he insisted:

> These schools became the focus of an intensive creative work whose leading trends had a fundamentally analytical character. The student youths were carried by the enthusiasm and creative energy the revolution had unleashed and the unbridled freedom of creation they enjoyed. This turned the schools into laboratories for architectural experimentation. Not a small part of responsibility for the ultimate sterility of these experiments falls on the architectural milieu of that time. The political unpreparedness to lead such blessed human material, which grew without understanding the essence of the tasks the revolution put before them, led the representatives of that faction to embrace the road of opportunism. They pushed the youth into plain petty-bourgeois negation of the cultural legacy. The artistic immaturity, the [influence] of the left-bohemian currents of Western art, hid from their view the most advanced, authentically Soviet architecture.

Kolli, a former member of the CIAM, having collaborated with Le Corbusier on the Centrosojuz, and who, in 1933, was warning visiting Charlotte Perriand to avoid political subjects in front of his ten-year old son,[91] or wrote a letter to Le Corbusier from Rome, in September 1935, beginning: "Now that I finally can write freely to you [...]"[92]—now accepted to play a servile role, betraying his formerly like-minded colleagues. He complained sheepishly about the modernists "who subjected the academic traditions of classicism, as well all the [traditional] styles of Russian architecture to violent ostracism.[93] They disparaged ancient orders as an intolerable thing of the past."

Further fustigating such "nihilistic" attitudes, Kolli lamented the nefarious influence "futurist art" had on architecture. He took as an example no less than Tatlin's Tower to the Third International, calling it sarcastically "the first architectural project embracing abstract symbolism, whose spiral was supposed to be the symbol of the revolution [...] a symbol of human emancipation [...]" and "that as such it was supposed to be better than a Renaissance monument!"

---

[90] RGALI, 674 op. 2 ed. hr. 31 pp. 27–78.
[91] Author's interview with Charlotte Perriand, June 1997.
[92] Op. cit. Udovički-Selb, "C'était dans l'Air du Temps" in M. McLeod, ed. *Charlotte Perriand*.
[93] It is worth noting, however, that the VHUTEMAS/VHUTEIN had actually a section where students could opt for a classical academic education.

Continuing along these lines, he argued that the best examples of the above incongruous radical-left tendencies (*levavchkie techenija*) were to be found in the Soviet capital. Due to a virtual absence of classical architecture, according to Kolli "such extremes could best prosper in Moscow." In addition, architects were "objectively prevented from being trained in high artistic mastery." Those who came out of I. A. Golosov's and Ladovskij's studios were a case in point. To buttress this assertion, he submitted an *ad hominem* argument pointing to Golosov's "compositionally inept 1923 'Palace of Labor' competition entry." He also attacked Ladovskij, "the leader of the analytical movement." In an act of bad faith and material inaccuracy, Kolli submitted as proof of Ladovskij's "pseudoscientific" propensities, the inaccurate fact that he "left nothing behind in terms of schoolwork or designs." This was, of course, highly erroneous. Rather the opposite was true: The VHUTEMAS/VHUTEIN, where Ladovskij played a central role, had left volumes of school work and designs, some presented even in the 1925 Soviet Pavilion in Paris.

Kolli further belittled the famous Leningrad INHUK (Institute of Artistic Culture) where Kandinsky, Tatlin, Matjushin, Malevich, Punin, Hidekel, and others had worked at various times as responsible for the "worse damage done to Soviet architecture: thus [opening the door] to formalism."

Kolli continued with similar invectives, against the "short-lived constructivist fad," and celebrated the birth of "Soviet architecture proper," in his twenty-six-page speech. He concluded with an assertive "Cronkite style," single sentence: "This is the way the various stages of Soviet architecture looked like in the last twenty years."[94]

The next speaker was announced as "Professor Steinberg, delegate from Soviet Ukraine." But a ten-minute break was suggested.

***

Finally came Viktor Vesnin's turn as member of the congress's presidium. What he was going to say was anything short of a thunderbolt out of a blue sky:[95]

Comrades,

The speech of Comrade N. Ja Kolli did not give us an accurate view of the important development of Soviet architecture in the twenty years following the October Revolution. While critiquing constructivism, the speaker failed to show the great social significance the phenomenon represented over this long period, one that involved almost all of the architectural creative forces of the country. Can something of such magnitude be considered to have been just a mere accident? No, comrades, it cannot. I would like to know who did not design as a constructivist throughout this period? Are there many architects who were not influenced by constructivism?

---

[94] The famous anchorman Walter Cronkite, at CBS news, would end his evening news famously by saying in a self-satisfied tone: "And that's the way it is on this day . . ."
[95] RGALI 674, op. 2, ed. hr. 34, pp. 15–24.

Alabjan's worst fears were coming true at a congress for which he had worked so relentlessly for half of a decade. He knew "the architecture masses" were still attached to modern architecture—that only they could practice assertively. But how had he allowed such a flagrant disavowal of his efforts to come to full view in front of five hundred delegates from the entire vast Union? And this from no less than a Soviet architectural legend—one of the three "Bratja Vesnini"—himself a member of the Supreme Soviet since 1936.

Pitiless, Vesnin continued, quoting "respected Academicians": Aleksej Viktorovich Shchusev who devoted "endless days to the great constructivism. Vladimir Alekseevich Shchuko along with Com. Gel'freih who both had their long career crowned with constructivism" [...] "Even Ivan Vladimirovich Zholtovskij betrayed Palladio (laughter and thunderous applauses) when he designed with Krasin a certain electric station."[96]

"And, should I mention that the speaker himself [Kolli] has been a devout constructivist?" (Huge laughter.)

The audience was warming up in excitement, giving Vesnin overwhelming support, while telling clearly to whomever wanted to hear where the loyalties of the "masses" laid. If they could not put it without some risk in their own speeches, they could vote with their applauses and liberating laughter.

Viktor did not spear either "Com. Alabjan, who was at the time the leader of VOPRA, and all the [constructivist] work he did in Erevan? Or for that matter Com. Mordvinov, VOPRA ideologist, with his post office in Harkov? Com. Simbircev, Com. Kocharijan, and Com. Mazmajan were all members of VOPRA who fought with words against constructivism, while their practice was in no way different from it." Another thundering applause shook the hall, telling something about the low esteem of VOPRA in the architects' minds.[97]

"Now take, for example, the author of the Palace of Soviets. [...]"

At this point, the page "17" is missing from the archives. Was it spirited away like the pages of encyclopedias with names of ostracized figures used to be torn away? We cannot assume that Vesnin was referring to the Palace of Soviets suprematist accents as we detected them. But there is little doubt that he was evoking, on the missing page, Iofan's avant-garde Barviha hospital. This was a highly contentious point, however, as Barviha was an undisclosed site serving exclusively the Politburo and the Central Committee. In a world of top secrecy and paranoia such page had to be eliminated.

The next, page eighteen, records further:

Among all of these well-known names, it would not be futile to pay particular attention to Nikolaj Jakovlevich [Kolli] who threw around capricious indictments

---

[96] The central electric heating station in Moscow (1926–1927).

[97] The two dactylographer seemed to have a good time as well, as they registered pointedly the quality of the laughter, and the length of the applauses.

against constructivism as if it had been just a vogue. During this time these architects did not sit idle. They worked; they raised buildings with greater or lesser success, but embraced constructivism.

Vesnin went on, addressing Kolli directly: "Nikolaj Jakovlevich, constructivism was not a fad; this was a fully legitimate phenomenon of an irresistible call to creative action after October. (Applauses.) It meant an indispensable reassessment of all the extant values in the field of artistic culture."

He insisted that the undoing of the old establishment could not spare architecture. Architects understood clearly that to continue working like before was wrong. It was indispensable to look for new roads, to demand a different architecture; to answer the call for a new life the working class demanded following the October Revolution. "The progressive architects showed spontaneously what the road should be, and followed the ways of constructivism as the most advanced orientation in the West at that time."

While the party leaders among architects now steadily and relentlessly eroded the base of the modernists, the latter relied on their moral and professional integrity and the strength they derived from their national and international authority, while despising the infantile and infantilizing rebukes of the SSA communist leadership. Whether they could objectively have promoted a broad public debate at all, as the one witnessed in 1928–1929,[98] remains an open question. In any case, when by January 1936 they began realizing what was happening, it was already too late. The growing oppressive conditions since Kirov's assassination in December 1934 certainly did not help. Still, wasn't Viktor Vesnin elected in 1936 to the Supreme Soviet, along with Alabjan?

The modernists were not to die voiceless:

Comrades, I do not know of a single good work—let me emphasize, I mean a good constructivist work—that was not useful to the Soviet man, to his needs, to his desires, to his demands. For us, the latter was always an axiom—this truth did not need to be demonstrated. [...]

Yet he had no illusions: "Today, when we evaluate that period, what appears perfectly clear to us is that constructivism did not succeed. Constructivism belongs to the past, but taught us a lot, and still teaches us some, with all of its positive values."

Having stated what had to be said about modern architecture, with a sense of resignation he was in a better position morally to call for the adoption of "socialist" realism without, of course, explaining what that was supposed to be. He simply evoked the trend's inventor in literature, Maxim Gorkij, and the Bolshevik Party as its sponsor, using the new phraseology over two more pages. With an expected salute to the new "Stalinian Constitution," he ended a speech of passionate courage.

---

[98] See Chapter 1.

Viktor Vesnin received a long, extended standing ovation as no one else did, except, to a certain extent, for Wright.[99] Not a single other speaker received any applause beyond a courteous end-of-speech clapping. If anything, he had proven that constructivism was still in the minds and hearts of the large part of the new generation in all corners of the vast country.

The next day *Pravda*, cutting off the entire part of his speech in defense of constructivism, quoted only his *mea culpa*, projecting a contrived Vesnin. The readers were served, as usual, with whatever they were supposed to know.

This passionate call to reason was to be the last, most vigorous attempt at saving the honor of modern architecture in the Soviet Union.

As opposed to Viktor Vesnin, Ginzburg simply left out any polemical or ideological discussion in his speech, and defended modern architecture dispassionately in its strictest technical dimension: the indispensable need for technological modernization, that is, industrialization of the Soviet building trades.

Foreign Delegates

The most significant contributions from the foreign delegates came from Frank Lloyd Wright[100] and Francis Jourdain.[101] The latter actually spoke in the name of the other French delegates all, like himself, close to or members of the French Communist Party.

The Association of Czechoslovak Contemporary Architects sent a letter several pages long in polite support.[102] A half page of formal good wishes came from the Slovak P.S.A. (*pracovné sdruženie architektorov*, written without capitals—in the Bauhaus fashion).[103] Bruno Taut had sent a long essay the previous year that was included in the congress proceedings. Not surprisingly, after his 1929 rebuttal of the work of the constructivists, he took the lukewarm, middle-of-the-road stance of generalities down twenty-five pages.[104] The only salient remarks were about his surprise in 1932 seeing that architects in Russia used steel and concrete in their projects, as if these scarce materials were in abundance; he was equally disturbed to see at the time that architects did not bother going to building sites, nor being aware necessarily when their project had broken ground. The subtext was that constructivists were mere "paper architects," thus in a way strengthening the official position.

Jourdain, who evoked his happy memories on the occasion of a speech he gave in Moscow ten years earlier, flattered his hosts with supportive superlatives rendered in

---

[99] RGALI, Congress, 674, op. 2, ed. hr. 34, p. 24.
[100] RGALI, Congress, 674, op. 2, ed. hr. 50, pp. 8–29.
[101] RGALI, Congress, 674, op. 2, ed. hr. 50, pp. 38–44.
[102] RGALI, Congress, 674, op. 2, ed. hr. 50, pp. 13–16.
[103] RGALI, Congress, 674, op. 2, ed. hr. 49, p. 1.
[104] RGALI Congress, 674, op. 2, ed. hr. 50-pp. 45-70.

graceful Gallic eloquence (his speech was not translated into Russian). This allowed him to challenge them on finding an appropriate plastic expression for their new society. This would silence "their detractors who tend to compare the socialist edifice with a military barracks or a convents, where everyone is expected to be of the same size and use the same tooth brush."[105] He exhorted the Soviets to show how "despicable and stupid" such assertions could be, by adhering to Marx's claim that "the free development of each person is the condition of the free development of all." In other words, whatever the arguments in a debate can be, critical or supportive of a modern expression, freedom of criticism was of essence for the further development of architecture. In his opinion, there were only two types of architects: "those who are Marxists and know it, and those who are Marxists without knowing it, because architecture is an inherently dialectical art." He also advocated the close interaction between the architect and the engineer "as was the case in Roman times when their aqueducts were masterpieces competing with their temples."

Jourdain finally came to his main point, obviously weary about the current tendencies in Soviet architecture: "The main lesson we have to draw from the past is that we should avoid at all costs to be dominated by it. All the great architectures [in history] have been modern architectures. A constant thriving to be modern has driven all the great works in history." And he took as an example the Gothic cathedrals. "Had it not been that way, humans would still be leaving in caverns. [...] If I am taking the liberty here to insist on these truisms you may find banal; I am doing so just to proclaim the hope that you will honor with force the great epoch in which you live."

Jourdain went on even more boldly claiming: "I told you that I am a fighter. As such, I am motivated to quote Lenin's words: 'The revolution has no use of flatterers.' So I believe that the fervor of my friendship towards you authorizes me to strongly warn you against the error of adhering too tightly to the past; an error that the bourgeoisie in my country stubbornly adhered to for too long. [...] No, the regime you are rightfully proud of will not express itself with a vocabulary borrowed, say, from the Roman Empire. No, living in the twentieth century, in a country that has liberated labor, you will gain nothing by borrowing from monuments that have been built by slaves." And he went on elaborating his point, warning that bad copies from the West will not do either. "By staying close to the needs and the hopes of the workers and peasants of your country," Jourdain mused, "you will no doubt get on the road of socialist realism. [...] The society you are building should not be looking to the past, it has to look decidedly to the future." He ended with quoting a sentence without citing it: "Life is about climbing up, not about climbing down."[106] *Pravda* did not publish his speech.

---

[105] RGALI, Congress, 674-2-50, 38–44.
[106] RGALI, Congress, 674 op. 2 ed. hr. 50 pp. 38, 70, 44.

Wright's Speech

Largely unaware of where he was, and what was happening around him beyond the former Nobility Court Building (Dvorjanskoe Sobranie) hosting the congress; the frantic delegates; the coffee breaks and cocktails with their chatty conversations (see Figure 5.3): the visits to the Moscow House of Architects with sweet-spoken Alabjan and world-savvy Iofan; the restaurant on Maxim Gorky's street, exclusively built and stocked for the congress (soon to become a pumpkin again at the event's closure); the 1935 Suhanovo vacation resort out of Moscow, accessible to those architects deemed most meritorious; and, of course, in the first place the overwhelming attention and adulation of his person.[107]

Thus, in bliss, Wright sat down to compose the first version of his speech.

My dear comrades,

I have traveled far, and managed my way across frontiers of five nations, [*from one great place of the world, the U.S.A., to greet another great hope of the same world, the U.S.S.R*—a sentence censored in *Pravda*] only to find the U.S.S.R. and the U.S.A. next-door neighbors, both moved into a central position among the nations of the Northern Hemisphere by Soviet aviation.[108]

As he had been already shown Alabjan's 1934 Red Army Theater and, of course, the model of Iofan's Palace of Soviets at the "House of Architects," he went on: "Now Soviet is to build fine buildings. A different matter. May I say, at this moment, a mere difficult matter. I am happy to be here with you, because I am already familiar with your struggle to find a suitable architecture for your new Soviet life."

He was "sympathetic" to the Soviet architectural plight, as he recognized the "clean slate" where the United States were at once upon a time. "We too had to choose between crawling back into the old shell of old culture and going bravely forward to the new. We needed to be ourselves a culture." They chose wrong; they adopted "the inferior path of the slave," the "official architecture" of his day being "a disgrace to the name of freedom." Then, inevitably touching a Soviet raw nerve by getting so close to Stalin's vested goal in architecture, Wright exclaimed: "Our boasted achievement in architecture—the skyscraper—what is it? A triumph of engineering and the defeat of architecture." Quoting the steel frame, wrapped in stones to "imitate the masonry mass of feudal towers," he asserted that they are "fascinating but false." And then a blow:

"I have seen a reflection of that falsity in your own work, the Palace of Soviets. This structure—only proposed I hope—is good if we take it as a modern version of St. George destroying the dragon, that is, today the leonine Lenin stamping the life out of a capitalist

---

[107] See op. cit. F. L. Wright, "Architecture and Life in the USSR," in *Architectural Record*, vol. 82. no. 4, October 1937, p. 59–63.
[108] RGALI, Congress, SSA, 674 op. 2 ed. hr. 50 pp. 8–11.

Figure 5.3 Coffee recess. Attending, from LEFT, Kolli, Iofan, Wright, Ol'ga Sasso-Ruffo Ogareva, Iofan's wife. (Private collection, photographer unknown)

skyscraper [from the top of the skyscraper]." He was speaking, unawares, about a project that filled the pages of journals and newspapers for almost a decade, along with relentlessly repeated competitions—the palace getting taller after each version—and, most of all, celebrated as a triumph of socialism.

Wright saw as well "in the subway, a tendency to repeat for the people underground what the nobles did for themselves, first in this hall in which we stand—an elegance suitable enough no doubt for their parasitic life." He opposed such tendencies to "the new integrity we are learning to call organic architecture," which could come "afresh with the new freedom of humanity. [...] The left wing of our movement toward an organic architecture [...] did not do more than make plain wall surfaces and flat tops and ornamental corner windows." He obviously had in mind the European "New Architecture," which the Soviets could handily take as a critique of constructivism. Less clear was his reference to "our right wing, which covers instead the buildings with ornaments"— possibly the *Jugendstil*, or art deco.

After addressing the hardships "organic architecture" faced in the United States, he exhorted his hosts "not to waste yourselves upon mere affairs of taste as we did."

He then moved to "another matter coming to light in our modern world—the inevitable decay of the city. Urban life has served its turn and cities both great and small are distinctly dated." He manifestly had in mind his Broadacre City, probably unaware of the disurbanist theory of the avant-garde that Ohitovich and Ginzburg had promoted at the start of the decade, and one that Alabjan had denigrated earlier in his own speech. Wright was even less aware that Kaganovich had resolved the issue in favor of megacities. Nor did Wright believe that it would be attainable soon in the US, blaming "private ownership raised to the Nth degree in all branches of life." He saw the Soviet Union as the ideal place to achieve organic architecture in the name of better existence, made possible by its "great new life."

Wright ended his four-page paper declaring: "Out of the new freedom that is the U. S. S. R. should come great art treasures for the future."

He then submitted his text for translation. The copy came back untranslated, but seriously edited, not to say censored. At least three people had read it, as the various handwritings testify.

Now the story of "leonine Lenin" killing the dragon, and Wright's "hope" that [the palace] was only a "proposal," was furiously crossed out for Wright's enlightenment. The modified part read: "This structure, idolizing leonine Lenin and elsewhere—in your subway for instance—was a testimony [sic], to repeat, for the people *underground,* what the nobles had in their palaces [. . .]." The word *underground* was so completely obliterated with ink that no one who did not read the original version could guess what the stamped-out word had been. Obviously, such place assigned to the people recalled too closely Fritz Lang's *Metropolis,* or, for that matter, the aforementioned Protozanov's *Aelita the Queen of Mars,* where the people indeed lived underground, brutally repressed by the nobility above.

So, to compensate for the loss of his Saint George and the Dragon story, Wright added a sentence to his claim about the "falsity" of steel covered with masonry: "Lenin deserves better." Needless to say, Wright may not have known either that Saint George was the saint protector of Moscow—inviting endless implications.[109] But the idea was not so far-fetched: During the civil war, a 1920 poster showed a horse rider of the red army killing the dragon of capitalism with a sword (Figure 5.4).

On the last page, to his sentence about the new freedom in Russia opening the way to organic architecture, Wright added a puzzling handwritten line: "The United States of Europe [sic] is [organic architecture's] only hope." The censor crossed the sentence with a pencil, adding a thick exclamation mark as if saying that the Amerikanets must have lost his bearings.

Wright was probably not shown the final translation's transgressions, which his Russian wife Olga Ivanovna could have detected.[110] So, Wright's sentence: "I have seen a reflection of that falsity in your own work palace of Soviets [sic]," became an inane "I saw a reflection of the architecture of skyscrapers in the project of the Palace of Soviets, a monument to the leonine Lenin."[111] It is not clear what was ultimately read at the congress, but *Pravda* went even further publishing something Wright did not have in his speech at

---

[109] RGALI, Congress, SSA, 674 op. 2 ed. hr. 50 pp. 21–29.
[110] It is also quite possible that Wright just did not care.
[111] RGALI, SSA, 674 op. 2 ed. hr. 50, pp. 20–25.

Figure 5.4 Soviet poster published towards the end of the civil war: Saint George as a red Bolshevik killing the dragon of capitalism. (Private collection)

all: "This falsity [of a steel structure veneered with stone] is as false as the [capitalist] economy that grew it." (Figure 5.5)[112]

Using the method we already encountered in the case of A. Vesnin and Leonidov, *Pravda* would interrupt the author's speech and fill the gap with the editor's own thoughts. So, Wright's defense of disurbanism was skipped, and his claims turned upside down: "Frank Lloyd Wright then evoked city planning. America, says Wright, is still very far from actual city planning. Its economic system prevents it from doing so. Private property makes it impossible." None of it was in his text.

With his last sentence in *Pravda*, not found in the version he gave to the translator, Wright was supposed to have declared: "I return home deeply impressed by your grandiose achievements, which reinforce the immense hopes I always had for the future of life on earth."[113]

---

[112] *Pravda*, June 23, 1937 No 171 (7137).
[113] *Pravda*, June 23, 1937 No 171 (7137).

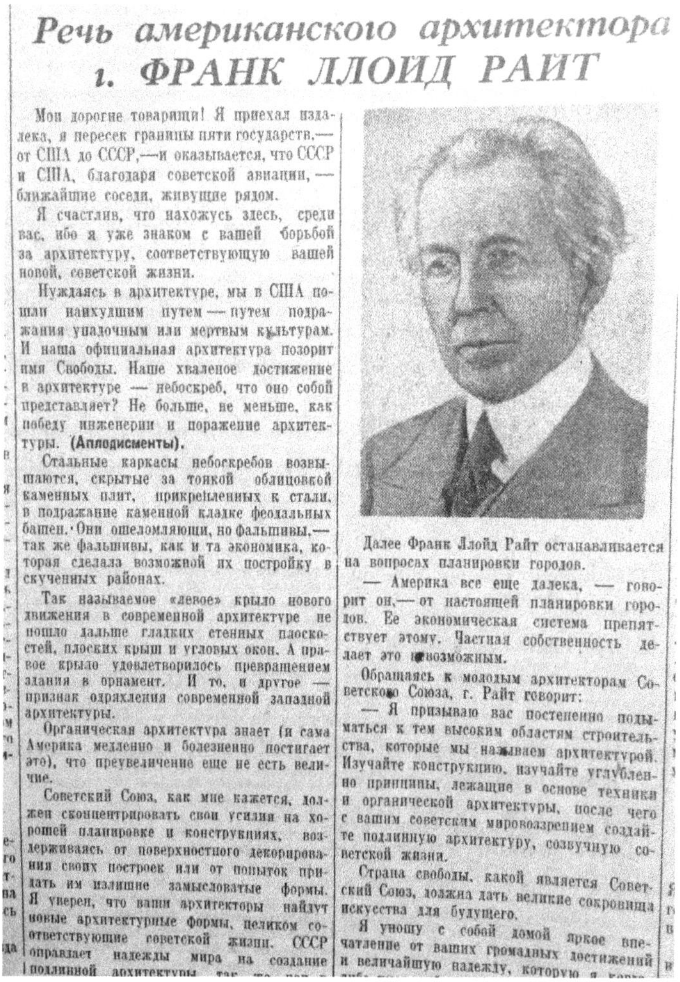

Речь американского архитектора
г. ФРАНК ЛЛОЙД РАЙТ

Мои дорогие товарищи! Я приехал издалека, я пересек границы пяти государств,— от США до СССР,—и оказывается, что СССР и США, благодаря советской авиации,— ближайшие соседи, живущие рядом.

Я счастлив, что нахожусь здесь, среди вас, ибо я уже знаком с вашей борьбой за архитектуру, соответствующую вашей новой, советской жизни.

Нуждаясь в архитектуре, мы в США пошли наихудшим путем — путем подражания упадочным или мертвым культурам. И наша официальная архитектура позорит имя Свободы. Наше хваленое достижение в архитектуре — небоскреб, что оно собой представляет? Не больше, не меньше, как победу инженерии и поражение архитектуры. **(Аплодисменты).**

Стальные каркасы небоскребов возвышаются, скрытые за тонкой облицовкой каменных плит, прикрепленных к стали, в подражание каменной кладке феодальных башен. Они ошеломляющи, но фальшивы,— так же фальшивы, как и та экономика, которая сделала возможной их постройку в скученных районах.

Так называемое «левое» крыло нового движения в современной архитектуре не пошло дальше гладких стенных плоскостей, плоских крыш и угловых окон. А правое крыло удовлетворилось превращением здания в орнамент. И то, и другое — признак одряхления современной западной архитектуры.

Органическая архитектура знает (и сама Америка медленно и болезненно постигает это), что преувеличение еще не есть величие.

Советский Союз, как мне кажется, должен сконцентрировать свои усилия на хорошей планировке и конструкциях, воздерживаясь от поверхностного декорирования своих построек или от попыток придать им излишне замысловатые формы. Я уверен, что ваши архитекторы найдут новые архитектурные формы, целиком соответствующие советской жизни. СССР оправдает надежды мира на создание подлинной архитектуры

Далее Франк Ллойд Райт останавливается на вопросах планировки городов.

— Америка все еще далека, — говорит он,— от настоящей планировки городов. Ее экономическая система препятствует этому. Частная собственность делает это невозможным.

Обращаясь к молодым архитекторам Советского Союза, г. Райт говорит:

— Я призываю вас постепенно подыматься к тем высоким областям строительства, которые мы называем архитектурой. Изучайте конструкцию, изучайте углубленно принципы, лежащие в основе техники и органической архитектуры, после чего с вашим советским мировоззрением создайте подлинную архитектуру, созвучную советской жизни.

Страна свободы, какой является Советский Союз, должна дать великие сокровища искусства для будущего.

Я уношу с собой домой яркое впечатление от ваших громадных достижений и величайшую надежду, которую я

Figure 5.5 Wright's "modified" speech in *Pravda*. (Author's scan)

Whatever the case, Wright received a huge applause confirming his celebrity status in the USSR.

***

After ten days of sustained daily sessions, the First Congress of the Union of Soviet Architects closed on June 25, 1937. For the first time (in Alabjan's Congress speech), "socialist" realism had been exemplified with two concrete architectural achievements—Iofan's 1937 Paris Pavilion and the last version of his Palace of Soviets. Both resonated with echoes of the avant-gardes.

Modern architecture, as we saw, would nonetheless survive to the end of the decade. The publication of Moisej Ginzburg's Kislovodsk sanatorium in 1940 would herald his own swan's song.

EPILOGUE

Upon returning to the United States, Wright published an article about his Soviet experience where he saluted "Comrade Stalin," calling the Soviet people "the liberated ones," and inviting Iofan to join him in working together on "organic architecture."[114] Having stopped in Paris on his way back home, he included in his article Iofan's Paris Pavilion. He lauded it as "a master architect's conception that walks away with the fair." Far from siding with those in the United States who claimed that Stalin had "betrayed the revolution," he retorted, "He betrayed it to the people."

Viktor Vesnin is said to have been sententiously reprimanded for his speech at the congress.[115] The only part *Pravda* published of that dramatic swan song of a constructivist was his admission of a final defeat. An era was sealed. Not having being a member of the communist party, he could not be usefully accused of being a "Trotskyite adventurist." To the contrary, he remained President of the Academy of Architecture, to which he had been elected the previous year. He kept his place as deputy of the Supreme Soviet, and continued his work at the People's Commissariat of Heavy Industry, supervising Stalin's "industrial revolution," fueled by slave work. His architectural practice, now without his brother Aleksandr, consisted mostly of competitions, none of which came to fruition. He edited two books on the history of architecture. In 1945, five years before his death at 52, he was awarded the Order of Lenin.[116]

Aleksandr, like Mel'nikov, refused to take part in the charade, and withdrew from architecture altogether. He dedicated himself to art in the privacy of his abode. His work was only exhibited long after his and Stalin's death, whom he survived by six years.[117]

Ginzburg continued his work at the NKTP, concentrating on industrial architecture, while publishing his Kislovodsk Sanatorium in 1940 under the same Commissariat's auspices. None of his later numerous projects and competitions, pursued even during the war, were ever realized.

---

[114] F. L. Wright, "Architecture and Life in the USSR," pp. 58–63.

[115] At the Congress, on June 21, 1937, Alabjan declared: "I believe that Viktor Aleksandrovich did not approach his and his comrades' work with self criticism." RGALI, 674, op. 2, ed. hr. 35, p. 86. I thank Vladimir Paperny for bringing to my attention this quote.

[116] A. G. Chinjakov. *Brothers Vesnin* (Moscow: Stroizdat), 1970. Victor Margolin, *The Slavic and East European Journal*, Vol. 32, no. 3 (Autumn, 1988), pp. 489–91. Selim Omarovich Khan-Magomedov, *Alexandr Vesnin and Russian Constructivism* (London: Lund Humphries), 1996.

[117] Selim Omarovich Khan-Magomedov, *Alexandr Vesnin and Russian Constructivism* op. cit. 1996.

The Improbable March to the Congress

Alabjan became vice-president of the Academy of Architecture (inheriting the position that the executed Aleksandrov had held). By 1948, having achieved celebrity, he married a twenty-two-years younger actress Ljudmila Celikovskaja who played the role of Tsarina in *Eisenstein's Ivan the Terrible*. In 1947, Alabjan had the merit of bringing to Moscow from their Norilsk exile his two Armenian comrades from VOPRA days, M. Mazmanjan and G. Kochar, setting them up in his own apartment. They had been arrested in 1937 as "Trotskyites."[118] He died in 1959, the same year as A. Vesnin.

Mordvinov, who built the Moscow Hotel Ukraine after the war (1953–1957)—today The Radisson—was harshly attacked in Nikita Khrushchëv's iconic November 4, 1955 speech, which chastised his monumental and onerously ornamented high-rise, pleasing to Stalin.[119]

Back from the trenches a wounded soldier, Leonidov pursued, in the first post-war years, an editorial activity, curating with other practitioners serial publications on Soviet cities—some of which are reproduced in the present book. He too returned to painting, using icon-making techniques he had learned in his village before coming to Moscow.[120] On his icon tablets, he often evoked his 1934 competition project, now rendered in dream-like forms he related to Tomaso Campanella's City of the Sun. He ended his life as an instructor of modeling in the cellars of the same building where he had studied under Aleksandr Vesnin, at the VHUTEMAS school of architecture.

---

[118] Mihail Vostrishev, *Celikovskaja—Series of famous people*.(Moscow: ZhZL), 2001, p. 87. The author published Alabjan's 1947 letter to the Supreme Court asking for permission to bring them to Moscow from Noril'sk, a city above the Arctic Circle.

[119] See Thomas P. Whitney *Khrushchev Speaks* op. cit., pp. 153–92.

[120] Andrei Gozak and Andrei Leonidov, *Ivan Leonidov: The Complete Work* (London, New York: Rizzoli), 1988.

CONCLUSION

The April 23, 1932 Central Committee decree on the dissolution of all—till then independent artistic groups—did not, nor did it later impose any stylistic direction. A single style was not even in the mind of the authors of the decree. Quite to the contrary, Lazar Kaganovich favored architectural plurality, and pragmatically recommended the support of the constructivists, even though he personally favored eclecticism. The creation of an All-Union of Soviet Architects cannot, therefore, be considered in itself as a turning point in the freedom of expression of the avant-gardes. Moisej Ginzburg having forcefully testified to this effect. In 1934, two years after the April decree, and one year into the new system of architectural production around the Mossovet ARHPLAN "masterskie," he maintained that architecture had "reached enviable social and creative heights."

Far from having been curtailed and disbanded, all the branches of the architectural avant-gardes—constructivists, rationalists, and independents, were each granted the control of five out of twelve ARHPLAN workshops. The quality and creative freedom of that new institution prompted Ginzburg, the most critical and intransigent among them, to claim that the new system of workshops granted ideal conditions for free, creative architectural work that surpassed the best of what had been available to him in the 1920s. Most significantly, he went so far as comparing favorably his ARHPLAN Masterska n. 3 to his own defunct OSA, "which I am identified with, and have worked successfully with, under the State Strojkom."

The door was not shut on the avant-gardes in 1932. They not only kept their occupations as teachers, project managers (notably Leonidov) and administrators of the All-Union of Soviet Architects, they, Mel'nikov included, were also granted chauffeured cars. In other words, they kept the status of state architects.

Beyond obvious totalitarian impulses, the likely rationale for dissolving the various architectural movements that appeared spontaneously in the 1920s and creating first a union of architects, and then an organized system of twelve free workshops, was to secure, at least in architecture and urban planning, the success of Stalin's First Five-Year plan. That plan needed, as was widely claimed, the concerted efforts of "all architectural forces." The promises were grandiose, as architects and urbanists were challenged not only with the thorough modernization of Moscow—including building its state-of-the-art subway—but also with constructing a vast program of new industrial cities. Architects and engineers from all over the world, including from the United States devasted by the Great Depression, were invited to join forces in building the USSR, allegedly "the sole country [at the time] boasting healthy finances," as the conservative French *Beaux-Arts* magazine declared in 1935.

Soviet Architectural Avant-Gardes

It seemed, now more than ever, that architects were fully entrusted with the decisive task of "pulling the Republic out of the mud," as Majakovskij wrote in a poem at the end of the Civil War. Competitions of all sorts, national and international, were organized in the USSR at a relentless pace. The authorities certainly knew that such contests maintained, like a mirage, the momentum of enthusiasm and hope where history did not "happen" but unfolded according to inexorable laws of dialectics in Hegelian and Marxist terms. Competitions could contribute to the illusion of revolutionary progress, blurring the nature of most of Stalin's redemptive campaigns. To a significant extent, the Five-Year plans, like the products of the incessant competitions, were doomed to remain on paper. The unrealized project for the Palace of the Soviets, itself born out of an international competition, could be seen as the most explicit metaphor of both. Still, even in the 1930s, the avant-gardes built far more than believed thus far.

Some of the most prominent Soviet architects remained long convinced that Stalin's "perestroika," commonly called "revolution from above," represented a genuine effort to revive and save the Revolution from what appeared to some in the leadership as the "menace" of the NEP. The question, by what means and at what pace should it be done, that is, whether to abolish the NEP or not, were among the main points of contention between Stalin and his allies vs. the "Right" in the Central Committee.

The official invitation sent to Frank Lloyd Wright and Le Corbusier, as well as to other foreign modernists—and only to modernists— to attend the first congress of the new union of architects, no doubt contributed to the conviction for some architects such as Boris Iofan, that sidelining modern architecture in their own country was only pragmatic and temporary. Still, Iofan was able to weave into his most "Stalinian" work, as we saw it, some of the important legacies of avant-garde art.

Albeit closely watched by the secret police,[1] the contact the avant-garde leaders had with the members of the so-called "modern movement" practitioners, abroad and those in the country, certainly maintained some illusion of still belonging to the modern world. On May 10, 1937, Alabjan, Shchusev and V. Vesnin invited Le Corbusier officially to join the congress.[2] Invitations to Le Corbusier in particular, actually kept coming during the entire 1930s, despite his Centrosojuz being vilified in the Soviet press, which he was not aware of until Nikolaj Kolli paid him a visit in 1934, in the wake of the Rome congress.

On the occasion of a trip to Paris, in the spring of 1935, Iofan also visited a surprised Corbusier who found Iofan quite sophisticated and charming, something he could not have expected from the author of the abhorred Palace of the Soviets whose photograph he kept in his drawers. Iofan urged the leader of French and European modernism to come to the Soviet Union even for a lecture series,[3] a clear sign among others that there was no formal prohibition in the USSR regarding modern architecture. In December

---

[1] On the occasion of his visit to Paris, Kolli told a perplexed Le Corbusier, who had been regularly sending him letters and books, why Kolli was not responding: all of it was delivered to him at the moment he was boarding the train on his way to the Rome congress in 1934.
[2] FLC P5-11
[3] FLC H2-9-373, 3–4

1935, while Stalin's Terror escalated, Le Corbusier was even invited to join the newly founded All-Union Academy of Architecture as "scientific correspondent," which he accepted, somewhat amused by the irony of the offer.[4] The Soviet authorities obviously cared to be perceived as a center of progress and labor emancipation, which was no doubt successful, at least until the launch of the Moscow trials and subsequent mass incarcerations.

"Socialist" realism, not unlike the vaunted "Proletarian" architecture it replaced, was a political rather than esthetic concept. VOPRA, a brainchild of Kaganovich, established to undermine and paralyze the avant-gardes at the start of the Cultural Revolution, had no genuine architectural program. This fact represented both VOPRA's strength and weakness. Strength, because it gave its promoters a high-pitched voice laced with deafening harangues; weakness, because, even when "Proletarian architecture" mutated into "socialist" realism, the latter's lack of definition repulsed and disoriented not only the young generation, but the middle-aged as well. They all harbored ideals of revolutionary transcendence through new architectural ideas, while standing on a very concrete platform of a modern architecture inaugurated in the 1920s. The SSA party cell, actually, had problems with its own youth, the Komsomols, who took refuge, away from nonsense, into the workshops of their elder avant-garde leaders.

The younger generation's attachment, party members or not, to its avant-garde leaders, was only logical. They were architects before anything else, and many had been educated by masters of Aleksandr Vesnin's stature, which in no way contradicted socialism per se. They were clear that what the architecture party cell was forcing onto them was "counter-revolutionary" in Leonidov's own words.

Passive resistance, absenteeism, and unspoken solidarity with their Masterskie leaders—lamented so adamantly in party meetings— were their way of responding to the senseless debates about an imposed directionless architectural trend endowed with mystical overtones. Even Higer, a sophisticated intellectual who once fought the "Proletarians'" absurdities, and defended Leonidov intelligently in the journal *SA*, had to admit in the later 1930s, that "in truth, the content of socialist realism in architecture is not quite *revealed* yet." In other words, he relegated "socialist" realism to a metaphysical realm in need of "revelation." Such intractable issue was brought up even in party meetings. While a member would reasonably remark that the problem was that "socialist realism was brought to us from another artistic field" (literature), he would collapse into mystical ecstasy by claiming in the next sentence, that even if "socialist" realism was "still undefined, any party member [could] feel it instinctively."

The same way Mussolini's inability to give a definition to his "chameleon-like" regime—to use Palmiro Togliatti's oft-quoted expression—allowed architects to compete in giving fascism their own architectural definition; the indeterminacy of the concept of "socialist" realism in architecture permitted plural answers throughout the decade.

---

[4] FLC I2-5-292

Ultimately, given Wright's unmitigated fame in the Soviet Union and Wright's own misgivings with European modern architecture, one could argue that his body of work, from a Soviet point of view, could have fit comfortably into such early all-embracing "socialist" realism, in opposition to Bauhaus-leaning "boxy" architecture.

The Kislovodsk sanatorium's Novecento front façades, and Ginzburg's comments about his own "socialist" realism, exemplifies this clearly. At that point, "socialist" realism seemed to be, at the outset, whatever you wanted it to be—as long as you were ready to spell the mantras, that is, invoke, like Ginzburg did, "Stalin's concern for the human person," or as a corollary, celebrate "the happy life we're all enjoying."

So, what happened? Why was modern, progressive architecture slowly declining over the decade?

We could isolate a few signals that constructivism was sliding to second rank, and was therefore becoming less attractive to architects seeking commissions. The most important signal occurred on February 28, 1932 (closely preceding the decree of April 23—thus blurring the lines) when Stalin's "Construction Council" disallowed all the results of the international competition, leaving a *tabula rasa*. That alone was more than enough for VOPRA to expunge modernism from their own projects.

Further, for an increasingly conservative society that Stalin was developing, with its rapidly mushrooming state bureaucracy,[5] European or Soviet modernism could hardly be one of the models for the long term. Retrograde competition juries reflecting the trend, were becoming the norm. Constructivism thus gradually ceased to bring prestige and awards, and therefor, following survival reflexes, "former constructivists" started deserting the field, while A. Vesnin and Leonidov sounded the alarm about the "gangrene" invading Soviet architecture.

These were no doubt propitious circumstances for the career goals of the SSA party leaders such as Alabjan, intent on supplanting the leaders of the avant-gardes. Using their newly acquired political preponderance, they exerted pressure on the central figures of constructivism, as well as on the architects of the younger generations across the board to admit "their errors," and abandon their architectural credo.

The likes of Alabjan knew very well that they could not compete with the leaders of the avant-gardes. Kaganovich only nailed it down more explicitly, when he recommended them to lower their ambitions about their congress, because no great architect was to be found among communists, unlike the case in the writers' triumphal congress. There was no Maxim Gorky among them. They legitimately feared (a fear, even panic, expressed repeatedly in party meetings until the last minute) that they would be outpaced at the congress by ideas and ideals of progressive architecture that were, logically, still broadly popular among architects at large. Viktor Vesnin's impromptu and passionate speech at the congress clearly confirmed that such fears were more than well founded. They had to stop such inclinations in their tracks, while carving for themselves a place of unchallenged social authority and prestige. Alabjan and his likes thus had to emasculate the moderns, in order to achieve

---

[5] See Robert Tucker, "The State Swells Up," in *Stalin in Power: Revolution from Above,1928-1941* (New York and London: W. W. Norton and Company), pp. 106–14.

professional preponderance and political ascendency that would give them access to the commissions most sought after. In a war of attrition with the avant-garde, the feeble and dubiously talented Nikolaj Kolli was their first and best victim. Having been member of the CIAM and having collaborated with Le Corbusier he feared potential liability.

The politically savvy Boris Iofan, on the other hand, who could have easily competed with the other modernists—he proved it with his Central Committee Barviha sanatorium—did not belong to the same circle—not even a member of the SSA party cell. Aleksej Rykov (executed in 1938) had brought him from Italy in the mid-1920s, and by 1929 Iofan was rising to become Stalin's unofficial architect, ultimately taking over the project of the Palace of the Soviets by 1934. Caught up in a golden cage, he used his position and talent to celebrate in unison Soviet Americanism while discretely recuperating suprematism.

Revivalist historicism in architecture was a well-established practice in Russia as complaints of the Harkov "Iniciativnaja Gruppa" had testified, long before Stalin and the party began intervening in the arts. Eclectical revivalism competed with modernism for prominent commissions as was the case of the Lenin Library. Therefore, in the absence of any rational definition of what the vaunted "realism" might be, the introduction of classicism, long considered in Russia as part of modernity—at least by contrast with the old Byzantine tradition—offered itself as a convenient escape for a growing number of "former constructivists" in a quest for commissions. This was clearly the case of "former constructivist" Daniil Fridman who, after having produced brilliant progressive architecture—such as notably the "Dom Korabl" in Ivanovo—ended arguing in party meetings in favor of classical architecture he perceived as the new norm.

While the trend was generalized in the decades to follow, in his 1954 speech Khrushchëv was able, perversely, to reprimand the architects—not Stalin's regime— and specifically Mordvinov (by then President of the Academy of Architecture) for their ornate and costly architecture.[6] Leonidov was somehow vindicated, if way too late. He died within two years of heart failure.

There were instances, as we saw, where workers in the building industry protested the cost eclectic architecture represented. There is little doubt, however, as shown in the case of Zholtovskij's popularly acclaimed 1934 Palladian Inturist housing,[7] that those who were not considering costs—in addition to their low level of architectural culture—did favor Renaissance revivals while abhorring "ascetic" (even "vegetarian") "boxy" architecture. Such opinion of "regular folks," not to say "the masses," would not have been in itself sufficient to derail progressive architecture.

The real influence, evidently, came from somewhere else. Suffice to look at the example of Ginzburg's 1930 Narkomfin settlement that befell the state bureaucracy. He was able to implement only one of the two planned buildings. The second building, raised perpendicularly to his pristine constructivist dwelling, was an undistinguished replica of a nineteenth-century tenement building the bureaucracy expected. This new ruling class

---

[6] See op. cit. Thomas, P. Whitney, ed. *Khrushchev Speaks* (Michigan: University of Michigan), 1963, pp. 167–96.
[7] In a 1934 Moscow parade, the marchers in a rally stopped to applaud the building.

was aiming at turning whatever was left of the revolution into revivals of the ancient regime, if masked by vocal rhetoric. They dictated the taste of the day, and weighed on modernism's gradual loss of sway. The best illustration of this tug of war were, as we saw it, the competitions for Metro stations and administrative buildings, be it in Moscow or Novosibirsk, where architects actually camouflaged their true intentions in the rendering of their competition entries. They made them appear more conservative than what they would actually end up building. Ginzburg went even further by hiding the outright modern aspects of his sanatorium behind the main façade, playing hide and seek, as it were, with the censor.

Ironically, in 1928, when the modernists called for the party to intervene in the polemic about progressive architecture on the occasion of the Lenin Library competition, they were convinced that a revolutionary party would necessarily reject historicism in the name of the modernity born in the wake of the revolution. The expected support was not granted. Quite to the contrary, they witnessed the emergence of a hydra—Kaganovich's VOPRA.

However, the slow pace of building in the USSR (projects designed in the late 1920s were often not completed until well into the next decade); mixed signals from power centers; the technical and scientific purpose of certain buildings (such as sanatoria); as well as the resilience of the revolutionary utopia in the imaginaries of the moderns, had a cumulative effect on preserving against all odds the modernist and anti-historicist trends, as late as the end of the 1930s. Only after the Second World War did the parvenu taste of the ever growing *nomenklatura*, eager to partake in the glittery aristocratic luxury, fully prevail, with extant constructivist buildings now "enriched" with absurdly added architectural ornaments.

***

The actual turning point occurred in the first semester of 1936, following Ginzburg's major essay in *Arhitekturnaja Gazeta* on the "Future Tasks of Soviet Architecture" that mightily alarmed the authorities. What transpired was that the constructivists, far from being content with a minor technical role in Soviet architecture, clearly advocated modern architecture as a fundamental, and dominant orientation of the country's built world.

From that point on, even the mention of constructivism was offensive. So, for a while, whatever architects produced, be it modern architecture such as Ginzburg's 1938 Ordzhonikidze in Kislovodsk, they had to accept to be formally confined, at least verbally, to "socialist" realism. This is exactly what Ginzburg did in his book about his Kislovodsk "Ordzhonikidze" sanatorium, published in 1940. Soviet architecture was, from then on, to belong exclusively to "socialist" realism, whatever that could have meant, and however the architectural work appeared. The issue was only, as Kolli's Introduction to the book testified, the degree to which Ginzburg had managed to get rid himself of an unspeakable deviation. The totalitarian seal was finally in place in architecture.

Only Viktor Vesnin broke the seal briefly, if with mighty force and courage at the congress. Vesnin's speech managed to play a powerful moment of catharses amongst architects from all over the immense country, deeply frustrated by the increasingly reactionary milieu that, in an undeclared way, favored passéisme. Vesnin's arguments thus resonated unambiguously within their own professional conscience, offering a sudden, if brief, breath of fresh air and sanity. Still, Vesnin was compelled to conclude his speech with the admission that constructivism had been, indeed, defeated.

BIBLIOGRAPHY AND SOURCES

Archives

Archives Nationales [Archives de France] Exposition Internationale de 1937, F12 12447; F12 12442 (For Soviet Pavilion).
AVERY Architectural & Fine Arts Library, Columbia University, Frank Lloyd Wright archives. Drawings MSS 2401. 136; 2401.204; 2401.205; U030C7; A076A08; A059D01; R039D04; R039C01; R039A05.
FLC, Fondation Le Corbusier H2-9-305; H2 I2-5-292; H2-9-373, 3–4.
GARF, Gosudarstvennyj Arhiv Rossijskie Federacii, Fond 5673–7952.
Gosudarstvennyj Muzej Arhitektury im. Shchuseva (Shchuseva Museum of Architecture) Fond: KP OF-6105.
Moscow Communist Party Archive Fond 17.
RAN Arhiv Rossijskoj Akademii Nauk, "Communist Academy" Fond 358.
RGALI Rossijskyj Gosudarstvennyj Arhiv Literatury i Isskustva. Fond SSA 674; VOKS 671.
RGASPI, Rossijskyj Gosudarstvennyj Arhiv Social'no-Politicheskoj Istorii Fond 81 (Kaganovich).
RGB, Rossijska Gosudarstvenna Biblioteka (Originally Lenin Library).

Main Libraries Consulted

CASVA Library (National Gallery Of Art).
Library of Congress.
RGB (State Library), Moscow.
Extension of the RGB (Press and Media).
New York Public Library.

Periodicals

Arhitektura SSSR 1933 ff.
Arhitektura za Rubezhom 1934–1937.
Arhitekturnaja Gazeta 1934–1940.
Iskusstvo v massy.
Izvestija Organ of the SNK (Government).
Komsomol'skaja Pravda Organ of the Communist Youth.
Pechat i Revolucija.
Pravda Organ of the Central Committee.
SA (Sovremenaja Arhitektura), 1926–1930.
Smena.
Sovetskaja Arhitektura 1931–1933.
Stroitel'stvo Moskvy 1927–1940.
Veshch/Objet/Gegenstand.

Bibliography and Sources

Primary Literature

A., A. "Obrazets vysokoj stroitel'noi kul'tury." *Stroitel'stvo Moskvy* 11, no. 6 (1934), pp. 12–14.
Afanas'ev K. ed. *Iz Istorii Sovetskoj Arhitektury: Dokumenti i Materialy, 1917–1925* (Moscow: Akademija Nauk SSSR), 1963.
Afanas'ev K. ed. *Iz Istorii Sovetskoj Arhitektury: Dokumenti i Materialy, 1926–1932* (Moscow: Akademija Nauk SSR), 1970.
Afanas'ev K. et al. ed. *Iz Istorii Sovetskoj Arhitektury, 1941–1945: Dokumenti i Materialy* (Moscow: Akademija Nauka), 1978.
Akademija Stroitel'stva i Arhitektury, *Sanatorii i Doma Otdyha,* (Moscow: Gosizdat, 1962.
"Against *Grupirovshchiny, for the consolidation of All Forces of the Architectural Front!*" Editorial, in *Arhitekturnaja Gazeta* no. 71, 22 December 1935.
"A Necessary Struggle: Protest Resolution on the VHUTEIN Dispute," Editorial, in *SA* 3 (1928), pp. 4–6.
Aksel'rod, I. A. *Arhitektura Strany Sovetov: Shkoly* (Moscow: Akademija Arhitektury SSSR), 1948.
Alabjan, K. S. "Protiv formalizma, uproshchenstva, eklektiki." *Arhitektura SSSR*, n. 4 (1936), pp. 1–6.
Aleksej Dushkin Arhitektor 1930–1950-h Godov: Arhitekturnye Proekty, Dokumenty, Zhivopis', Grafika Exhibition Catalogue (Moscow: Russian Academy of Architecture and Building Sciences), 2004.
Antiova, P. I. et al. ed. *Dvorec Sovetov: Svesojuznij Konkurs 1932 g.* (Moscow: SSA and All Union Cooperative of Plastic Arts), 1933.
Aranovich, D. M., "Konstruktivizm kak metod laboratornoj i pedagogicheskoj raboty." *Sovremennaja Arhitektura,* no. 6 (1927): 160–66.
Aranovich, D. M., "Ot konstruktivizma k socijalisticheskomu realizmu." *Arhitekturnaja Gazeta,* 23 June 1937, 3.
Aranovich, D. M., "Socialisticheskij realizm v arhitekture." *Arhitekturnaja Gazeta,* 23 June 1937, 2.
Aranovich, D. M., Klassika i industrializacija." *Arhitekturnaja Gazeta*, 23 June 1937, 3.
Arhitektor, "Kakofonija v Arhitekture." in *Pravda,* 20 February 1936.
Arkin, David. *Iskusstvo bytovoj veshchi: ocherki noveishej hudozhestvennoj promyshlennosti.* (Moscow: Orgiz-Izogiz), 1932.
Arkin, David "'Gabriel' i Ledoux," in *Problemy Arhitektury: Sbornik Materialolov*, 1 (Moscow) 1936. *Arhitekturnaja Gazeta,* no. 70. December 17, 1935. p. 3. Moscow Conference of Architects.
"ARU: Obshchestvo Arhitektorov Urbanistov," Editorial, *Sovetskaja Arhitektura* 1, no. 1–2 (1931).
Ashchepkov, E., Under the editorial supervision of Ivan Leonidov, Viktor Vesnin, David Arkin: *Arhitektura Gorodov SSSR Novosibirsk* (Moscow: Akademija Arhitektury SSSR and Institut Istorii i Teorii Arhitektury), 1949.
Atarov, N. *El Palacio de los Soviets* (Second edition) (Montevideo: Ediciones Pueblos Unidos), no date.
Barhin, G. B. *Rabochie Zhilishcha* (Moscow: Voprossy Truda), 1925.
Barabanova, Ekaterina "Igarka, la costruzione di una città nell' estremo nord dell' Unione Sovietica," in De Magistris, Alessandro, and Irina Korob'ina, ed. *Ivan Leonidov:1902–19,* (Milano: Electaarchitettura), 2009.
Breinas, Simon, *Architectural Record,* Vol. 82. no. 4, October 1937, pp. 58–63. p. 65.
Bretanickij, L., Under the editorial supervision of Ivan Leonidov, Viktor Vesnin, David Arkin: *Arhitektura Gorodov SSSR: Baku* (Moscow: Akademija Arhitektury SSSR and Institut Istorii i Teorii Arhitektury), 1949.
Buharin, Nikolaj "Notes of an Economist," in *Pravda* 30 September 1928,
Central Committee Decree "O Rabote po Perestrojke Byta", in *Pravda* on 29 May 1930, no. 145.
Chinjakov, A. G. *Bratja Vesnini* (Moscow: Stroizdat), 1970.

Bibliography and Sources

Dikovskij, S. "Arhitekturnye urody." in *Pravda,* 3 February 1936.
Etlin, Richard. *Modernism in Italian Architecture, 1890–1940* (Cambridge: MIT Press), 1991.
Gan, Aleksej, *Constructivism / Konstruktivizm.* Translation and Introduction by Christina Lodder (Barcelona: Tenov), 2013.
Ginzburg, M. Ja., *Stil' i epoha* (Moscow: Gosizdat), 1924.
Ginzburg, M. Ja., "Funktsional'nyj metod i forma." *Sovremennaja Arhitektura* 1, no. 4 (1926), pp. 89–92.
Ginzburg, M. Ja., "Konstruktivizm kak metod laboratornoj i pedagogicheskoj raboty." *Sovremenaja Arhitektura,* no. 6 (1927), pp. 160–66.
Ginzburg, M. Ja., "Zelenyj gorod: Socialisticheskaja rekonstrukcija Moskvy." *Sovremennaja Arhitektura,* no. 1–2 (1930), pp. 17–36.
Ginzburg, M. Ja., "Industrializacija zhilishchnogo stroitel'stva." *Arhitekturnaja Gazeta,* 28 June 1937, 2.
Ginzburg, M. Ja., "Nasledie i novatorstvo." *Arhitektura SSSR* 8, no. 7 (1940), pp. 51–52.
Ginzburg, M. Ja., "Socialisticheskij Realizm" v "Arhitekture." *Arhitekturnaja Gazeta,* 23 June 1937, 2.
Ginzburg, M. Ja., *Arhitektura Sanatorija: NKTP v Kislovodske* (*The Architecture of the Sanatorium: NKTP in Kislovodsk*) (Moscow: Academy of Architecture, USSR), 1940.
Ginzburg, M. Ja., *Style and Epoch,* Oppositions Books. Translated by Anatole Senkevitch (Cambridge, MA: MIT Press), 1982. Original published in Moscow, 1924.
Ginzburg, M. Ja., V. A. Vesnin, and A. A. Vesnin. "Problemy sovremennoj arhitektury." *Arhitektura SSSR* 2, no. 2 (1934): 63–69.
Ginzburg, M. Ja., *Zhilishche* (Moscow: Gosstrojizdat), 1934.
Ginzburg, M. Ja., "Zadachi Sovetske Arhitektury" [The tasks of Soviet Architecture], in *Arhitekturnaja Gazeta,* 27 November, no. 27 1935 p. 3.
Gol'ts, G. P. "Tvorcheskij otchet." *Arhitektura SSSR* 3, no. 5 (1935), pp. 17–20.
Gol'ts, G. P. "Lakonizm v arhite0kture." *Arhitekturnaja Gazeta,* 3 June 1935, 2.
Gorskij S., "Otrubite ej kryl'ja, in *Smena* no. 4, 1931, pp. 22–23.
Hazanova, V. I. *Sovetskaja arhitektura pervoj pjatiletki: Problemy goroda budushchego* (Moscow: Nauka), 1980.
Higer, Roman. "Formalizm: Ideologija upadochnichestva v sovetskoj arhitekture." *Sovremennaja Arhitektura,* no. 4 (1929): 142–46.
Iofan, B. M. "Sanatorij v Barvihe." *Arhitektura SSSR* 1, no. 6 (1933): 24–26, pp. 1–4.
"Itogi vsesojuznogo tvorcheskogo soveshchanija arhitektorov." *Arhitektura SSSR,* no. 7(1935), pp. 1–4.
Jalovkin, F. "VOPRA i OSA." *Sovremennaja Arhitektura,* no. 5 (1929), p. 171.
Jaralov, Ju, Under the editorial supervision of Ivan Leonidov, Viktor Vesnin, David Arkin: Arhitektura Gorodov SSSR, *Erevan* (Moscow: Akademija Arhitektury SSSR and Institut Istorii i Teorii Arhitektury), 1948.
Kaganovich, Lazar, *Pamjatnye Zapiski* (Moscow: Vagrius), 1996.
"K itogam diskussii." *Arhitekturnaja Gazeta,* 3 March 1936, 1.
"La Réaction esthétique en U.R.S.S." *L'Architecture d'Aujourd'hui,* no. 5 (1933), p. 106.
Kettering Karen L. "An Introduction to the Design of the Moscow Metro in the Stalin Period: "The Happiness of Life Underground," in *Studies in the Decorative Arts* Vol. 7, no. 2 (Spring–Summer 2000), pp. 2–20.
Ladovskij, N. A. "Osnovy postroenija teorii arkhitektury." *Izvestjia ASNOVA,* no. 1 (1926), pp. 3–6.
Lavrent'ev, A. N. *Aleksej* [series Tvorci Avangarda] (Moscow: Izdatel'skij proekt "Ruskij Avangard"), 2010.
Lebedev, A. I., ed. *Voprosy arhitektury* (Moscow: OGIZ), 1935.
"Lestnica, vedushchaja nikuda': arhitektura vverh nogami." *Komsomol'skaja Pravda,* 18 February 1936, 4.
"Let's Create a Federation," *SA* 3 (1929), p. 89.

Bibliography and Sources

Lissitzky, El, *Dva Kvadrata* (Berlin), 1922.
Maca, I., ed. *Sovetskoe iskusstvo za 15 let: Materialy i dokumentcija* (Moskva: Izogiz), 1933.
"Mebel' Fakulteta po Obrabotke Dereva i Metalla VHUTEINa," in *Stroitel'stvo Moskvy*, October 1929, pp. 9–12.
Mel'nikov, K. "Ob arhitekture i ob sebe (25 March 1936)," in *Konstantin Stepanovich Mel'nikov: arhitektura moej zhizni, tvorcheskaja koncepcija: tvorcheskaja praktika,* ed. A. A. Strigalev and I. V. Kokkinaki, (Moscow: Iskusstvo), 1985, pp 126–29.
Meyer, Hannes, "Bauen, Bauarbeiter und Techniker in der Sowjetunion," in *Das Neue Russland* 8–9, (1931).
Mikkola, Kirmo. "Konstruktivismi Suomen Modernissa: Arkkitehtuurissa Kuvataiteesa ja Taideteollisuudessa," in *Muotja Rakenne* (Helsinki, Finland: Ateneumin Taidemuseo), 1981.
Miljutin, N. A. *Sotsgorod: The Problem of Building Socialist Cities.* Translated by Arthur Sprague (Cambridge, MA: M.I.T. Press), 1974.
Miljutin, N. A. *Sotsgorod: Problema stroitel'stva socialisticheskih gorodov : osnovnye voprosy racionalnoj planirovki i stroitel'stva naselennyh mest SSSR.* (Moskva: Gosudarstvennoe izdatel'stvo), 1930.
Miljutin, Nikolaj, "Fundamental Questions about the Building of Housing and the *Byt*," *Sovetskaja Arhitektura* no. 1–2, 1931.
Miljutin, Nikolaj, "Theoretical Fundaments in the Theory of Soviet Architecture," in *Sovetskaja Arhitektura* no.6, 933, p. 5.
Mordvinov, A. G. "Leonidovshchina i eë vred." *Iskusstvo v massy,* no. 12 (1930), pp. 12–15.
Mordvinov, A. G. "Nashi zadachi." *Akademija arhitektury* 1, no. 1–2 (1934): 4–6.
Mordvinov, A. G. "VOPRA: Nashi zadachi." *Sovetskaja arhitektura* 1, no. 1–2 (1931), pp. 65–66.
Mordvinov, Grigorevich Arkadij. "Leonidovshchina i eë vred," *Iskusstvo v Massy* (Art to the Masses), in the column "Let Us Destroy a Foreign Ideology," no. 12 (1930), pp. 12–15.
Mordvinov, Grigorevich Arkadij, "Bauhaus: k Vystavke v Moskve." *Sovetskaja Arhitektura* 1–2, 1931, pp. 8–11.
Murzin, M. Ju. "Psikho-tekhnicheskaja laboratoriia arhitektury (V poriadke postanovki voprosa)." *Izvestija ASNOVA,* no. 1 (1926), p. 7.
Murzin, M. Ju. *Nashe Nasledie: "Dorogoj Lazar' Moiseevich" V epistoljarnom Zhanre s komentarjami Jurija Murzina* (Moscow), 2006.
Nikiforov, N. *Kul'turnaja Revolucija i Ozdorovlenie Byta* (Moscow: Gosudarstvenoe Medicinskoe Izdatel'stvo), 1929.
Nikiforov, N., *V istokov formirovanija ASNOVA i OSA: dve arhitekturnye gruppy INHUKa.* (Moscow: Arhitektura), 1994.
Nikiforov, N., *ZHIVSKUL'PTARH, 1919–1920: Pervaja tvorcheskaja organizacija sovetskogo arhiteknurnogo avangarda* (Moscow: Arhitektura), 1993.
Nikolaev, V. "Konstrukcija Dvorca Sovetov na Stal'nom Karkase," in *Arhitektura SSSR,* 2, 1937.
Novickij, Pëtr "Restavratory / Vosstanoviteli i Shkola Arhitektury VTH," in *Stroitel'stvo Moskvy,* Jul. 1929, 12–13.
"O perestrojke literaturno-hudozhestvennyh organizacii, Postanovlenie CK VKP(b) ot 23 aprelja 1932 goda," in *Iz istorii sozdanija Sojuza sovetskih arhitektorov,* ed. T. Samohina (Moscow: Sojuz moskovskih arhitektorov), "Trockist-avantjurist Ohitovich razoblachen." *Arkhitekturnaja Gazeta,* 8 April 1935, 2.
Ohitovich, M., "K probleme goroda: o sposobah vosprijatija arhitekturnogo opyta." *Sovremennaja Arhitektura,* no. 4 (1929): 130–34.
"Ot redaksii," editorial, in *SA* no. 5 1930, pp. 2–4.
Prezidium OSA. "Sozdadim federatsiiu revoliutsionnykh arkhitektorov." *Sovremennaja Arhitektura,* no. 3 (1929): 89.
"Programmno-ideologicheskaja ustanovka sektora ASNOVA." *Sovetskaja Arhitektura* 1, no. 1–2 (1931): 46–47.

"Programma proektirovanija Dvorca Sovetov SSSR v Moskve," in *Dvorec Sovetov: Vsesojuznyj Konkurs*, 1932

"Protiv neprincipielnogo eklektizma" [Against Unprincipled Eclecticism], SA 3 (1928), 92.

"Protiv formalizma, uproshchenstva, i eklektiki" *Arhitekturnaja Gazeta,* 28 February 1936, 1–3.

"Protiv formalizma." *Arhitekturnaja Gazeta,* 23 February 1936, 1–2.

Rebajn, Ja. *Rostov-na-Donu* [Arhitektura Gorodov SSSR series] (Moscow: Gosudarstvenoe Izdatel'stvo), 1950.

Rempel' L. I. *Arhitektura Poslevoennoj Italii* [Post-War Architecture in Italy] (Moscow: Academy of Architecture), 1935.

"Rezoljucija s''ezda po dokladam o zadachah sovetskoj arhitektury." *Arhitektura SSSR* 5, no. 7–8 (1937), pp.4–5.

Roshchin, "Functionalism is not a Road," in *Isskustvo v Massy* no. 6, 1930.

Shalavin and Lamtsov, "About the Roads of Development of Socialism," in *Pechat i Revolucija,* no. 9, 1929.

Shchusev, A. V. "Protiv asketicheskoj arhitektury." *Stroitel'stvo Moskvy* 10, no. 2–3 (1933): 17.

Shchusev, A., "The Roads of Soviet Architecture," *Arhitekturnaja Gazeta* no. 70, 17 December 1935, p. 3.

Sokolov, N. B. *Sochi—Macesta: Ocherk Arhitektury* (Moscow: Gosizdat), 1950.

Sovet stroitel'stva Dvorca Sovetov. "Ob organizacii rabot po okonchatel'nomu sostavleniju proekta Dvorca Sovetov SSSR v gor. Moskve." *Stroitel'stvo Moskvy,* no. 3 (1932), pp. 15–16.

Stalin, Joseph, Vissarionovich, *Sochinenija* (Moscow: Gosizdat), 1951.

Stalin, Joseph, *Sochinenija* (Moscow: Institut Marksa-Engel'sa-Lenina Pri TsK VKPB(b), Tom X, 1946–52).

Taut, Bruno, "Stroitel'stvo i Arhitektura Novoj Moskvy," *Stroitel'stvo Moskvy,* Feb. 1929, pp. 11–12.

Troickij, N. V. *Voronezh* [Arhitektura Gorodov SSSR series] (Moscow: Gosudarstvenoe Izdatel'stvo), 1959.

Vesnin A. and V. Vesnin. "Forma i soderzhanie," in *Arhitekturnaja Gazeta* no. 20, April 8, 1935, p. 6.

Vesnin, A. "Novyj Stil' Epohi," in *Sovetskoe Iskusstvo,* November 17, 1934, p. 2.

Vlasov, Aleksandr, ed. *Sovetskaja Arhitektura, 1917–1957* (Moscow: Gosizdat), 1957.

Volodin, P. *Sverdlovsk* [Under the editorial supervision of Ivan Leonidov, Viktor Vesnin, David Arkin] *Arhitektura Gorodov SSSR* series, (Moscow: Akademija Arhitektury SSSR and Institut Istorii i Teorii Arhitektury), 1948.

Wright, Frank Lloyd, "Architecture and Life in the USSR," in *Architectural Record,* vol. 82. no. 4, October 1937, pp. 58–63.

Wright, Frank Lloyd. "First Answers to Questions by Pravda." From *Collected Writings, Volume II: 1931–1939.* (Rizzoli International Publications, Inc. New York, NY: 1993), pp. 141–42. Published originally in 1933.

Zapletin, I. "Dvorec Sovetov SSSR (Po materialam konkursa)," in *Sovetskaja Arhitektura* no. 2–3, 1932.

Zhdanov, A., M. Gorky, N. Buharin, K. Radek, A. Stetsky, *Problems of Soviet Literature: Reports and Speeches at the First Soviet Writers' Congress* (Moscow/Leningrad: Cooperative Publishing Society of Foreign Workers in the USSR), 1935.

Žižek, Slavoj. "The Two Totalitarianisms," in *LRB,* vol. 27 no. 6, 17 March 2005.

Secondary Literature

Adkins, Helen, et al. *Naum Gabo and the Competition for the Palace of Soviets*, Moscow, 1931–1933. Berlin: Berlinische Galerie, 1993.

Bibliography and Sources

Afanas'ev, K. N., and V. E. Hazanova. *Iz istorii sovetskoj arhitektury 1926–1932 gg. : dokumenty i materialy : Tvorcheskie ob'edinenji.* (Moscow: Nauka), 1970.

Aleksandrov, P. A., and S. O. Khan-Magomedov. *Ivan Leonidov* (Moskva: Strojizdat), 1971.

Alexopulos, Golfo, Julie Hessler, and Kiril Tomoff *Writing the Stalin Era: Sheila Fitzpatrick and Soviet Historiography* (New York: Palgrave Macmillan), 2011.

Anderson, Richard, *Architecture in Print: Design and Debate in the Soviet Union* (Columbia University, 2005).

Anderson, Richard. "The Journal States its Aims: Partisanship and the Party Line in the Soviet Architectural Press," in *Architecture in Print: Design and Debate in the Soviet Union, 1919–1935: Selections from the Collection of Stephen Garmey,* ed. Richard Anderson and Kristin Romberg, (New York: Miriam and Ira D. Wallach Art Gallery Columbia University), 2005, pp. 25–36.

Anderson, Richard, *Russia,* [Series: Modern Architecture in History] (Glasgow: Reaktion Books), 2015.

Anderson, Richard. "USA/USSR: Architecture and War," *Grey Room,* no. 34 (Winter 2009): 80–103.

Aratov, N. S., *El Palacio de los Soviet* (Montevideo: Pueblos Unidos) 1945, second edition.

Astaf'eva-Dlugach, M. I. et al. ed. *Zodchie Moskvy* (Moscow: Moskovskij Rabochij), 1988.

Attwood, Lynne. *Gender and Housing in Soviet Russia: Private Life in a Public Space.* (Manchester: Manchester University Press), 2010.

Avangard i Aviajacija (Moscow: Ievrejskij Muzej i Centr Tolerantnosti), 2014.

Banks, Miranda, ed. *The Aesthetic Arsenal: Socialist Realism under Stalin,* exhibition catalogue (New York: The Institute for Contemporary Art), 1994.

Bann, S, and Bowlt, J. E. *Russian Formalism: A Collection of Articles and Texts* (Edinburgh), 1973.

Barenberg, Alan. *Gulag Town, Company Town: Forced Labor and Its Legacy in Vorkuta* (New Haven: Yale University Press), 2014.

Barron S., ed. *The Avant-Garde in Russia, 1910–1934: New Perspectives,* (Cambridge & London: MIT Press), 1980. Walter,

Baudelaire, Charles *L'Albatros,* from *Fleurs du mal.* Translation by Eli Siegel (Definition Press), 1968.

Benevolo, Leonardo, *Storia dell'architettura moderna* (Bari: Laterza) 1960.

Benjamin Walter, *Moscow Diary,* ed. Gary Smith, trans. Richard Sieburth, (Cambridge: Harvard University Press), 1986).

Benton, Kathleen, *Moscow, an Architecture History* (London: I B Tauris) 1990.

Bocharov, Ju., Khan-Magomedov *Nikolaj Miljutin* [Series Tvorci Avangard] (Moscow: "Arhitektura-S"), 2007.

Bongraber, Christian & Schadlich, eds. *Avantgarde II: 1924–1937; Sowjetische Architektur* (Stuttgart: G. Hatje), 1993.

Borngraber, Christian. "Constructivistes et académistes dans le Métro de Moscou au milieu des années trente," in *URSS, 1917–1978: La ville, l'architecture,* J. L. Cohen, M. De Michelis, M. Tafuri, eds. (Paris: L'Equerre and Rome: Officina Edizioni), 1979.

Borngräber, Christian. "Auslandische Architekten in der UdSSR: Bruno Taut, die Brigaden Ernst May, Hannes Meyer und Hans Schmidt," in *Wem gehört die Welt : Kunst und Gesellschaft in der Weimarer Republik,* ed. Jurgen Kleindienst, (Berlin: Die Gesellschaft), 1977, pp. 109–42.

Bouvard, Josette, *Le Métro de Moscou: La construction d'un mythe soviétique,* (Paris: Sextant), 2005.

Bowlt, John E. and Olga Matich, ed. *The Russian Avant-Garde and Cultural Experiment* (Stanford, CA: Stanford University Press), 1996, 194–218.

Bown, Cullerne Matthew, *Art under Stalin* (New York: Holmes & Meier), 1991.

Brandenberger, David. *National Bolshevism: Stalinist Mass Culture and the Formation of Modern Russian National Identity, 1931–1956.* Cambridge: Harvard University Press, 2002.

Buchli, Victor. "Moisej Ginzburg's Narkomfin Communal House in Moscow: Contesting the Social and Material World." *Journal of the Society of Architectural Historians* 57, no. 2 (1998), pp. 160–81.

Buck-Morss, Susan. *Dreamworld and Catastrophe: The Passing of Mass Utopia in East and West* (Cambridge, MA: MIT Press), 2002.

Bulgakowa Oksana "Spatial Figures in Soviet Cinema of the 1930s," in *The Landscape of Stalinism: The Art and Ideology of Soviet Space*, ed. Evgeny Dobrenko and Eric Naiman, (Seattle: University of Washington Press, 2003),

Burger, Peter. *Theory of the Avant-Garde* (Minneapolis: University of Minnesota Press), 1984.

Castillo, Greg. "Classicism for the Masses: Books on Stalinist Architecture," *Design Book Review* no. 35/36 (Winter–Spring 1995), 78–88.

Castillo, Greg, "Gorky Street and the Design of the Stalin Revolution," in *Streets: Critical Perspectives on Public Space*, ed. Zenep Celik, Diane Favro, and Richard Ingersoll, (Berkeley and Los Angeles: University of California Press, 1994), 57–70.

Central Committee Decree "On the Reconstruction of daily life (*byt*)" ["O Rabote po Perestrojke Byta"], Published in *Pravda* on 29 May 1930, no. 145.

Cherpkunova, I. *Kluby Postroennye po Programme Profsojuzov, 1927–1930* (Moscow: Nauchno issledovatel'skij Muzej Arhitektury Imenni A.V Shchuseva) 2010.

Chinjakov A. G. *Brat'ja Vesniny* (Moscow: Izdatel'stvo Literatury po Stroitel'stvu), 1970.

Chepkunova, I. V., M. A. Kostyuk, E.Ju. Zheludkova, ed. *Moskovskoe Metro Podzemnyj Pamjatnik Arhitektury* (Moscow: Svjaz Epoh), 2016.

Ciucci, Giorgio, Francesco dal Co, Marco De Michelis, Viteslav Rochazka, Hans Schmidt, Manfredo Tafuri et al. ed. *Socialismo, Città, Architettura, URSS 1931–1937: Il contributo degli architetti europei* (Rome: Officina Edizioni), second edition, 1972.

Clark, Katerina. "The Avant-Garde and the Retrospectivists as Players in the Evolution of Stalinist Culture," in *Laboratory of Dreams: The Russian Avant-Garde and Cultural Experiment*, ed. John E. Bowlt and Olga Matich, 259–76. (Stanford CA: Stanford University Press), 1996.

Clark, Katerina. "The 'New Moscow' and the New 'Happiness': Architecture as a Nodal Point in the Stalinist System of Value." *Petrified Utopia: Happiness Soviet Style*, edited by Marina Balina and Evgeny Dobrenko, 189–200. (London: Anthem Press), 2009.

Clark Katerina. *Moscow the Fourth Rome: Stalinism. Cosmopolitanism, and the Evolution of Soviet Culture 1931–1941* (Cambridge, MA: Harvard University Press), 2011.

Cohen J. L., M. De Michelis, M. Tafuri, eds., *URSS, 1917–1978: La ville, L'architecture* (Paris: L'Equerre and Rome: Officina Edizioni) 1979.

Cohen, Jean-Louis "America: A Soviet Ideal," *AA Files* 5 (Jan. 1984).

Cohen, Jean-Louis. *Building a new New World* (New Haven: Yale University Press), forthcoming May 2020.

Cohen, Jean-Louis, "L'Oncle Sam au pays des Soviets: Le temps des avant-gardes," in *Américanisme et modernité : l'ideal americain dans l'architecture*, ed. Jean-Louis Cohen and Hubert Damisch (Paris: Flammarion), 1993, pp. 403–35.

Cohen, Jean-Louis. "L'Aventure Soviétique (1934–1937) ou l'attente déçue," in *André Lurçat (1894–1970): Autocritique d'un Moderne*, (Paris-Liège: IFA-Madraga), 1995, "pp. 177–209.

Cohen, Jean-Louis. *L'Architecture d'André Lurçat (1894–1970): L'autocritique d'un moderne* (Liège: Pierre Mardaga), 1995.

Cohen, Jean-Louis. "La forme urbaine du "réalisme 'socialiste'," in Cohen, J.-L., M. De Michelis and M. Tafuri, dir., *URSS 1917–1978, l'architecture, la ville*, Rome, Paris: Officina Edizioni, L'Equerre, 1979, p. 140–99.

Cohen, Jean-Louis. *Scenes of the World to Come: European Architecture and the American Challenge, 1893–1960*. (Paris: Flammarion/Canadian Center for Architecture), 1995.

Cohen, Jean-Louis. "Le commissaire prend le crayon," in *Sotsgorod: le problème de la construction des villes socialistes* (Paris: Editions de l'imprimeur), 2002.

Cohen, Jean-Louis *Building the Revolution: Soviet Art and Architecture 1915–1935*. (London: Royal Academy of Arts), 2011.

Bibliography and Sources

Cohen, Jean-Louis. *Le Corbusier and the Mystique of the USSR* (Princeton: Princeton University Press), 1992.

Cohen, Jean-Louis, "Late Constructivism and 'Socialist' Realism 1930–37," *Architecture and Urbanism* no. 253 (October 1995), 11–21.

Cohen, Jean-Louis. "Useful Hostage: Constructing Wright in Soviet Russia and France," in *Frank Lloyd Wright: Europe and Beyond*, edited by Anthony Alofsin. Berkeley: University of California Press, 1999.

Cohen, Yves, "The Soviet Fordson: Between the Politics of Stalin and the Philosophy of Ford, 1924–1934," in *Ford, 1903–2003: The European History*, ed. Hubert Bonin, Yannick Lung and Holliday, Steven, pp. 531–58. (Paris: P.L.A.G.E.), 2003.

Colton, Timothy J. *Moscow: Governing the Socialist Metropolis*. (Cambridge: Harvard University Press,) 1995.

Conquest, Robert, *The Great Terror: A Reassessment* (Oxford: Oxford University Press), 40th edition, 2008.

Conn, Steven. *Americans Against the City: Anti-Urbanism in the Twentieth Century* (Oxford: Oxford University Press), 2014.

Cooke, Catherine. "'Form is a function X': The Development of the Constructivist Architect's Design Method." *Architectural Design* 53, no. 5–6 (1983), pp. 34–49.

Cooke, Catherine. Guest edited, *Russian Avant-Garde: Art and Architecture* (London: Architectural Design and Academy Editions), 1983.

Cooke, Catherine. "Mediating Creativity and Politics: Sixty Years of Architectural Competitions in Russia," in *The Great Utopia: The Russian and Soviet Avant-Garde, 1915–1932*, (New York: Guggenheim Museum), 1992, pp. 681–715

Cooke, Catherine. *Russian Avant-Garde: Theories of Art, Architecture and the City* (London: Academy Editions), First edition, 1995.

Cooke, Catherine, "Beauty as a Route to 'the Radiant Future': Responses of Soviet Architecture," *Journal of Design History* vol. 10, no. 2 (1997), pp. 137–60.

Cooke, Catherine (with Susan E. Reid). "Modernity and Realism," in *Russian Art and the West: A Century of Dialogue in Painting, Architecture, and the Decorative Arts,* edited by Rosalind P. Blakesley and Susan E. Reid, 172–194. (DeKalb: Northern Illinois University Press), 2007

Crankshaw, Edward, and Talbott, Strobe. ed. *Khrushchëv Remembers* (Boston: Little, Brown), 1970.

Day, Andrew Elam. "The Rise and Fall of Stalinist Architecture," in *Architectures of Russian Identity: 1500 to the Present,* edited by James Cracraft and Daniel Rowland, 172–190 (Ithaca, NY: Cornell University Press), 2003.

De Feo, Vittorio *U.R.S.S. Architettura, 1917–1936* (Rome: Editori Riuniti), 1963.

De Haan, Heather, *Stalinist City Planning: Professionals, Performance, and Power.* (Toronto: University of Toronto Press), 2013.

De Magistris, Alessandro, ed. *La Costruzione della Città Totalitaria: Il Piano di Mosca e il Dibattito sulla Città Sovietica tra gli Anni Venti e Cinquanta* (Milano: Città Studi Edizioni), 1995.

De Magistris, Alessandro, *URSS, Anni ⊠30-⊠50: Paesaggi dell'Utopia Staliniana* (Milano: Mazzotta) 1997.

De Magistris, Alessandro, "Il Dibattito Achitettonico degli Anni '30–'50 nelle pagine di Architettura SSSR," in *Casabella* no. 602, year LVII.

De Magistris, Alessandro, "Mosca Anni Trenta: Realismo e burocratizzazione." *Rassegna* 20, no. 75 (1998) pp.70–85.

De Magistris, Alessandro, and Irina Korob'ina, ed. *Ivan Leonidov:1902–1959* (Milano: Electaarchitettura), 2009.

De Michelis, Marco and Pasini, Ernesto, *La Città Sovietica, 1925–1937* (Venice: Marslio Editori), 1981.

Djilas, Milovan, *Conversations with Stalin* (New York: Harcourt, Brace), 1962.

Djilas, Milovan, *The New Class: An Analysis of the Communist System* (New York: Praeger), 1957.
Dluhosch Eric and Rotislav Svácha, *Karel Teige 1900/1951: L'Enfant Terrible of Czech Modernist Avant-Garde* (Cambridge: MIT Press, 1999).
Dobrenko Evgeny and Eric Naiman ed. *The Landscape of Stalinism: The Art and Ideology of Soviet Space* (Seattle and London: University of Washington Press), 2003.
Dobrenko, Evgeny. *The Political Economy of Socialist Realism* (New Haven: Yale University Press), 2007.
Dushkina, N. O. *Zhizn Arhitektora Dushkina: 1904–1977* (Moscow: Izdatel'stvo "A-Fond"), 2004.
Duskin, J. Eric. *Stalinist Reconstruction and the Confirmation of a New Elite, 1945–1953*. (New York: Palgrave), 2001.
Dunham, Vera S. *In Stalin's Time: Middleclass Values in Soviet Fiction* (Durham: Duke University Press), 1990.
Ejgel', Isaak. Ju. *Boris Iofan* (Moscow: Stroizdat), 1978.
Erlich, Victor *Russian Formalism: History and Doctrine* (New Haven and London: Yale University), 1981.
Fitzpatrick, Sheila. "Becoming Cultured: Socialist Realism and the Representation of Privilege and Taste," in *The Cultural Front: Power and Culture in Revolutionary Russia* (Ithaca: Cornell University Press), 1992, pp. 216–37.
Fitzpatrick, Sheila. *Everyday Stalinism: Ordinary Life in extraordinary Times: Soviet Russia in the 1930s* (Oxford: Oxford University Press), 1999.
Fitzpatrick, Sheila. *On Stalin's Team: The Years of Living Dangerously in Soviet Politics* (Princeton and Oxford: Princeton University Press), 2015.
Fitzpatrick, Sheila *The Russian Revolution* (Oxford and New York: Oxford University Press), 1982 & 1994.
Fitzpatrick, Sheila, "Cultural Revolution as Class War," in Fitzpatrick, ed. *Cultural Revolution in Russia: 1928–1931* (Bloomington: Indiana University Press), 1984.
Fitzpatrick, Sheila, ed. *Cultural Revolution in Russia, 1928–1931* (Bloomington: Indiana University Press), 1984.
Fitzpatrick, Sheila, *The Cultural Front: Power and Culture in Revolutionary Russia* (Ithaca and London: Cornell University Press), 1992.
Fitzpatrick, Sheila, *Stalinism: New Directions*, (London: Routledge), 2000, pp. 1–14.
Freeman, Joshua, *Behemoth: A History of the Factory and the Making of the Modern World* (New York & London: W. W. Norton & Company), 2018.
Furst, Juliane. "Late Stalinist Society: History, Policies, and People," in *Late Stalinist Russia: Society between Reconstruction and Reinvention*, edited by Juliane Furst (London: Routledge), 2006, 1–20.
Getty, J. Arch. *Origins of the Great Purges: The Soviet Communist Party Reconsidered, 1933–1938*. (Cambridge: Cambridge University Press), 1985.
Getty, J. Arch., and Oleg Naumov, *The Road to Terror: Stalin and the Self-destruction of the Bolsheviks, 1932–1939*, (New Haven and London: Yale University Press), 1999.
Getty, J. Arch., "*Samokritika* Rituals in the Stalinist Central Committee, 1933–38." *Russian Review* 58, no. 1 (1999), pp. 49–70.
Getty, J. Arch. *Practicing Stalinism: Bolsheviks, Boyars, and the Persistence of Tradition* (New Haven: Yale University Press), 2013.
Geyer, Michael and Sheila Fitzpatrick, *Beyond Totalitarianism: Stalinism and Nazism Compared* (Cambridge: Cambridge University Press), 2009.
Gide, André, *Retour de l'Urss* (Paris: Gallimard), 1936.
Goldman, Wendy Z. *Inventing the Enemy: Denunciation and Terror in Stalin's Russia* (New York: Cambridge University Press), 2011.
Gozak, Andrei and Andrei Leonidov. *Ivan Leonidov: The Complete Work* (London, New York: Rizzoli), 1988.

Bibliography and Sources

Gozak A. *Narkomtjazhprom Leonidova: Shedevry Avantgard* (Moscow: MU/AR) 2011.
Groys, Boris. "The Birth of Socialist Realism from the Spirit of the Russian Avant-Garde," in *Laboratory of Dreams: The Russian Avant-Garde and Cultural Experiment*, ed. John E. Bowlt and Olga Matich (Stanford CA: Stanford University Press), 1996.
Groys, Boris. *Petersburg, Crucible of Cultural Revolution* (Cambridge, MA: Harvard University Press), 1995.
Groys, Boris. *The Total Art of Stalinism: Avant-Garde, Aesthetic Dictatorship, and Beyond* (London-New York: Verso), 2011.
Hazanova, V. E. *Sovetska Arhitektura Pervoj Pja tiletki: Problemy Goroda Budushchego* (Moscow: Nauka), 1980.
Hendrix, John Shannon and Lorens Eyan Holm. *Architecture and the Unconscious* (London: Ashgate), 2016.
Herf, Jeffrey. *Reactionary Modernism: Technology, culture, and politics in Weimar and the Third Reich* (Cambridge: Cambridge University Press), 1984.
Hoisington, Sona. "'Ever Higher': The Evolution of the Project for the Palace of Soviets," *Slavic Review* 62, no.1 (Spring 2003).
Hudson, Hugh. *Blue Prints and Blood: The Stalinization of Soviet Architecture, 1917-1937* (Princeton University Press), 1994.
Ikonnikov, Andrej. *Arkhitektura Moskvy XX vek* (Moscow: Moskovskij rabochij, 1984).
Ikonnikov, Andrej. Vladimirovich. *Russian Architecture of the Soviet Period.* (Moscow: Raduga Publishers), 1988.
Ital'janskij, Andrej. *Dvorec Sovetov* [Il Palazzo Italiano dei Soviet] Collection of the family Armando Barzini. Exhibition catalogue (Moscow: Mu Ar), 2007.
Johnson, Donald. "Frank Lloyd Wright in Moscow," *JSAH*, Vol. 54 March 1987, 65–79.
Kachurin, Pamela. *Making Modernism Soviet: The Russian Avant-Garde in the Early Soviet Era, 1918-1928* (Evanston, IL: Northwestern University Press), 2013.
Kaganovich, L. M. *Socialist Reconstruction of Moscow and other Cities in the U.S.S.R* (New York: International Publishers), 1931.
Kazus', I. A. *Sovetskaja Arhitektura 1920ih godov: organizatsija proektirovanija* (Moscow: Progress-Tradicija), 2009.
Khan-Magomedov, Omarovich, Selim. *Andrej Burov* [Series Tvorci Avangarda] (Moscow), 2012.
Khan-Magomedov, Omarovich, Selim. *Alexandr Vesnin and Russian Constructivism* (London: Lund Humphries), 1996.
Khan-Magomedov, Omarovich, Selim. *Arhitektura sovetskogo avangarda* (Moskva: Strojizdat), 1996.
Khan-Magomedov, Omarovich, Selim. *Il'ja Golosov* (Moscow: Strojizdat), 1988.
Khan-Magomedov, Omarovich, Selim. *Mihail Ohitovich* [Series Tvorcy Avangarda] (Moscow: "Arhitektura-C"), 2009.
Khan-Magomedov, Omarovich, Selim. *Nikolaj Ladovskij* [Series Tvorcy Avangarda] (Moscow: "Arhitektura-C"), 2007.
Khan-Magomedov, Omarovich, Selim. *Racionalizm: (racio-arhitektura) "Formalizm"* (Moscow: "Arhitektura-S"), 2007.
Khan-Magomedov, Omarovich, Selim. *Vhutemas* (Paris: Edition du Regard), 1990.
Khan-Magomedov, Omarovich, Selim. "K istorii vybora mesta dlja Dvorec Sovetov," in *Arhitektura i Stroitel'stvo Moskvy*, Jan. 1988, pp. 21–23.
Khan-Magomedov, Omarovich, Selim. "Ivan Leonidov, un architetto sovietico, 1902-1959," in *Ivan Leonidov, 1902-1959*, ed. Alessandro de Magistris and Irina Korobina (Milano: Mondadori Electa), 2009.
Khlevniuk, Oleg. "The Gulag and Non-Gulag as One Interrelated Whole." *Kritika* 16, 3 (Summer 2015) pp. 479-98.
Khmel'nitsky, Dmitrij, ed. *Ivan Zholtovskij: Arhitektor Sovetskogo Palladianstva* (Berlin / Moscow: Dom publishers & Gosudarstvenij Muzej Arhitekturi), 2013.

Khmel'nitskij, Dmitrij. *Arkhitektura Stalina: psikhologija i stil'* (Moscow: Progress-Traditsija), 2007.
Khmel'nitsky, Dmitrij. *Zodchij Stalin, Ocherki vizual'nost* (Moscow: Novoe literaturnoe obozrenie), 2007.
Kiaer, Christina, "Was 'Socialist Realism' Forced Labour? The Case of Aleksandr Deineka in the 1930s." *Oxford Art Journal* 8, no. 3 (2005), pp. 321–45.
Kiaer, Christina. *Imagine no Possessions: The Socialist Objects of Russian Constructivism* (Cambridge MA: MIT Press), 2005.
Kirov, S. M. *Izabranye stat'i i rechi: 1912–1934.* (Moscow: Gosizdat), 1957.
Khrushchëv, Nikita Sergeevich. Ed., Crankshaw, Edward, and Talbott, Strobe. *Khrushchev Remembers*. First edition. (Boston: Little, Brown), 1970.
Kopp, Anatole. *Changer la vie, changer la ville: de la vie nouvelle aux problèmes urbains, U.R.S.S. 1917–1932* (Paris: Union générale d'éditions), 1975.
Kopp, Anatole. *L'Architecture de la période stalinienne* (Grenoble: Presses Universitaires de Grenoble), 1978.
Korobyna, Irina and Aleksandr Rappaport, *Paviliony SSSR na Mezhdunarodnyh Vistavkah* (Moscow: Museum of Architecture), 2013.
Kotkin, Stephen. *Stalin: Waiting for Hitler* (New York: Penguin Press), 2017.
Kotkin, Stephen. *Magnetic Mountain: Stalinism as a Civilization* (Berkley, Los Angeles, London: University of California Press), 1995.
Kotkin, Stephen. *1991 and the Russian Revolution: Sources, Conceptual Categories, Analytical Frameworks* in *The Journal of Modern History*, Vol. 70, no. 2 (June 1998), pp. 384–425.
Kuznetsov, Pavel, Irina Korobyna and Irina Chepkunova. *Arhitektor Konstantin Mel'nikov: Pavil'ony, garazhi, kluby i Zhil'e Sovetskoj Epohi* (Moscow: MU/AR), 2015.
Le Corbusier. "The Atmosphere of Moscow," trans. Edith Schreiber Aujame, *Precisions on the Present State of Architecture and City Planning* (Cambridge: MIT Press, 1991).
Le Corbusier, Léger, Lurçat, Aragon et al. *Présentation de Serge Fauchereau La Querelle du réalisme* [Une collection des Éditions du Cercle d'Art] (Paris: Diagonales), 1987.
Lizon, Peter. "Quest for an Image to Serve a Revolution: Design Competitions for the Palace of the Soviets," *Journal of Architectural Education* 35 (1982), pp. 10–16.
Lizon, Peter. *The Palace of the Soviets: The Paradigm of Architecture in the USSR* (Colorado Springs: Three Continents Press), 1992.
Mandelstam, Nadezhda. *Hope Against Hope* (London: The Harvill Press), second edition, 1999.
Margolin, Victor. *The Slavic and East European Journal*, Vol. 32, no. 3 (Autumn, 1988), pp. 489–91.
Margolin, Victor. *The Struggle for Utopia: Rodchenko, Lissitzky, Moholy-Nagy, 1917–1946.* (Chicago and London: The University of Chicago Press), 1997.
McCannon, John. "To Storm the Arctic: Soviet Polar Exploration and Public Visions of Nature in the USSR, 1932–1939," in *Cultural Geographies* 2, no. 1 (1995), pp. 15–31.
Medvedev, Roy. *Let History Judge: The Origins and Consequences of Stalinism* (New York: Alfred A. Knopf), 1972.
Medvedev, Roy. *Staline et le Stalinisme: origines, histoire, conséquences* (Paris: combats SEUIL), 1979.
Merridale, Catherine. *Moscow Politics and the Rise of Stalin: The Communist Party in the Capital, 1925–32* (London: Macmillan) 1990.
Milioutine, Nikolaï. *Sotsgorod: Problème de la Construction des Villes* (Paris: les Editions de l'Imprimeur), 2002.
Merridale, Catherine. *Red Fortress: History and Illusion in the Kremlin* (New York: Metropolitan Books), 2013.
Nevzgodin, I. V. "Architect Boris Gordeev." *Proekt Sibir*, no. 6 (2000), pp. 24–27.
Nevzgodin, I. V. *Arhitektura Novosibirska* (Novosibirsk: Siberian section of the Ran), 2005.
Nevzgodin, I. V. *Konstrutivizm v Arhitekture Novosibirska* (Novosibirsk), 2013.

Bibliography and Sources

Orel'skaja, Ol'ga. *Akhitektura epohi sovetskogo avangarda v Nizhnem Novgorode* (Nizhnij Novgorod: Promgrafika), 2005.
Owen Hatherley. *Landscapes of Communism: A History through Buildings* (New York & London: The New Press), 2015.
Paperny, Vladimir. *Kul'tura Dva* (Moscow: Novoe literaturnoe obozrenie), 2011.
Paperny, Vladimir. "Narkomfin Narratives: Dreams and Realities," in Udovički-Selb, Danilo, ed. *The Narkomfin House: Moisej Ginzburg and Ignatij Milinis* (Austin/Berlin: O'Neil Ford/Wasmuth), 2015.
Paperny, Vladimir, *Architecture in the Age of Stalin: Culture Two* (Cambridge: Cambridge University Press), 2002.
Pare, Richard, Photography, Exhibition Curator, *Building the Revolution*, Exhibition Catalogue (London: Royal Academy), 2012.
Plamper, Jan. *The Stalin Cult: A Study in the Alchemy of Power* (Stanford/New Haven: Stanford University/Yale University Press), 2012.
Podgorskaja, N. O. *Pavil'ony SSSR na Mezhdunarodyh Vystavkah* (Moscow: Manezh and Shchusev Museum of Architecture), 2013.
Prokofiev, A Chief engineer, *The Palace of Soviets* (Moscow: Foreign Languages Publishing House), 1939.
Quilici, Vieri. *Il Costruttivismo* (Bari: Lateza editori), 1991.
Quilici, Vieri. "The Magazine SA: a Constructivist Creation." *Rassegna* 11, no. 38 (1989), pp.10–25.
Quilici, Vieri. ed., Exhibition Catalogue *Mosca: Capitale dell' Utopia* (Milano: Arnoldo Mondadori Arte), 1991.
Rees, E. A. *Iron Lazar: A Political Biography of Lazar Kaganovich* (New York: Anthem Press), 2012.
Reid, Susan E. "Toward a New (Socialist) Realism: The Re-engagement with Western Modernism in the Khrushchev Thaw," in *Russian Art and the West: A Century of Dialogue in Painting, Architecture, and the Decorative Arts,* ed. Rosalind P. Blakesley and Susan E. Reid (DeKalb: Northern Illinois University Press), 2007, pp. 217–39.
Rempel', L. I. *Arhitektura Poslevoennoj Italii* (Moscow: All-Union Academy of Architecture), 1934.
Robin, Regine. *Socialist Realism: An Impossible Aesthetic.* (Stanford University Press), 1992.
Rosenberg, William G. "NEP Russia as a 'Transitional' Society," in *Russia in the Era of NEP: Explorations in Soviet Society and Culture,* edited by Sheila Fitzpatrick, Alexander Rabinowitch, and Richard Stites (Bloomington: Indiana University Press), 1991, pp. 1–11.
Ruthers, Monica. "The Moscow Gorky Street in late Stalinism," in *Late Stalinist Russia: Society between Reconstruction and Reinvention,* edited by Juliane Furst (London: Routledge), 2006.
Sabsovich L. M., N. A. Miljutin et al. *La Costruzione della Città Sovietica 1929–31,* ed. Paolo Ceccarelli (Padova: Marsilio Editori), 1970.
Samohina, T., ed. *Iz istorii sozdanija Sojuza sovetskih arhitektorov* (Moscow: Sojuz moskovskih arkhitektorov), 2007.
Samonà, Alberto, ed. *Con due saggi di Vittorio Gregotti e di Vieri Quilici Il Palazzo dei Soviet,1931–1933* (Roma: Officina Edizioni), 1976.
Schlögel, Karl, *Moscow, 1937,* First published in German as *Terror und Traum 1937* (Munich: Carl Hanser Verlag), 2008. (English edition: Malden, MA: Polity), 2012.
Sedov, Vladimir, "Armando Brazini i Boris Iofan" *Proekt klassika* 21 (2007), pp. 136–55.
Seiner, Ursula. "The 'Neues Bauen' by Other Means – the International Building Brigades in the Soviet Union," in *Daidalos,* no.54 (Dec. 15, 1994), 42–51.
Senkevitch, Anatole. "Aspects of Spatial Form and Perceptual Psychology in the Doctrine of the Rationalist Movement in Soviet Architecture in the 1920s." *Via 6* (1983), pp. 78–115.
Shvidkovskij, Dmitrij. *Russian Architecture and the West* (New Haven and London: Yale University Press), 2007.

Starr, Frederick. "Visionary Town Planning during the Cultural Revolution," in *Cultural Revolution in Russia, 1928–1931*, ed. Sheila Fitzpatrick (Bloomington: Indiana University Press), 1978, pp. 207–40.
Starr, Frederick. *Mel'nikov: Solo Architect in a Mass Society* (Princeton: Princeton University Press), 1981.
Starr, Frederick. "Le Corbusier and the USSR: New Documentation." *Cahiers du Monde russe et soviétique* 21, no. 2 (1980), pp. 209–21.
Starr, Frederick "The Social Character of Stalinist Architecture," in *AA Quarterly*, 1979, pp. 36–48.
Steiner, Peter. *Russian Formalism, A Metapoetics* (Ithaca and London: Cornell University Press), n.d.
Stites, Richard. *Revolutionary Dreams: Utopian Vision and Experimental Life in the Russian Revolution* (Oxford: Oxford University Press), 1989.
Tafuri, Manfredo and Francesco Dal Co. *Modern Architecture*. 2 vols. (New York: Electa/Rizzoli), 1986.
Tafuri, Manfredo. *Architecture and Utopia: Design and Capitalist Development* (Cambridge, MA: MIT Press), 1976.
Tafuri, Manfredo. "Avanguardia e Formalismo, Fra la NEP ed il Primo Piano Quinquenale," in *La Ville L'Architecture: URSS, 1917–1978*, ed. L. L. Cohen, M. De Michelis, M. Tafuri (L'Equerre/ Officina Edizioni), 1985.
Tarkhanov, Alexej and Sergei Kavtaradze. *Architecture of the Stalin Era*. (New York: Rizzoli), 1992.
Teige, Karel, and Jan Kroha. *Avantgardni arhitektura*, Josef Cisarovsky ed. (Prague: Češkoslovensky Spisovatel), 1969.
Tolstoj, Vladimir Pavlovich, ed. *Vystavochnye ansambli SSSR, 1920 – 1930-e gody: materialy i dokumenty* (Moscow: Galart), 2006.
Tucker, Robert C. *Stalin in Power: The Revolution from Above, 1928–1941* (New York and London: W. W, Norton and Company), 1990.
Tucker, Robert, C. *Stalin in Power: The Revolution from Above, 1928–1941* (New York and London: W. W. Norton & Company), 1992.
Tupitsyn, Margarita, ed. *El Lissitzky: Beyond the Abstract Cabinet: Photography, Design, Collaboration* (New Haven: Yale University Press), 1999.
Tupitsyn, Margarita, *Gustav Klutsis and Valentina Kulagina: Photography and Montage after Constructivism* (New York: Steidl and ICP), 2004.
Tupitsyn, Margarita, *Rodchenko & Popova: Defining Constructivism* (London: Tate Publishing), 2009.
Udovički-Selb, Danilo. "Les Constructivistes face à Staline: Sanatoriums méconnus des Années Trente de Moscou au Caucase," in *Les Hôpitaux Modernes: Survie et restauration* (Paris: Cité de l'Architecture/Palais de Tokyo), 1990.
Udovički-Selb, Danilo. "C´était dans l'Air du Temps, Charlotte Perriand and the Popular Front," in *Charlotte Perriand: An Art of Living*, Mary McLeod, ed. (New York: Abrams), 2003.
Udovički-Selb, Danilo. "Facing Hitler's Pavilion: The Uses of Modernity in the Soviet Pavilion at the 1937 Paris World's Exhibition," in *Journal of Contemporary History* (*JCH*) Special Edition, Vol. 47, no. 1, Jan. 2012.
Udovički-Selb, Danilo. "Projets et Concours," in *Exposition de Paris, 1937: Cinquantenaire*, ed., Bertrand Lemoine, Exhibition Catalogue (Paris: Musée d'Art Moderne/IFA), 1987.
Udovički-Selb, Danilo. "Les Engagements de Charlotte Perriand pour L'Exposition de 1937: Le Corbusier, Les Jeunes '37, Le Front Populaire." Exhibition Catalogue (Paris: Centre Pompidou), 2007.
Udovički-Selb Danilo. "Between Modernism and Socialist Realism: Soviet Architectural Culture Under Stalin's "Revolution from Above: 1928–1938," in *Journal of Architectural Historians* Vol. 68, no.4, December 2009.
Udovički-Selb, Danilo. ed. *The Narkomfin House: Moisej Ginzburg and Ignatij Milinis* (Austin/Berlin: O'Neil Ford/Wasmuth), 2015.

Bibliography and Sources

Udovički-Selb, Danilo *"L'Exposition de 1937 n'aura pas lieu:* The Invention of Paris International Expo and the Soviet and German Pavilion," in *Architecture of Great Expositions* (London: Ashgate), 2015.

Udovički-Selb, Danilo, "Between Vanguard and Establishment: Boris Iofan's Two Pavilions—Paris 1937 and New York's 1939," in Alla Aronova and Alexander Ortenberg, eds, *A History of Russian Exposition and Festival Architecture: 1700-2014,* London: Routledge, 2018, pp. 168-87.

Velikanov A. A. *Dvorec Sovetov SSSR: Sozdanie Nevozmozhnogo* [no date, no publisher] ISBN 987-5-91529-031-9; UDK 725,03(47+57); BBBK 85.113(2)6.

Voevodina, T. V. et al. *Pamjatniki Istorii, Arhitektury i Monumental'nogo Isskustva Novosibirskoj Oblasti,* Volume 1, (Novosibirsk: Gorod Novosibirsk), 2011.

Vostrishev, Mihail. *Ljudmila Celikovskaja: Zhizn' Zamechatelnyh Ljudej* (Moscow: Molodaja Gvardija), 2001.

von Geldern, James. "Putting the Masses in Mass Culture: Bolshevik Festivals, 1918-1920," *Journal of Popular Culture* 31, no. 4 (1998).

Weissberg, Alex. *Conspiracy of Silence,* with a preface by Arthur Koestler (London: Hamish Hamilton), 1952.

Whitney, Thomas, P. ed. *Khrushchev Speaks* (Michigan: University of Michigan), 1963.

Wood, Paul, "The Politics of the Avant-Garde," in *The Great Utopia: The Russian and Soviet Avant-Garde, 1915-1932* (New York: Guggenheim Museum), 1992, 1-24.

Wood, Paul. "The Politics of the Avant-Garde," in *The Great Utopia: The Russian and Soviet Avant-garde, 1915-1932* (New York: Guggenheim Museum), 1992, pp. 1-24.

Yurchak, Alexej. *Everything Was Forever, Until It Was No More: The Last Soviet Generation* (Princeton: Princeton University Press, 2006).

Doctoral Dissertations

Anderson, Richard, "The Future of History: The Cultural Politics of Soviet Architecture, 1928-1941." Doctoral Dissertation, Columbia University, 2010.

Day, Andrew Elam. "Building Socialism: The Politics of the Soviet Cityscape in the Stalin Era." PhD dissertation, Columbia University, 1998.

Haran, Barnaby Emmett, "The Amerika Machine: Art and Technology between the USA and the USSR, 1926 to 1933." PhD Thesis, University College London, 2008.

Suzuki, Yuya. "Konkurs na dvorec sovetov 1930-x gg. v Moskve i mezhdunarodnij arkhitekturnij kontekst." PhD dissertation, State Institute for the Study of Art, Moscow, 2014.

Vronskaya, Alla "The Productive Unconscious: Architecture, Experimental Psychology and Techniques of Subjectivity in Soviet Russia, 1919-1935." Doctoral Dissertation, MIT, 2014.

Vronskaya, Alla G. "Invisible Colors: The Narkomfin House-Painting Experiment," in *Narkomfin, Moisej J. Ginzburg, Ignatij F. Milinis,* O'NFM_6, ed. Danilo Udovički (Austin/Berlin, Tubingen: Center for American Architecture and Design/Ernst Wasmuth Verlag), 2016.

Zheludkova, Elena, "Predistorija Stroitel'stva Moskovskogo Metropolitena: Dorevolucionnye Proekty i Diskussii 1920-h Godov," in *Moskovskoe Metro Podzemnyj Pamjatnik Arhitektury,* I. V. Chepkunova, M. A. Kostjuk, E. Ju. Zheldukova, ed. (Moscow: Kuckovo Pole), 2016.

Zubovich, Katherine, "Moscow Monumental: Soviet Skyscrapers and Urban Life under High Stalinism." UC Berkley, 2016.

INDEX

The letter *f* following an entry indicates a page that includes a figure.

Aalto, Alvar 87, 89
   Finnish Pavilion, New York 87
   Paimio Sanatorium 70, 89
"About the Development if the Ideology of Constructivism in Contemporary Architecture" (Leonidov, Ivan) 29
Aelita Queen of Mars (Protazanov, Jakov) 133, 195
"Against Vulgarizers and Slanderers: A Few Clarifications to our Critics" (Higer, Roman) 29–31
Ageev, Dmitrij 111
   Kuzbassugol housing 111*f*–12
Alabjan, Karo 2, 18, 44, 46, 175, 199, 204
   Arhitektura SSSR 125, 126–7
   ARHPLAN 138
   Assembly of Moscow Architects 169–70
   Builders' Club 18
   CIAM 178
   First Congress of the Union of Soviet Architects 134, 145–7, 148, 180, 182*f*, 184–5, 189
   gruppirovke 181
   Red Army Theater 51, 65, 144
   Sovetskaja Arhitektura 32
   Sovremenaja Arhitektura 24
   SSA 43, 145–7, 148, 150–1
   VHUTEMAS 164
   VOPRA 18
   Wright, Frank Lloyd 177
Aleksandrov, Jakov 2, 134, 147, 148, 157, 175
   Arhitekturnaja Gazeta 135
   classicism 149
   constructivism 162–3, 165
All-Union Academy of Architecture 47
All-Union of Soviet Architects (SSA). *See* SSA
All-Union Society of Proletarian Architects (VOPRA). *See* VOPRA
America 48–9, 57, 61, 63–4, 105, 127 (*see also* skyscrapers)
   aviation 182–3*f*
   Wright, Frank Lloyd 177, 193
Antonov, I. P.
   NKVD housing compound ("Gorodok Ckekistov" [Chekist's Townlet]) 114–16
Antonov, P. P.
   Moscow House of Books 127

architects 139–40, 142, 153, 203
Architectural Building Institute (ASI) 24
Architecture of the Cities of the USSR, The (Leonidov, Ivan/Arkin, David/Vesnin, Viktor) 42
"Architecture of the Revolutionary Years, The" (Higer, Roman) 130
Arhitektony (Malevich, Kazimir) 61, 62*f*, 64, 103, 105*f*
ARHITEKTOR
   "Cacophony in Architecture" 167–8
Arhitektura Poslevoennoj Italii (*Post-War Architecture in Italy*) (Rempel, L. I.) 75–6
Arhitektura Sanatorija NKTP (Ginzburg, Moisej) 70–2, 206
Arhitektura SSSR 5, 6, 43–4, 124–31, 157
   "Creative Tribune" 138–43
   "socialist" realism 131–4
Arhitektura za Rubezhom (*Architecture from Abroad*) 47*f*
Arhitekturnaja Gazeta 134–6, 151, 154, 157, 162
   ARHPLAN 136–8
   censorship 171, 172–3
   formalism 174
   Vesnin, Aleksandr 171
ARHPLAN 2, 45, 136–8, 162, 201
Arkin, David 125, 129, 134, 160–1, 168
   Architecture of the Cities of the USSR, The 42
   Arhitekturnaja Gazeta 135
   Wright, Frank Lloyd 177
art 19–20, 31, 141–2
   Mordvinov, Arkadij 34–5
ARU (Association of Architects-Urbanists) 56
ASI (Architectural Building Institute) 24
ASNOVA (Association of New Architecture) 15, 18, 55
   kitchen factory 78, 79*f*
Assembly of Moscow Architects 169–75
Association of Architects-Urbanists (ARU) 56
Association of New Architecture (ASNOVA) 15, 18, 55
aviation 182–3*f*

Bajdukov, G. F. 182
Baku 12*f*, 118–19*f*, 143

Index

Barhin, Mihail 134
Barshch, Mihail 130
Barviha Sanatorium (Iofan, Boris) 65f–7f, 189
Bauhaus 10, 33–5
Beljakov, A. V. 182
Вещ/Gegenstand/Objet 80
"Billboard Building". See *Pravda* headquarters, Leningrad
"Black Square" (Malevich, Kazimir) 2, 93, 96
Bobrov, A. I. 113–14
Bolshevik Revolution 7, 105–6
Bosin
 Kujbyshev (Samara) housing 119
Bourgeois, Victor 48
Budennovskij Prospekt, Rostv-n-Donu residential buildings 116–18
Buharin, Nikolaj 7, 81, 84
Builders' Club (Alabjan, Karo) 18
"Building and Construction Policies of the Country" conference 154
Burov, Andrej 50, 147, 150
 Tverskaja (Gorky) Street, Moscow 50
Byzantine 51

"Cacophony in Architecture" (ARHITEKTOR) 167–8
Camera del Lavoro (Carminati, Antonio) 76f
Campanella, Tomaso
 City of the Sun 199
capitalism 139, 176, 177, 184
Carminati, Antonio
 Camera del Lavoro 76f
Casa del Fascio (Terragni, Guiseppe) 109
Celikovskaja, Ljudmila 199
Central Committee
 decree of 1930 26, 27–8
 decree of 1932 1–2, 43, 44, 201
Central Post Office, Harkov (Mordvinov, Arkadij) 18
Central Telegraph (Rerberg, Ivan) 13
Centrosojuz (Commissariat of Light Industry [Narkomlegprom]) (Le Corbusier) 125, 127, 167–7, 202
Chalkushjan, H. H.
 Rostov-na-Donu hotel 116f
Cherkesjan, I. E.
 Rostov-na-Donu hotel 116f
Chernishev, Leonid 134
Chistye Prudy Metro station (Kolli, Nikolaj/Sammer, František) 99–101
Chlakov, V. P. 182
Christ the Saviour church 56
CIAM (Congrès internationaux d'architecture moderne) 10, 46, 47–8, 178–9
cinema 4, 142
CIRPAC (International Association for New Architecture) 48, 135, 178

City of the Sun (Campanella, Tomaso)fdecre 199
classical architecture 139, 140
classicism 51, 149, 150, 205
 Alabjan, Karo 185
 Wright, Frank Lloyd 176
collectivization 8, 43
color 131
Commissariat of Heavy Industry. See Narkomtjazhprom (NKTP) building
Commissariat of Light Industry [Narkomlegprom]) (Le Corbusier) 125, 127
competitions 202, 204, 206
composition 176
Congrès internationaux d'architecture moderne (CIAM) 10, 46, 47–8
constructivism 2, 3–4, 19, 67, 83, 107–8, 149, 204, 206
 Alabjan, Karo 145, 146, 151, 184–5, 189
 Aleksandrov, Jakov 162
 Arhitektura SSSR 127
 Baku 118–19f
 curtailing 123
 estrangement (*ostranenie*) 141
 First Congress of the Union of Soviet Architects 143–4
 foreign influence 185
 Gan, Aleksej 129
 Ginzburg, Moisej 71, 129, 151–3, 158
 Kaganovich, Lazar Moisejevich 2, 47, 101, 154
 Kolli, Nikolaj 71, 189–90
 Kujbyshev (Samara) 108, 119
 Leonidov, Ivan 172
 Lisagor, Solomon 159–62, 165, 166
 Ljudvig, Genrih 161–2, 165
 Miljutin, Nikolaj 129–30
 Mordvinov, Arkadij 34, 39, 189
 New York Pavilion (1939) 107
 Novosibirsk 108–14f
 Palace of Culture (ZIL) 84, 85
 Pravda 167–8
 Rostov-na-Donu 116f–18
 Shchuko, Vladimir 189
 Shchusev, Alexej 158, 160, 189
 SSA 157–8
 Sverdlovsk (Ekaterinburg) 108, 114–16
 Taut, Bruno 191
 Vesnin, Aleksandr 164–5, 171
 Vesnin, Viktor 185, 188–91, 207
 Vesnin brothers 128, 129, 184
 VOPRA 189
 Voronezh 117f, 118
"Constructivism and Eclecticism" (Lisagor, Solomon) 160–1, 165, 166–7
corporate architecture 5, 48, 61, 101, 107 (*see also* skyscrapers)
 Iofan, Boris 66

Index

"Creative Tribune" (Vesnin, Viktor/Vesnin, Aleksandr/Ginzburg, Moisej) 138–43
cubism 34
cultural revolution 7, 9

David (Michelangelo) 141
decree of 1930 26, 27–8
decree of 1932 1–2, 43, 44, 201
decree of 1935 120
Defense Complex, Moscow (Vesnin brothers) 127
Deineka, Aleksandr 97
Delaunay, Sonia
  "Rhythm" 99
disurbanism 129, 162, 184, 194–5 (*see also* urbanism)
Dnieper Hydroelectric Plant (Vesnin brothers) 16 n. 27
Dom Sojuzov (Kazakov, M. F.) 181
Dushkin, Aleksej 2–3, 94
  Kropotnitskaja/Dvorec Sovetov Metro station 92–3*f*, 94*f*
  Majakovskaja Metro station 92, 93, 94–8, 111
Dva Kvadrata (Two Squares) (Lissitzky, E 96
Dvorec Sovetov Metro station (Dushkin, Aleksej) 92–3*f*, 94*f*
Dzherzhinskaja Metro station (Ladovskij, Nikolaj) 98–9, 100*f*

Eastern, Cor van 48
eclecticism 39–40, 149
  Alabjan, Karo 185
  Arhitektura SSSR 125
economic crisis 176, 184, 201
Eden, Anthony 94
editing 4, 67
Eisenstein, Sergei
  Ivan the Terrible 199
Enudkidze, A. 135
Erevan 12*f*
estrangement (*ostranenie*) 141
ethnic architecture 6
European New Architecture (Neue Bauen) 68, 139, 194

famine 43
Finland 89
Finnish Pavilion, New York (Aalto, Alvar) 87
First Congress of the Union of Soviet Architects 123, 134, 143–8, 181–91, 194*f*, 204
  Arhitekturnaja Gazeta 134–6, 174
  foreign delegates 175–81, 191–7, 202
  postponements 123, 136
  Vesnin, Viktor 188–91, 198, 204, 206–7
  Wright, Frank Lloyd 175–8, 193–7*f*, 202
Fitzpatrick, Sheila 7
Five-Year Plans 91, 201, 202

"Flying Cities" (Krutikov, Georgij) 25
Fomin, Ivan 96, 134, 149 n. 85
forced labour camps 28, 81
formalism 3, 4, 19, 33, 150, 151 (*see also* Russian Formalists)
  Alabjan, Karo 184
  Arhitektura SSSR 125
  Arhitekturnaja Gazeta 174
  Fridman, Daniil 173
  Leonidov, Ivan 169, 171, 172
  Lurçat, André 173–4
  Mel'nikov, Konstantin 171
  Mordvinov, Arkadij 39, 169
  Vesnin, Aleksandr 170–1
Fridman, Daniil 21, 147, 150, 173, 181
  classicism 205
  Standard High School Building, Moscow 120*f*
Fridman, Fidman and Markov 13*f*, 14
functionalism 16, 71, 127–8, 171–2
  Alabjan, Karo 126
  Ginzburg, Moisej 71–3
  Higer, Roman 29, 31
  Miljutin, Nikolaj 129–30
  Mordvinov, Arkadij 34, 35
  sanatoria 71, 72
furniture 25, 67*f*, 70*f*
futurism 34, 187

Gan, Aleksej, 129
  Konstruktivizm 4
Gelfreich, Vladimir 56, 189
George, Saint 195, 196*f*
Gideon, Siegfried 48
Ginzburg, Moisej 45, 108, 128, 170, 198, 201
  Alabjan, Karo 184
  Arhitektura Sanatorija NKTP 70–2, 2198, 06
  Arhitektura SSSR 128–9, 137
  ARHPLAN 45, 137, 162
  Assembly of Moscow Architects 169–70, 174
  "Building and Construction Policies of the Country" conference 154
  "Creative Tribune" 138–43
  First Congress of the Union of Soviet Architects 134, 146, 147, 191
  formalism 169
  Gosstrah Housing 128
  housing 141
  Italian architecture 75–7, 80
  Kislovodsk sanatorium 198, 204, 206
  Leonidov, Ivan 41, 169, 170
  "Liberated Creativity" 2
  Mel'nikov, Konstantin 169
  "Metropoliten" 92
  Narkomfin 4, 26–7*f*, 32, 72, 142, 170, 205
  nepartijci (non-party sympathizers) 46
  Novecento architecture 75–7, 80

Index

"Ordzhonikidze" Sanatorium 3, 68–81*f*, 206
organic architecture 71, 72–4, 124–5
"Organic in Architecture and in Nature, The" 124–5
OSA 26, 137
Palace of Labor 128
"socialist" realism 70–4
Sovetskja Arhitektura 32
Sovremenaja Arhitektura (*SA*) 10, 141
SSA 45, 164
Style and Epoch 74
"Tasks of Soviet Architecture, The" 151, 157–8, 164
"Which legacy, Egyptian? Gothic? Greco-Roman?"
Zhilishche (*Abode*) 141
Golosov, Il'ja 45, 55*f*, 92, 188
Golosov, Panteleimon 53–4*f*
Gordeev, Boris A. 108, 112
　"Housing for Artists" 112, 113*f*
　Kuzbassugol housing 111*f*–12
　OGPU housing 112–13, 14*f*
　Regional Executive Committee Oblispolkom (Oblastnij Ispolitel'nij Komitet) 108–10
　Sibzoloto employee housing 113
"Gorodok Ckekistov" (Chekist's Townlet) (Antonov, I. P./Sokolov, V. D.) 114–16
GOSPLAN building (Langman, Arkadij) 49–50*f*, 63*f*
GOSPLAN garage (Mel'nikov, Konstantin) 3, 121*f*–2
Gosstrah Housing (Ginzburg, Moisej) 128
Gramsci, Antonio 7
Great Stalinist Constitution, The 44
Greece 51
Grinzaid, Je. M. 95
Gropius, Walter 34, 78*f*, 84
gruppirovke 44, 137, 180, 181

Hamilton, Hector 48, 56–7*f*, 61
Heap, Jane
　"Machine-Age Exposition" 63
"Hegel and Architecture" (Vercman, I.) 130
Higer, Roman 29, 203
　"Against Vulgarizers and Slanderers: A Few Clarifications to our Critics" 29–31
　"Architecture of the Revolutionary Years, The" 130
　Arhitektura SSSR 130–3
　Mel'nikov, Konstantin 131–3
historic architecture 141
historical legacy 5–6, 139, 147, 153
historicism 51
history 139
Hood, Raymond
　Rockefeller Center 49*f*, 57, 61, 62*f*, 63, 104

Hope Against Hope (Mandelstam, Nadezhda) 161
Hotel Moskva (Shchusev, Alexej) 49, 50–1, 127
housing 26–8
　Ginzburg, Moisej 141
　Golosov, Il'ja 55*f*
　Gosstrah Housing 128
　high-rise 61, 62*f*
　Intourist housing 205
　Kujbyshev (Samara) 119
　Miljutin, Nikolaj 32
　Novosibirsk 111*f*–14*f*
　socialist 10
　Sverdlovsk (Ekaterinburg) 114–16
　Wright, Frank Lloyd 176
　Zholtovskij, Ivan 51
"Housing for Artists" (Turgenev, Sergej/Gordeev, Boris A.) 112, 113*f*

industrial design 25
INHUK (Institute of Artistic Culture) 188
"Iniciativnaja Gruppa" 205
International Association for New Architecture (CIRPAC) 48, 135, 178
"International Exposition of the Arts and Technology in Modern Life", Paris (1937) 102*f*, 103
Intourist housing (Zholtovskij, Ivan) 205
Iofan, Boris 3, 48, 63, 66, 202, 205
　Barviha Sanatorium 65*f*–7*f*, 189
　First Congress of the Union of Soviet Architects 134
　Lenin Library 21
　Narkomtjazhprom (NKTP) building 63*f*
　New York Pavilion (1939) 28, 45, 83, 106–7*f*
　Palace of the Soviets. *See* Palace of the Soviets
　Paris Pavilion (1937) 1, 3, 45, 66, 83, 101–6, 197, 198
　Wright, Frank Lloyd 178
Italian architecture 75–7, 80
Ivan the Terrible (Eisenstein, Sergei) 199

Jourdain, Francis 135, 179, 191–2

Kaganovich, Lazar Moisejevich 8, 15, 26, 101, 201, 204
　Arhitektura SSSR 125–6
　ARHPLAN 2, 45
　"Building and Construction Policies of the Country" conference 154
　constructivism 2, 47, 101, 154
　First Congress of the Union of Soviet Architects 143–5
　Leonidov, Ivan 38
　power 23, 32, 48
　SSA 143, 158
　style 50, 51
　VOPRA 3, 8, 17, 20

Index

Kazakov, M. F. 181
    Dom Sojuzov 181
Kirov, Sergej 61
Kirovskaja Metro station (Kolli, Nikolaj/Sammer, František) 99–101
Kislovodsk Sanatorium (Ginzburg, Moisej) 198, 204, 206
Klucis, Gustav 45–6
Kochar, Gevorg 18, 199
Kolli, Nikolaj 70–1, 125, 202, 205, 206
    First Congress of the Union of Soviet Architects 134, 186–8, 189
    Kirovskaja/Chistye Prudy Metro station 99–101
    "Tasks of Soviet Architecture, The" 187–8, 189–90
Komarova, Lidija 163, 164, 166
    "Triada Konstruktivizma" 157–8, 164–5
Kommuna (Mel'nikov, Konstantin) 185
Komsomols, the 147, 148, 203
Konstruktivizm (Gan, Aleksej) 4
Kozelkov, G. 36
Krasin, Borisovich 165, 189
Krasnaja Vorota Metro station (Ladovskij, Nikolaj) 98, 99*f*
Kravec, S. M. 91, 92
    Kropotnitskaja Metro station 92
Krejcar, Jaromir 135
    Teplice sanatorium 127
Krjukov, Mihail 134
Kropotnitskaja Metro station (Dushkin, Aleksej) 92–3*f*, 94*f*
Krupskaja, Nadezhda 7, 32
Krushchëv, Nikita 1, 83, 199, 205
Krutikov, Georgij
    "Flying Cities" 25
Kujbyshev (Samara) 108, 119
Kurochkin, M. V. 168
Kuzbassugol housing 111*f*–12

Ladovskij, Nikolaj 15 n. 22, 45, 93, 108, 188
    Dzherzhinskaja/Lubjanka Metro station 98–9, 100*f*
    First Congress of the Union of Soviet Architects 134, 188
    Krasnaja Vorota Metro station 98, 99*f*
    "Metropoliten" 92
"Lamps of Architecture" (Ruskin, John) 72
Lang, Fritz
    Metropolis 195
Langman, Arkadij 48
    GOSPLAN building, Moscow 49–50*f*, 63*f*
Laprade, Albert
    "Pavillion de la Paix" 107
Le Corbusier (Charles-Édouard Jeanneret) 46–7, 86–7, 139, 171, 202–3
    Arhitekturnaja Gazeta 135

Centrosojuz (Commissariat of Light Industry [Narkomlegprom]) 125, 127, 167–8, 202
    First Congress of the Union of Soviet Architects 179, 202
    Mundaneum 129
    Villa La Roche 78, 79*f*
    "Villas Suspendues" 77
Lef 131
legacy 56, 139, 147, 153
Lenin, Vladimir 7
Lenin Library 9, 10–16, 20–3, 127
Leningradskaja Pravda "Billboard Building". See *Pravda* headquarters, Leningrad
Leonidov, Ivan 3, 35–42, 44, 45, 199, 205
    "About the Development if the Ideology of Constructivism in Contemporary Architecture" 29
    Alabjan, Karo 169
    Architecture of the Cities of the USSR, The 42
    Arhitektura SSSR 124, 125, 130, 131
    Assembly of Moscow Architects 169–73, 174
    First Congress of the Union of Soviet Architects 134
    formalism 3, 169, 171
    furniture 70*f*
    Ginzburg, Moisej 41, 169, 170
    Lenin Library 11, 22
    Mordvinov, Arkadij 36–7, 38–40, 168
    Moscow Hermitage 125
    Narkomtjazhprom (NKTP) building 40*f*, 70, 71*f*, 125, 126, 131, 169
    nepartijci (non-party sympathizers) 46
    Palace of Culture (ZIL) 36, 37–8, 130
    Vesnin, Aleksandr 36, 37, 171
    VHUTEMAS 164
    VOPRA 10
"Leonidovism and Its Harm" (Mordvinov, Arkadij) 37
Leonidovshchina 35–42
Libera, Adalberto 55*f*
    Palazzo del Littorio 75
"Liberated Creativity" (Ginzburg, Moisej) 2
Lisagor, Solomon 158, 159–63
    "Constructivism and Eclecticism" 160–1, 165, 166–7
Lissitzky, El 41, 80, 130
    Arhitektura SSSR 124
    Dva Kvadrata (Two Squares) 96
    "Victory over the sun" theater set 103, 104*f*
Ljudvig, Genrih 161–2, 163, 165, 166
London 178, 179
lotus flowers 92–3
Lubjanka Metro station Ladovskij, Nikolaj 98–9, 100*f*
Lunacharskij, Anatolij 15, 51
Lurçat, André 173–4, 179

Index

Maca, Ivan 21, 134
"Machine-Age Exposition" (New York exhibition) 63
Mahorka pavilion (Mel'nikov, Konstantin) 44
Majakovskaja Metro station (Dushkin, Aleksej) 92, 93, 94–8, 111
Malevich, Kazimir
   Arhitektony 61, 62*f*, 64, 103, 105*f*
   "Black Square" 2, 93, 96
   "Soviet Artists in Recent Years" 64*f*
   "Victory over the Sun" theater set 103, 104*f*
   "White on White" 2, 93, 94*f*
Mandelstam, Nadezhda
   Hope Against Hope 161
MAO (Moskovskoe Arhitekturnoe Obshchestvo) 11
Marxism 144–5, 192
Masterskie (workshops) 92, 136–8, 147, 201
Matveev
   Kujbyshev (Samara) housing 119
May, Ernst 108
Mazmanjan, M. 199
Mel'nikov, Konstantin 2, 44, 46, 83, 167–8
   Alabjan, Karo 169, 185
   Arhitektura SSSR 131–3
   ARHPLAN 45
   formalism 171
   GOSPLAN garage 3, 121*f*–2
   Kommuna 185
   Mahorka pavilion 44
   "Metropoliten" 92
   Narkomtjazhprom (NKTP) building 122, 130, 132*f*, 167
   Paris Exposition 44
   Rusakov workers' club and theater 169
Merzhanov, Miron
   Voroshilov Sanatorium and Rest Home 68*f*, 107
Metro stations 91–2, 101
   Dushkin, Aleksej 2–3, 92
   Dzherzhinskaja/Lubjanka Metro station 98–9, 100*f*
   Kirovskaja/Chistye Prudy Metro station 99–101
   Krasnaja Vorota Metro station 98, 99*f*
   Kropotnitskaja/Dvorec Sovetov Metro station 92–3*f*, 94*f*
   Majakovskaja Metro station 92, 93, 94–8, 111
Metropolis (Lang, Fritz) 195
"Metropoliten" 83, 90–101, 186, 194, 195
Meyer, Hans 34–5, 51
Michelangelo
   David 141
Milinis, Ignatij
   Narkomfin 4, 26–7*f*, 32
Miljutin, Nikolaj 31, 32, 44
   Arhitektura SSSR 129–30
   Sovetskja Arhitektura 124, 130

modernism 1 n. 3, 103, 190, 204–6
   First Congress of the Union of Soviet Architects 146
   Iofan, Boris 66
   Lenin Library 10
modernity 1 n. 3, 61, 90, 103, 106, 120
Molotov, Vjacheslav 58
montage 4
Mordvinov, Arkadij 2, 10, 18, 189, 199
   Arhitektura SSSR 124, 129
   Bauhaus 33–4
   Central Post Office, Harkov 18
   as head of IZO 26
   Krushchëv, Nikita 205
   Leonidov, Ivan 36–7, 38–40, 168
   "Leonidovism and Its Harm" 37
   Mel'nikov, Konstantin 168
   "O Melkoburzhuaznom napravlenii v Arhitekture—Leonidovshchina" (About the Petit Bourgeois Current in Architecture—Leonidovism) 38
   Tverskaja (Gorky) Street, Moscow 50
   VOPRA 18
Moscow 127, 131
Moscow Commissariat of Agriculture (Shchusev, Alexej) 108, 127
Moscow Hermitage (Leonidov, Ivan) 125
Moscow House of Books (Velikovskij, B. M./Antonov, P. P./Zhuralev, A. A.) 127
Moscow "Metropoliten". *See* "Metropoliten"
Moser, Karl 135
Moskovskoe Arhitekturnoe Obshchestvo (MAO) 11
Mostorg Department Store, Moscow (Vesnin brothers) 127
Muhina, Vera 95, 103
Mundaneum (Le Corbusier) 129

Narkomfin (Ginzburg, Moisej/Milinis, Ignatij) 4, 26–7*f*, 32, 72, 142, 170, 205
Narkomlegprom (Commissariat of Light Industry) (Le Corbusier) 125, 127, 167–8
Narkomtjazhprom (NKTP) (Commissariat of Heavy Industry building). *See* NKTP building
"national" architecture 12*f*
nationalism 183
nature 141
NEP (New Economic Policy) 7, 202
nepartijci (non-party sympathizers) 46
Neue Bauen (European New Architecture) 68, 139, 194
Nevskij, Valdimir 15–16, 21, 22–3
New Economic Policy (NEP) 7, 202
"New Moscow" (Pimenov, Jurij) 49–50
New York 48–9
   "Machine-Age Exposition" 63

Index

New York Pavilion (1939) (Iofan, Boris) 28, 45, 83, 106–7*f*
Nikitin, N. V. 112
1930 decree 26, 27–8
1932 decree 1–2, 43, 44, 201
1935 decree 120
NKTP (Narkomtjazhprom) (Commissariat of Heavy Industry) building 122, 125, 126, 131, 132*f*
    Iofan, Boris 63*f*
    Leonidov, Ivan 40*f*, 70, 71*f*, 125, 126, 131, 169
    Mel'nikov, Konstantin 122, 130, 132*f*, 167
NKVD housing compound ("Gorodok Ckekistov" [Chekist's Townlet]) (Antonov, I. P./Sokolov, V. D.) 114–16
Novecento architecture 75–7, 80
Novitskij, Pavel 22, 25
Novosibirsk 108–14*f*

"O Melkoburzhuaznom napravlenii v Arhitekture—Leonidovshchina" (About the Petit Bourgeois Current in Architecture—Leonidovism) (Mordvinov, Arkadij) 38
OGPU housing (Turgenev, Sergej/Gordeev, Boris A.) 112–13, 14*f*
Ohitovich, Mihail 68, 129, 161
OPOJAZ (Society of Poetic Language) 4
Ordzhonikidze, Sergo 70
"Ordzhonikidze" Sanatorium (Ginzburg, Moisej) 3, 68–81*f*, 206
organic architecture 71, 72–4, 124–5, 194, 195
"Organic in Architecture and in Nature, The" (Ginzburg, Moisej) 124–5
Orlov, G. 21
orphism 99
OSA (Society of Contemporary Architects) 15, 25, 26, 56, 137
Oud, J. J. 135–6

Paimio Sanatorium (Aalto, Alvar) 70, 89
Palace of Culture (ZIL) (Vesnin brothers) 3, 52–3, 83, 84–90*f*
    Higer, Roman 139
    Kaganovich, Lazar Moisejevich 168
    Leonidov, Ivan 36, 37–8, 130
Palace of Friendship (Zoltovskij, Ivan) 13
Palace of Labor 61, 127, 128, 162, 188
Palace of the Soviets (Iofan, Boris) 3, 47–8, 55–64, 104, 202
    "socialist" realism 197
    Stroitel'stvo Moskvy 105
    VOPRA 9, 18
    Wright, Frank Lloyd 49, 193–4, 195
Palazzo del Littorio (Libera, Adalberto) 75
Palazzo della Signoria 141
Palladio, Andrea 51

Paris "International Exposition of the Arts and Technology in Modern Life" (1937) 102*f*, 103
Paris Pavilion (1937) (Iofan, Boris) 1, 3, 45, 66, 83, 101–6, 197, 198
patriotism 184
"Pavillion de la Paix" (Laprade, Albert) 107
Pavlov, Ivan 20
perestrojka 3, 7–9, 27, 202
Perret, Auguste 135, 186
Pimenov, Jurij
    "New Moscow" 49–50
Popov-Shaman, A. I.
    "Utjuzhok" 117*f*, 118
Pravda 154–5, 167–8, 172, 190
    Wright, Frank Lloyd 176–7, 195–6, 197*f*
Pravda headquarters, Leningrad (Vesnin brothers) 53, 89, 127
Pravda headquarters, Moscow (Golosov, Panteleimon) 53–4*f*
proletarian architecture 9, 16, 19–20 (*see also* VOPRA)
    Mordvinov, Arkadij 35
    Novitskij, Pavel 22
Proletkult 17
Protazanov, Jakov
    Aelita Queen of Mars 133, 195
purges 80–1, 184

RA (*Revolucionaja Arhitektura*) 24
rationalism 3
Red Army Theater (Alabjan, Karo) 51, 65, 144
Regional Executive Committee Oblispolkom (Oblastnij Ispolitel'nij Komitet) (Gordeev, Boris A.) 108–10
Rempel, L. I. 75
    Arhitektura Poslevoennoj Italii (*Post-War Architecture in Italy*) 75–6
"Renassiance" Gosbank (Zoltovskij, Ivan) 13
Rerberg, Ivan 11
    Central Telegraph 13
rest homes 65, 68*f* (*see also* sanatoria)
revivalism 205
Revolucionaja Arhitektura (*RA*) 24
"Rhythm" (Delaunay, Sonia) 99
"Rights" (*Pravie*) opposition 32–3
"Roads to Soviet Architecture, The" (Shchusev, Alexej) 154, 158–9, 160
Rockefeller Center (Hood, Raymond) 49*f*, 57, 61, 62*f*, 63, 104
Rome International Congress of Architects 150 n. 90
Rostov-na-Donu 116*f*–18
Royal Institute of British Architects 179
Rozanov, S. N. 91
Ruskin, John
    "Lamps of Architecture" 72

Index

Russian Formalists 4, 33, 74, 128, 170 (*see also* formalism)
Rykov, Aleksej 7, 205

SA (*Sovremenaja Arhitektura*) 10, 24, 29–33, 141
    Leonidov, Ivan 37–8
Sammer, František
    Kirovskaja/Chistye Prudy Metro station 101
sanatoria 65, 72
    Barviha Sanatorium 65*f*–7*f*, 189
    Kislovodsk Sanatorium 198, 204, 206
    "Ordzhonikidze" Sanatorium 3, 68–81*f*, 206
    Paimio Sanatorium 70, 89
    Teplice Sanatorium 127
    Voroshilov Sanatorium and rest home 68*f*, 107
Scheper, Hinnerk 141
schools 120
science 140
Shahtij trial 9 n. 8
Shakespeare, William 153
Shchuko, Vladimir 90–1, 189
    Lenin Library 11, 13*f*–16, 21, 22
    Palace of the Soviets 56, 60
Shchusev, Alexej 11, 158, 166
    "Building and Construction Policies of the Country" conference 154
    First Congress of the Union of Soviet Architects 134
    First Congress of the Union of Soviet Architects 186, 189
    Hotel Moskva 49, 50–1, 127
    Moscow Commissariat of Agriculture 108, 127
    "Roads to Soviet Architecture, The" 154, 158–9, 160
Sheinfains, R. A. 95
Shirjaev, Arkadij. N.
    West-Siberian Railroad Administration 110*f*–11
Shklovskij, Viktor 4, 170
Sibzoloto employee housing (Gordeev, Boris A.) 113
Simonov Monastery 52*f*, 53*f*
simplism 168
Sinijavskij, Mihail 131
skyscrapers 48–9*f*, 57, 59, 61–4*f*, 193–4
social class 28, 147
socialist housing 10
"socialist" realism 1, 2, 20, 44, 147, 185–6, 203, 206
    Alabjan, Karo 185–6, 197
    Assembly of Moscow Architects 174
    Ginzburg, Moisej 70–4, 153, 204
    Higer, Roman 133–4
    Iofan, Boris 66
    Mordvinov, Arkadij 34
    Soviet Writers Congress 138
    Turkenidze, A. 181

Vesnin, Aleksandr 172
Vesnin, Viktor 190–1
VOPRA 9
Wright, Frank Lloyd 204
Society of Contemporary Architects (OSA) 15, 25, 26
Society of Poetic Language (OPOJAZ) 4
Sokolov, V. D.
    NKVD housing compound ("Gorodok Ckekistov" [Chekist's Townlet]) 114–16
Sovetskja Arhitektura 31–2, 44, 124, 130
Soviet architecture 149
"Soviet Artists in Recent Years" (Leningrad exhibition) 64*f*
Soviet Pavilion, New York (1939) (Iofan, Boris) 28, 45, 68, 106–7*f*
Soviet Pavilion, Paris (1937) (Iofan, Boris) 1, 3, 45, 66, 83, 101–6, 197, 198
Soviet Writers Congress 138, 144
Sovremenaja Arhitektura (*SA*). See *SA*
SSA (All-Union of Soviet Architects) 2, 123, 124, 143–51, 164–6, 201
    CIAM 47–8
    constructivism 157–8, 204
    creation 43
    "Creative meetings" 136
    Ginzburg, Moisej 45, 157–8
    Komsomols, the 147, 148, 203
    "socialist" realism 2, 138
    Vesnin, Viktor 43, 45
Stalin, Joseph 7, 8, 28, 48–9, 181
    Bolshevik Revolution 105
    "Building and Construction Policies of the Country" conference 154
    Five-Year Plans 91, 201, 202
    Klucis, Gustav 45–6
    patriotism 184
    purges 80–1, 184
    style 50
Stalinism 1
Stalinization 1
Stam, Mart 178–9
Standard High School Building, Moscow (Fridman, D.) 120*f*
state bureaucracy 204, 205–6
Stepanova, Varvara 32
Stroitel'stvo Moskvy 14–15, 105
Style and Epoch (Ginzburg, Moisej) 74
Suetin, Nikolaj 103, 105*f*
suprematism 3, 34, 63, 64
    Iofan, Boris 103, 104
Sverdlovsk (Ekaterinburg) 108, 114–16
synthesis 103–7, 116, 141–2, 169, 176

"Tasks of Soviet Architecture, The" (Ginzburg, Moisej) 151, 157–8, 164

Index

"Tasks of Soviet Architecture, The" (Kolli, Nikolaj) 187–8
Tatlin's Tower 162, 187
Taut, Bruno 191
technology 140
Teplice Sanatorium (Krejcar, Jaromir) 127
Terragni, Guiseppe
  Casa del Fascio 109
"Triada Konstruktivizma" (Komarova, Lidija) 157–8, 164–5
Turgenev, Sergej 112
  "Housing for Artists" 112, 113f
  OGPU housing 112–13, 14f
Regional Executive Committee Oblispolkom (Oblastnij Ispolitel'nij Komitet) 108–10
Turkenidze, A. 164, 180–1
Tverskaja (Gorky) Street, Moscow 50
type, the 140–1

United States. *See* America
unprincipled architects 150
urbanism 107–8, 184, 194–5, 196, 201 (*see also* disurbanism)
"Utjuzhok" (Popov-Shaman, A. I.) 117f, 118

Vago, Pierre 179
VANO (all-Soviet Architectural Scientific Society) 23–4, 43
Velikovskij, B. M.
  Moscow House of Books 127
Vercman, I.
  "Hegel and Architecture" 130
Vesnin, Aleksandr 10, 11, 86–7, 146, 147, 198 (*see also* Vesnin brothers)
  Assembly of Moscow Architects 170–2
  "Creative Tribune" 138–43
  formalism 170–1
  Leonidov, Ivan 36, 37, 171
  SSA 164–6
  VHUTEMAS/VHUTEIN/ASI 165
Vesnin, Leonid 11 (*see also* Vesnin brothers)
Vesnin, Viktor 11, 44, 134, 185, 198 (*see also* Vesnin brothers)
  Architecture of the Cities of the USSR, The 42
  "Creative Tribune" 138–43
  First Congress of the Union of Soviet Architects 188–91, 198, 204, 206–7
  SSA 43, 45
Vesnin brothers 11, 13f, 127–8, 184
  Arhitektura SSSR 127
  ARHPLAN 45
  Defense Complex, Moscow 127
  Dnieper Hydroelectric Plant 16 n. 27
  Lenin Library 127
  "Metropoliten" 92
  Mostorg Department Store, Moscow 127

nepartijci (non-party sympathizers) 46
Palace of Culture. *See* Palace of Culture
Palace of Labor 127, 128, 162
Pravda headquarters, Leningrad 53, 89, 127
"Which legacy, Egyptian? Gothic? Greco-Roman?" 5–6
VHUTEIN (Higher Artistic and Technical Institute) 11, 160, 165
  resolution 11–13, 24–6
VHUTEMAS (Higher Artistic and Technical Workshops) 10, 11, 24, 160, 162, 164 (*see also* VHUTEIN)
  Kolli, Nikolaj 187
  Ladovskij, Nikolaj 188
  Leonidov, Ivan 36
  Vesnin, Aleksandr 165
"Victory over the Sun" theater set (Lissitzky, El/Malevich, Kazimir) 103, 104f
Villa La Roche (Le Corbusier) 78, 79f
"Villas Suspendues" (Le Corbusier) 77
Vlasov, Aleksandr 108, 130–1, 134, 150, 185
VOKS (Institute for the Relations with Foreign Cultural Organizations and Individuals) 134, 175, 179
VOPRA (All-Union Society of Proletarian Architects) 4, 9, 43, 189, 203, 206
  creation 8. 16–23
  classicism 23
  Declaration of Principle 19–20
  Kaganovich, Lazar Moisejevich 3, 8
  Palace of the Soviets 56
  VANO 23–4
  VHUTEMAS/VHUTEIN 24–6
Voronezh 117f, 118
Voroshilov, Kliment 68
Voroshilov Sanatorium and Rest Home (Merzhanov, Miron) 68f, 107

West-Siberian Railroad Administration (Shirjaev, Arkadij. N.) 110f–11
"Which legacy, Egyptian? Gothic? Greco-Roman?" (Ginzburg, Moisej/Vesnin brothers) 5–6
"White on White" (Malevich, Kazimir) 2, 93, 94f
women 32
workshops (*Masterskie*) 92, 136–8, 147, 201
Wright, Frank Lloyd 3, 9, 10, 198
  Arhitekturnaja Gazeta 135
  aviation 183
  economic crisis 194
  First Congress of the Union of Soviet Architects 175–8, 179, 193–7f, 202
  Hotel Moskva 50, 127
  skyscrapers 49
  "socialist" realism 204
  Soviet Pavilion, Paris (1937) 102, 198

Index

Zaslavskij, Abram 134, 171
Zhilishche (*Abode*) (Ginzburg, Moisej) 141
Zholtovskij, Ivan 51–2, 90–1, 151, 189
    First Congress of the Union of Soviet Architects 134
    Intourist housing 205

Palace of Friendship 13
Palace of the Soviets 48, 55, 56, 60
"Renassiance" Gosbank 13
Zhuralev, A. A.
    Moscow House of Books 127
ZIL (Palace of Culture). *See* Palace of Culture

www.ingramcontent.com/pod-product-compliance
Lightning Source LLC
Chambersburg PA
CBHW072140290426
44111CB00012B/1928